IMMIGRANT AMERICA

Immigrant America

A Portrait

THIRD EDITION

Revised, Expanded, and Updated

Alejandro Portes and
Rubén G. Rumbaut

UNIVERSITY OF CALIFORNIA PRESS Berkeley   Los Angeles   London

University of California Press, one of the most distinguished university presses in the United States, enriches lives around the world by advancing scholarship in the humanities, social sciences, and natural sciences. Its activities are supported by the UC Press Foundation and by philanthropic contributions from individuals and institutions. For more information, visit www.ucpress.edu.

University of California Press
Berkeley and Los Angeles, California

University of California Press, Ltd.
London, England

Library of Congress Cataloging-in-Publication Data

Portes, Alejandro, 1944–
  Immigrant America : a portrait / Alejandro Portes and Rubén G. Rumbaut.—3rd ed., rev., expanded, and updated.
        p.   cm.
  Includes bibliographical references and index.
    ISBN-13: 978-0-520-24283-8 (cloth : alk. paper),
  ISBN-10: 0-520-24283-1 (cloth : alk. paper)
    ISBN-13: 978-0-520-25041-3 (pbk. : alk. paper),
  ISBN-10: 0-520-25041-9 (pbk. : alk. paper)
    1. Immigrants—United States—History.   2. United States—Emigration and immigration—History.
  3. Americanization—History.   I. Rumbaut, Rubén G.
  II. Title.

JV6450.P67   2006
304.8'73—dc22   2006006955

Manufactured in the United States of America

15   14   13   12   11   10   09   08   07   06
10   9   8   7   6   5   4   3   2   1

Contents

Illustrations

FIGURES

PHOTOGRAPHS following pages 102 and 284.

Tables

Preface to the Third Edition

We began to write this book more than twenty years ago—between the Mariel boat lift and the passage of the Immigration Reform and Control Act of 1986, at a time of "compassion fatigue" and heightened concern over undocumented immigration from Mexico, in the heyday of Southeast Asian refugee resettlement and of less visible flows of tens of thousands of escapees from murderous wars in Central America who were not deemed bona fide political refugees in the context of the Cold War. Not long before, in 1970, the U.S. Census had found that the foreign-born accounted for only 4.7 percent of the total population—the lowest proportion since 1850, when it first recorded the country of birth of U.S. residents. But in the preface to the first edition, we noted that after a lapse of half a century, this "permanently unfinished" society was being transformed yet again by immigration. We had already been systematically studying the phenomenon for years—indeed, we had lived it—but we could not foresee with precision just how "unfinished" a society it was, or how transformed it would become, or how dramatically the larger world would change. In this third edition, we bring this extraordinary story up-to-date.

Immigration is a transformative force, producing profound and unanticipated social changes in both sending and receiving societies, in intergroup relations within receiving societies, and among the immigrants themselves and their descendants. Immigration is followed predictably not only by acculturative processes on the part of the immigrants but also by state policies that seek to control the flows and by varying degrees of nativism and xenophobia on the part of established residents, who may view the alien newcomers as cultural or economic threats. And immigration engenders ethnicity—collectivities who perceive themselves and are perceived by others to differ in language, religion, "race," national origin or ancestral homeland, cultural heritage, and memories of a shared historical past. As we show in this book, their modes of incorporation across generations may take a variety of forms—some leading to greater homogenization and solidarity within the society (or within segments of the society), others to greater ethnic differentiation and heterogeneity.

Each edition of *Immigrant America* has reported the results of the latest decennial census. In 1980, the foreign-born population totaled 14.1 million, or 6.2 percent of the national total; by 1990, it had grown to 19.8 million (7.9 percent); by 2000, to 31.1 million (11.1 percent); and as of this writing, to approximately 37 million (12.5 percent) and growing by more than a million per year. More immigrants came in the 1980s than in any previous decade but one—1901–1910, the peak years of mass migration from Europe when the foreign-born population reached 14.7 percent of the U.S. total; and more immigrants came in the 1990s than in any other decade—a total that may be surpassed in the present decade, adding to the largest immigrant population in history. More consequential still, as we elaborate in these pages, is the commensurate growth of the second generation of their children born and raised in the United States, who are rapidly becoming a key segment of the American society and workforce in the twenty-first century.

While the sheer numbers and rates of growth are impressive, the dynamics of immigration and incorporation processes and policies do not take place in a vacuum but must be understood in the complex contexts of global historical change. Ten years ago, in the preface to the second edition, we pointed to such large-scale changes and events as the end of the Cold War and the first Persian Gulf War; the collapse of the Soviet Union and the Mexican economy; and the passage of new laws, multinational agreements, and the normalization of relations with the governments of Vietnam and Cambodia (but not with Cuba), among others. Since that time, the world has changed again, in ways that have

BYOB: Adult Summer Reading Challenge VIRTUAL Book Discussion

Monday, August 7, 6:30 p.m. – 7:30 p.m.

Let's Celebrate Summer and CPL's 150th Celebration!
Join us for a book discussion about one or two books you
read for the Adult Summer Reading Challenge. Please choose
from various reading categories from our **Summer at CPL
Reading Challenge Board.**

The discussion will take place on Zoom.

For registration information, go to **https://bit.y/3MNMH4k.**

For more information about
our summer events go to
bit.ly/adultsummer2023.

Events for Adults

Follow CPL

Celebrating
150
Years!

CHICAGO
PUBLIC
LIBRARY

profoundly affected the contexts of reception of newcomers to the United States—particularly in the wake of the attacks of September 11, 2001, which led to wars in Afghanistan and Iraq, heightened domestic security concerns, the passage of the PATRIOT Act (and pending legislation to further tighten immigration controls, declare English as the official national language, and even build a fence across the U.S.-Mexico border), and the reorganization of the U.S. immigration and naturalization bureaucracy within a new Department of Homeland Security. But we also discern the continuity of other patterns that give predictability and structure to immigration flows and adaptation processes, including the sustained demand for immigrant labor by U.S. employers, the enabling presence of social networks of family and friends, the strong tradition of American religious pluralism, and the overriding significance of historical ties between the United States and the countries that account by far for its principal immigrant communities today.

In this third edition, we have transformed the book to take into account the profound changes in immigrant America over the past decade. Every chapter has been thoroughly revised, expanded, and updated to reflect the latest available national and regional information, including the 2000 U.S. Census and the most recent Current Population Surveys. We have added sections addressing such topics as patterns of incarceration and paradoxes of acculturation. Where appropriate, we make use of new survey data, including the results of the recently completed third wave of our Children of Immigrants Longitudinal Study (CILS), which followed for more than ten years a panel representing scores of immigrant nationalities on both coasts of the United States from adolescence to early adulthood. We have added several new chapters, from an opening chapter that aims to humanize the object of our study through a set of engaging but factual stories; to a new and overdue chapter on religion and immigration, a central topic neglected by the research literature until recently; and a concluding chapter that examines the clash of dominant ideologies and public debates about immigrant exclusion and assimilation with the history and political economy of U.S. immigration, and that suggests alternative policies for both the first and second generations grounded on a firmer grasp of underlying realities.

We seek to make reasoned sense of complex and often controversial issues and to make our portrait of immigrant America at the dawn of a new century accessible not just to specialists but to a general audience whose understanding of today's immigrants can be clouded by media clichés, popular stereotypes, and a new climate of fear. As in the previous editions, the purpose of this book will be fulfilled if the reader finds here a stimulus to gain additional knowledge about the newest members of American society.

Preface to the Second Edition

Six years have passed since we completed, in January 1989, the manuscript for the first edition of *Immigrant America*. In that brief span, the world changed—and so did immigrant America.

The Cold War ended, yet refugee admissions increased significantly; a massive amnesty program for three million formerly unauthorized immigrants was implemented; the Immigration Act of 1990 increased regular immigrant visas by 40 percent over the levels reached in the 1980s; and despite a variety of official efforts to stem the flow, undocumented immigration has not only grown but diversified since 1989. From the collapse of the former Soviet Union at the beginning of the 1990s to the collapse of the Mexican economy at mid-decade; from the passage of the Immigration Act of 1990 and the 1993 North Atlantic Free Trade Agreement to the normalization of relations with the governments of Vietnam and Cambodia; from the ill-fated voyage of the *Golden Venture*, the smuggling ship carrying Chinese immigrants that ran aground off the coast of New York, to the interdiction of thirty thousand Cuban *balseros* in the Florida Straits and the reversal of a favorable thirty-year U.S. policy toward Cuban émigrés; from Tiananmen Square to the Persian Gulf War to the U.S. interventions in Somalia and Haiti; all of these are but bits and pieces of a larger set of forces that—alongside the sustained demand for immigrant labor by U.S. employers, the vagaries of U.S. foreign policies and public opinion, the enabling presence of social networks of family and friends—have had substantial if often unintended repercussions for immigration flows and policies.

The vertiginous pace of recent historical change requires that we bring our analysis up-to-date, a task that has become all the more compelling in view of the sharply politicized and increasingly acrimonious public debate on immigration issues in the 1990s. Indeed, the past several years have witnessed not only an *acceleration* of immigration flows into the United States—the twenty million foreign-born persons counted by the 1990 U.S. Census formed the largest immigrant population in the world, and admissions during the 1990s appear certain to eclipse the record set in the first decade of this century—but also an *intensification* of public alarm and nativist resistance to it, exacerbated by the prolonged recession of the early 1990s and capped by the passage in 1994 of Proposition 187 in California, home to fully a third of the nation's immigrants. As a result, immigration has risen to the top of the policy agenda and become a salient campaign issue in the 1996 presidential elections.

Accordingly, we have revised the text to reflect the latest available evidence, making extensive use of the wealth of new data from the 1990 census, the Immigration and Naturalization Service, and other sources from a rapidly accumulating research literature through the mid-1990s. The result is a thorough updating of the book; most of the several dozen tables and figures in the first six chapters are new or have been wholly revised, as is their accompanying text. Moreover, two new chapters have been especially written for this second edition. Chapter 7 examines the new second generation of children of immigrants now coming of age in American cities, a vastly understudied topic that nonetheless is key to a serious understanding of the long-term consequences of contemporary immigration for American society. Chapter 8 concludes with an effort not only to assess critically the sometimes paradoxical effects of present policies but also to confront and to specify the policy implications of our own analysis, placing our findings in historical perspective and seeking to tease out the complex dynamics of U.S.-bound immigration.

Throughout, we maintain our original analytical approach, focusing on immigration as a process, not an event, and on the diversity of today's immigrants—their social origins and contexts of exit and their adaptation experiences and contexts of incorporation. We noted in the preface to the first edition that we sought to grasp at once the diversity and the underlying structures of the new immigration, and to make it accessible to a broader audience whose understanding of today's immigrants can be clouded by common media clichés and widespread stereotypes. That was and remains the aim of this book.

Preface to the First Edition

America, that "permanently unfinished" society, has become anew a nation of immigrants. Not since the peak years of immigration before World War I have so many newcomers sought to make their way in the United States. Each year during the 1980s, an average of six hundred thousand immigrants and refugees have been legally admitted into the country, and a sizable if uncertain number of others enter and remain without legal status, clandestinely crossing the border or overstaying their visas. The attraction of America, it seems, remains as strong as ever—as does the accompanying ambivalence and even alarm many native-born Americans express toward the newest arrivals. Unlike the older flows, however, today's immigrants are drawn not from Europe but overwhelmingly from the developing nations of the Third World, especially from Asia and Latin America. The heterogeneous composition of the earlier European waves pales in comparison to the current diversity. Today's immigrants come in luxurious jetliners and in the trunks of cars, by boat, and on foot. Manual laborers and polished professionals, entrepreneurs and refugees, preliterate peasants and some of the most talented cosmopolitans on the planet—all are helping reshape the fabric of American society.

Immigrant America today differs from that at the turn of the century. The human drama of the story remains as riveting, but the cast of characters and their circumstances have changed in complex ways. The newcomers are different, reflecting in their motives and origins the forces that have forged a new world order in the second half of this century. And the America that receives them is not the same society that processed the "huddled masses" through Ellis Island, a stone's throw away from the nation's preeminent national monument to liberty and new beginnings. As a result, theories that sought to explain the assimilation of yesterday's immigrants are hard put to illuminate the nature of contemporary immigration.

Certainly much has been said and written about the newest inflows, in both the popular and academic media, and nonspecialists are beginning to get glimpses of the extraordinary stories of ordinary immigrants in the contemporary American context. Missing still is an effort to pull together the many strands of our available knowledge about these matters, to grasp at once the diversity and the underlying structures of the new immigration, and to make it accessible to a general public. Such is the aim of this book.

A subject as complex and controversial as recent immigration to the United States cannot, of course, be exhaustively considered within the scope of this or any other single volume. Nor is it our purpose to present the results of original research, to assess systematically the myriad impacts of post–World War II immigration on American institutions, or to cover in any significant depth the trajectories of each of the scores of national groups that are in the process of becoming, with or without hyphens, the newest members of American society. Instead, we have sought to comb through a vast literature and to offer a synthesis of its major aspects in a way that is both comprehensive and comprehensible. Throughout, our focus on today's immigrants is on the diversity of their origins and contexts of exit and on the diversity of their adaptation experiences and contexts of incorporation. Although the emphasis is on contemporary trends, the discussion seeks to understand present realities in historical perspective and in the context of competing theories of immigrant adaptation.

The book consists of seven chapters. "Who They Are and Why They Come" is the basic issue addressed in chapter 1, and a typology of contemporary immigrants that serves to organize the subsequent analysis of their processes of economic, political, social, cultural, and psychological adaptation is proposed. Chapter 2, "Moving," examines their points of destination and patterns of settlement, and the formation and function of new ethnic communities in urban America. Chapter 3, "Making It in America," looks at the incorporation of immigrants in the American economy and seeks to explain their differences in education, occupation, entrepreneurship, and income within specific contexts of reception. That is, the economic adaptation of immigrants needs to be understood not merely in terms of their resources and skills but as it is shaped by specific government policies, labor market conditions, and the characteristics of ethnic communities. Chapter 4, "From Immigrants to Ethnics," analyzes immigrant politics, including the underlying questions of identity, loyalty, and determinants of current patterns of naturalization among newcomers who are "in the society but not of it."

Chapter 5, "A Foreign World," switches lenses to focus on the psychology of immigrant adaptation, looking at the emotional consequences of varying modes of migration and acculturation, the major determinants of immigrants' psychological responses to their changed circumstances, and immigrant patterns of mental health and help seeking in different social settings. Chapter 6, "Learning the Ropes," proceeds to a detailed discussion of English acquisition, the loss or maintenance of bilingualism across generations, and new data on the educational attainment of diverse groups of young immigrants in American public schools. The concluding chapter seeks to clarify the origins of that most controversial segment of today's immigration—the illegals—and to assess how this inflow and its recorded counterpart are likely to affect the nation in years to come.

This, then, is a portrait of immigrant America in the waning years of the twentieth century. Like any portrait, selective in its hues and brushstrokes, it is an interpretation of a subject too rich and elusive to be rendered in a single picture. Our goal has been not to reach exclusively colleagues and specialists but rather a broader audience whose understanding of today's immigrants can be clouded by common media clichés and widespread stereotypes. If the reader finds in this book a challenge to these prevailing views and a stimulus to gain additional knowledge about the newest members of this society, its purpose will have been fulfilled.

Acknowledgments
for the Third Edition

As noted in the preface, successive editions of this book have dovetailed with each of the last three decades and the changes in immigration and global society that they have brought about. This third edition, appearing in the midst of the first decade of a new century and a new millennium, has had to address the multiple changes in the form and content of immigration brought about by sweeping transformations of the global system. Patient readers of this and prior acknowledgment pages will also note that each edition has been preceded and supported by major empirical projects: the first, by Portes's study of Mariel Cuban and Haitian entrants in South Florida and by Rumbaut's study of Vietnamese, Laotian, and Cambodian refugees and their children in Southern California in the 1980s; the second, by the first two panels of Portes and Rumbaut's Children of Immigrants Longitudinal Study (CILS), focused on the new second generation, which followed a sample on both coasts of the United States representing a number of different nationalities. This third edition is no exception, as it draws heavily on the third and final survey for the same study (CILS-III), completed after a decade-long span from the original one, at a time when our respondents had reached early adulthood.

As with past editions, our debts of gratitude for the present one are mainly due to those who made this final study possible. We thank Eric Wanner, president of the Russell Sage Foundation (RSF), who embraced the idea of this new survey from the start, and to the RSF's board, who provided the funds to make it possible. After data collection for the CILS-III survey was completed, RSF first and then the National Science Foundation provided vital support for analyzing the data and bringing results to publication. These data provide the core of chapter 8, dealing with the new second generation (formerly chapter 7), are extensively used in chapter 9 on immigrant religion, and inform our final conclusions and policy recommendations.

As with prior waves of the same study, the CILS-III survey was conducted in tandem in two regions of the country, South Florida and Southern California. The South Florida panel, centered in Miami, was directed by William Haller who, with skill and tenacity, led the effort to track and reinterview thousands of respondents to a successful conclusion. Haller was supported by a team of interviewers housed at the Institute for Public Opinion Research (IPOR) of Florida International University. We are indebted to IPOR's director, Hugh Gladwin; its assistant director, Ann Goraczko; and their staff for the skill and perseverance in conducting fieldwork for the study.

Patricia Fernández-Kelly led an ethnographic field team to Miami that carried out detailed interviews with fifty-five respondents stratified by age, socioeconomic status, and nationality. The team included Bill Haller, Lisa Konczal, and Salih Eissa. Materials from this ethnographic module are used extensively in chapters 8 and 9, and we draw on them for our final policy conclusions. We have a particular debt of gratitude to Patricia and Bill without whose skills and commitment the extensive and demanding fieldwork for the study would not have been completed.

The Southern California segment of the project, centered in San Diego, depended on the indispensable collaboration of a staff led by Linda and Norm Borgen. Their work in tracking, locating, and surveying respondents not only in Southern California but throughout the United States was exceptional, and it was followed by their conduct of 134 in-depth, open-ended interviews with a diverse subsample of CILS respondents. This last effort was supported by a grant from the MacArthur Foundation Research Network on Transitions to Adulthood. After completion of fieldwork, Golnaz Komaie, Charlie V. Morgan, Sheila J. Patel, and Karen J. Robinson at the University of California, Irvine, and Jeanne Batalova of the Migration Policy Institute in Washington, D.C., also provided valuable research assistance.

The authors benefited from a summer fellowship at Oxford University in 2000 for Alejandro Portes, where the idea of going ahead with a new CILS survey began to take form; and from year-long stays by Rubén Rumbaut at the Russell Sage Foundation, where he was a visiting scholar in 1997–1998, and at the Center for Advanced Study in the Behavioral Sciences at Stanford University in 2000–2001. The latter fellowship was generously supported by the Hewlett Foundation.

In addition to CILS-III, a revised chapter on linguistic acculturation and a new chapter on immigration and religion for the present edition incorporate data from the Immigration and Intergenerational Mobility in Metropolitan Los Angeles (IIMMLA) survey supported by another major grant from the Russell Sage Foundation. Rumbaut has served as principal investigator for this project, along with Frank Bean and a team of collaborators that includes Susan Brown, Leo Chávez, Louis DeSipio, Jennifer Lee, and Min Zhou.

A number of colleagues have generously given of their time to read and comment on various chapters of this edition. We thank, in particular, Jen'nan Ghazal Read, Louis DeSipio, and Frank Bean at the University of California, Irvine; Min Zhou at the University of California, Los Angeles; and Patricia Fernández-Kelly, Douglas S. Massey, and Miguel Angel Centeno at Princeton University.

As with prior editions, the photos included in the present one come from the archives of Steven J. Gold of Michigan State University. A prominent scholar of immigration and ethnicity, Steve has distinguished himself by combining his research and scholarship with a passion for photography. His keen sociological eye is revealed in these photos that, in manifold ways, put "faces" to the ideas and figures discussed in the text.

The publication of this book by the University of California Press marks the continuation of a productive two-decade relationship sustained thanks to our longtime editor, Naomi Schneider. She has provided unfailing support to the idea of preparing this revised and expanded edition and has given us needed encouragement to overcome the obstacles and challenges in its path. A dear friend, Naomi has our gratitude for her faith in us and in this project.

Last but not least, Barbara McCabe at Princeton University typed and organized successive drafts of each chapter, organized the bibliography, and readied the other ancillary materials required for bringing the book into production. Another dear friend and long-time collaborator, Barbara distinguishes herself for her efficiency, her serenity under stress, and the charm with which she discharges the most demanding duties.

The book is dedicated to the memory of our immigrant mothers, Eulalia and Carmen, to whom the first two editions were dedicated while they were still with us. In these last lines, we wish to acknowledge as well our wives, Patricia and Irene, who, along the many years that it took to complete the empirical study and then the book, sustained us with their devotion and their strength. To them our love.

Alejandro Portes
Princeton University

Rubén G. Rumbaut
University of California, Irvine

April 2006

Acknowledgments
for the Second Edition

This new edition has relied extensively on original research carried out during the 1990s by the authors. In particular, since 1989 we have collaborated on a continuing study of children of immigrants in Southern California and South Florida—the largest such survey to date—results from which form the core of chapter 7. We gratefully acknowledge the financial support of the Andrew W. Mellon Foundation, the Russell Sage Foundation (889.503), the Spencer Foundation, and the National Science Foundation (SBR 9022555), which jointly made this study possible. We are very much indebted to the administrators, principals, and teachers and staff of scores of secondary schools in the San Diego Unified School District and the Dade County and Broward County school districts for their unstinting cooperation throughout the various phases of data collection. We are grateful as well for the generous assistance extended to us by the sociology departments of San Diego State University, Florida International University, Michigan State University, and the Johns Hopkins University, through which the study has been conducted.

In San Diego, we have benefited from the extraordinary commitment and competence of our research staff, especially James Ainsworth, Linda Borgen, Norm Borgen, Kevin Keogan, and Laura Lagunas. We appreciate as well the work of a team of over two dozen interviewers fluent in Spanish, Tagalog, Vietnamese, Cambodian, Lao, Hmong, and other Asian languages representative of the immigrant families that have settled in the San Diego area. While the mix of languages is less diverse in South Florida, the effort and capabilities of our research staff there are no less noteworthy. Our colleague, Lisandro Pérez, who directed fieldwork in that area from the start, deserves much credit for the success of this challenging research program. So does his Florida International University team of Liza Carbajo, Ana María Pérez, Victoria Ryan, and the trilingual team of interviewers who took the final stage of the survey to successful completion.

At Johns Hopkins, Richard Schauffler, Dag MacLeod, and Tomás Rodríguez were responsible for data entry and editing and the management of data files. Their dedicated and professional work made possible the timely analysis of survey data for inclusion in this new edition. We also appreciate the comments on the new chapter 7 by Guillermina Jasso, Aristide Zolberg, Charles Tilly, Douglas Massey, and Patricia Fernández-Kelly.

In addition, chapter 5 and 6 have been revised to reflect more recent research supported by grants awarded to Professor Rumbaut, respectively, by the U.S. Department of Health and Human Services, Bureau of Health Care Delivery, Division of Maternal and Child Health, for a study of infant health risks and outcomes among low-income immigrants, carried out in collaboration with Professor John R. Weeks of San Diego State University; and by the U.S. Department of Education, Office of Educational Research and Improvement, for a study of school contexts and educational achievement among language-minority immigrant students in San Diego city schools. Their support is gratefully acknowledged.

Additional original photography was contributed specifically for this new edition by Steven J. Gold, to whom we are once again greatly indebted. The images captured by his camera in communities throughout the country illustrate the diversity of immigrant America today. Finally, we owe a special debt of gratitude to our editors at the University of California Press, Naomi Schneider and William Murphy, who gave us unfailing support during the preparation of this new edition, and to Angie Decker at Johns Hopkins, who is really the key person without whose dedication and effort in assembling disparate text corrections, references, maps, and tables, the final manuscript could not have been produced. We can only hope that the contents of this new edition are up to the quality of her work.

Acknowledgments
for the First Edition

In the years since we first conceived the idea of this book, many unexpected events have affected its progress. As often happens, its execution proved far more time-consuming and difficult than originally planned. However, we have had the support of many people and institutions along the way. In California, Chanthan S. Chea, Duong Phuc, Vu Thanh Thuy, and Prany Sananikone gave a first powerful impulse to the project by organizing field visits to the Vietnamese and Cambodian business communities of San Diego and Santa Ana. These experiences persuaded us that there was here an unwritten human story, different from that depicted in official statistics and media reports, that needed to be told. Tong Vang supplemented these visits with interviews and translations of views of Hmong refugees, some of which are included in chapter 5.

Much of the writing took place while Portes conducted field surveys of recently arrived Mariel Cubans and Haitian refugees in South Florida. Data from these projects and qualitative observations garnered while conducting them have been extensively used in the book. For financial support to implement these surveys, we acknowledge the Sociology Program of the National Science Foundation (grant #SES-8215567), of the National Institute of Mental Health (MH-41502), and the Sloan Foundation (87-4-15). In Miami, the president of Florida International University (FIU), Modesto Maidique; the dean of the Arts and Sciences School, James Mau; and the chair of the Sociology and Anthropology Department, Lisandro Pérez, deserve our thanks for making available the facilities of the institution and for their unwavering support during the months of fieldwork.

The close ties of this project with FIU also involved many members of its faculty, in particular Douglas Kincaid, Anthony Maingot, Mark Rosenberg, and Alex Stepick. Together with the previously cited officials, they helped us unravel the intricacies of ethnic relations in Miami and the distinct characteristics of its different foreign communities. Stepick and his wife, Carol Dutton Stepick, directed three successive surveys of post-1980 Haitian refugees. Their close ties with leaders of the Haitian community and their dedication and patience made possible the successive completion of each stage under unusually adverse conditions. The parallel Cuban surveys were led by Juan Clark of Miami-Dade Community College. The expertise of Clark and his team of interviewers made it possible to gain access and obtain reliable data from a large sample of Mariel refugees, a group afflicted at that time by numerous difficulties of adaptation.

We have also made extensive use of results from two large surveys of recently arrived Southeast Asian refugees conducted by Rumbaut in Southern California. For financial support, we acknowledge the National Institute of Child Health and Human Development (#HD-15699), the U.S. Office of Refugee Resettlement (#100-86-0214), and the San Diego State University (SDSU) Foundation. Kenji Ima of SDSU was the co-investigator in one of these studies. Both owe much to the commitment and ability of a staff of Indochinese interviewers and translators recruited from the refugee communities of San Diego.

Many colleagues have helped us by reading and commenting on various chapters. At Hopkins, we thank Andrew Cherlin, William Eaton, Patricia Fernández-Kelly, and Melvin Kohn for their valuable input. At SDSU, we acknowledge the advice of Richard L. Hough, John R. Weeks, and James L. Wood. Elsewhere, Charles Hirschman, Leif Jensen, Ivan Light, Silvia Pedraza-Bailey, Peter J. Rose, Rubén D. Rumbaut, Marta Tienda, and William A. Vega also read and commented on several parts of the manuscript. All have our deep appreciation but are exempted from any responsibility for the contents.

Original photography was contributed specifically for this book by several individuals, adding a visual dimension to our portrait of immigrant America in ways that mere words cannot. We wish to thank Estela R. García and Luis E. Rumbaut for scenes of immigrant communities in Miami and Washington, D.C., Steven J. Gold for his photos of diverse immigrant groups in California and along the Mexican border, Erica Hagen for her portraits of Southeast Asians awaiting resettlement to the United States in various refugee camps in Thailand, and the *San Diego Union* and Michael Franklin for his photos of Mexican migrant farmworkers in Southern California.

At the University of California Press, Naomi Schneider adopted the idea of the book as her own and has given it indispensable encouragement. We are thankful to her, as well as to the press's reviewers, who provided numerous useful suggestions. Anna Stoll not only typed multiple versions of each chapter but coordinated the many tasks required by the supporting field projects and the various stages of the manuscript. Thanks to her diligence and competence, the idea of this book has become reality.

1

Nine Stories

1

After spending eleven days in jail for antigovernment activities, Remedios Díaz Oliver and her husband, Fausto, left Cuba in 1961. A graduate of two Havana business schools, she went to work as a bookkeeper for Richford Industries, a container distributor. Fausto found work at Bertram Yacht, located nearby; that meant the couple could manage with a single old car. Within a year, Remedios had been moved to Richford's international division. Fausto took his two weeks' vacation, and the couple traveled to Central America with a bag of Richford's samples. They returned with $300,000 in orders from pharmaceutical companies in Honduras and Costa Rica. By 1965, Remedios had been appointed Richford's vice president of domestic sales, in addition to serving as president of the Latin American division.

These were the years in which former militant exiles were looking for permanent employment. From her Havana days, Remedios knew many people with the skills to make a business succeed. In 1966, she persuaded Richford to advance $30,000 in credit to one such person, with the promise that if he defaulted, she would cover the debt with her own salary. The man paid, the account grew, and so did her commission.

1

Following this experience and at her prodding, Richford agreed to advance credit to exiled clients.

In 1976, however, Richford was sold to a division of Alco Standard Corp. of Omaha, Nebraska. The new employer required Remedios to sign a contract guaranteeing that she would not compete with Alco Standard if she left the company. Instead of signing, Remedios decided to quit and form her own company. The construction trailer in which American International Container opened did not look like much, except that its owner had far more solid connections in the local market than the buttoned-down midwestern company did. By 1978, American International had taken over the inventory of Alco Standard after driving it out of Miami. Remedios became the exclusive Florida distributor for some of the biggest names in packaging, including Owens-Illinois and Standard Container. Her company had warehouses in Miami, Orlando, and Tampa and annual sales of over $60 million.

Remedios has been president of Dade County's American Cancer Society, the Hispanic division of the Red Cross, and the social committee of the Big Five—the private club created in Miami in nostalgic remembrance of the Havana Yacht Club and its four extinct counterparts in Cuba.[1]

2

Karen Kim had not yet been born when her father's sister met and married a soldier in the U.S. Army who was stationed in South Korea. Soon after, in 1973, her pioneering aunt immigrated to the United States as a military bride, from where she would regularly send news to her family in Pusan comparing life in America with the authoritarian regime of Park Chung Hee. She also filed to obtain immigrant visas for her mother and brothers, and, in 1977, most of the family immigrated to Los Angeles. Karen's father, mother, and sister soon followed, but Karen, who was a baby at the time, was left in the care of a grandmother and would not rejoin her parents until 1979, when they had settled in and found work.

Mr. Kim, Karen's father, started out at the bottom, like many other immigrants. In Korea, where he had a high school education, he had worked as a bus mechanic; his first job in Los Angeles was at an auto body shop. Meanwhile, Karen's mother—who in Korea had worked in a toothpaste factory's assembly line—had been working as a seamstress in several sweatshops in L.A.'s garment district. Both her parents' employers were Korean. In 1986, Karen's parents took over ownership of a small juice and snack shop located in the downtown garment district. Mr. Kim's older brother had bought the shop from another Korean immigrant in 1982. In 1989, Karen's aunt—the pioneer bride who had set all this in motion—became the owner of a bakery next door to Mr. Kim's shop. And in 1992, Mr. Kim's younger brother followed suit and bought a coffee shop nearby.

"For twenty years," Karen said, "this has been my parents' existence: six days a week, working from 5 A.M. to 5 P.M. in a little shop on the first floor of a building that houses several sweatshops, selling *jugos*, *tortas*, *café*, and *pan*." When Karen and her sister had to help their parents at the shop, they found it a grueling experience, waking up at five in the morning and working twelve hours making coffee, squeezing juice, sweeping the floors. Most of their customers work in the sweatshops above their store, and their exchanges take place in three languages, Spanish, English, and Korean. Like her uncles and aunt, both her parents work together at the shop, employing only one or two other persons, usually Korean or Mexican immigrants. "They live in a mainly Mexican neighborhood, attend an all-Korean church, get their news from Korean newspapers and television programs, and work in an area where most of their customers are Spanish speaking, so their English proficiency is low."

Like her aunt two decades earlier, Karen has been doing some pioneering of her own. In 1994, Karen was the first in her family to become a naturalized citizen, legalizing the American name she had adopted since fourth grade. She later became the first to graduate from college and recently the first to go to graduate school. A few weeks after she had entered a Ph.D. program, her proud father asked her over dinner, "Dr. Karen, what will you study?" And then, Karen said, "he told me that no matter what I ended up doing, I should tell our story, the story of my family's journey to America."

3

After finishing medical school, Amitar Ray confronted the prospect of working *ad honorem* in one of the few well-equipped hospitals in Mumbai or moving to a job in the countryside and to quick obsolescence in his career. He opted instead for preparing and taking the Educational Council for Foreign Medical Graduates (ECFMG) examination, administered at the local branch of the Indo-American Cultural Institute. He passed it on his second attempt. In 1972, there was a shortage of doctors in the United States, and U.S. consulates were directed to facilitate the emigration of qualified physicians from abroad.

Amitar and his wife, also a doctor, had little difficulty obtaining permanent residents' visas under the third preference of the U.S. immigration law, reserved for professionals of exceptional ability. He went on to specialize in anesthesiology and completed his residence at a public hospital in Brooklyn. After four years, nostalgia and the hope that things had improved at home moved the Rays to go back to India with their young daughter, Rita. The trip strengthened their professional and family ties, but it also dispelled any doubts as to where their future was. Medical vacancies were rare and paid a fraction of what he had earned as a resident in Brooklyn. More important, there were few opportunities to grow professionally because he would have had to combine several part-time jobs to earn a livelihood, leaving little time for study.

At fifty-one, Amitar is now an associate professor of anesthesiology at a midwestern medical school; his wife has a local practice as an internist. Their combined income is in the six figures, affording them a very comfortable lifestyle. Their daughter is a senior at Bryn Mawr, and she plans to pursue a graduate degree in international relations. There are few Indian immigrants in the midsized city where the Rays live; thus, they have had to learn local ways in order to gain entry into American social circles. Their color is sometimes a barrier to close contact with white middle-class families, but they have cultivated many friends among the local faculty and medical community.

Ties to India persist and are strengthened through periodic trips and through the professional help the Rays are able to provide to colleagues back home. They have already sponsored the immigration of two bright young physicians from their native city. More important, they make sure that information on new medical developments is relayed to a few selected specialists back home. However, there is little chance that they will return, even after retirement. Work and new local ties play a role in this decision, but the decisive factor is a thoroughly Americanized daughter whose present life and future have very little to do with India. Rita does not plan to marry soon; she is interested in Latin American politics, and her current goal is a career in the foreign service.

4

In Guadalajara, Juan Manuel Fernández worked as a mechanic in his uncle's repair shop, making the equivalent of $150 per month. At thirty-two and after ten years on the job, he decided it was time to go into business on his own. The family, his uncle included, was willing to help, but capital for the new venture was scarce. Luisa, Juan's wife, owned a small corner grocery; when money ran out at the end of the month, she often fed the family off the store's shelves. The store was enough to sustain her and her children but not to capitalize her husband's project. For a while, it looked as if Juan would remain a worker for life.

Today Juan owns his own auto repair shop, where he employs three other mechanics, two Mexicans and a Salvadoran. The shop is not in Guadalajara, however, but in Gary, Indiana. The entire family—Luisa, the two children, and a brother—have resettled there. Luisa does not work any longer because she does not speak English and because income from her husband's business is enough to support the family. The children attend school and already speak better English than their parents. They resist the idea of going back to Mexico.

Juan crossed the border on his own near El Paso in 1979. No one stopped him, and he was able to head north toward a few distant cousins and the prospect of a factory job. To his surprise, he found one easily and at the end of four months was getting double the minimum wage in steady employment. Almost every worker in the plant was Mexican, his foreman was Puerto Rican, and the language of work was uniformly Spanish. Three trips from Gary to Guadalajara during the next two years persuaded him that it made much better sense to move his business project north of the border. Guadalajara was teeming with repair shops of all sorts, and competition was fierce. "In Gary," he said, "many Mexicans would not get their cars fixed because they did not know how to bargain with an American mechanic." Sensing the opportunity, he cut remittances to Mexico and opened a local savings account instead.

During his last trip, the "migra" (border patrol) stopped him shortly after crossing; that experience required a costly second attempt two days later with a hired "coyote" (smuggler). The incident put a stop to the commuting. Juan started fixing cars out of a shed in front of his barrio home. Word got around that there was a reliable Spanish-speaking mechanic in the neighborhood. In a few months, he was able to rent an abandoned garage, buy some equipment, and eventually hire others. To stay in business, Juan has had to obtain a municipal permit and pay a fee. He pays his workers in cash, however, and neither deducts taxes from their wages nor contributes to Social Security for them. All transactions are informal and, for the most part, in cash.

Juan and Luisa feel a great deal of nostalgia for Mexico, and both firmly intend to return. "In this country, we've been able to move ahead economically, but it is not our own," she says. "The gringos will always consider us inferior." Their savings is not in the bank, as before the shop was rented, but in land in Guadalajara, a small house for his parents, and the goodwill toward many relatives, who receive periodic remittances. They figure that in ten years they will be able to return, although they worry about their children, who may be thoroughly Americanized by then. A more pressing problem is their lack of "papers" and the constant threat of deportation. Juan has devised ingenious ways to run the business despite his illegal status, but it is a constant problem. A good part of his recent earnings is in the hands of an immigration lawyer downtown, who has promised to obtain papers for a resident's visa, so far without results.

5

Dr. Benigno Aguinaldo shut down his medical practice in Manila and moved to the United States. Now forty-one, he works as a nurse at a medical center in Los Angeles and makes $50,000 a year—four times what his physician's salary was in the Philippines. "I am not planning for myself anymore," he said. "I am planning for my kids." Back home, Benigno had noticed more and more newspaper advertisements seeking nurses in the United States, promising high salaries, sponsorship for visas, flights to Guam to take the U.S. nursing boards, and moving expenses. When he asked his father what he should choose—to be an R.N. in America or a doctor in his own country—his father told him, "Son, the opportunity is in America, not here."

Benigno had a decent standard of living in the Philippines, and he and his wife employed a full-time housekeeper and a nanny for their three children. But as the economy worsened in the late 1990s, many patients switched to government hospitals offering free care, and the Aguinaldos started worrying about how they were going to put their kids through college. So he enrolled in a new fast-track program for physicians that allowed M.D.s to get nursing degrees by taking night and weekend classes for eighteen months. Benigno attended one with more than one hundred other doctors, among them his medical school mentor. So many doctors have taken up nursing in recent years—with the intention of switching careers and countries—that Philippine nursing students without M.D.s have complained that the curve is being driven up on the national exam, which they must pass to graduate.

When Benigno arrived in California, he found that several doctors in his nursing class—an obstetrician, a pediatrician, an ophthalmologist, an anesthesiologist, and an orthopedic surgeon—had already been hired as nurses at the same medical center in Los Angeles. Once he passed the required U.S. nursing boards—which Philippine doctors tend to pass with flying colors—the hospital sponsored him for a work visa and signed him on. Soon afterward, he bought a three-bedroom house with a yard. His family arrived eight months later.

For Benigno, more difficult than the adjustment of moving to the United States has been the loss of professional status. "We feel a lot of shame," he said, remembering his first day on the job, when he was ordered to wash the patients. "I never imagined myself changing someone's diapers," he said. "It is a real adjustment, draining the urine from the urine bags, scratching their backs. Lots of patients like to be scratched." He does not want to be a nurse forever, and he is now often at Starbucks keeping himself awake with double espressos while he studies for the U.S. medical boards in the hope of eventually practicing medicine in his new country. In the meantime, he's hopeful for his children's futures. His fifteen-year-old daughter's main problem, he says, is that her public high school here is too easy.

6

Rubén González ran away from the small town of La Esperanza after an incursion from an army patrol left several of his neighbors dead. Escaping the civil war in his native El Salvador, Rubén eventually crossed into Mexico and then traveled to the U.S. border. Although he came escaping persecution in his country, he was denied political asylum by U.S. authorities and had to recross the border as an illegal alien. From there he trekked to Los Angeles, where he survived through a series of temporary jobs in restaurants, landscaping companies, and construction. A small farmer in his native town, he had only an elementary school education and no urban job skills.

Eventually he found steady employment in a large gardening and landscaping company, where by dint of diligent and steady work he rose to supervisor. With his savings and despite his illegal status, he created his own small, informal gardening company, González Lawns, which, in turn, employs two young Salvadorans. The end of the civil war in his country brought about major changes in Rubén's life. The new Salvadoran government pleaded with the United States to grant its expatriates legal residence so that they could stay and continue to send remittances home. Implausibly, Salvadoran government officials argued that their expatriates should be granted asylum because of a "well-founded fear of persecution in their country."

Rubén benefited from these events by first receiving a temporary residence permit and then being lucky enough to have his new asylum application granted. In a year's time, he became a legal permanent resident. He was now able to return to El Salvador and eventually brought his entire family to Los Angeles. With his legal status and increasing prosperity, Rubén has become a prominent figure in the local Salvadoran community. When the La Esperanza Development Committee was created by migrants from his hometown, he was elected president. This position has played a key role in helping Rubén fend off discrimination.

A stocky, dark man with heavy mestizo features, he suffers routine prejudice from Americans: clerks follow him around in stores, and the police have stopped and questioned him on several occasions. Despite these and other disadvantages, he plans to remain in Los Angeles and raise his children there. He explains:

> I really live in El Salvador, not in L.A. Sure, the gringos discriminate against us, but when we have the regular fiestas to collect funds for La Esperanza, I am the leader and am treated with respect. When I go back home to inspect the works paid with our contributions, I am as important as the mayor. In L.A., I earn money and educate my children, but my thoughts are really back home. Besides, it's only three hours away.

Rubén takes his two children back to El Salvador every summer to meet with grandparents and so that they "do not forget the place where we came from." He plans to retire there.

7

Emmanuel Murat is a twenty-five-year-old black man of Haitian descent residing in Miami. He is a surgical technician at a local hospital, preparing and stocking operating rooms before surgeries. After high school, Emmanuel attended Barry University in Miami, earning a bachelor's degree in biology. Strongly encouraged by his parents to pursue medicine, Emmanuel completed the pre-med track at Barry in the hope of attending medical school in the near future.

Emmanuel's family had come to the United States seeking a more comfortable life. His father had worked for the Haitian government in Port-au-Prince, amassing the money necessary to relocate to the United States in 1986. The family (Emmanuel, his father, mother, older brother, and grandmother) lived in New York for four years before moving to Miami in 1992, Emmanuel's first year of high school. They settled into a small single-family home in a West Indian neighborhood, where they still live.

Despite his humble background, Emmanuel did not have to look for a job until college, when he started working at a nearby Target store. After graduating from Barry, he found a full-time position at a pharmaceutical plant. Emmanuel, who lives with his parents, supports only himself for the time being. He hopes to support his parents in the near future. "We Haitians believe in family. We believe that when you grow up, if your parents need help, you should be able to take care of them." Emmanuel's family does not receive any government assistance or other outside help, in spite of its financial struggle. "We don't really give to charity, either. There is just no extra money in this house."

Emmanuel believes that Haitians face challenges to which other groups are not subjected: "When Haitians come from Haiti, we don't have the educational background that, for example, Cubans or Jamaicans have. I speak French at home; most Haitians speak Creole. We don't really get the chance to learn English." Despite these challenges, Emmanuel is convinced that his parents' stress on education, religion, and family values has provided him with all the advantages necessary for achieving success. Education, he explained, is the key to success, which he perceives as "having a fairly good career and being able to provide for yourself." Considering the future of Haitian Americans, he says, "I don't think political organization or anything like that is going to make any difference." Emmanuel urges his peers to ignore discrimination and acts of hostility. "That's all distraction. I would tell people to just stay in school and try to succeed on their own."

8

Martín Cuadra lives with his family (father, mother, little sister, and dog) in a small house that is part of a large real estate development where all units look identical, as is common in lower middle-class areas of Miami. Martín was five years old when his family decided to emigrate. In Nicaragua, his father was a middle-class professional, and the family was stable. The father ran into trouble with the Sandinista regime and was forced to leave the country. In Miami, he started working at a bakery for $3 an hour. Martín had to take care of his infant sister while his father worked, but "little by little things progressed until we were able to buy a house." The father is now an accountant working at a bank, and his mom works as a cook in a hospital. His sister attends Miami-Dade Community College. The family have not yet become U.S. citizens, but they expect to do so soon.

Martín attended high school at Coral Park Senior High in Miami, graduating in 1996. Since then, he has been juggling work (at Toys "R" Us), school, and technical training in sound engineering to advance his career as a disc jockey. He works in clubs in Miami Beach and has done some parties in New York, Los Angeles, and Orlando. He's active and well-known in the local music scene but is waiting for his big break, to be discovered by the "right people." A creative, artistic career that places no limits to his potential is "plan A." But he knows that the odds are against any one person succeeding in the entertainment industry, so sound engineering is "plan B."

Martín says he'll give himself until age thirty to work primarily on his dream career. "If I do get to thirty and still see myself in the bottom rung of the industry, then I go to plan B, which is already in process." He is single with no children and lives at home with his parents. He contributes some money to the household to help with rent or food when he can, but it's not something that is asked of him. Martín holds his parents in the highest esteem because "my family has taught me the value of unconditional love. A lot of parents don't understand what unconditional love is, and I've been fortunate to have parents that do." He sees himself as very close to success. "God put me in this place for a reason, and I'm kind of getting the idea of what that reason is."

After the September 11 attacks, Martín Cuadra became more connected to his new country than ever before. "It just made me see what the United States means. It's a place where your dreams can come true, and a lot of people in the world, I guess, are envious of that. Some people take advantage of the freedom in the United States, but with me, I value the opportunity to live in a free country and, yes, make money, but money is not more important than freedom."

9

Justin Cheung, now twenty-four years old, came to the United States as a Taiwanese "parachute kid" when he was twelve. His parents, who owned homes in Taiwan and the United States, left Justin and his younger brother in the care of their fourteen-year-old brother in San Diego. Together, the brothers lived in a townhouse while attending junior high and high school. They were left to fend for themselves, with the help of frequent visits by their mother and generous financial assistance to pay bills, buy groceries, and meet any other educational expenses. Justin's parents have professional careers. His mother has a college degree and worked as a teacher in Taiwan, while his father is a physician.

Justin and his brothers came to the United States with green cards (immigrant visas) when their uncle was able to successfully sponsor them. Once in the United States, the three brothers stayed in line because they were worried about getting into trouble and exposing their situation. Justin's older brother eventually graduated from college and is currently in medical school in another state, while his younger brother recently graduated with a major in economics.

Justin is single, has never been in a serious relationship, and has been focused on school since coming to the United States. In high school, he earned straight As with perfect attendance because, he says, "I didn't have my parents here. I couldn't get in trouble too much." He never had a job during high school and even spent his summers in school. Although he wanted to go to Stanford or an Ivy League school, he excelled at the University of California in cell biology and graduated with department honors at the age of twenty-two. He worked for one year as a research assistant to buy some time and get some experience while he waited to get into an Ivy League medical school on the East Coast. He was accepted and has just completed his first year there.

Justin maintains a hectic schedule, with six hours of daily class; two to three hours of daily study; volunteer work tutoring elementary school kids; involvement in various clubs; and some time for swimming, jogging, soccer, and basketball. He has no regrets about his past and feels as though nothing bad or unusual has ever happened to him. Moreover, he feels successful being in medical school, aims to have a good career, and is "trying to figure out what kind of a doctor I'm going to be."

2

Who They Are and Why They Come

After a lapse of half a century, the United States has again become a country of immigration. In 1990, the foreign-born population reached 19.8 million, or 7.9 percent of the total. By 2005, the number had grown to 37 million, or 12.5 percent of the total. Although not yet reaching the situation a century ago, when immigrants accounted for 14.7 percent of the American population, that figure is being approached fast, while the impact of contemporary immigration is significant and growing. Numerous books and articles have called attention to this revival and sought its causes—first in a growing American economy and second in the liberalized provisions of the 1965 Immigration Act. A common exercise is to compare this "new" immigration with the "old" inflow of the early twentieth century. Similarities include the predominantly urban destination of most newcomers, their concentration in a few port cities, and their willingness to accept the lowest-paying jobs. Differences are more frequently stressed, however, for the "old" immigration was overwhelmingly European and white, whereas the present inflow is, to a large extent, nonwhite and comes from countries of the Third World.

The public image of contemporary immigration has been colored to a large extent by the Third World origins of most recent arrivals.

Because the sending countries are generally poor, many Americans believe that the immigrants themselves are uniformly poor and uneducated. Their move is commonly portrayed as a one-way escape from hunger, want, and persecution and their arrival on U.S. shores as not too different from that of the tired, "huddled masses" that Emma Lazarus immortalized at the base of the Statue of Liberty. The "quality" of the newcomers and their chances for assimilation are sometimes depicted as worse because of their non-European past and the illegal status of many.

The reality is very different. The nine stories related in chapter 1, each a composite of real-life experiences, are certainly not representative of all recent immigrants. Clearly, not all newcomers are entrepreneurs, doctors, or skilled mechanics. Similarly, not all of them or their children manage to circumvent the challenges of poverty and discrimination and integrate successfully. Still, these are not isolated instances. Underneath its apparent uniformity, contemporary immigration features a bewildering variety of origins, return patterns, and modes of adaptation to American society. Never before has the United States received immigrants from so many countries, from such different social and economic backgrounds, and for so many reasons. Although pre–World War I European immigration was by no means homogeneous, the differences among successive waves of Irish, Italian, Jews, Greeks, and Poles pale by comparison with the current diversity. For the same reason, theories coined in the wake of the Europeans' arrival at the turn of the twentieth century have been made largely obsolete by events during the last decades.

Increasingly implausible, for example, is the view of a uniform assimilation process that different groups undergo in the course of several generations as a precondition for their social and economic advancement. Today we meet first-generation millionaires who speak broken English, foreign-born mayors of large cities, and top-flight immigrant engineers and scientists in the nation's research centers. There are also those, at the other extreme, who cannot even take the first step toward assimilation because of the insecurity linked to an uncertain legal status.

This book describes that diversity. Many of the nationalities of today's immigrants have one of their most densely populated cities in the United States. Los Angeles's Mexican population is next in size to Mexico City, Monterrey, and Guadalajara. Havana is not much larger than Cuban Miami, and Santo Domingo holds a precarious advantage over Dominican New York. This is not the case for all groups; others, such as Asian Indians, Iranians, Argentines, and Israelis, are more dispersed throughout the country. Reasons for both these differences and other characteristics of contemporary immigrant groups are not well understood—in part because of the recency of their arrival and in part because of the common expectation that their assimilation process would conform to the well-known European pattern. But immigrant America is a very different place today from the America that came out of Ellis Island and grew up in the tenements of New York, Chicago, and Boston a century ago.

THE ORIGINS OF IMMIGRATION

Why do they come? A common explanation singles out the 1965 change in American immigration law as the principal factor. According to this view, today's immigrants come because they can, whereas before 1965, legal restrictions prevented them from doing so. Although the 1965 law certainly explains some qualitative and quantitative changes in immigration during the last four decades, it is an insufficient explanation.[1] Not everyone in even the major sending countries has immigrated or is planning to do so. Compared with the respective national populations, those who decide to migrate generally represent a minuscule proportion. In 2000, international agencies calculated that there were 175 million international migrants worldwide, representing just 3 percent of the global population.[2] The question can thus be reversed to ask not why so many come but why so few have thus far decided to undertake the journey, especially when difficult economic and political conditions prevail in many sending countries.

Moving abroad is not easy, even under the most propitious circumstances. It requires making elaborate preparations, enduring much expense, giving up personal relations at home, and often learning a new language and culture. Not so long ago, the lure of higher wages in the United States was not sufficient by itself to attract foreign workers and had to be activated through deliberate recruitment. Mexican immigration, for example, was initiated by U.S. growers and railroad companies who sent recruiters into the interior of Mexico to bring needed workers. By 1916, five or six weekly trains full of Mexican workers hired by the agents were being run from Laredo to Los Angeles. According to one author, the competition in El Paso became so fierce that recruiting agencies stationed their employees at the Santa Fe bridge, where they literally pounced on immigrants as they crossed the border.[3]

The question then remains: What are the factors motivating some groups but not others to seek entry into the United States? The most common answer is the desperate poverty, squalor, and unemployment of many foreign lands. Two authors offer this somber assessment:

> We call the poorest countries of the world "developing countries," as though the use of a progressive adjective could make a country progressive. But the overwhelming evidence is that most of these countries are not "developing" countries but "never-to-be-developed" countries. Most of the world's poor will stay poor for our lifetimes and for several generations to come, and there is nothing the developed nations can do to alter this fact.[4]

They go on to argue that as these countries "sink into squalor, poverty, disease, and death," their poor will seek to migrate en masse to the United States and other developed countries to escape these terrible conditions.[5] Many academic accounts tend to share the same basic view of migration as a consequence of foreign destitution and unemployment.

In less alarmist terms, neoclassical economic theories have generally assumed that labor migration flows occur because of an imbalance between labor demands and wages in sending and receiving areas. From this view, it follows that the greater the imbalance between the two, the greater the probability of migration. At the individual level, neoclassical theory translates into the prediction that people in less developed countries will rationally calculate the gap between their present wages and those that they could earn abroad, times the probability that they would obtain employment there. If the expected wages, discounted for the costs of migration, are higher than present ones, the individual will move.[6]

These predictions are made despite ample evidence that actual labor migrations do not occur in this manner. If they did, the poorest countries in the world and, within them, the poorest groups would be the prime sources of migration. They are not. As evidence in later chapters will show, migration, in general, and the flow coming to the United States, in particular, do not originate mostly in the poorest countries or most destitute regions. They often come from middle-income nations and among groups that are relatively advantaged with respect to the source population. This explains why the average educational and skill credentials of the immigrant population of the United States at present are not much inferior to those of the native-born. For example, in 2003, the proportion of the foreign-born with a college degree, 26.5 percent, was essentially the same as the native-born, 26.8 percent. By that year, immigrants with twenty or more years in the United States had closed the earnings gap with the native-born, with both groups having median earnings of approximately $32,000.[7]

As we will see subsequently, these averages conceal major differences among immigrant nationalities, but even those from the most modest origins—for instance, illegal labor migrants from Mexico and Central America—tend to have educational levels that are higher on average than their respective sending populations. Contrary to the cataclysmic image of an "invasion" by the world's poor and downtrodden suggested by the abstract notion of individual rational calculation, empirical research has shown wide differences in the onset and incidence of migration from local communities in the same country and at comparable levels of economic development. How does the story of rational individualism square with the fact that, while many towns in Mexico or El Salvador produce a regular flow of United States–bound migrants, others in the same countries and in similar economic circumstances have few or no migrants abroad?[8]

The first reason that the poorest of the poor seldom migrate is that they lack the necessary contacts and information to make such a move meaningful. The option of moving abroad in order to improve their economic situation is not self-evident and is foreign to many of the world's poor. Second, even if they somehow become aware of the migration alternative, they would still lack the economic means to implement it. International migration, whether legal or unauthorized and whether coming from near or faraway countries, is generally an expensive proposition, not within everyone's reach.[9]

An alternative explanatory framework, labeled the "new economics of migration," focuses on the household rather than on the individual as the primary unit of analysis and views migration as *one* economic strategy among several that peasant and working-class households may use to capitalize productive investments or acquire expensive items, such as a dwelling or an automobile.[10] The same theory emphasizes *relative* rather than absolute deprivation, pointing out that households frequently send a member abroad in order to generate sufficient income to "catch up" with the levels of consumption and lifestyles that are already present and visible among others nearby.

Although superior to neoclassical predictions as to who migrates and when, the new economics leaves open the question of how households learn that a migration economic alternative exists in the first place.

Without such knowledge, families and households could not possibly incorporate "sending a member abroad" into their pool of economic options. For that alternative to emerge, three things need to happen:

- First, a demand for migrant labor must exist. Contrary to the "invasion" theory, the fact is that labor migrants come not so much because they want to as because they are wanted. This demand exists at the bottom of the labor market for menial, low-paying jobs and, at higher levels, for professional and technical occupations in short supply in the nation—such as nurses and software engineers. Economist Michael Piore has compellingly argued that the demand for foreign workers is "chronic and unavoidable" in the advanced economies, an intrinsic structural need fueled by the proliferation of low-paying, menial service openings and the increasing resistance of native workers to accept these types of jobs.[11]

- Second, labor demand must be made known. In earlier periods, the "higher wages and better meals" paid for work in American industry were not enough to activate a labor flow so that paid recruiters had to be sent abroad to apprise foreign peasants and workers of those facts. This was the origin of the massive southern Italian migrant flow at the turn of the twentieth century, as well as of the Mexican movement north still occurring today.[12] More recently, the mass media and innovations in communication technologies have succeeded in disseminating information about labor market opportunities in the advanced world far more efficiently than in the past. To these developments are added the social networks built by migrants themselves that can act as veritable human transmission belts, conveying information about job opportunities in New York or California to the most remote villages and towns in a number of sending countries.[13]

- Third, the opportunities must be desirable. Desirability is less a question of the gross earnings disparity between sending and receiving countries than of the *meaning* that these economic advantages have for households and communities. On the one hand, a self-sufficient and relatively isolated farming community may see no great advantage in risking life and limb on a perilous journey abroad. On the other hand, when external competition forces such communities to adopt modern production methods requiring large capital investments or when new consumption expectations cannot be met within the confines of the local economy, then there is every incentive to send one or more family members abroad.[14]

The penetration of capitalist institutions from the developed world into less developed lands has played a major role in this process. Television and mass advertising bring to these populations information about lifestyles in the rich nations and create new consumer desires that can hardly be met with paltry local resources. This "relative deprivation," as Alba, Stark, and others argue, represents a major force stimulating out-migration. In a sense, "what goes around comes around." Efforts by transnational corporations to expand their markets abroad through advertising and promotion of new consumer needs create a direct incentive for migrating in search of the incomes that would make satisfaction of these imported aspirations possible.[15] For this reason, it is no longer necessary for employers in the United States to send labor recruiters abroad since it is sufficient for them to regulate an abundant labor supply at their doors, activated by the penetration of modern capitalist institutions into the less developed countries.

Once these three conditions have been met, migration flows can become self-sustaining and virtually unstoppable. Migrants abroad and those who have returned home pass along to potential movers the necessary information on job opportunities, housing, and transportation, lowering the costs of the next journey. Established migrant communities similarly facilitate the settlement and labor market incorporation of newcomers. Thus, what starts as a movement of "pioneers," mostly young males, comes to encompass the general population, including women and entire families. Douglas Massey and his colleagues have developed a "cumulative causation" model of the process in which labor migration, once started, becomes its own major determinant in the future.[16] Once migrant networks have consolidated, they can become sufficiently powerful to sustain the movement *in the absence* of the original economic incentives. Family imperatives, transnational entrepreneurial opportunities, and other considerations linked to the web of transactions between sending areas and their expatriate communities take over as engines of the movement.[17]

With some variants, this tripartite causal model of activated labor demand, cultural penetration of sending countries, and development of social networks apply to the migration of the highly skilled as well as to that of manual laborers. Because *relative*, not absolute, deprivation lies at the core of most contemporary immigration, its composition tends to be positively selected in terms of both human capital and motivation. It is thus not surprising that most of today's immigrants, even the undocumented, have had some education and come from cities, for these are precisely the groups most thoroughly exposed to lifestyles and consumption patterns emanating from the advanced world. These are also the groups for whom the gap between aspirations and local realities is most poignant and among whom one finds the individuals most determined to overcome this situation. Educated and skilled workers and small farmers are generally better informed about employment opportunities abroad than the illiterate and the destitute.

The form that this gap takes varies, of course, across countries and social groups. For skilled workers and small farmers, migration is the means to stabilize family livelihoods and meet long-desired aspirations —a car, a TV set, domestic appliances of all sorts, additional land and implements. For urban professionals, it provides a means of reaching life standards commensurate with their past achievements and of progressing in their careers. Seen from this perspective, contemporary immigration is a direct consequence of the dominant influence attained by the culture of the advanced West in every corner of the globe.[18]

Back in the nineteenth century, the United States was a growing industrializing country that needed labor, but because its lifestyle was not a global standard and its economic opportunities were not well known, it had to resort to direct recruitment. The enormous variety of today's immigrants and the fact that they come spontaneously, rather than through recruitment, reflect the attraction of American lifestyles and their gradual conversion into a world standard. Immigrants do not come to escape perennial unemployment or destitution in their homeland. Most undertake the journey instead to attain the dream of a new lifestyle that has reached their countries but that is impossible to fulfill in them. Not surprisingly, the most determined individuals, those who feel the distance between actual reality and life goals most poignantly, often choose migration as the path to resolve this contradiction. For this reason, immigrants tend to be positively selected, their drive to succeed giving rise to many stories similar to those recounted in the first chapter.

IMMIGRANTS AND THEIR TYPES

Within this general picture are significant differences in migration goals and their relative fulfillment. Any typology implies simplification, but it is useful at this point to present a basic classification of contemporary immigrants to organize the upcoming analysis of modern processes of adaptation. Each basic type is represented by several nationalities; conversely, a national group may include individuals representing different types. These are distinguished by a series of common characteristics of socioeconomic origin and motives for departure that tend to be associated with different courses of adaptation in the United States.

Contemporary immigrants to the United States differ along two main dimensions. The first is their personal resources, in terms of material and human capital, and the second is their classification by the government. The first dimension ranges from foreigners who arrive with investment capital or are endowed with high educational credentials versus those who have only their labor to sell. The second dimension ranges from migrants who arrive legally and receive governmental resettlement assistance to those who are categorized as illegal and are persecuted accordingly. In the recent past, only persons granted refugee status or admitted as legal asylees have received any form of official resettlement assistance.[19] Most legal immigrants are admitted into the country but receive no help. Since 1996, they have also been barred from welfare programs such as Supplemental Security Income (SSI) or Medicaid to which citizens are entitled.

Cross-classifying these dimensions produces the typology presented in table 1. Representative nationalities are included in each cell, with the caution that migrants from a particular country may be represented in more than one. The following description follows the horizontal axis, based on human capital skills, noting the relative legal standing of each distinct type. A final section discusses the special case of refugees and asylees.

LABOR MIGRANTS

Manual labor immigration corresponds most closely to popular stereotypes about contemporary migrants. The movement of foreign workers in search of menial and generally low-paying jobs has represented the bulk of immigration, both legal and undocumented, in recent years. The Immigration Reform and Control Act (IRCA) of 1986 was aimed primarily at discouraging the surreptitious component of this flow, while compensating employers by liberalizing access to legal temporary workers. A decade later, Proposition 187, an initiative passed by the California electorate in 1994, sought to discourage undocumented

TABLE I. A TYPOLOGY OF CONTEMPORARY IMMIGRANTS TO THE UNITED STATES

Legal status	Human capital		
	Unskilled/ semi-skilled laborers	Skilled workers and professionals	Entrepreneurs
Unauthorized	Mexican, Salvadoran, Guatemalan, and Haitian workers	Chinese, Dominican, and Indian physicians and dentists practicing without legal permits	Chinese, Indian, Mexican operators of informal business in ethnic enclaves and neighborhoods
Legal, temporary	H-2 West Indian cane cutters and Mexicans and Indians admitted for temporary harvest work	Chinese, Indian, Filipino, Mexican software engineers and technicians with valid, temporary work permits	
Legal, permanent	Mexicans and Central Americans legalized under amnesty provisions of 1986 Immigration Act	Argentine, Chinese, Filipino, and Indian physicians, engineers, nurses admitted under occupational preferences of 1990 Immigration Act	Chinese, Dominican, and Korean owners of legal firms in ethnic enclaves
Refugees, asylees	Laotian, Cambodian, Vietnamese, and Somali refugees; Central American asylees	Pre-1980 Cuban, post-1990 Russian, Ukrainian, and Iranian professional refugees	Cuban and Vietnamese owners of legal firms in ethnic enclaves and in the general market

immigration by barring illegal aliens from access to public services. We discuss the intent and effectiveness of these two measures in chapter 10. For the moment, it suffices to note the principal ways manual labor immigration has materialized in recent years.

First, migrants can simply cross the border on foot or with the help of a smuggler or overstay a U.S. tourist visa. In official parlance, illegal border crossers have been labeled *EWIs* (entry without inspection); those who stay longer than permitted are labeled *visa abusers*. In 2002, the U.S. Immigration and Naturalization Service (INS) located 1.06 million deportable aliens, of which 1.03 million were EWIs. Predictably, the overwhelming majority of illegal border crossers—exactly 96 percent—were Mexicans.[20]

A second channel of entry is to come legally by using one of the family reunification preferences of the immigration law (left untouched, for the most part, by the 1986 IRCA reform and reaffirmed by the Immigration Act of 1990). This avenue is open primarily to immigrants who have first entered the United States without legal papers or for temporary periods and who have subsequently married a U.S. citizen or legal resident. Marriage automatically entitles the immigrant to a legal entry permit; spouses of U.S. citizens are given priority because they are exempt from existing quota limits. Studies of legal Mexican immigrants arriving in the 1970s found that up to 70 percent of respondents had lived in the United States prior to legal entry. The vast majority of these immigrants come with visas granted to spouses of U.S. citizens or U.S. legal residents.[21]

By the early 1990s, the situation was not very different. Ninety-three percent of the 69,784 legal Mexican immigrants who arrived in 1993 entered under family preferences or as immediate relatives of U.S. citizens. An additional 56,777 were also legalized in 1993 under IRCA's amnesty provisions, of whom 69 percent were immediate family members who entered as "legalization dependents" under a provision of the Immigration Act of 1990. In 2002, out of a total of 219,380 Mexicans admitted for legal residence, 58,602 (26.7 percent) came under the worldwide quota as family-sponsored entries, and an additional 150,963 (68.8 percent) arrived outside quota limits as immediate relatives of U.S. citizens.[22]

The last avenue for labor migration is to come as a contract laborer. A provision in the 1965 Immigration Act allowed for the importation of temporary foreign laborers when a supply of "willing and able" domestic workers was not available. This provision was maintained and actually liberalized by the 1986 reform. In both cases, the secretary of labor must certify that a labor shortage exists before immigration authorizes the entry of foreign workers. Because the procedure is cumbersome, especially in the past, few employers sought labor in this manner. An exception is the sugar industry in Florida, for which "H-2" workers (so labeled because of their type of visa) became the mainstay of its cane-cutting labor force for many years. Most of these contract workers came from the West Indies.[23] The 1990 Immigration Act placed a cap of sixty-six thousand temporary H-2 workers per year. However, the number of unauthorized farmworkers has grown to such an extent as to encourage many agricultural employers to dispense with the cumbersome legal procedures for temporary labor. The de facto situation is that undocumented Mexican and Central American labor, previously confined to the Southwest and Midwest, has now reached all corners of the country, replacing traditional sources of rural labor in Florida as well as along the eastern seaboard.[24]

The principal magnet drawing foreign manual workers to the United States is undoubtedly the level of North American wages relative to those left behind. Despite its fast depreciation in real terms, the U.S. minimum wage of close to six dollars per hour continues to be six to seven times that prevailing in Mexico, which is, in turn, higher than most in Central America. The actual wage that many U.S. employers pay their foreign workers exceeds the legal minimum and is significantly higher than that available for skilled and even white-collar work in Mexico and other sources of this type of immigration. For this reason, relatively educated foreigners are willing to accept frequently harsh labor conditions. To them, the trek to the United States and the economic opportunities associated with it often represent the difference between stagnation or permanent poverty in their home countries and attainment of their individual and family goals.[25]

As seen previously, this international wage gap acquires meaning in the context of the economic and cultural penetration of Mexico and other sending countries that creates strong incentives for households of modest means to avail themselves of the migration alternative. That option receives additional impulse from the consolidation of migrant networks and from the strong demand for manual labor on the U.S. side of the border. That demand originates not only in agriculture but in construction, labor-intensive industries, and a wide gamut of urban services. Employers consistently state that American workers are either unavailable or unwilling to perform harsh menial jobs. Garment contractors, small electronic firms, and other employers of immigrants have argued further that they would have to close their doors or move abroad if their foreign labor supply were cut off.

Contrary to the situation in the late 1980s, when the INS actively sought to penalize employers of illegal labor and staged frequent raids against such firms, subsequent enforcement efforts increasingly concentrated on the U.S.-Mexico border, allowing successful border crossers a fairly free hand in finding employment. This situation, which has only been partially reversed in the last two years, accounts in part for the movement of Mexican laborers to all parts of the nation. Simultaneously, it has placed employers in the enviable position of having a motivated labor supply at their doorstep, whose members bear all risks of the journey.[26]

Not surprisingly, labor migrants receive low wages, many live below the poverty line, and they are commonly uninsured. Census statistics show that immigrant nationalities that are composed primarily of this type of migrant are in a much inferior economic situation relative to the native-born. Thus, for example, the poverty rate among the U.S. native-born in 2002 was 11.1 percent, but among Mexican immigrants, it reached 24.4 percent; among Dominicans, 25.8 percent. While 12.2 percent of the native-born population was without health insurance, 53.4 percent of Mexicans, 53.7 percent of Salvadorans, and 55.8 percent of Guatemalans lacked this coverage.[27]

Willingness to work for low wages and with few benefits, together with diligence and motivation, are what makes these workers so desirable to American employers. Under such conditions, it is not surprising that manual labor immigration has continued and grown from year to year. This flow does not represent an "alien invasion" because an invasion implies moving into other people's territory against their will. In this instance, the movement is very much welcomed, if not by everyone, at least by a very influential group—namely, the small, medium, and large enterprises in agriculture, services, and industry that have come to rely on and profit from this source of labor. The match between the goals and economic aspirations of migrant workers and the needs and interests of the firms that hire them is the key factor sustaining the flow year after year.

PROFESSIONAL IMMIGRANTS

A preference category of the U.S. visa allocation system is reserved for "priority workers; professionals with advanced degrees, or aliens of exceptional ability." This category has provided, until recently, the main entry channel for the second type of immigrant. Unlike the first, the vast majority of its members come legally and are not destined to the bottom rungs of the American labor market. Labeled "brain drain" in the countries of origin, this flow of immigrants represents a significant gain of highly trained personnel for the United States. In 2002, 34,452 "persons of extraordinary ability," "outstanding researchers," "executives," and their kin plus an additional 44,468 professionals holding advanced degrees and their families were admitted for permanent residence. Although, in relative terms, employment-related immigration only represents about 13 percent of the legal total since 2000, it has been the main conduit for the addition of highly trained personnel to the U.S. labor force. Their entry helps explain why a quarter of the U.S. foreign-born population are college graduates or higher and why about 25 percent of foreign-born workers are in managerial and professional specialty occupations.[28]

Foreign professionals seldom migrate because of unemployment back home. The reason is that they not only come from higher educational strata but also are probably among the best in their respective professions in order to pass difficult entrance tests, such as the qualifying examinations for foreign physicians. The gap that makes the difference in their decision to migrate is not the absolute income differential between prospective U.S. salaries and what they earn at home. Instead, it is the relative gap between available salaries and work conditions *in their own countries* and those that are normatively regarded as acceptable for people with their level of education.[29]

Professionals who earn enough at home to sustain a middle-class standard of living and who are reasonably satisfied about their chances for advancement seldom migrate. Those threatened with early obsolescence or who cannot make ends meet start looking for opportunities abroad. A fertile ground for this type of migration is a country in which university students are trained in advanced Western-style professional practices but then find the prospects and means to implement their training blocked because of poor employment opportunities or a lack of suitable technological facilities.[30]

Because they do not come to escape poverty but to improve their careers and life chances, immigrant professionals seldom accept menial jobs in the United States. However, they tend to enter at the bottom of their respective occupational ladders and to progress from there according to individual skills. This scenario explains why, for example, foreign doctors and nurses are so often found in public hospitals throughout the country. An important feature of this type of immigration is its inconspicuousness. We seldom hear reference to a Filipino or an Indian immigration "problem," although more than 1.3 million Filipinos and a comparable number of Indians now live in the United States. The reason is that professionals and technicians, heavily represented among these nationalities, seldom cluster in highly visible ethnic communities.[31]

As the cases of Amitar Ray and Benigno Aguinaldo in chapter 1 exemplify, professional immigrants are among the most rapidly assimilated. Reasons include their occupational success and the absence of strong ethnic networks to reinforce the culture of origin. Yet, "assimilation" does not mean severing relations with the home country. On the contrary, because accomplished professional immigrants have the means to do so, they frequently attempt to bridge the gap between past and present through periodic visits back home and the maintenance of active ties with family, friends, and colleagues there. During the first generation at least, these "transnational" activities allow immigrant professionals to juggle two social worlds and often to make a contribution to the development of their respective fields in their own countries.

During the 1990s, several important exceptions emerged in this general pattern among this second type of immigrant. First, some refugee groups—such as Iranians, Iraqis, and those coming from the former Soviet Union—included high proportions of educated, professional immigrants. They must be added to those admitted under regular occupational preferences since they also contribute to the pool of highly skilled talent in the U.S. labor market. Unlike regular immigrants, however, refugees and asylees are generally barred from returning to their home countries; hence, their capacity to engage in transnational activities is far more restricted.[32]

At the other extreme, we find professional and technical specialty workers arriving under the temporary "H-1B" program. This new category, created by the 1990 Immigration Act and subsequently expanded, has become the principal conduit for the arrival of tens of thousands of foreign engineers, computer programmers, and medical personnel in recent years. In regional terms, Asia and, to a lesser extent, Eastern Europe and South America have been the principal sources of this new high-skilled inflow. The numerical ceiling for petitions for this type of visa was originally set at 65,000; it was increased to 115,000 in 1999 and then to 195,000 in 2002. The actual number of beneficiaries in 2002 was 197,357. In the same year, the total number of "temporary workers and trainees" reached 582,250.[33]

This high figure reflects the hunger for trained labor in the high-tech and other expanding sectors of the U.S. economy that seem impervious to recent business downturns. Increasingly, this demand is being channeled through temporary entry programs rather than through the more traditional occupational preference categories. Over seventy-five thousand (38 percent) of H-1B workers in 2002 were in computer-related fields, with an additional twenty-five thousand (13 percent) in architecture, engineering, and surveying. Ninety-eight percent had a bachelor's degree or higher, and 42 percent held a postgraduate degree.[34] As a group, temporary professional workers can be expected to sustain extensive ties with their home countries because of their short-term stays and expected return. For the same reasons, they are less likely to establish deep roots in places where they settle. Yet they are not as inconspicuous as permanent professional migrants. Because of their high numbers and concentration in certain high-tech industries, H-1B workers have become more visible and, on occasion, have been targets of resentment and opposition by native workers, who complain of unfair competition.[35] Paralleling the situation of unauthorized, unskilled labor migrants at the bottom of the labor market, the tenuous legal status of these professional workers gives employers a freer hand in setting their wages and work conditions.

Finally, as shown in table 1, some foreign professionals are in the country illegally or have not managed to meet the high accreditation requirements of their respective fields. Doctors, dentists, and other professionals in this situation may choose, as an alternative to unskilled manual work, to practice without licenses. Their clients are, almost always, other immigrants, mostly from the same country, who trust these professionals and find in them a preferable, low-cost option to regular health care. Unauthorized medical, dental, and other professional practices are thus highly localized in areas of immigrant concentration.[36]

Despite these different situations, foreign professionals have generally done very well occupationally and economically in the United States. India and the Philippines have been prime sources of this type of migrant under both permanent and temporary legal entry programs. In 2000, the Filipino population of the United States had median family earnings of $66,000, while Asian Indians reached $64,420. Both figures significantly exceeded the national average of $50,046 in that year. While median earnings for all male foreign workers were approximately $7,000 below the national figure, those coming from Asia—a prime source of professional immigration—exceeded the median by about $3,500.[37]

ENTREPRENEURIAL IMMIGRANTS

Near downtown Los Angeles is an area approximately a mile long where all commercial signs suddenly change from English to strange pictorial characters. Koreatown, as the area is known, contains the predictable number of ethnic restaurants and grocery shops; it also includes a number of banks, import-export houses, industries, and real estate offices. Signs of "English spoken here" assure visitors that their links with the outside world have not been totally severed. In Los Angeles, the propensity for self-employment is three times greater among Koreans than among the population as a whole. Grocery stores, restaurants, gas stations, liquor stores, and real estate offices are typical Korean businesses. Koreans also tend to remain within the community because the more successful immigrants sell their earlier businesses to new arrivals.[38]

A similar urban landscape is found near downtown Miami. Little Havana extends in a narrow strip for about five miles, eventually merging with the southwest suburbs of the city. Cuban-owned firms in the Miami metropolitan area increased from 919 in 1967 to 8,000 in 1976 and approximately 28,000 in 1990. By 1997, they had reached 72,639. Most are small, averaging 4.5 employees at the latest count, but they also include factories employing hundreds of workers. Cuban firms are found in light and heavy manufacturing, construction, commerce, finance, and insurance. An estimated 60 percent of all residential construction in the metropolitan area is now done by these firms.[39] The entrepreneurial success of Remedios Díaz Oliver, described in one of chapter 1's vignettes, is representative of dozens of similar stories.

Areas of concentrated immigrant entrepreneurship are known as *ethnic enclaves*. Their emergence has depended on three conditions: first, the presence of a number of immigrants with substantial business expertise acquired in their home countries; second, access to sources of capital; and third, access to labor. The requisite labor is not too difficult to obtain because it can be drawn initially from family members and, subsequently, from more recent immigrant arrivals. Sources of capital are often not a major obstacle, either, because the sums required initially are small. When immigrants do not bring them from abroad, they can accumulate them through individual savings or obtain them from pooled resources in the community. In some instances, would-be entrepreneurs have access to financial institutions owned or managed by conationals. Thus, the first requisite is the critical one. The presence of a number of immigrants skilled in what sociologist Franklin Frazier called "the art of buying and selling" can usually overcome other obstacles to entrepreneurship.[40] Conversely, their absence tends to confine an immigrant group to wage or salaried work, even when enough capital and labor are available.

Entrepreneurial minorities have been the exception in both early twentieth-century and contemporary immigrations. Their significance is that they create an avenue for economic mobility unavailable to other groups. This avenue is open not only to the original entrepreneurs but to later arrivals as well. The reason is that relations between immigrant employers and their coethnic employees often go beyond a purely contractual bond. When immigrant enterprises expand, they tend to hire their own for supervisory positions. Today Koreans hire and promote Koreans in New York and Los Angeles, and Cubans do the same for other Cubans in Miami, just as sixty years ago the Russian Jews of Manhattan's Lower East Side and the Japanese of San Francisco and Los Angeles hired and supported those from their own communities.[41]

An ethnic enclave is not, however, the only manifestation of immigrant entrepreneurship. In other cities, where the concentration of these immigrants is less dense, they tend to take over businesses catering to low-income groups, often in the inner cities. In this role as "middleman minorities," entrepreneurial immigrants are less visible because they tend to be dispersed over the area occupied by the populations they serve. Koreatown in Los Angeles is not, for example, the only manifestation of entrepreneurship among this immigrant group. Koreans are also present in significant numbers in New York City, where they have gained increasing control of the produce market, and in cities such as Washington, D.C., and Baltimore, where they have progressively replaced Italians and Jews as the principal merchants in low-income inner-city areas. Similarly, roughly two-thirds of Cuban-owned firms are concentrated in Miami, but they are also numerous in other cities, such as Los Angeles, Jersey City, and West New York. The percentage of firms per thousand Cuban population is actually higher in these secondary concentrations than in Miami.[42]

According to the Current Population Survey, the rate of self-employment for Korean adult immigrants (26.5 percent) is almost 2.5 times the corresponding rate for natives, 11.1 percent. Other highly entrepreneurial immigrant groups include Iranians (24.6 percent), Pakistanis (19.4 percent), and Russians (18.9 percent).[43] Data from the U.S. Census show high rates of male self-employment in the 1990s among Koreans (34.2 percent), Chinese (15.3 percent), and Cubans (18.2 percent). In all three groups, the self-employed exceeded the annual earnings of male wage workers by approximately $12,000. Other studies of the entire foreign-born population have consistently documented the economic advantage of the self-employed over wage workers as well as the much stronger propensity of male migrants to engage in entrepreneurial activities.[44]

The emergence of ethnic enclaves and other forms of immigrant entrepreneurship has been generally fortuitous. While the 1990 Immigration Act includes a preference category for "employment creating" investors, very few foreigners have availed themselves of this option. This is, in part, a consequence of the high capital requirements to qualify. In the late 1990s, this preference attracted barely a thousand new immigrants per year. No explicit entry preference exists for small entrepreneurs with little or no capital, and none is likely to be implemented in the future. In general, entrepreneurial minorities come under preferences designated for other purposes. Koreans and Chinese, two of the most successful business-oriented groups, have availed themselves of the employment-based preference categories for professionals and skilled workers and, subsequently, of the family reunification provisions of the 1965 and 1990 immigration laws. Cubans came as political refugees and were initially dispersed throughout the country. It took this group more than a decade after arrival to regroup in certain geographic locations, primarily South Florida, and then begin the push toward entrepreneurship.

More recent refugee groups, such as the Vietnamese and Russians, have also followed the entrepreneurial path, creating new enclaves on both coasts. The principal Vietnamese concentration is in Orange County, California, around the town of Westminster. The main Russian enclave is found in Brighton Beach, Brooklyn. Research on the Vietnamese in California has found the same pattern of economic success of ethnic entrepreneurs reported among other groups.[45] Finally, even some unauthorized immigrants go into business on their own. The story of Juan Manuel Fernández in chapter 1 is not an isolated incident since other undocumented migrants have also sought to escape low-wage work by setting themselves up as independent mechanics, gardeners, handymen, and house cleaners. Naturally, entrepreneurship cannot be expected to yield the same benefits for these migrants as for those enjoying legal status. Their businesses are small and informal, and, as in the case of Fernández, they are constantly in fear of losing everything if they are found and deported.

A more recent literature has shown that a high proportion of successful migrant firms depend for their operation on transnational ties, primarily with the owners' home country. They commonly import goods for sale in the immigrant community or in the open market, export high-tech U.S. goods to the home nation, and draw on contacts there for sources of capital and labor. A 2002 study of entrepreneurial activities among Latin American immigrants in the United States found that up to 58 percent of firms in these communities relied on these transnational ties for their continued viability and growth.[46] We will return to the consequences of ethnic enterprise and transnationalism when we examine immigrants' economic and political adaptation in chapters 4 and 5.

REFUGEES AND ASYLEES

The Refugee Act of 1980, signed into law by President Jimmy Carter, aimed at eliminating the former practice of granting asylum only to escapees from Communist-controlled nations. Instead, it sought to bring U.S. policy into line with international practice, which defines a *refugee* as anyone with a well-founded fear of persecution or physical harm, regardless of the political bent of his or her country's regime. In practice, however, during the two Reagan administrations, the United States continued to grant refugee status to escapees from Communism, primarily those from Southeast Asia and Eastern Europe, while making it difficult for others fleeing right-wing regimes, such as those from Guatemala and El Salvador. Being granted asylum has significant advantages over other immigration channels. The central difference is that while refugees have legal status and the right to work, and they can avail themselves of the welfare provisions of the 1980 act, those denied asylum have none of these privileges and, if they stay, are classified as illegal aliens.[47]

Being a refugee is therefore not a matter of personal choice but a governmental decision based on a combination of legal guidelines and political expediency. Depending on the relationship between the United States and the country of origin and the geopolitical context of the time, a particular flow of people may be classified as a political exodus or as an illegal group of economically motivated immigrants. Given past policy, it is not surprising that there are few escapees from rightist regimes, no matter how repressive, living legally in the country. Major refugee groups have arrived, instead, after the Soviet army occupation of Eastern Europe, after the rise to power of Fidel Castro in Cuba, and after the takeover by Communist insurgents of three Southeast Asian countries.

The end of the Cold War and the demise of the Soviet Union has brought about a more diversified and less ideological orientation to U.S. refugee policy. Although still driven by geopolitical interests and expediency, this policy has room for broader humanitarian considerations. Thus, the national origins of the current refugee flow have become more diversified and include countries that are not necessarily adversarial to the United States. Still, the number of refugees pales by comparison to that of regular immigrants and, especially, to the growing category of temporary workers. In 2001, the United States allowed entry for 68,925 refugees, compared with 1,064,318 admitted for legal permanent residence (of which 411,059 were new arrivals) and 739,421 "temporary workers and trainees" plus their families. In 2002, reflecting the impact of the September 11, 2001, terrorist attacks, the number of refugee petitions approved and actual refugee arrivals dropped again, this time drastically. Refugee admissions in 2002 numbered only 26,839, a 61 percent decline from the prior year.[48] Unless international circumstances change, it is unlikely that refugee admissions will climb anytime soon to the levels reached during the Cold War.

The legal difference between a refugee and an asylee hinges on the physical location of the person. Both types are recognized by the government as having a well-founded fear of persecution, but whereas the first still lives abroad and must be transported to the United States, the second is already within U.S. territory. This difference is important because it makes the refugee flows conform more closely to the government's overall foreign policy, while would-be asylees confront authorities with a fait accompli to be handled on the spot. Thus, prior to 1990, refugees were mostly opponents and victims of Communism in the Soviet Union and its allies, including Cuba and Vietnam; in the early 1990s, they came primarily from Russia and the successor states of the former Soviet Union, as U.S. refugee policy was used to stabilize and ease economic conditions for the fragile new governments in these countries. By the late 1990s, the refugee flow had diversified to include significant numbers from Bosnia-Herzegovina, Somalia, Iran, and Iraq. Between 1995 and 1999, close to one hundred thousand Bosnians, fifteen thousand Somalis, and twenty thousand Iranians and Iraqis were admitted under this category.[49]

Asylee applications during the 1990s were, by contrast, dominated by migrants from Central America, primarily El Salvador, Guatemala, and Nicaragua. These movements originated in violent civil wars in these countries that pushed large numbers to move abroad and eventually seek entry in the United States. Their wishes did not accord, however, with the interests of the U.S. government at the time, which routinely denied their requests. The end of the civil wars and return of political democracy in all three countries was followed by urgent entreaties by the new governments to U.S. authorities to grant the asylum requests of their conationals. While reasons for asylum had been largely removed by the end of the armed conflicts, the new Central American leaders argued that their economies desperately needed the remittances sent by their migrants, living and working in the United States as unauthorized aliens.[50]

During the 1990s, 195,000 Salvadorans, 165,000 Guatemalans, and 16,000 Nicaraguans filed or refiled their asylum requests. U.S. immigration authorities were not too impressed by their claims or those of their respective governments, as shown by the fact that only one-fifth of these applications were approved in the case of Nicaraguans and less than one-tenth in those of Guatemalans and Salvadorans. Overall, the rate of approval of asylum applications for immigrants already living in the United States or presenting themselves at border entry points was approximately 25 percent during the last decade.[51]

As shown in table 1, refugees and asylees vary greatly in terms of human capital endowment. Some, such as the pre-1980 waves of Cuban exiles and recent Iranian, Iraqi, and Russian refugees, are well educated, and many possess professional and entrepreneurial skills. Other groups, such as Cambodian, Laotian, and Hmong refugees or would-be Guatemalan and Salvadoran asylees, are composed primarily of small farmers and rural laborers with little formal education. In every case, the distinct advantages conferred by refugees or asylee status include not only the right to stay and work but a program of generous resettlement and welfare assistance, health benefits, and the right to attain permanent legal residence in one year.[52]

Refugee professionals and entrepreneurs have generally made good use of these privileges to reestablish themselves and prosper in their respective lines of work. Refugee groups arriving with little or no human capital have at least managed to survive under the welfare provisions of the program. Although, as we shall see, the acculturation and entry into the labor market of some of these groups may have been delayed by access to these benefits, some policies have provided them with the opportunity to rebuild their families and communities, creating a key source of social capital for themselves and their children to cope with their new environment.

OVERVIEW

In 2005, well over a hundred foreign countries and possessions sent immigrants to the United States. Aside from basic statistical data supplied by INS and the Census Bureau, little is yet known about most of these groups. Tracing their individual evolution and patterns of adaptation is a task well beyond the scope of this book. Instead, we delineate the basic contours of contemporary immigration by focusing on major aspects of the adaptation experience. The emphasis throughout is on diversity both in the immigrants' origins and in their modes of incorporation into American society. The typology outlined in this chapter will serve as our basic organizing tool as we follow immigrants through their locations in space, their strategies for economic mobility, their efforts at learning a new language and culture, their decision to adopt U.S. citizenship or not, and their struggle to raise their children in the United States and, inevitably, as Americans.

Although significant differences exist within each major type of immigration, we have reason to believe that each type outlined in table 1 shares a number of characteristics with others in a similar position. Thus, skilled professionals coming to the United States with permanent residence permits tend to follow occupational, locational, and social adaptation patterns that are similar to each other and quite different from those of unskilled workers, even those of the same nationality. Similarly, refugee entrepreneurs are likely to cluster in ethnic enclaves that resemble each other, despite differences in language, culture, and places of arrival. As we will see in chapter 4, legal status and governmental reception are just two of the components of an immigrant group's mode of incorporation. However, they are decisive because they frequently determine the other levels, as well as the possibility that migrants can put to use the human capital that they brought from abroad.

A description of contemporary immigration and its diversity would be incomplete if it did not address the question of what it all means for the rest of American society. In other words, is it good or bad for the country to continue receiving hundreds of thousands of immigrants from all over the world? As in the early twentieth century, periods of high immigration have inevitably triggered a nationalistic reaction and increasing hostility toward foreigners. As in that earlier era, their presence is seen today as a threat to national culture and the unity of the nation. Not surprisingly, there have been growing calls for restriction in recent years, coming from both policy and academic circles, as well as from the mass media.[53]

Echoing tracts directed against Irish and Italian immigrants a century ago, today's nativists argue that immigrants do not really want to learn English or assimilate culturally and that their inferior cultural heritage will undermine the integrity of an Anglo-Protestant nation. These tirades inevitably conclude with a call for drastic restrictionism.[54] As we will see in later chapters, the accusation that today's Latin immigrants do not want to learn English or integrate into the American mainstream runs against all empirical evidence and hardly deserves consideration. In contrast, it is true that the majority of certain groups, such as Mexicans and Central Americans, are labor migrants and thus arrive with relatively low levels of human capital. As we will see in chapter 8, their children also experience serious barriers to successful adaptation.[55]

Before taking the neonativists' recommendations at face value, however, it is important to consider the actual short- and long-term consequences of immigration for the nation. We do this in detail in the last chapter, but, to anticipate the conclusions of that analysis, we will show that immigration, as a whole, has been positive for American society in the past and continues to be so at present. There are exceptions, to be sure, and they will be noted. Yet, a persuasive case can be made that the United States would not be the strong, vibrant nation that it is without the contributions made by its millions of immigrants. Today they fill the labor needs of the giant American economy, rejuvenate the population, and add new energies and diversity to American culture. Without immigration, the United States would come to resemble the profile of rich but aging European societies hobbled by stagnant economies and a declining population, whose support in old age looms as a major economic and social problem.[56]

Immigrant America faces many challenges, not the least of which is the prospect for successful adaptation of its second generation. But, on balance, the flow of energy, talent, and labor from abroad creates more solutions than problems and represents an indispensable component of the nation's future. Ironically, many of the most ardent restrictionists today are themselves the children and grandchildren of immigrants. They would do well to reflect more carefully on what was said by the self-appointed guardians of "Anglo-Protestant" institutions of their parents and grandparents and on how the story finally turned out. For predictions about the dire consequences of immigration have been commonplace and consistently proven wrong. Similar predictions advanced today with such a sense of certainty and urgency are likely to follow the same course.

3

Moving
Patterns of Immigrant Settlement
and Spatial Mobility

n his 1926 study *Migration and Business Cycles*, Harry Jerome concluded that the inflow of population was "on the whole dominated by conditions in the United States. The 'pull' is stronger than the push."[1] By that time, the gradual integration of the world economy had advanced sufficiently to make many Europeans aware of economic opportunities on the other side of the Atlantic, so deliberate recruitment became unnecessary. The question remains, however, about the destination of these flows. Labor economists frequently write as if immigrants have perfect information about labor market conditions in the receiving country and adjust their locational decisions accordingly.

The reality is very different because a number of factors other than wage differentials impinge on the actual destination of migrant flows. This chapter examines the locational distribution of immigrant groups with an emphasis both on diversity among nationalities and types of migration and on the unequal distribution of the foreign population in space. Although our main interest is on contemporary trends, we must go back in time, because the roots of the locational patterns of immigrants arriving today are often found in events that took place in the last century.

THE PIONEERS

The settlement decisions of contemporary immigrants are decisively affected by the ethnic concentrations established by their compatriots in the past. Because earlier flows consisted overwhelmingly of manual laborers, it is important to examine first how these foreign working-class communities came to settle where they did. A first significant factor was geographic propinquity. It is not by chance that the bulk of turn-of-the-century European immigrants settled along the mid– and north Atlantic seaboard, while their Asian counterparts settled in California and other Pacific states. It is also not surprising that the bulk of early Mexican immigration concentrated in the Southwest, especially along the border. For immigrant workers, proximity to the homeland has two important economic consequences. First, for those who come on their own, it reduces the costs of the journey; second, for everyone, it reduces the costs of return, which most labor migrants plan to undertake at some point. In those cases in which migration occurs along a land border, as with Mexicans, proximity to the sending area also provides a familiar physical and climatic environment.

The impact of propinquity is most vividly reflected in those immigrant communities established right by the waterside, at points of debarkation in port cities of both coasts. The "Little Italys" huddled close to the water in Boston, New York, Philadelphia, and Baltimore, as well as the "Chinatowns" of San Francisco and other cities, offer living testimony of a type of immigration that, having reached U.S. shores, would go no farther.[2]

This is not the whole story, however, because many other groups pushed inland. For foreign laborers, the decisive factor for the latter type of settlement was recruitment either in the home country or at ports of entry. The concentration of some Central and Eastern European peoples in the Midwest reflects the turn-of-the-century development of heavy industry in this area—first steel and later automaking. This concentration, coupled with the minimal skills required for most new industrial jobs, made recruiting cheap immigrant labor attractive to employers. Consequences of this recruitment pattern last to our day: only 4 percent of the foreign-born population in 2000 lived in Ohio, but it is the home state of 15 percent of the nation's Croatians, 14 percent of the Hungarians, 15 percent of the Serbs, 22 percent of the Slovaks, and 45 percent of the Slovenians, whose ancestors had come a century earlier.[3]

Similarly, during the nineteenth century, labor recruitment by the Hudson and other canal companies moved contingents of Irish and Italian workers inland along the routes followed by canal construction. In the West, Chinese coolie workers also moved inland after mass recruitment by the railway companies.[4] The Union Pacific and the Central Pacific recruited Mexicans, trainloads of whom were dispatched from El Paso and other border cities. About the same time, Finnish workers made their appearance in northern Wisconsin, Minnesota, and the Michigan Peninsula, hired by the copper mine and timber companies.[5]

Not every group arriving during the nineteenth century consisted exclusively of wage workers, however. Those coming before the Civil War in particular were often able to take advantage of cheap land in the West to go into business for themselves. This was especially the case for German settlers arriving since before the Revolutionary War. Germans were able to push inland toward the sparsely settled lands of Ohio, Indiana, Illinois, and beyond. In their wake, the landscape of the Midwest became dotted with rural farm enclaves in which the settlers' language and customs dominated.[6]

The influence of what were, in fact, the entrepreneurial migrations of its day has also lasted to the present. Descendants of the original settlers and those coming later on during the nineteenth century represent the paramount ethnic concentrations throughout the Midwest. In the west north-central states (Wisconsin, Minnesota, Iowa, the Dakotas, and Nebraska), between 35 and 45 percent of the population reported German ancestry in 2000, figures that quintuple those corresponding to the English.[7] German Americans have been by far the dominant ethnic group in Cincinnati (39 percent), Indianapolis (27 percent), Milwaukee (45 percent), Minneapolis–St. Paul (39 percent), and St. Louis (36 percent).[8]

A similar pattern of independent Midwest farm settlement was followed by early Scandinavian and Czech immigrants. Scandinavian enclaves in the west north-central region and especially in Minnesota attracted immigrants from the same nationalities throughout the twentieth century; their descendants represent today the fourth-largest ancestry group in the region and the third largest (15 percent) in Minneapolis–St. Paul. Czech farming made its appearance in Wisconsin around the mid-1800s; from Racine and earlier farming enclaves, Czechs pushed inland toward the Nebraska frontier and then to Oklahoma and Texas. As late as 1990, Czech ancestry still accounted for about 25 percent of the populations of several rural counties in these states.[9]

In the Far West, Japanese immigrants attempted to follow the same path by buying land and engaging in independent farming during the early 1900s. In their case, however, land was neither plentiful nor empty. Japanese farmers faced the united opposition of domestic growers, who had welcomed their arrival as laborers but who resisted violently their shift into self-employment:

> So long as the Japanese remained willing to perform agricultural labor at low wages, they remained popular with California ranchers. But . . . many Japanese began to lease and buy agricultural land for farming on their own account. This enterprise had the two-fold result of creating Japanese competition in the produce field and decreasing the number of Japanese farmhands available.[10]

As a result, the California state legislature passed the Alien Land Law of 1913 restricting Japanese land acquisition. This legal instrument was refined in 1920, when these immigrants were forbidden to lease land or act as guardians of native-born minors in matters of property.[11] These measures drove many Japanese off the land and into urban small businesses, but the development of an urban enclave economy was also stunted by the end of Japanese immigration, following the Gentleman's Agreement of 1907. As a consequence of these restrictions, Japanese Americans, although a highly successful group, currently number fewer than one million and, with the exception of Hawaii, represent a minuscule proportion of the population of the states where they concentrate.[12]

Pioneer migrants—whether settling close to places of arrival, following labor recruiters inland, or charting an independent course through farming and urban trade in different locations—had a decisive influence on later migrants. Once a group settled in a certain place, the destination of later cohorts from the same country often became a foregone conclusion. Migration is a network-driven process, and the operation of kin and friendship ties is nowhere more effective than in guiding new arrivals toward preexisting ethnic communities. This process may continue indefinitely and accounts for the high concentration of most foreign groups in certain regions of the country and their near absence from others.

FOLLOWING IN THE FOOTSTEPS

At the time of the Mexican Revolution in the early 1900s, large contingents of Mexican refugees migrated northward to find employment in the slaughterhouses of Chicago, the breweries of Milwaukee, and the steel mills of Gary, Indiana. Communities established then continue to serve as magnets for Mexican migrants today. Despite the distance and the different climatic conditions, remote villages in the interior of Mexico continue sending their residents, year after year, for a stint of work in the cities of the Midwest.[13]

The same pattern is found in the East, where small Jamaican, Dominican, and Haitian colonies in New York City provided the nucleus for guiding mass labor migration in recent decades. Again distance and a colder climate were no obstacle for these Caribbean migrants to follow in the wake of their predecessors. Out West, most contemporary Asian and Pacific Islander migrations, such as the Japanese and the Filipinos, continue to be overwhelmingly concentrated in their areas of traditional settlement.[14]

The influence of preexisting networks on locational patterns tends to be decisive among contemporary labor migrants because they are not guided by recruiting agents but by spontaneous individual and family decisions, usually based on the presence in certain places of kin and friends who can provide shelter and assistance. Exceptions to this pattern are found most often among other types of immigrants. During the last fifteen years, unauthorized Mexican labor migration, formerly concentrated in the West and Southwest, has increasingly moved east to become a truly national presence. As we will see in later chapters, this displacement is partially a consequence of significant changes in immigration law and its enforcement. Even then, however, deliberate recruitment and kin and friendship networks have continued to play a central role in the location decisions of current Mexican immigrants.

Professionals, such as physicians, engineers, and scientists, tend to rely less on the assistance of preexisting ethnic communities than on their own skills and qualifications. They frequently come only after securing job offers from U.S. employers and tend to be more dispersed throughout the country than manual labor migrants. Although no national contingent is formed exclusively by professionals and their families, a few—such as recent Indian immigrants—approximate this pattern and provide examples of its characteristic dispersion.[15]

Entrepreneurial minorities tend to settle in large urban areas that provide close proximity to markets and sources of labor. Like working-class migrants, foreign entrepreneurs are often found in the areas of principal ethnic concentration because of the cheap labor, protected markets, and access to credit in these areas. This is the case, for example, of Koreans, concentrated in Los Angeles; Chinese entrepreneurs in Los Angeles, San Francisco, and New York; and Cubans in Miami. However, other business-minded immigrants choose to move away from the principal areas of ethnic concentration in quest of economic opportunity. The latter are commonly found in the role of middleman merchants and lenders to the domestic working class. Koreans and Chinese in several East Coast cities and Cubans in Puerto Rico provide examples.[16]

Finally, the early locational patterns of political refugees and seekers of political asylum are often decided for them by government authorities and private resettlement agencies. In the past, the goal of official resettlement programs has been to disperse refugee groups away from their points of arrival to facilitate their cultural assimilation and attenuate the economic burden they are supposed to represent for receiving areas. This official decision accounts for the multiplicity of locations in which groups such as the Cubans and the Vietnamese are found today. Gradually, however, refugees tend to trek back toward areas closer to their homeland and more compatible in terms of climate and culture. The presence of ethnic communities of the same nationality or a related one has frequently played a decisive role in promoting these secondary migrations.

The rapid growth of the Cuban population in Miami–Dade County, Florida, and of the Vietnamese population in Orange County and San Jose, California, can be traced directly to this process. By 1979, on the eve of the Mariel boat lift, half of the Cuban-origin population of the United States was found in the Miami metropolitan area, a result primarily of return migration by refugees originally resettled elsewhere; by 2000, the national share of Cuban Americans in the Miami area had grown to 60 percent. Similarly, by 1990, Orange County alone had more Vietnamese refugees than any state except all of California combined, with its hub in the communities of Santa Ana and Westminster ("Little Saigon"), where the Nguyens outnumbered the Smiths two to one among Orange County home buyers; it was followed by San Jose, where the Nguyens outnumbered the Joneses in the phone book fourteen columns to eight. By 2000, Orange County and San Jose accounted for one-fifth of all Vietnamese in the country. Calle Ocho (S.W. 8th Street) in Miami is the heart of "Little Havana"; Bolsa Avenue in Westminster has been called the Vietnamese capital of America.[17]

CONTEMPORARY SETTLEMENT PATTERNS: A MAP OF IMMIGRANT AMERICA

These various causal processes have led to a settlement pattern among recent immigrants to the United States that combines two apparently contradictory outcomes: concentration, because a few states and metropolitan areas receive a disproportionate number of the newcomers; and diffusion, because immigrants are found in every state and because different immigrant types vary significantly in their locational decisions.

Figures 1 and 2 provide a striking pair of images of immigrant settlement by county in the contiguous forty-eight states in 2000. The first map shows the absolute number of the foreign-born population residing in each county; the second shows the relative proportion of the foreign-born as a percentage of each county's total population. While vast expanses of the country, particularly in the heartland, contain relatively few immigrants in absolute or relative terms, other regions exhibit extraordinary concentrations, especially along the coasts. Large concentrations are apparent throughout much of the entire state of California, most notably along its southern corridor from Los Angeles to San Diego; as well as in South Florida; the northeastern coastal corridor extending from Washington, D.C., through Philadelphia, New York City, and Boston; and the greater metropolitan areas of Chicago, Detroit, Houston, Dallas–Fort Worth, Phoenix, Atlanta, Minneapolis–St. Paul, and Seattle. High relative proportions are especially evident in less populated counties along the Mexican border from Texas to California and, more recently, in some nontraditional areas of pioneering immigrant settlement, notably in North Carolina and Georgia in the South, and in Colorado and Nevada in the Southwest.

Table 2 documents the concentrations at the state level of the twelve largest immigrant groups. The 2000 U.S. Census counted a foreign-born population of 31.1 million people, and California alone was home to nearly 30 percent of them, although only 10 percent of the native-born population lived there. Indeed, California was the principal state of settlement of nine of the ten largest immigrant nationalities. The state of New York absorbed another 12.4 percent of the nation's foreign-born, while being home to only 6 percent of the native-born. Texas followed with 9.3 percent of the foreign-born total, compared with 7.2 percent of the native-born. Those three states combined to account for a little more than half of all immigrants in the country. Another 18 percent of the foreign-born were found in Florida, Illinois, and New Jersey,

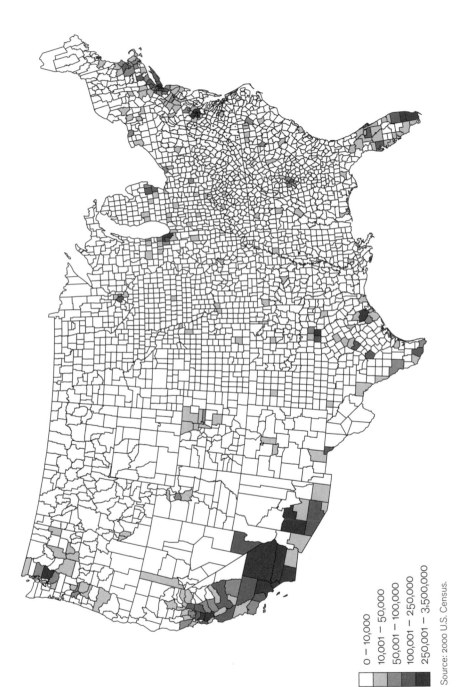

Figure 1. The foreign-born population in the United States by county, 2000

0 – 10,000
10,001 – 50,000
50,001 – 100,000
100,001 – 250,000
250,001 – 3,500,000

Source: 2000 U.S. Census.

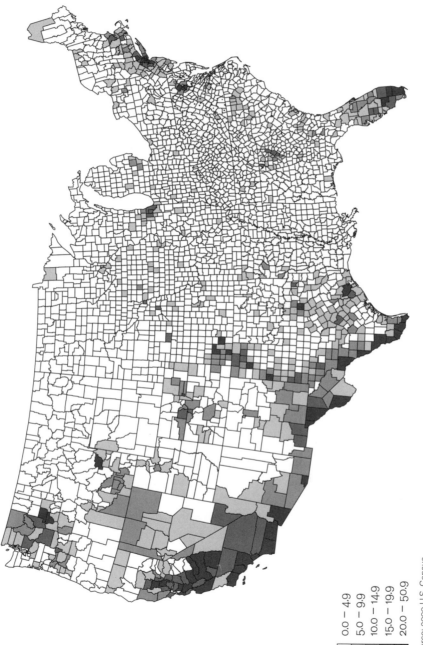

Figure 2. The foreign-born in the United States as a percentage of total county population, 2000

0.0 − 4.9
5.0 − 9.9
10.0 − 14.9
15.0 − 19.9
20.0 − 50.9

TABLE 2. STATES OF PRINCIPAL SETTLEMENT OF THE TWELVE LARGEST IMMIGRANT GROUPS, 2000

Country of birth	N	% of total immigrants	States of principal settlement					
			First	%	Second	%	Third	%
Mexico	9,163,463	29.4	California	42.8	Texas	20.4	Illinois	6.7
Philippines	1,374,213	4.4	California	48.5	New York	5.2	New Jersey	5.0
India	1,027,144	3.3	California	19.5	New Jersey	11.7	New York	11.5
China[a]	997,301	3.2	California	33.2	New York	23.4	New Jersey	4.1
Vietnam	991,995	3.2	California	42.5	Texas	10.9	Washington	4.1
Cuba	872,716	2.8	Florida	73.5	New Jersey	6.4	California	4.7
Korea	870,542	2.8	California	31.3	New York	11.6	New Jersey	5.9
Canada	820,713	2.6	California	17.6	Florida	11.8	New York	6.8
El Salvador	815,570	2.6	California	44.0	Texas	12.2	New York	9.2
Germany	705,110	2.3	California	14.1	New York	9.8	Florida	9.2
Dominican Republic	685,952	2.2	New York	59.4	New Jersey	12.8	Florida	9.3
Former USSR[b]	618,302	2.0	New York	29.3	California	16.1	Illinois	6.0
Total foreign-born	31,133,481	100.0	California	28.5	New York	12.4	Texas	9.3
Total native-born	250,288,425	100.0	California	10.0	Texas	7.2	New York	6.0

SOURCE: 2000 U.S. Census, 5% Public Use Microdata Sample.

[a]Immigrants from mainland China only.
[b]Immigrants from Russia and Ukraine.

so that nearly two-thirds of all immigrants nationally resided in only six states in 2000.

These six states have been the primary destination states for legal immigrants in every year since 1971. In 2002, 65 percent of the 1,063,732 foreign-born persons admitted for legal permanent residence went to the same half-dozen states in approximately the same proportions: California (27.4 percent), New York (10.8 percent), Florida (8.5 percent), Texas (8.3 percent), New Jersey (5.4 percent), and Illinois (4.4 percent). At the other extreme, no state received fewer than two hundred immigrants, the least favored being Wyoming (281) and Montana (422).[18]

Within this general picture, some immigrant nationalities are far more concentrated than others. Of the dozen largest groups in 2000, three-fourths of all Cubans were in Florida; three-fifths of all Dominicans were in New York, with another 13 percent next door in New Jersey; and between 40 and 50 percent of Filipinos, Salvadorans, Mexicans, and Vietnamese were in California, as were a third of the Chinese and Koreans. By comparison, and for reasons noted earlier, Indian immigrants were much more dispersed, as were the long-settled populations of Canadians and Germans.

Figure 3 portrays the national composition of immigrant flows to seven major receiving urban areas. Together these cities accounted for 34 percent of all legal immigration during 2002. With some variations, this settlement pattern remains representative of those registered throughout the 1980s and 1990s. Along with numerical concentration, there is much diversity in the origins of immigrants going to these seven cities.

Mexicans form by far the largest contingent settling in Los Angeles —the premier destination of immigrants—as well as in the third and sixth areas of destination—Chicago and Houston, respectively. The play of geography and prior ethnic settlement is also reflected in the major flows to each city. In Los Angeles, Asian immigrants account jointly for over one-fourth of the total; in Chicago, they are also present but share pride of place with Mexicans and a major European group— Poles, who have traditionally settled in this area. The same forces underlie the composition of immigration to San Jose (Silicon Valley) and the greater San Francisco Bay Area, a traditional place of settlement for Asians, where Indians, Chinese, Vietnamese, and Filipinos account jointly for a large share of the inflow.

Three of the five principal immigrant flows to New York City—the second major receiving area—come from the Caribbean, with those

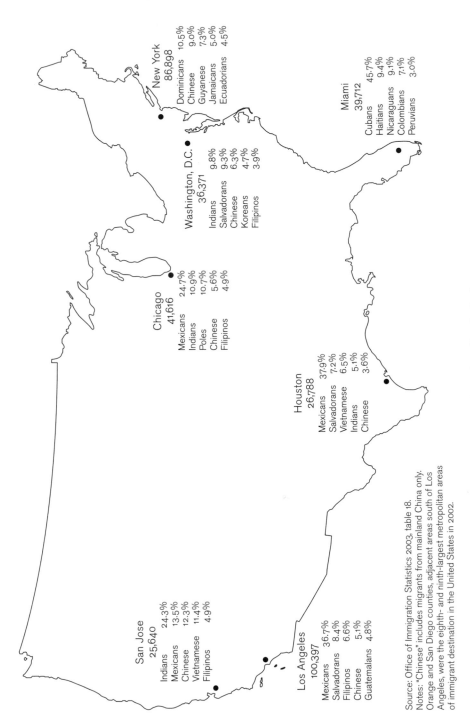

New York
86,898

Dominicans 10.5%
Chinese 9.0%
Guyanese 7.3%
Jamaicans 5.0%
Ecuadorians 4.5%

Miami
39,712

Cubans 45.7%
Haitians 9.4%
Nicaraguans 9.1%
Colombians 7.1%
Peruvians 3.0%

Washington, D.C.
36,371

Indians 9.8%
Salvadorans 9.3%
Chinese 6.3%
Koreans 4.7%
Filipinos 3.9%

Chicago
41,616

Mexicans 24.7%
Indians 10.9%
Poles 10.7%
Chinese 5.6%
Filipinos 4.9%

Houston
26,788

Mexicans 37.9%
Salvadorans 7.2%
Vietnamese 6.5%
Indians 5.1%
Chinese 3.6%

San Jose
25,640

Indians 24.3%
Mexicans 13.5%
Chinese 12.3%
Vietnamese 11.4%
Filipinos 4.9%

Los Angeles
100,397

Mexicans 36.7%
Salvadorans 8.4%
Filipinos 6.6%
Chinese 5.1%
Guatemalans 4.8%

Source: Office of Immigration Statistics 2003, table 18.
Notes: "Chinese" includes migrants from mainland China only.
Orange and San Diego counties, adjacent areas south of Los
Angeles, were the eighth- and ninth-largest metropolitan areas
of immigrant destination in the United States in 2002.

Figure 3. Composition of legally admitted immigrant flows to seven major metropolitan destinations, 2002

from the Dominican Republic accounting for a tenth of the total, followed by Jamaica and Guyana. Different Caribbean and Latin American origins typify immigration to Miami, except that here Cubans are by far the dominant nationality. These flows continue to reflect, with notable precision, the power of pioneer settlement patterns for each of these nationalities.

Perhaps the most peculiar case is Washington, D.C., where most immigrant communities are of recent vintage and where, unlike other East Coast destinations, Caribbean groups are not predominant. Instead, migration to Washington is dominated by entrepreneurial Asian groups along with former political refugees. Salvadorans and Vietnamese represent the latter trend. Although there is some logical affinity between the motives for departure of these politically motivated outflows and their settlement in the nation's capital, the actual processes leading to this outcome have not been studied in detail so far.[19]

LOCATIONAL DECISIONS OF IMMIGRANT GROUPS

An alternative portrait of the settlement process emerges when we examine locational decisions of the major immigrant groups themselves, rather than major areas of destination. Although there is overlap between both forms of arranging the data, the two vary because national contingents differ in their levels of concentration and their propensity to locate in metropolitan areas. Table 3 presents the relevant information for 2002. Four of the twelve largest immigrant groups arriving in that year—Mexicans, Filipinos, Salvadorans, and Koreans— shared a preferred place of destination: Los Angeles. New York was the first choice of four other groups: immigrants from mainland China, the Dominican Republic, Ukraine, and Russia. The last four groups— the Indians, Vietnamese, Cubans, and Bosnians—preferred San Jose, Orange County, Miami, and Chicago, respectively. When we look further at immigrant groups' second and third preferred destinations (not shown in table 3), we find that only five of the twelve groups did not have Los Angeles as one of their preferred destinations; seven did not include New York, but three of them settled in neighboring New Jersey cities on the other side of the Hudson River.

Next to Los Angeles and New York comes San Jose, the second choice of the Vietnamese and third choice of the Chinese, and San Diego, the second for Filipinos and third for Mexicans. Washington, D.C., was the second choice of Salvadorans and Koreans. Finally, several cities are the

TABLE 3. METROPOLITAN DESTINATIONS OF THE TWELVE LARGEST IMMIGRANT GROUPS, 2002

| Nationality | N | Most common destination | | % at top three destinations | % at metropolitan destinations | % at other nonmetropolitan destinations | As % of total immigration |
		Metropolitan area	%				
Mexican	219,380	Los Angeles	17	27	64	9	21
Indian	71,105	San Jose	9	22	76	2	7
Chinese[a]	61,282	New York	13	26	71	3	6
Filipino	51,308	Los Angeles	13	21	71	8	5
Vietnamese	33,627	Orange County, CA	10	26	72	2	3
Salvadoran	31,168	Los Angeles	27	49	49	2	3
Cuban	28,272	Miami	64	71	28	1	3
Bosnian	25,373	Chicago	6	17	80	3	2
Dominican	22,604	New York	40	50	48	2	2
Ukraine	21,217	New York	14	31	65	4	2
Korea	21,021	Los Angeles	17	31	64	5	2
Russia	20,833	New York	12	19	75	6	2

SOURCE: U.S. Office of Immigration Statistics 2003, table 2.

[a]Immigrants from mainland China only.

specific destinations of only one group for reasons of settlement history or propinquity. Cubans are the single-largest immigrant group in both Miami and Tampa. Third settlement choices have alternated in the past with other locations for several nationalities.

The locational decisions of all major contemporary inflows reflect both historical patterns of settlement and types of contemporary immigrants. Most concentrated and least rural are Cubans, over 60 percent of whom have settled in Miami. In 2002, as in prior years, recorded immigration from Cuba did not correspond to actual arrivals but was formed instead by former political refugees who adjusted their legal status. As refugees, Cubans were far more dispersed following the deliberate resettlement policy of government agencies. The high concentration of Cubans as "immigrants" thus reflects voluntary individual decisions to migrate back to South Florida. As a result, the majority of Miami's population is today of Cuban origin, and close to half of the metropolitan population of Dade County is classified as Hispanic. Undoubtedly, geographic and climatic reasons have played a role in the process, but more important seems to have been the business and employment opportunities made available by the emergence of an ethnic enclave economy in the area.[20]

Next in concentration are Dominicans, a group whose rapid growth has taken place during the last three decades and that is composed primarily of industrial operatives and urban laborers. Employer recruitment and the existence of an older Dominican colony in New York City appear to have been the decisive factors channeling Dominican migration toward the Northeast.[21]

Indian immigrants represent one of the most spatially dispersed groups, as well as the group with the highest proportion of university graduates and professionals, whose numbers in the United States more than doubled during the 1990s. The Indian pattern of settlement corresponds to that expected from professional immigrants. Though less than 10 percent settled in their preferred destination, that location—San Jose—also reflects the occupational composition of Indian immigration, since it is tied to employment in the high-tech industries of Silicon Valley.

The Chinese exhibit both a clear preference for New York City and a moderately high level of concentration in their next major places of destination—the San Francisco Bay Area and Los Angeles. Like Indians, a high proportion of recent Chinese immigrants possess university degrees; like Cubans, they are often bound toward those areas where an ethnic enclave economy already exists. In this case, traditional

Chinatowns and emerging ones in suburban areas seem to provide the lure for the entrepreneurially inclined, as well as those seeking wage work in ethnic firms.[22]

The largest national contingents are relatively similar in their levels of metropolitan concentration, although this convergence is not the outcome of the same historical process. The largest group by far—Mexicans—is formed overwhelmingly by workers and their families. The proportion of professionals and managers among occupationally active Mexican immigrants remained the lowest among all major immigrant groups in 2000, as it had been in prior years; the percentage of urban workers and farm laborers was, however, the highest. Originally a rural-bound flow, Mexican immigration has become mostly urban bound in recent years, with the vast majority of new arrivals going to metropolitan areas. The considerable dispersion of this group can be attributed to its size and its long-standing character as a source of wage labor throughout the Southwest and Midwest and, since the 1990s, to its growing extension to new areas of settlement in the South and Northeast.

Filipinos represent another large group with a long history of settlement in the United States. Earlier arrivals, in particular those going to Hawaii, were mostly rural workers.[23] Unlike Mexicans, however, contemporary Filipino immigrants are a diverse group, combining family reunification with a sizable contingent of new professionals. A tradition of serving as subordinate personnel in the U.S. Navy accounts for sizable Filipino concentrations in Pacific fleet ports—in particular, San Diego.

Koreans are an entrepreneurial group of more recent vintage, with a sizable number of professionals. Their main destination remains Los Angeles, where an ethnic enclave economy grew rapidly during the 1980s and 1990s. Koreans have also become prominent in produce retailing and other middleman small businesses in East Coast cities. Washington and New York followed Los Angeles as their destinations in 2002; they were also the single-largest foreign group arriving in large mid-Atlantic cities such as Philadelphia and Baltimore.[24]

Like Cubans, the Vietnamese are not newly arrived immigrants but mostly former refugees who have adjusted their legal status. The influence of government resettlement programs in the spatial distribution of refugee groups can be seen clearly in this instance. About 10 percent of 2002 Vietnamese immigrants planned to settle in Orange County, their preferred location. Earlier evidence had suggested that the Vietnamese, like the Cubans in the past, began leaving areas of initial settlement and concentrating in other cities, primarily in California. A decade before, in 1993, the proportion of Vietnamese settling in Orange County had reached 18 percent, with adjacent Los Angeles and San Diego absorbing an additional sizable share of these former refugees.[25] However, by 2001, the share of new Vietnamese immigrants who chose Orange County and San Jose dwindled to about 7 percent each.

In general, however, refugee groups that are sponsored and resettled initially through official programs tend to exhibit higher levels of spatial dispersion at the start of their American lives than subsequently. This pattern is illustrated in table 4, which presents data on preferred states of residence of the five largest refugee groups admitted in 1987, 1993, and 2001. All three Southeast Asian nationalities, generally resettled through officially sponsored programs, chose California as their preferred destination, but much smaller fractions were initially settled there. Over time, however, family sponsorships led to increasing concentrations in their preferred locales. In 1987, only 6 percent of Hmong refugees from Laos were resettled in Fresno, but by 1993, the proportion going to Fresno had quadrupled to 25 percent. The proportion of Iranians settling in Los Angeles increased by 10 percent between 1987 and 1993. Like immigrants of the same nationality, Cuban "refugees" in 1987 were not new arrivals but mostly individuals who had come during the Mariel boat lift and then adjusted their earlier "entrant" status. After the initial resettlement period, Mariel refugees were free to select their place of residence. Like other Cubans, they gravitated heavily toward South Florida. As table 4 shows, 78 percent of all 1987 Cuban refugees and 76 percent of all 1993 Cuban refugees settled in Miami, as did 66 percent of all Cubans admitted in 2001.

Geopolitical events since the early 1990s changed the composition of refugees admitted into the United States. The flows of Cambodians and Laotians slowed to a trickle, whereas new waves of refugees were ushered in from the new republics of the former Soviet Union. They were joined by Bosnians, Croats, Serbs, Iraqis, and Somalis coming as refugees in the wake of U.S. interventions in their respective countries. For these recent arrivals, a pattern of dispersal to new destinations, similar to that experienced by earlier refugee groups, was the norm. In 2001, the two most common destinations for newly admitted refugees from the former Yugoslavia were Chicago (9 percent) and St. Louis (5 percent); for those from the former USSR, it was New York (16 percent) and Sacramento (13 percent); and for Iraqis, Detroit (19 percent)

TABLE 4. METROPOLITAN DESTINATIONS OF THE FIVE MAJOR
REFUGEE GROUPS ADMITTED IN 1987, 1993, AND 2001

Nationality	N	Most common destination	(%)	Second most common destination	(%)
1987					
Cuban	26,952	Miami, FL	78.5	New York	5.9
Vietnamese	20,617	Orange County, CA	9.2	Los Angeles	7.4
Cambodian	12,206	Stockton, CA	9.3	Los Angeles	6.0
Laotian	6,560	Minneapolis–St. Paul, MN	12.1	Fresno, CA	6.4
Iranian	5,559	Los Angeles	40.3	New York	5.8
1993					
Soviet Union	45,900	New York	24.5	Los Angeles	8.7
Vietnamese	30,249	Orange County, CA	17.9	San Jose, CA	10.3
Cuban	11,603	Miami, FL	76.5	Jersey City, NJ	3.7
Laotian	6,547	Fresno, CA	24.6	Minneapolis–St. Paul, MN	9.4
Iranian	3,875	Los Angeles	60.9	New York	6.2
2001					
Former Yugoslavia[a]	29,830	Chicago	8.8	St. Louis, MO-IL	5.0
Cuban	22,687	Miami, FL	66.0	Tampa, FL	3.6
Former Soviet Union[b]	19,057	New York	15.8	Sacramento, CA	13.5
Vietnamese	10,351	Orange County, CA	7.0	San Jose, CA	6.8
Iraqi	3,060	Detroit, MI	19.4	San Diego, CA	12.2

SOURCES: U.S. Immigration and Naturalization Service 1988, table 40; 1994, table 37; 2002, table 33.

[a]Includes immigrants from Bosnia-Herzegovina, Croatia, and Yugoslavia (Serbia, Kosovo, and Montenegro).
[b]Includes immigrants from Ukraine, Russia, Belarus, and other former republics of the Soviet Union.

and San Diego (12 percent). If history is any guide, it is likely that these groups will subsequently gravitate toward locations selected for reasons of history and propinquity, thereby increasing their respective levels of ethnic concentration.

PREFERRED PLACES

Immigration to the United States is today an urban phenomenon, concentrated in the largest cities. In 2002, less than 5 percent of legal immigrants went to live in nonurban areas, and 40 percent settled in just ten metropolitan locations. In particular, recent years have seen the gradual end of what was a significant component of pre–World War I immigration: rural-bound groups coming to settle empty lands or work as farm laborers.

This trend is probably less marked among undocumented immigrants, many of whom continue working in agriculture. No reliable figures are available on the size and occupational distribution of the undocumented population, but a series of studies conducted among returning immigrants in their places of origin indicates both a continuing rural presence and an increasing urban concentration. Many undocumented immigrants apparently begin as rural workers but gradually drift into the cities, attracted by higher wages and better working conditions.[26] As noted in chapter 2, there is a close interaction between legal and illegal immigrants from the same countries. A large proportion of legal migration from countries such as Mexico and the Dominican Republic is composed of formerly undocumented immigrants who managed to legalize their situation. Hence, the spatial distribution of the recorded component of these inflows gives us a partial glimpse of what takes place underground.[27]

The bias of contemporary immigration toward a few metropolitan places is not a phenomenon of recent years but one that has occurred regularly during the last three decades. Year after year, with remarkable regularity, the same cities emerge as the preferred sites of destination of the total inflow and of its major national components. Table 5 illustrates this trend with data for selected years, beginning in 1967. During the subsequent thirty-five years, approximately one-fourth to one-third of total immigration concentrated in the three principal areas of destination. Until the 1990s, New York always remained the preferred site, while the next two places alternated among Los Angeles, Chicago, and Miami. The single most significant change during the period is the

TABLE 5. DESTINATIONS OF MAJOR IMMIGRANT GROUPS IN SELECTED YEARS

Nationality	Year	N	As % of total immigration	% in top three destinations	Most common destinations		
					First	Second	Third
Mexican	1967	42,371	11.7	19.6	Los Angeles	Chicago	El Paso
	1975	62,205	16.1	22.7	Los Angeles	Chicago	El Paso
	1979	52,096	11.3	17.3	El Paso	Los Angeles	Houston
	1984	57,557	10.6	27.9	Los Angeles	Chicago	El Paso
	1987	72,351	12.0	33.0	Los Angeles	El Paso	San Diego
	1993	126,561	14.0	31.4	Los Angeles	Chicago	Houston
	1997	146,865	18.4	22.5	Los Angeles	Chicago	Houston
	2002	219,380	20.6	27.0	Los Angeles	Riverside	San Diego
Cuban	1967	33,321	9.2	59.0	Miami	New York	San Juan
	1975	25,955	6.7	57.9	Miami	New York	San Juan
	1979	15,585	3.4	59.1	Miami	New York	San Juan
	1984	10,599	1.9	51.8	Miami	Jersey City	New York
	1987	28,916	4.8	86.0	Miami	New York	Tampa
	1993	13,666	1.5	81.5	Miami	Jersey City	Tampa
	1997	33,587	4.2	78.8	Miami	Tampa	Palm Beach
	2002	28,272	2.7	71.3	Miami	Tampa	Jersey City
Dominican	1967	11,514	3.2	90.6	New York	San Juan	Miami
	1975	14,066	3.6	84.7	New York	San Juan	Jersey City
	1979	17,519	3.8	80.6	New York	San Juan	Bergen-Passaic
	1984	23,147	4.3	78.7	New York	San Juan	Bergen-Passaic

	Year	Number					
	1987	24,858	4.1	76.0	New York	San Juan	Bergen-Passaic
	1993	45,420	5.0	71.1	New York	San Juan	Boston
	1997	27,053	3.4	65.6	New York	San Juan	Boston
	2002	22,604	2.1	49.8	New York	Bergen-Passaic[a]	Boston
Filipino	1967	10,865	3.0	25.6	San Francisco	Honolulu	New York
	1975	31,751	8.2	20.1	San Francisco	Los Angeles	Honolulu
	1979	41,300	9.0	17.8	San Francisco	Los Angeles	Honolulu
	1984	42,768	7.9	28.1	Los Angeles	San Francisco	Honolulu
	1987	50,060	8.3	30.0	Los Angeles	San Francisco	San Diego
	1993	53,457	7.0	26.0	Los Angeles	New York	San Diego
	1997	49,117	6.2	24.8	Los Angeles	Honolulu	San Diego
	2002	51,308	4.8	20.9	Los Angeles	San Diego	Chicago
Total	1967	361,972	26.1		New York	Miami	Chicago
	1975	386,194	28.2		New York	Los Angeles	Chicago
	1979	460,348	25.5		New York	Los Angeles	Miami
	1984	543,903	29.8		New York	Los Angeles	Chicago
	1987	601,516	33.2		New York	Los Angeles	Miami
	1993	904,292	30.9		New York	Los Angeles	Chicago
	1997	798,378	27.0		New York	Los Angeles	Miami
	2002	1,063,732	21.5		Los Angeles	New York	Chicago

SOURCE: U.S. Office of Immigration Statistics, Yearbook of Immigration Statistics (Washington, D.C.: U.S. Government Printing Office, 1968, 1976, 1980, 1985, 1988, 1994, 1998, 2003).

[a] San Juan was not listed in 2002 in the OIS statistical yearbook.

consolidation of Los Angeles as the most preferred destination of immigrants overall by 2002.

Table 5 presents trends for the four major nationalities for which data are available during the entire period. Mexicans went from 12 percent of total immigration in 1967 to over 20 percent in 2002, all the while increasing their absolute numbers from some forty thousand to more than two hundred thousand per year. Dominicans maintained approximately the same proportion of total immigration throughout these years, peaking in 1993 and decreasing slightly through 2002. Filipino immigration experienced a significant absolute increase between 1967 and 1987 and then stabilized at about fifty thousand immigrants per year. Cuban immigrants—mostly adjusted former refugees—declined significantly until the mid-1980s and then increased again to about 5 percent of total immigration in 1987. This quantum leap is an outgrowth of the Mariel exodus, which also accounts for an extraordinary rise in spatial concentration. Over 70 percent of recent Cuban immigrants cluster in just three cities, with the overwhelming majority going to Miami. As seen previously, Dominicans come close to Cubans in level of concentration, although their strong preference for New York has declined in recent years. Filipinos and Mexicans are far more dispersed; yet, with some exceptions, their preferred areas of destination remain the same. Los Angeles consolidated its place during this period as the major area of settlement for both groups, and San Diego surged ahead to third place for Mexicans and second place for Filipinos, replacing more traditional destinations.

Reasons for the spatial concentration of immigrant flows, the strong urban bias of recent ones, and the consistency of their destinations over time are all linked to the characteristic economics of immigration. Like native youths, newly arrived immigrants are newcomers to the labor market who tend to search for immediately available opportunities. Regardless of their qualifications and experience, recent immigrants generally enter at the bottom of their respective occupational ladders. Thus, foreign manual workers are channeled toward the lowest-paying and most arduous jobs; immigrant professionals—such as engineers, programmers, physicians, and nurses—also must accept less desirable entry jobs within their professions and even outside them.[28] Lastly, entrepreneurs also start small, with shops catering to their own community or in riskier middleman ventures in the inner city.

In the absence of deliberate recruitment or other ad hoc factors, entry jobs at the bottom of the respective ladders are more easily accessible in large urban agglomerations and in those experiencing rapid economic growth. Once immigrants from a particular nationality "discover" the existence of such opportunities, migration becomes self-perpetuating through the operation of ethnic networks. It is thus not surprising that the principal concentrations of the largest immigrant groups at present are found in Los Angeles, a large metropolitan area that has experienced sustained economic expansion in recent decades. It is not surprising, either, that Cubans concentrate in Miami, another fast-growing city that has become the center of U.S. trade with Latin America. Washington, D.C., is also an attractive area of destination for entrepreneurially oriented groups because of the presence of a large inner-city minority population, along with a sizable segment of well-paid government workers.

Less obvious are the forces leading to the continuation of New York–bound immigration, given the industrial decline of the area in recent history. Between 1980 and 1990, the most affected sector in New York was manufacturing, where employment decreased by almost one-third. New York's industrial decline raises the question of why immigrants persist in going there instead of following manufacturing jobs to their new locations in the Carolinas, Florida, or Texas. One reason is that, despite declines in both population and employment, New York continues to be the nation's largest urban agglomeration. Another is that large established ethnic communities continue to serve as a magnet for new immigrants from their home countries. More important, however, amid industrial decline there has been significant economic growth spurred by other sectors, including services and construction. From 1977 to 1987, close to two-thirds of all new jobs created in New York were in the information industries. In 1990, total construction activity was up by more than 25 percent over the 1980 level. Between 1981 and 1990, demand for office space remained strong,[29] Manhattan alone gaining more than fifty-three million square feet of new office space.

About half of the jobs generated in distributive and producer services in New York City are in the highest-paid earning classes; this is particularly true in the so-called FIRE sector (finance, insurance, and real estate) and in transportation, communications, and utilities. However, about 45 percent of employment in producer services and 65 percent in consumer services are formed by jobs paying minimum or near-minimum wages. Approximately 20 percent of employment in construction is also in this low-wage class, a figure that increases significantly among nonunion workers.[30]

Immigrants have found in these low-paying jobs a continuing and expanding entry point into New York's labor market; in turn, their presence has been a significant element fueling the city's economic expansion. In addition to producer services, consumer services, and construction, renewed industrial activity is also a source of entry-level work, but one that takes place through subcontracting, sweatshops, home work, and other informal arrangements. Several field studies point to a heavy concentration of immigrants among both owners and workers in this informal industrial economy.[31] Thus, recent economic growth in New York has been accompanied by a profound reorganization of production and distribution activities in a number of sectors. As Sassen states, "The large influx of immigrants from low-wage countries over the last fifteen years . . . cannot be understood separately from this restructuring. . . . It is the expansion in the supply of low-wage jobs generated by major growth sectors that is one of the key factors in the *continuation* of the current immigration to New York."[32] Waldinger has argued that an ethnic division of labor in this context allows immigrants to gain entry into lower-level service jobs ahead of native minorities. A hiring queue allocates jobs among ethnic groups in terms of desirability. Factors such as the shape of the queue (the relative sizes of the groups), resources, ethnic networks, and discrimination determine where a group will fall in the resulting hierarchy.[33]

PERSISTENT ETHNICITY

A final question is what locational trends can be expected in the future. In other words, will recent immigrants and their descendants continue to be disproportionately concentrated in a few metropolitan places, or will they gradually disperse throughout the country? Theories of immigrant assimilation have consistently assumed the latter outcome. Insofar as immigrants and their children become more like native Americans, their patterns of spatial mobility will become more similar to those of the rest of the population. In this view, the gradual disappearance of concentrated immigrant communities represents the spatial counterpart of cultural assimilation as foreign groups "melt" into the host society. Some writers describe the process as an elementary version of queuing theory, with older immigrant groups leaving urban ethnic areas to new ones:

> There has also been an historical pattern of one group replacing another in neighborhoods, jobs, leadership, schools, and other institutions. Today's neighborhood changes have been dramatized by such expressions as "white flight" but these patterns existed long before. . . . In nineteenth century neighborhoods where Anglo-Saxons had once fled as the Irish moved in, the middle-class Irish later fled as the Jews and Italians moved in.[34]

We showed previously that new immigrants tend to be persistent in their choice of spatial location. This pattern says little, of course, about the long-term preferences of particular groups once they have settled in the country for generations. To explore this question, we must move back in time and examine locational patterns of groups that have been in the United States for longer periods. A recent study provides initial support for the assimilation hypothesis by reporting a negative correlation between time in the country and spatial concentration as measured by the index of dissimilarity (D) from the American population as a whole. For ten European nationalities, most of which were already well represented in the country at the time of independence, the correlation between these two variables is $-.72$.[35] However, the same study goes on to report that immigrant groups' initial settlement patterns have had a decisive influence on the ethnic composition of each of the country's regions. For example, with few exceptions, the five largest ancestry groups within each regional division include groups that were among the five largest immigrant contingents already living in the area in 1850, 1900, or 1920. Thus, German and Irish are among the largest ancestry groups in New England, where they were also among the principal immigrant nationalities in each of these earlier years. Norwegians and Swedes are strongly represented in the west north-central region at present, just as their ancestors were at the turn of the century.[36]

What is true of regions is also true of specific nationalities. Descendants of late nineteenth- and early twentieth-century immigrants, particularly those coming from the Mediterranean and from non-European countries, tend to remain in their original areas of settlement. At present, the five most highly concentrated ethnic groups are Mexicans, Portuguese, Japanese, Filipinos, and Norwegians. As seen previously, Mexicans and Filipinos continue to arrive in large numbers and still go to the places in which they were concentrated a half century ago. The remaining groups are, however, descendants of immigrants who arrived in the United States mostly before World War II. Despite long residence in the country, they cluster in the same areas as their forebears. Three-fourths of all Portuguese Americans reside at present in only four states: Massachusetts and Rhode Island in the East and California and Hawaii in the West; a similar proportion of Japanese Americans is found in just the latter two states.[37]

Within major areas of settlement, outward movement and dispersal have occurred, of course, and this pattern has been taken as evidence of full assimilation. However, the telling fact is that, after several generations, particular nationalities continue to be associated with specific patches of national territory, giving them their distinct idiosyncrasies and cultural traits. Such stable locations are a far cry from the image of a thoroughly homogenized "melted" population with identical proportions of the same original nationalities found everywhere.

We have few grounds to believe that the resilience of these ethnic communities is likely to disappear in the future. The American population as a whole is gradually moving away from the Northeast and Midwest toward the South and Southwest. If present trends continue indefinitely, New England and the mid-Atlantic region will see their combined share of the total population reduced from 21 to just 10 percent, and the west south-central and Pacific regions will increase theirs from 24 to 36 percent. However, this spatial displacement will not lead to greater dispersion of ethnic communities. If trends observed since the late 1980s continue, their overall spatial concentration will either not change or actually increase.

Three trends account for this somewhat unexpected outcome. First, ethnic groups concentrated in regions losing population are less likely to leave so that, over time, their relative proportion increases. Second, when members of an ethnic minority move, they are more likely to go to areas where their own group is already numerous, including those experiencing out-migration. Third, when an ethnic group moves en masse from its traditional area, it does not become necessarily dispersed but often regroups in another region. The outcome of these trends, when projected into the future, is that nationalities such as the Poles will tend to remain heavily concentrated in the Northeast and Midwest, the Norwegians in the west north-central states, and the Cubans in the Southeast; Jews of mostly Russian origin will tend to abandon the mid-Atlantic region to reconstitute themselves as a major ethnic group in the Pacific.[38]

An instructive example involves the 130,000 Indochinese refugees who arrived in the United States in 1975. Upon arrival, they were sent to four major reception centers, from which they were resettled in 813 separate locations spread throughout all fifty states. Data collected at the reception centers show that less than half of these refugees (47.3 percent) were sent to the state of their choice. By 1980, however, 45 percent lived in a state other than the one to which they had been sent. Nearly 40 percent had moved to areas of high ethnic concentration in California. Conversely, the proportion that lived in dispersed communities with fewer than five hundred refugees of the same nationality dropped from 64.7 to 40.1 percent. Secondary migration trends during the 1980s and 1990s continued reinforcing the predominance of a few areas of Indochinese concentration.[39]

Given these past experiences and the propensity of major contemporary immigrations to remain clustered, we have little reason to expect a dispersal of recent immigrants and their children. Contrary to conventional assimilation views, the safest prediction is that ethnic communities created by present immigration will endure and will become identified with their areas of settlement, giving to the latter, as other immigrants have before them, a distinct cultural flavor and a new "layer" of phenotypical and cultural traits.

CONCLUSION: THE PROS AND CONS OF SPATIAL CONCENTRATION

The question of why ethnic communities tend to stay put in certain parts of the country can be discussed jointly with advantages and disadvantages of this pattern because the two issues are closely intertwined. Overall, the entire process of immigrant settlement is "sticky" because new arrivals tend to move to places where earlier immigrants have become established, and later generations do not wander too far off. Following assimilation theory, one could argue that this pattern is irrational because economic opportunities, especially for the American-born generations, are often greater elsewhere. Individualistic aspirations should lead to dispersal because upward economic mobility often requires spatial mobility.[40]

An alternative logic, however, contradicts this reasoning. By moving away from places where their own group is numerically strong, individuals risk losing a range of social and moral resources that make for psychological well-being as well as for economic gain. A large minority that becomes dispersed risks lacking a significant presence or voice anywhere; on the contrary, even a small group, if sufficiently concentrated, can have economic and political influence locally. For members of the immigrant generation, spatial concentration has several positive consequences: preservation of a valued lifestyle, regulation of the pace of acculturation, greater social control over the young, and access to community networks for both moral and economic support.

For subsequent generations, preservation of the ethnic community, even if more widely dispersed, can also have significant advantages. Among the entrepreneurially inclined, ethnic ties translate into access to sources of working capital, protected markets, and pools of labor.[41] Others also derive advantages from an enduring community. There is strength in numbers, especially at the ballot box, and this fact allows minority groups to assert their presence and their interests in the political process. As chapter 5 will show, politics can also serve as an avenue of individual upward mobility when other paths remain blocked. The ascendance of urban Irish politicians in the late nineteenth century and that of their Italian counterparts later on provide the classic examples.[42] The highly concentrated Cuban population in South Florida has followed the same path.

The question of relative advantages and disadvantages can be turned around, however, and asked from the point of view of mainstream society. Many writers have expressed fears of continuing immigration precisely because it leads to growing ethnic concentration, which, they believe, will alter the cultural fabric of the nation. At worst, secessionist movements have been anticipated in those areas where immigrants and their descendants become the majority.[43]

There is little doubt that the best way of minimizing the social and cultural impact of immigration is either to stop it or to disperse new arrivals, but this approach also minimizes the potential long-term contribution that immigrant communities can make. Throughout the history of the United States, communities created by foreign groups have been a significant force in promoting the growth and economic vigor of cities such as New York, Boston, San Francisco, and Los Angeles, as well as entire regions such as the Midwest. Once immigrants have settled and integrated economically, their traditions and folkways have entered local culture. After a while, these syncretic products become institutionalized and are proudly presented as "typical" of the local lore. St. Patrick's Day parades, German beerfests, Chinese New Year celebrations, Mardi Gras carnivals, Mexican fiestas, and the like, are so many manifestations of this process. Without the past and present contribution of immigrant groups, the dynamism and vibrancy of American culture would have given way to a uniform, gray landscape.

But what about separatism? During the first two decades of the twentieth century, immigrants came to represent over one-fifth of the American labor force, and they and their children composed absolute majorities of the country's urban population. This situation, in which the foreign presence relative to the native population vastly exceeded that found today, did not give rise to any secessionist movement. Immigrants focused their energies instead on carving an economic niche for themselves; their children learned English and gradually entered native social circles and the local political process. Perhaps the most telling case against nativist fears is that of Mexican Americans in the Southwest. Despite the large size of this minority, its proximity to the home country, and the fact that these territories were once Mexico's, secessionist movements within the Mexican American population have been insignificant.

During World War II and the Korean War, Mexican American youths could easily have avoided military service by taking a short ride into Mexico; instead, they contributed tens of thousands of both soldiers and battle casualties to the nation's war effort.[44] The latest illustrations of this trend come in the form of the commanding officer of American troops in Iraq in 2003 and early 2004, Lt. Gen. Ricardo Sánchez—who is a second-generation Mexican American from a poor immigrant family settled right by the U.S.-Mexico border—and many "green card marines"—such as José Angel Garibay and Jesús Angel González, both twenty-two, who were born in Mexico, grew up in poverty in Southern California, and were among the first to die in action in Iraq at the start of the war in 2003.[45]

Ethnic communities have been much less the Trojan horses portrayed by the xenophobes than effective vehicles for long-term adaptation. As Greeley states, "It could be said that the apparent inclination of men . . . to consort with those who, they assume, have the same origins provides diversity in the larger society and also creates substructures that meet many functions the larger society would be hard put to service."[46] He also notes, however, that "the demons of suspicion and distrust prove very hard to exorcise from interethnic relationships."[47] At a time when such "demons" are again on the rise, we may do well to recall past experience, where spatial concentrations of immigrants from all over the globe did not lead either to political separatism or to cultural alienation. Within their respective areas of settlement, ethnic communities created by immigration have grown and diversified; later generations' efforts to maintain a distinct culture have been invariably couched within the framework of loyalty to the United States and an overarching American identity. Today's immigrants will follow the same path.

4

Making It in America
Occupational and Economic Adaptation

A s we noted in chapter 2, a common perception of contemporary immigration is that it is predominantly a low-skilled labor flow and that its quality is declining over time. This perception not only is common among the public at large but has been given academic credibility as well. Some time ago, an economist described his version of the trend as follows:

> As one moves from one country to another . . . one begins to believe that there is something in common among jobs held by migrants in widely diverse geographic areas and very different historical periods: the jobs tend to be unskilled, generally but not always low-paying and to connote inferior social status; they often involve hard or unpleasant working conditions and considerable insecurity.[1]

In testimony before Congress, another economist put forth a different version of this argument: "The labor market quality of immigrant cohorts has changed substantially over time and has declined in the last 20 or 30 years; the kinds of skills and the kinds of people we are getting now are different from the kinds of skills and the quality of immigration we were getting 30 or 40 years ago."[2]

Forty years ago there was little immigration, of course, and what there was came under a quota system that effectively barred most nationalities. Statements about an overwhelmingly low-skilled flow may be applicable to undocumented immigration, but, like those about "declining quality," they neglect the sizable recorded immigration of recent years. The socioeconomic profile of the foreign-born is quite different from what such statements would make us believe. In 2000, the proportion of college graduates among all immigrants was the same as in the total U.S. population. More significantly, that proportion was higher among immigrant cohorts arriving in the 1990s. In 2000, the proportion of the foreign-born in professional specialty occupations was almost on a par with the same figure for the native-born, both about 20 percent. These facts contradict popular stereotypes about immigration as a Third World "invasion" by the poor and downtrodden as well as equally biased academic stereotypes about the "low quality" of contemporary immigration. The reality is very different and can only be accounted for by the diversity of types of immigration described in chapter 2.

In this chapter, we examine in detail the most recent evidence pertaining to the education, labor force participation, occupational status, and incomes of the foreign-born population. We explore determinants of occupational and income achievement of immigrants and propose an alternative interpretation that contrasts an exclusively individualistic approach with one that takes into account the sociological reality of different contexts of reception experienced by different immigrant minorities.

IMMIGRANTS IN THE AMERICAN ECONOMY

EDUCATION

Great diversity is evident within the general picture of an educationally advantaged population. If most immigrants are not illiterate, they are not all college graduates. Variation in educational background highlights again the central theme of great heterogeneity among the foreign-born. In table 6, for example, the Taiwanese appear as the most educated immigrants because close to 100 percent are high school graduates; if the indicator is college rather than high school graduation, then Asian Indians take first place.

TABLE 6. EDUCATIONAL ATTAINMENT OF PRINCIPAL FOREIGN NATIONALITIES IN 2000

Country of birth	Total persons	% college graduates[a]	% high school graduates[a]	% immigrated 1990–2000
Total native-born	250,288,425	24.4	83.3	
Total foreign-born	31,133,481	24.1	61.8	42.4
Above U.S. average				
India	1,027,144	69.1	88.2	54.9
Taiwan	325,234	66.7	93.6	35.8
Nigeria	135,791	57.8	93.5	54.0
Iran	285,176	50.6	86.4	26.6
Pakistan	229,206	50.5	81.5	57.0
Hong Kong	201,358	50.4	84.4	33.8
Former Soviet Union	618,302	47.3	84.0	69.7
Philippines	1,374,213	45.7	86.8	35.4
Korea	870,542	42.9	86.1	37.4
Japan	346,453	42.7	90.6	50.0
China	997,301	41.6	68.4	48.8
Near U.S. average				
United Kingdom	567,240	36.6	90.2	27.8
Canada	820,713	33.6	82.5	29.9
Brazil	209,612	32.2	79.9	65.3
Germany	705,110	26.8	83.5	18.8
Ireland	153,311	23.6	78.4	22.3
Peru	275,111	23.1	80.4	46.7
Poland	472,544	22.1	73.1	36.7
Colombia	515,206	21.8	72.0	45.1
Greece	166,023	19.8	59.1	9.7
Vietnam	991,995	19.2	61.6	44.7
Cuba	870,203	18.7	59.0	26.6
Jamaica	554,897	17.8	72.1	31.4
Below U.S. average				
Italy	476,033	13.9	54.0	8.6
Haiti	422,841	13.7	62.3	39.7
Ecuador	292,246	12.8	61.4	46.7
Cambodia	137,365	10.4	48.5	16.5
Dominican Republic	685,952	9.5	48.1	42.7
Honduras	281,428	8.1	43.7	57.0
Portugal	175,812	7.8	44.2	11.7
Laos	205,931	7.6	47.2	21.0
Guatemala	480,004	6.1	36.9	49.6
El Salvador	815,570	5.0	34.7	40.4
Mexico	9,163,463	4.2	29.7	48.6

SOURCE: 2000 U.S. Census, 5% Public Use Microdata Sample.

[a] Persons age twenty-five or older.

The largest foreign-born group—Mexicans—has the lowest level of schooling, according to both indicators. This result is due not to Mexico having a singularly bad educational system but to its having a border with the United States of nearly two thousand miles, allowing peasants and workers of modest origins to come in search of work. By and large, the Mexican immigrant population of the United States is composed of the peasants and workers who are on this side of the border at any given time, plus their families. As seen in chapter 2, this population has been in the past highly mobile, engaging in a cyclical back-and-forth movement across the border.[3] The generalization that low-educated immigrants come mostly from Latin America is contradicted, however, by the presence of European nationalities in the bottom educational category. Immigrants from Italy and Portugal, in particular, are noteworthy for their low average educational attainment. These represent, for the most part, remnants of earlier flows. Southeast Asian refugees from Cambodia and Laos are also in this bottom category. Nationalities that are close to the educational mean come predominantly from traditional countries of emigration in northeastern Europe and from Canada. In this category are also several Latin American countries, the most numerically important of which are Cuba, Colombia, and Peru.

The portrait of education among the foreign-born presented in table 6 is puzzling and does not lend itself to ready interpretation. The view that the educational level of immigration has been declining over time does not find support in these data, either in terms of general averages or when disaggregated by national origins. The last column of table 6 presents the proportion of immigrants coming during 1990–2000 as a rough indicator of recency of arrival. Close to 50 percent or more of the best-educated groups—such as those from India, Nigeria, Pakistan, and China—arrived in recent years. Notable in that respect is the highly educated flow from the former Soviet Union, 70 percent of which arrived in the nineties. By contrast, high proportions of those groups with lower averages of education were already in the country before 1990.

This conclusion is also supported by results in table 7 that indicate higher proportions of college and high school graduates among immigrants who arrived during the last ten years than among the entire foreign-born population. Note, however, the marginal declines of these proportions among immigrants from Africa and Latin America, partially compensated for by significant increases in the number of edu-

TABLE 7. EDUCATIONAL ATTAINMENT OF IMMIGRANTS
AGE TWENTY-FIVE AND OLDER, 2000

	All immigrants		Immigrated 1990–2000	
Region of birth	% completed college	% completed high school	% completed college	% completed high school
All immigrants	24.1	61.8	28.2	62.5
Asia	43.3	78.9	47.0	78.9
Africa	43.0	86.7	36.3	84.2
Europe, Canada, and Australia	29.9	77.7	44.9	87.7
Latin America and Caribbean	9.8	44.1	10.0	41.6

SOURCE: 2000 U.S. Census, 5% Public Use Microdata Sample.

cated immigrants from Europe and Canada. These tendencies reflect the interplay of a complex array of factors, including the growing presence of dependent kin in certain immigrant flows. Dependents tend to lower the average educational level of their respective national groups. This is especially the case among nationalities composed originally of immigrants of very high educational attainment, as those coming from Asia and Africa. The rapid rise in education among Europeans is a direct consequence of the breakup of the Soviet Union, which triggered massive outflows from Russia and the successor republics. The resulting ups and downs in the educational composition of migrant flows cannot be appropriately summarized by any simplistic conclusion about "declining quality."

A full interpretation of educational differences among the foreign-born requires consideration of a plurality of factors. There are actually two different levels of explanation: that of differences between nationalities and that of differences among individuals.

At the first or aggregate level, relevant factors involve the countries of both origin and destination. Concerning the latter, immigration policies and labor demand are the most important explanatory variables. Prior to 1965, U.S. immigration policy made it difficult for Asians and Africans to come. After that date, a new immigration policy opened the doors on the basis of two criteria: family reunification and occupational qualifications. Unlike European and certain Latin American nationalities, Africans and Asians had few families to reunite with in the United

States; hence, the only path open to them was that of formal credentials. This situation explains the high average levels of education of most Asian and African immigrants. It also helps account for its slight decline in the last few years as family reunification and, hence, the arrival of dependents gained growing significance.

Apart from regular immigration, the U.S. government has also chosen to admit certain groups at particular times for political considerations. As seen in chapter 2, most of these refugee groups have come from Communist-dominated countries. The educational profile of each such nationality depends on the evolution over time of the inflow. Initial waves of refugees tend to come from the higher socioeconomic strata; as the movement continues, however, they are increasingly drawn from the lower classes. The decline in schooling tends to be faster when refugees originate in poor countries where the well educated represent a small proportion of the total population. In combination, these factors explain the low average levels of education of some Southeast Asian refugee groups (such as Cambodians and Laotians), the average educational levels of Vietnamese and Cubans, and the high educational profile of recently arrived Iranians, Soviet Jews, Ethiopians, and Afghans. During the 1990s, the momentous process leading to the demise of Communism in Eastern Europe was aided by a U.S. policy that greatly facilitated the arrival of Soviet citizens as refugees. These were positively selected by the U.S. consulates in Russia and other former Soviet republics, which explains the high educational level of this new immigrant cohort. As Asians before them, Russians had few relatives to reunite with in the United States, which accounts for the continuing positive educational selectivity of this new inflow.[4]

Finally, demand for low-wage labor in agriculture and other U.S. industries has given rise, as seen earlier, to a sustained underground flow. Not surprisingly, this demand has had its greatest impact in less developed countries near America's borders rather than in distant or more developed nations. Although undocumented migration tends to be temporary rather than permanent, a substantial number of migrants eventually settle down in the United States and manage to legalize their situation.[5] Given the size of the undocumented inflow and the modest educational origins of most participants, it is not surprising that, even if only a minority change their status to legal residence, they will have a strong downward effect on the aggregate statistics. This pattern helps explain the low average education of legal immigrants from Mexico, the Dominican Republic, and most of Central America, countries that have been the primary sources of undocumented migration in the past.

Geopolitical concerns and labor demand in the United States do not solely explain the diversity of educational achievement among the foreign-born. The relative opening of American borders after 1965 may have been a godsend to the highly educated in certain countries, but it was a matter of indifference to others. Similarly, American growers' demand for low-wage rural workers had a significant impact on Mexico but a very limited one on Canada. Finally, the relative decline in the numbers of European immigrants after 1965 took place despite the expanded facilities for immigration from these countries—through either family reunification or occupational preferences. Clearly, an increasingly prosperous European population did not see changes in U.S. law as a cause for much excitement.

The greatest impact of the new preference system was elsewhere—namely, on the less developed countries of Asia and Africa. Unlike Western Hemisphere nations, for which the doors were never closed, the possibilities to migrate to the United States from Africa or Asia had been absent until this time. The 1965 act changed this situation, and the well educated in these countries took note. After the demise of Communism and the ensuing harsh period of economic adjustment, the same thing happened to educated citizens of the former Soviet Union. During the 1990s, they came to join Asians and Africans among foreign groups with the highest proportion of college graduates. For illustration, table 8 lists the twenty-four nations contributing the highest proportions of college graduates to the United States in 2000. These countries share three notable characteristics. First, they are all distant, being located, without exception, in Asia, Africa, or the former Soviet Union. Second, these immigrants are of recent origin, as indicated by the proportion that emigrated after 1980; nearly all came after that date, with proportions ranging from 60 percent for Iran to 96 percent for Azerbaijan, Uzbekistan, and Saudi Arabia. Third, they are all less developed countries, including several, such as Bangladesh, Zimbabwe, and Kenya, that are among the poorest in the world.

As shown in table 8, for many of these countries, substantial percentages of the respective sending populations are illiterate, and the per capita product (at purchasing power parity) did not exceed U.S.$4,000 in 2002. The table also makes clear that among the sources of college-educated immigrant professionals to the United States in the last decades, India has pride of place. The 710,000 college graduates among

TABLE 8. FOREIGN-BORN GROUPS WITH HIGHEST PROPORTIONS OF COLLEGE-
EDUCATED PERSONS IN 2000, AND CHARACTERISTICS OF COUNTRIES OF ORIGIN

Country	Total immigrants in United States	% college graduates among foreign-born[a]	% immigrated to United States 1980–2000	GDP per capita ($), ca. 2002[a]	% literate population, ca. 2003[b]
India	1,027,144	69.1	80.8	2,600	59.5
Taiwan	325,234	66.7	75.0	18,000	86.0
Singapore	20,801	59.8	84.0	25,200	93.2
Egypt	114,132	59.6	66.5	4,000	57.7
Nigeria	135,791	57.8	85.3	900	68.0
Cameroon	12,241	57.6	92.9	1,700	79.0
Georgia	9,739	56.4	90.6	3,200	99.0
South Africa	62,429	55.9	78.6	10,000	86.4
Kuwait	21,604	53.4	91.8	17,500	83.5
Bulgaria	34,949	53.0	84.9	6,500	98.6
Malaysia	49,883	52.2	87.0	8,800	88.9
Uganda	11,799	52.2	74.6	1,200	69.9
Tanzania	11,025	51.7	78.7	600	78.2
Saudi Arabia	21,881	51.2	96.0	11,400	78.8
Kenya	41,081	51.0	86.5	1,100	85.1
Iran	285,176	50.6	60.4	6,800	79.4
Pakistan	229,206	50.5	86.7	2,000	45.7
Nepal	11,859	50.3	94.1	1,400	45.2
Algeria	11,187	49.8	80.8	5,400	70.0
Zimbabwe	11,166	49.4	82.0	2,100	90.7
Sri Lanka	25,380	49.0	80.9	3,700	92.3
Azerbaijan	14,118	48.1	95.5	3,700	97.0
Bangladesh	91,440	47.4	93.3	1,800	43.1
Uzbekistan	22,770	46.1	96.5	2,600	99.3

SOURCES: U.S. Census of the Population, 5% Public Use Microdata Sample; Central Intelligence Agency 2003.

[a] Purchasing power parity, 2002.
[b] Persons age fifteen or older who can read and write.

Indian immigrants in 2000 exceed the sum total of the next highest fifteen nations and more than triple, in absolute numbers, the next largest contributor, Taiwan. The rapid rise of the university-educated Indian population in the United States is a direct consequence of the implementation of the H-1B program, discussed in chapter 2, as well as the regular occupational preferences of the 1990 Immigration Act. The source country of this flow—a vast, distant, and poor nation with a 40 percent illiteracy rate—is emblematic of the major sources of professional immigration today. It is thus clear that the lure of occupational and economic opportunities in the United States, created by the new preference systems for the highly skilled, had its greatest impact in those parts of the world where such opportunities are most scarce and where the well educated have had few other alternatives.[6]

A second approach to explaining educational differences is identifying individual background factors that affect the process. Some time ago, Hirschman and Falcón analyzed educational attainment among twenty-five religioethnic groups in the United States, including both recent immigrants and descendants of earlier arrivals. A sample size close to seven thousand cases and information on a number of relevant variables make the results of this study worth careful attention.[7]

Not surprisingly, parental schooling and then father's occupational characteristics were the most important individual factors accounting for educational differences across groups. Parental schooling alone explained about a third of these differences. The net advantages of Jews, Asians, and British ancestry groups were thus due, in large measure, to their having been reared by parents with above-average levels of education. Conversely, the large disadvantage of Italians, Eastern Europeans, and Mexicans was reduced by about half once parental schooling was statistically controlled.

Also significant was the finding that immigrant generation did not affect education. There was a rise in average schooling from the first to the third generations and a decline in the fourth and subsequent ones. The net impact of generation was not, however, of much consequence. This result indicates that time in the United States does not compensate for low educational endowments among earlier immigrant generations. First-generation newcomers from higher socioeconomic backgrounds are generally better educated, on average, than established ethnic groups from more modest origins. After controlling statistically for a series of individual factors, Hirschman and Falcón found that the original differences in education were significantly reduced but that important ones remained. For example, Asians who were statistically "equal" to others in parental schooling and other background factors retained a 1.6-year educational advantage over the rest; Mexicans suffered a 1.4-year disadvantage.[8]

A more recent study that we conducted on the educational attainment of second-generation youths found similar results. Our study followed more than 5,200 children of immigrants attending public and private schools in the metropolitan areas of Miami–Fort Lauderdale and San Diego over a ten-year period. In agreement with Hirschman and Falcón's earlier results, we found that immigrant parents' education and occupational status played a decisive role in the academic achievement of their offspring, as did being raised in an intact family (both biological parents present). To these effects were added those of gender and educational aspirations in early adolescence. Females generally achieved significantly higher grades and overall education, as did students with higher ambition early in life.

After controlling for these and a number of other variables, we still observed significant differences among nationalities in academic performance, dropout rates, and completed years of education. Chinese, Korean, Vietnamese, and Cuban students whose parents came in the early exile waves had significantly higher academic performance and overall attainment, as measured by years of completed education by age twenty-four. Mexican Americans, and to a lesser extent Nicaraguan-origin youths, did worse on average on both counts.[9] These persistent nationality differences point to the operation of contextual factors not captured by individual or family variables. In other words, the particular characteristics and experiences of immigration of foreign groups play a significant role in academic attainment, above and beyond the effects of family on individual predictors. We will return to this point after examining occupational status and incomes next.

OCCUPATION AND ENTREPRENEURSHIP

In 2000, 61 percent of the foreign-born population in the United States was in the labor force, a figure slightly below the national average. Labor force participation was higher among immigrants from Africa (71 percent) and Asia (63 percent) and especially high among certain nationalities such as Indians (69 percent), Nigerians (79 percent), and Egyptians (65 percent). Immigrant unemployment in 2000 was 6.8 percent, a significantly higher rate than for the native-born (5.7 percent).

There is variation around this figure, but immigrant groups differ much less in their commitment to work and their ability to find employment than in other dimensions.

A partial exception to this pattern is refugees from Laos and Cambodia, whose labor participation rate falls below 60 percent. They are joined in this category by Dominicans, who also registered the highest unemployment rates. Indeed, in the boon years of the late 1990s, it was Latin American and Caribbean immigrants who had the greatest difficulty in finding employment. As seen in table 9, the Dominican unemployment rate more than doubled the national average, and that for Mexicans, Haitians, and Hondurans exceeded it by more than 60 percent. Recall that these are among the nationalities that contributed most heavily toward the low-skilled manual labor inflow during the last decades. By the turn of the century, the supply of this kind of migrant worker was clearly exceeding the demand, at least as far as formal recorded employment is concerned.[10]

The same diversity among nationalities in levels of education seen previously is found when we examine types of occupation in the United States. Given the close association between both variables, it is not surprising that highly educated groups are those most frequently represented in professional and managerial occupations. The wide occupational diversity among the foreign-born conceals a basic bimodal pattern in which certain groups concentrate at the top of the occupational distribution, while others are found mostly at the bottom. Table 9 illustrates this pattern with data for selected groups of more than one hundred thousand persons in 1990. Immigrant nationalities that exceed the proportion of professionals in the American labor force by a significant margin come from Asia, the Middle East, and Europe. Noteworthy again is the occupational profile of Indians, where professionals represent over half of occupationally active immigrants, and that of the Taiwan Chinese, where they represent 45 percent.

At the other extreme are nationalities from Latin America and Southeast Asia, where the relative number of those in high-level occupations is 60 percent or less than the national average. Note that the low presence of these groups at the top of the occupational distribution is not correlated with weak labor force participation. Latin American immigrants, with the exception of Dominicans, are among the most active in the U.S. labor market. It bears repeating that the clear bimodal pattern revealed by these results and by the occupants of the top and bottom of the American educational and occupational hierarchies are, to a large

TABLE 9. LABOR FORCE PARTICIPATION
AND PROFESSIONAL SPECIALTY OCCUPATIONS
OF SELECTED IMMIGRANT GROUPS, 2000

Country of birth	Number of persons	% in U.S. labor force[a]	% unemployed (looking for work)[a]	% in professional specialty occupations[b]
Total native-born	250,288,425	63.9	5.7	21.7
Total foreign-born	31,133,481	60.6	6.8	19.1
Above U.S. average[c]				
India	1,027,144	69.1	3.8	51.3
Taiwan	325,234	63.2	3.7	45.5
Nigeria	135,791	78.7	6.1	40.1
China	997,301	58.8	4.5	36.8
France	147,755	59.3	3.4	36.4
Canada	820,713	55.8	3.1	35.8
Former Soviet Union	618,302	52.5	6.4	35.8
Egypt	114,132	64.7	5.2	35.4
Iran	285,176	63.8	4.8	34.7
United Kingdom	567,240	61.5	3.2	34.6
Below U.S. average[c]				
Haiti	422,841	65.1	9.6	14.6
Cambodia	137,365	57.6	7.0	14.0
Laos	205,931	59.2	6.4	11.7
Nicaragua	224,447	61.3	8.5	11.2
Ecuador	292,246	62.3	8.5	10.4
Portugal	175,812	63.1	5.0	9.6
Dominican Republic	685,952	56.0	12.9	9.4
Honduras	281,428	64.3	10.6	6.4
Guatemala	480,004	63.3	8.3	5.8
El Salvador	815,570	64.2	8.1	5.7
Mexico	9,163,463	60.0	9.4	4.7

SOURCE: 2000 U.S. Census, 5% Public Use Microdata Sample.

[a] Persons age sixteen or older.
[b] Employed persons age sixteen or older.
[c] Ranked in terms of professional specialty occupations.

extent, the result of geographic accident. India, Pakistan, Egypt, and Nigeria, among other senders of well-educated immigrants, are as poor or poorer on a per capita basis than Mexico, the Dominican Republic, or Ecuador. They are one or several oceans away, with no possibility of entering the United States by land or via a short commercial flight.

The proximity of the United States to Mexico and the countries of the Caribbean Basin and the hegemony exercised by the American economy and culture over nearby countries have influenced peasants and low-skilled workers in these countries far more than those in distant lands. Up to now, it is rare the Egyptian or Indian peasant or manual worker who makes it to New York or Los Angeles, places where people of the same class extraction but coming from Mexico, Haiti, and the Dominican Republic are numerous.[11]

Table 10 presents an alternative portrayal of the occupational composition of contemporary immigration by listing the ten largest countries of out-migration by the proportion of regular immigrants admitted under the occupational references of the law versus those admitted for family reasons or as refugee adjustments. Occupational preference visas are regularly granted to college-educated professionals and highly skilled workers. The average educational and occupational composition of family-related immigration tends to be much lower. The second panel of the table lists the major countries contributing professional talent to the U.S. labor market through the temporary H-1B program and the educational composition of this inflow.

Both parts of the table convey essentially the same message. While over 90 percent of legal immigration from Mexico and the Dominican Republic comes under family preferences and, conversely, the relative proportion of occupational preference migrants from these countries is minimal, the proportion of occupational preferences among Canadians and Asians exceeds 20 percent, reaching a remarkable 60 percent among Indian immigrants. The sole exception to this pattern in table 10 is Vietnam, a major source of political refugees during the 1980s and 1990s from which recent migrants are primarily relatives of former refugees who have naturalized. The continuing refugee flow from Cuba is also reflected in these figures, where Cuban "immigrants" are mostly adjusted refugees already in the country. As noted previously, the educational and occupational composition of recent Cuban migration has been significantly lower than among the earlier middle-class waves arriving during the 1960s and 1970s.[12]

Indian professionals far outdistance, in absolute and relative terms, the number from other nationalities coming with temporary labor contracts. Among Latin American nations, only Colombia is a significant contributor to this type of immigration. These results not only underline the bimodal pattern of contemporary immigration but point to a clear division of labor among the principal contributing nations: India

TABLE 10. PRINCIPAL COUNTRIES OF EMIGRATION BY CATEGORY OF ADMISSION AND PRINCIPAL NATIONAL CONTRIBUTORS TO TEMPORARY PROFESSIONAL EMIGRATION (H-1B) BY LEVEL OF EDUCATION, 2002

Regular immigrants		Category of admission		
Country of origin	*Total admissions, 2002*	*Employment-related preferences (%)*	*Family-related preferences or relatives of U.S.citizens (%)*	*Refugee adjustment (%)*
All countries	1,063,732	16.4	63.3	11.8
Mexico	217,318	3.2	95.6	—
India	66,864	59.5	37.7	—
China, People's Republic	55,994	32.1	66.4	1.2
Philippines	48,674	23.0	76.6	—
Vietnam	32,425	0.3	76.2	21.6
El Salvador	30,539	5.1	43.9	—
Cuba	27,520	0.1	8.6	88.3
Canada	27,296	49.5	47.7	—
Dominican Republic	22,474	1.0	98.6	—
South Korea	20,114	41.6	58.2	—

Temporary (H-1B workers)		Level of education	
Country of origin	*Total admissions, 2002*	*College degree (%)*	*Master's degree or higher (%)*
All countries	197,537	98	48
India	64,980	99	48
China, People's Republic	18,841	100	85
Canada	11,760	94	39
Philippines	9,295	99	15
United Kingdom	7,171	92	36
South Korea	5,941	98	59
Japan	4,937	97	37
Taiwan	4,025	99	71
Pakistan	3,810	99	50
Colombia	3,320	98	29

SOURCE: Office of Immigration Statistics 2003, tables 8 and J.

(and, to a lesser extent, China) is the prime source of professional/ technical immigration, and Mexico (and, to a lesser extent, El Salvador and the Dominican Republic) is the major source of low-skilled labor migrants. Few studies have been conducted on the individual occupational achievement of immigrants, but those that exist point toward the overwhelming importance of formal education, work experience, and knowledge of English.[13] Even though this pattern is the predominant one, ethnographic evidence also shows that professionals who are part of predominantly low-skilled migrant flows may fail to secure legal permits to practice in the United States and may become unlicensed service providers for their respective communities. As noted in chapter 2, undocumented doctors and dentists commonly find themselves in this situation.

As important as the status of the jobs that newcomers occupy is their relative propensity for self-employment. It is a familiar sociological observation that immigrant minorities are more prone than the native population to work for themselves. In the 1820s, 80 percent of free white Americans were self-employed, but the proportion declined continuously, at least until 1970. In that year, the self-employed represented only 7.8 percent of the employed American labor force. The figure was, however, 8.5 percent among the foreign-born, 12 percent among Chinese and Japanese immigrants, and over 15 percent among those of Greek and Russian origin.[14]

The rate of self-employment is important as an indicator of economic self-reliance and also as a potential means for upward mobility. In general, immigrants who own their own established businesses earn significantly more than those working for wages. A study of immigrant earnings in the early 1990s found consistent and significant differences between self-employed entrepreneurs and salaried workers among seven major foreign nationalities, including Mexicans, Dominicans, Cubans, Chinese, and Koreans. Among Chinese immigrants, for example, the self-employed had average annual earnings of $43,151, in comparison with $29,721 for salaried workers; among Cubans, the respective figures were $36,558 and $26,510. After the analysis controlled for an array of predictors commonly included in earnings equations, such as education, work experience, and length of U.S. residence, the differences declined but did not disappear. Chinese entrepreneurs who were statistically equal in background characteristics to salaried workers still made $8,900 more per year; Cuban entrepreneurs made $7,500 more than their equivalent salaried conationals.[15]

As in other forms of labor market achievement, there is significant variation in this dimension as well. Table 11 presents the relevant figures. In 2000, the rate of self-employment among the native-born economically active population was 93.4 per thousand, a considerable jump from the rate ten years earlier, but the figure among the foreign-born was still higher. The table presents, first, all immigrant groups with at least twenty thousand self-employed persons and whose rates of entrepreneurship exceeded the U.S. average by at least thirty points; second, nationalities closest to the U.S. average with at least ten thousand self-employed persons; and third, those whose rate of entrepreneurship falls below the national average by ten points or more. Diversity in this table is highlighted both by the large gap between the most and least entrepreneurial immigrant nationalities and by the internal composition of each of the three categories.

The self-employment rate among Greeks, Koreans, and Iranians—the three most entrepreneurial groups—quadruples that of Laotians and Haitians at the bottom of the distribution. Entrepreneurship among the top nationality in the bottom category, Salvadorans, is forty points below Cubans, at the bottom of the top group. Highly entrepreneurial immigrant groups come from all over the world, including Europe, Asia, the Middle East, and Latin America. The close-to-average category is equally heterogeneous. Only the bottom groups indicate some geographic affinity, with a high concentration of immigrants from Latin America and the Caribbean. Note that in *absolute* terms, the number of self-employed Mexicans far surpasses that among any other nationality and that there are sizable numbers of entrepreneurs among Filipinos, Salvadorans, and Dominicans as well. These numbers get buried, however, in the relative statistics because of the very large size of the respective populations.

The meaning of self-employment in the 1990 U.S. Census remains somewhat obscure because no distinction is made, for example, between odd jobbers working for a casual wage and professionals with an established practice. Therefore, it is not possible to say a priori whether high rates of self-employment among a particular group represent a means of material survival or a vehicle for economic advancement. The survey of minority business ownership, conducted by the Bureau of the Census every five years, refines this information by distinguishing between firms with or without paid employees and by providing information on their relative size. Unfortunately, these data have been gathered only for a few specific minorities and not for all immigrant or ancestry groups.

TABLE 11. SELF-EMPLOYMENT AMONG SELECTED IMMIGRANT GROUPS, 2000

Country of birth	Number of self-employed	Rate of self-employment per thousand population[a] employed
Total native-born	13,665,432	93.40
All foreign-born	2,114,799	96.96
Above U.S. average		
Greece	27,711	253.37
Korea	120,715	205.15
Iran	41,893	203.15
Italy	48,224	178.40
Brazil	24,299	160.35
Poland	42,065	134.73
Germany	59,354	134.64
Canada	70,209	132.90
Pakistan	19,380	131.44
Taiwan	31,288	128.60
Cuba	74,626	127.29
Near U.S. average		
Colombia	41,690	111.07
Former Soviet Union	35,998	104.30
Portugal	13,566	103.74
Vietnam	73,242	99.03
China	66,290	98.79
India	75,682	97.73
Peru	20,367	97.29
Nigeria	10,041	91.62
Below U.S. average		
Salvador	52,902	82.43
Thailand	8,781	81.60
Ecuador	17,586	81.12
Dominican Republic	37,799	80.00
Nicaragua	13,094	78.53
Trinidad	10,849	72.14
Honduras	15,128	71.13
Mexico	440,046	68.95
Jamaica	28,302	65.66
Guyana	9,100	56.98
Philippines	54,165	50.64
Panama	3,864	49.95
Laos	7,164	49.11
Haiti	14,756	47.92

SOURCE: 2000 U.S. Census, 5% Public Use Microdata Sample.

[a] Employed persons age sixteen or older.

Nevertheless, this information provides a useful point of comparison, as shown in table 12.

The main findings from these data are that minorities with the highest rates of self-employment—defined in this case by total number of firms per one hundred thousand population—are also the ones with the highest rates of ownership of firms with paid employees. There is also a rough correspondence with the 2000 figures in terms of the relative positions of the nationalities listed in both tables. This correlation suggests that self-employment rates are an acceptable, if still imperfect, measure of established business ownership. In 1997, Japanese, Asian Indians, Koreans, and Chinese owned the highest relative number of firms with paid employees among the groups studied. Among Latin groups, Cubans had the highest rate of business ownership—with or without employees. In absolute terms, Mexican immigrants had the highest number of firms and second-highest total gross business receipts (next to the Chinese).

In relative terms, however, Mexican business ownership is the lowest among all groups considered, as the number of entrepreneurs is again buried in a vast immigrant population.[16] Among Asian groups, Filipinos again have the least relative propensity for entrepreneurship. For example, the rate of ownership of firms with employees among Filipinos is less than one-sixth that among Asian Indians and Japanese and less than one-fifth the rate among Chinese and Koreans. However, rates of business ownership among even the least entrepreneurial of these foreign groups exceed the figure for the largest domestic minority, African Americans, as shown in the bottom row of table 12. Following, in part, the Mexican pattern, American blacks have the largest absolute number of firms, but their relative rate is the lowest among all groups considered, including Mexicans.

Several theories have been advanced to explain the differential propensity for self-employment and entrepreneurship among various groups. The most common explanation is the distinct cultural endowment of certain nationalities that leads them to seek avenues for profitable enterprise while others remain content with wage employment. As Light has noted, all these cultural theories trace their origin, directly or indirectly, to Max Weber's thesis about the Protestant work ethic and its effect on the development of capitalism.[17]

A first problem with culturalistic theories, however, is that they are always *post factum*; that is, they are invoked once a group has achieved a notable level of business success, but they seldom anticipate which

TABLE 12. MINORITY FIRM OWNERSHIP AND INDICATORS OF FIRM PERFORMANCE, 2001

Group	All firms			Firms with paid employees			
	Total number of firms	Firms per 100,000 population	Gross receipts (total million dollars)	Number of firms	Firms per 100,000 population	Employees per firm	Gross receipts (total million dollars)
Asian							
Korean	135,571	156.6	45,936	50,076	57.5	6.7	40,746
Asian Indian	166,737	162.3	67,503	67,189	65.4	7.3	61,760
Japanese	85,538	247.2	43,741	23,309	67.4	11.2	41,295
Chinese	252,577	165.8	106,197	90,582	59.4	7.6	98,233
Vietnamese	97,764	98.6	9,323	18,948	19.1	4.2	6,768
Filipino	84,534	61.5	11,078	14,581	10.6	7.6	8,966
Latin American							
Cuban	125,273	144.0	26,492	30,203	34.7	5.8	23,873
Central or South American	287,314	94.5	40,998	42,916	14.1	5.6	34,798
Mexican	472,033	51.5	73,707	90,755	9.9	7.7	62,271
African American	823,499	23.9	71,215	93,235	2.7	7.7	56,378

SOURCES: 2000 U.S. Census, 5% Public Use Microdata Sample; U.S. Bureau of the Census 2000, 2001a, 2001b.

ones will do so. A second problem is the diversity of national and religious backgrounds of entrepreneurially oriented groups. Among minorities with high rates of business ownership, we find Jews and Arabs, southern and northern Europeans, Asians, and Latin Americans. They practice Protestantism, Catholicism, Greek Orthodoxy, Buddhism, Confucianism, Shintoism, and Islam. If a set of unique entrepreneurial "values" must be associated with each of these distinct religiocultural backgrounds, it is difficult to see what is left out as a point of comparison. This theoretical untidiness is compounded by the presence of other groups of similar cultural or religious origins that are not significantly represented among minority business owners. Why, for example, are Chinese Buddhists prone to entrepreneurship, but not Buddhist Cambodians; why Catholic Cubans and not Catholic Dominicans? A theory that must invent a unique explanation for each positive instance or for each exception ends up explaining nothing.[18]

For this reason, sociologists have moved away from exclusively culturalistic interpretations to try to find in the situational characteristics of different immigrant groups the key to their economic behavior. One such theory, advanced by Bonacich and her associates, is that groups that consider themselves and are regarded by others as temporary residents have every incentive to engage in business and accumulate profits. According to this view, such groups are set apart from the native majority, and they themselves long to go home, a situation that promotes their distinct economic behavior.[19]

This theory explains, for example, why immigrant groups in the United States are more entrepreneurially oriented than domestic minorities, such as blacks. It fails to explain, however, differences in business ownership between Jews and other European immigrant groups at the turn of the twentieth century or between Cubans and Mexicans at present. Unlike most pre–World War I immigrants, who aimed to return to their countries once they had "made it in America," Eastern European Jews came escaping czarist oppression and did not intend to return.[20] Similarly, Mexican immigrants have been, until recently, part of a cyclical flow, with many planning to return to or retire in Mexico. Cuban refugees—at least after the failure of the 1961 Bay of Pigs invasion— left the island with few prospects for return. These and other empirical examples contradict the "sojourner" theory of immigrant entrepreneurship. Alternatively, other authors, such as Michael Piore, have argued that sojourners, as "birds of passage," are in fact more willing to engage in low-wage labor and other forms of temporary employment than in long-term business planning.[21]

A second situational theory emphasizes the social disadvantages newcomers face in a strange society and their negative economic consequences. Minorities are frequently discriminated against in the labor market and are thus either excluded from employment or relegated to the least attractive jobs. Given this situation, it is not surprising that they find self-employment, even in marginal businesses, an attractive alternative. According to this "disadvantage theory," originally proposed by Ivan Light and others, self-employment is not, at least initially, an avenue for economic mobility but a means for material survival. Groups that are discriminated against tend to pool their resources, forming rotating credit associations and other similar cooperative organizations in order to provide mutual support.[22]

This theory explains the high propensity for self-employment among Asian minorities, such as the Chinese and the Japanese, who were subjected to a great deal of discrimination and even direct persecution during the first decades of the twentieth century. However, it fails to explain the low rates of self-employment among Filipinos and Mexicans, also discriminated minorities and also subjected to persecution in different periods. Nor does it provide a satisfactory account for the very low levels of entrepreneurship among American blacks, despite their being the prototypical victims of prejudice. In contrast, several nationalities with high rates of business ownership—such as the Lebanese, Greeks, Koreans, and Cubans—do not seem to have suffered much political or economic persecution in the United States. Hence, just as in the cases of education and occupation, we find that existing theories account only partially for the significant variability in self-employment and business ownership among the foreign-born. Factors other than those identified so far must be brought into play in order to achieve a satisfactory explanation of both occupational status and entrepreneurship. We will return to this point later.

INCOME

The best summary measure of the relative position of an immigrant group in the United States is probably its average income level. Given the variability of education, occupation, and business ownership among the foreign-born, it is not surprising that average incomes also vary widely, although the patterns observed are not what other factors would suggest. Table 13 presents the available evidence from the 2000 U.S. Census in 1999 dollars. Median immigrant incomes lag about $3,700 for families and about $1,800 for households in comparison with the total U.S. population. When figures are aggregated by continents, Asian immigrants have the highest household incomes, followed by Europeans. Asian *individual* incomes are actually lower than Europeans' on the average, indicating the importance of income pooling among Asian families. Latin American immigrants rank at the bottom of both distributions and also exhibit much higher poverty rates.

This level of aggregation is somewhat deceptive because it conceals significant differences within geographic regions. Table 13 lists foreign groups of one hundred thousand people or more in 1990 that occupied the top and bottom of the household income distribution, as well as those that came close to the national median ($49,000). Although a number of factors, including household size, household composition, and length of time in the country, affect these average figures, it is noteworthy that the top category is occupied mostly by the same nationalities that were well represented at the top of the educational and occupational distributions. Several of these groups (such as the Iranians, Taiwanese, Israelis, Canadians, and the Greeks) also have very high rates of self-employment.

Close to the national median income is an array of Latin American, Asian, and European nationalities. In contrast to the advantaged position of the Taiwanese, immigrants from the People's Republic of China have middling incomes and average poverty levels. Notable in this middle group is the presence of the three Southeast Asian refugee groups. Despite very low levels of education, especially among Cambodians and Laotians, they have managed to ascend economically to about the national median. However, poverty rates among these groups is still significantly higher than in the country as a whole. Present in this group as well are several "old" European nationalities, such as German and Italians, close to half of whom have reached retirement age.

The bottom income category is reserved primarily for immigrants from Mexico, Central America, and the Caribbean. All these groups, without exception, suffer poverty rates above the national average. These are especially high among groups composed primarily of manual labor migrants, such as Mexicans, Dominicans, and Hondurans. The low average income levels among nationals from the former Soviet Union, despite their above-average level of education, is attributable to

TABLE 13. MEDIAN ANNUAL HOUSEHOLD INCOMES AND POVERTY RATES OF PRINCIPAL IMMIGRANT NATIONALITIES AND REGIONS OF ORIGIN, 1999

Region/country of birth	Persons (N)	Income		Age
		Median household income ($)	Poverty rate[a] (%)	60 years and older (%)
Total native-born	250,288,425	49,298	15.1	16.4
All immigrants	31,133,481	44,999	20.1	14.8
Asia	8,155,503	57,002	15.5	13.3
Europe, Canada, and Australia	5,931,905	51,004	12.9	32.9
Africa	883,092	46,067	19.8	6.7
Latin America and Caribbean	16,162,981	38,914	25.1	9.4
Above $55,000				
Philippines	1,374,213	70,003	7.4	17.5
India	1,027,144	70,002	10.0	8.9
Taiwan	325,234	65,138	17.3	6.9
Hong Kong	201,358	64,998	13.6	5.6
United Kingdom	567,240	62,240	8.4	29.6
Ireland	153,311	59,929	9.8	41.5
Israel	112,965	59,832	15.9	10.0
Iran	285,176	59,773	13.9	18.4
France	147,755	59,294	13.0	27.4
Canada	820,713	56,996	10.3	33.0
Between $44,000 and $55,000				
Japan	346,453	54,117	18.8	18.6
Vietnam	991,995	53,993	16.3	9.8
China	997,301	51,025	16.6	23.4
Poland	472,544	50,006	10.2	30.4
Germany	705,110	49,813	11.2	40.2
Italy	476,033	49,122	9.9	49.3
Korea	870,542	49,005	17.7	12.0
Peru	275,111	48,644	14.1	12.4
Jamaica	554,897	47,991	14.9	15.5
Ecuador	292,246	46,267	19.1	10.5
Cambodia	137,365	45,088	24.8	9.4
Laos	205,931	44,803	24.8	8.3
Below $44,000				
Colombia	515,206	43,242	20.3	11.6
El Salvador	815,570	41,992	21.8	5.3
Guatemala	480,004	41,043	23.8	4.9
Former Soviet Union	618,302	40,978	23.1	26.5
Cuba	870,203	40,005	18.2	34.6
Haiti	422,841	39,981	22.2	12.0
Honduras	281,428	38,986	26.9	6.1
Mexico	9,163,463	36,004	28.9	6.2
Dominican Republic	685,952	34,311	29.3	10.2

SOURCE: 2000 U.S. Census, 5% Public Use Microdata Sample.

[a]Percentage of persons below the federal poverty line.

their recency of arrival and, hence, low levels of U.S.-specific work experience. The presence of a formerly advantaged group such as Cubans in this bottom category reflects the passing from the scene of the earlier elite exile professionals and entrepreneurs and their substitution by a predominantly low-skill labor flow. The aging of the earlier exile waves is reflected in the high proportion of retirement-age Cubans, comparable to that of "old" European groups.[23]

Several studies have attempted to establish the effect of individual characteristics on the earnings of the foreign-born. One of the classic studies is that by Chiswick, who analyzed male immigrant earnings in 1970 on the basis of such characteristics as education, work experience, and time since immigration. He found that education had a positive effect on earnings among immigrants but that the effect was not as high as among the native-born. Every year of education increased earnings by about 7 percent among natives, but only by 5.5 percent among the foreign-born. Similarly, the positive effect of work experience was "discounted" for immigrants whose earnings increased less per year of past work than among natives. For all immigrants, earnings increased by about 7 percent after five years in the United States, 13 percent after ten years, and 22 percent after twenty years.[24]

This study also found that, after controlling statistically for individual background characteristics, immigrants from Mexico, Cuba, Asia, and Africa had significantly lower earnings than the rest. Chiswick attributed Cubans' gap to the recency of their arrival because 80 percent of this group had arrived in the decade prior to the 1970 census. Cubans with ten to fifteen years of U.S. residence had already reached economic parity with the native-born. Most significant, however, was the finding that the earnings gap for Mexicans—by far the largest non-European immigrant group—did not decline significantly with time in the United States. Chiswick attributed this large and persistent gap to a Mexican "ethnic-group effect."[25]

Subsequent studies have generally confirmed this finding. In an econometric analysis of the earnings of Spanish-origin males, Reimers found that, after she controlled for education, work experience, and other background traits, Mexican men earned about 6 percent less than non-Hispanic whites; Cubans, about 6 percent more. There were no such differences among women, in part because average earnings of native-born and immigrant women alike were so low.[26] A more recent analysis based on data from the Current Population Survey (CPS) in the 1990s by Bean and Stevens finds the predictable effects of education in raising earnings among the foreign-born. In 1998, college-educated male immigrants from Latin America had average incomes of $50,215, compared with $19,481 among those with less than a high school education; for Asian immigrants, the corresponding figures were $60,600 versus $20,707. However, all first-generation migrants registered income gaps relative to similarly educated native whites, and the distance persisted across all income categories. Latin American immigrants, regardless of their education, made about 75 percent of the earnings of comparable native whites; for Asians, the figure rose to about 80 percent.[27]

In agreement with past studies, Bean and Stevens found that the gap was particularly large for Mexicans and that it existed across all educational categories. Thus, college-educated Mexican immigrants had earnings that were, on average, only 60 percent of those of similar natives in 1989; for those with a high school education, the gap declined marginally, to about 69 percent. The relatively low ability of predictive models, based on individual variables, to account for economic differences across immigrant groups and between them and the native-born, plus the persistent earnings disadvantage suffered by groups such as Mexicans, points, once again, to the need for a more encompassing explanation. This task must focus on contextual factors that go beyond individual characteristics that immigrants brought from abroad or their present levels of skill and effort. We turn to this matter next.

EXPLAINING THE DIFFERENCES: MODES OF INCORPORATION

There are two ways to "make it" in America, at least legally. The first is the salaried professional/managerial route; the other is independent entrepreneurship. Without doubt what immigrants bring with them in terms of motivation, knowledge, and resources is a decisive feature affecting whether they will gain entry into one or another path of economic mobility. The typology of immigration presented in chapter 2 is essentially a qualitative summary of these basic resource endowments. For example, manual immigration is generally characterized by low levels of education and occupational skills and an absence of prior entrepreneurial experience. This scarcity of human capital, characterizing immigrants of modest origin, makes raw physical power their principal marketable asset in the American labor market.

Professional immigration is characterized by high levels of education and skill. These resources may not translate immediately into highly paid positions because of language difficulties and lack of job-seeking experience. Over time, however, education and professional training tend to give these immigrants a significant edge in gaining access to better-paying positions. Similarly, entrepreneurial flows are distinguished by a substantial number of immigrants with prior business experience. These skills may remain dormant for a while, as new arrivals struggle with language and customs at the receiving end. However, with increasing time and familiarity with the host economy, many are able to reenact past experience by eventually moving into self employment.

Hence, time is an important variable influencing socioeconomic achievement, but it is so for some groups more than for others. As the previously discussed research shows, earnings tend to increase with the number of years since arrival. However, the process is likely to be more accelerated for those who possess skills and resources than for those who must rely on their physical energy. Among refugee groups, time has a different meaning at the collective level because it is often associated with a declining socioeconomic background. Earlier refugees tend to come from the elite and middle classes; later cohorts increasingly resemble the mass of the sending country's population. The fate of these late arrivals depends, to a large extent, on the kind of community created by their conationals. This contingent outcome already calls attention to the significance of the contexts of reception met by newcomers.

An emphasis on the different modes in which immigrants can become incorporated into the host society is a way to overcome the limitations of exclusively individualistic models of immigrant achievement. The basic idea is simple: individuals with similar skills may be channeled toward very different positions in the labor market and in the stratification system, depending on the type of community in which they become incorporated. This process can help explain differences in occupation, business ownership, and income among immigrants who are statistically "equal" in a host of individual characteristics. However, it is not sufficient to point to the importance of context, just as it is not enough to attribute persistent income differences to an "ethnic group effect." We must move beyond this level of generalization to specify at least what some of these contextual factors are and how they actually operate.

CONTEXTS OF RECEPTION

For immigrants, the most relevant contexts of reception are defined by the policies of the receiving government, the conditions of the host labor market, and the characteristics of their own ethnic communities. The combination of positive and negative features encountered at each of these levels determines the distinct mode of newcomers' incorporation. Governments are important because their policies determine whether sizable immigration flows can begin at all and, once under way, the forms that they will take. Regular legal migrant flows can only exist, of course, with the consent of governments. In some cases, sustained underground labor flows have also taken place with tacit official consent.[28] When this agreement does not exist, clandestine immigration is organized and shaped, at every step, by the need to bypass the state's enforcement machinery. In every instance, governmental policy represents the first stage of the process of incorporation because it affects the probability of successful immigration and the framework of economic opportunities and legal options available to migrants once they arrive.

Although a continuum of possible governmental responses toward foreign groups exists, three basic options surface: exclusion, passive acceptance, and active encouragement. When enforced, exclusion precludes immigration or forces immigrants into a wholly underground existence. The second alternative is defined by the act of granting access, explicitly or implicitly, without any additional effort to facilitate or impede the process. Most economically motivated immigration to the United States in recent years has taken place under this alternative. The third governmental option occurs when authorities take active steps to encourage a particular inflow or to facilitate its resettlement. At various times during the nineteenth and twentieth centuries, the U.S. government was directly involved in recruiting laborers or skilled workers deemed to be in short supply domestically.[29]

During the last three decades of the twentieth century, active governmental intervention to stimulate migration or facilitate its resettlement was restricted to selected refugee inflows. Governmental support is important because it gives newcomers access to an array of resources that do not exist for other immigrants. However, the interaction of this contextual dimension with individual characteristics can lead to very different outcomes. For refugees with professional or business skills, governmental assistance represents a means to accelerate social integration and economic mobility; for those lacking these resources, it can be a means to perpetuate social dependence and economic marginalization.[30]

Labor markets represent the second dimension of contexts of reception. Clearly, several features affect the economic prospects for immigrants. These features—such as stage in the business cycle, demand for specific kinds of labor, and regional wage differentials—have been discussed at length in the economic literature as potential determinants of earnings. However, there is a sociological aspect of labor markets that is perhaps more significant—namely, the manner in which particular immigrant groups are typified. Employers as a whole may be indifferent toward a particular group, or they may have a positive or negative view of it. Positive or negative typification of a specific minority can take, in turn, different forms. For example, widespread discrimination may hold that certain groups are able to perform only low-wage menial labor ("Mexican work" or, in an earlier time, "coolie labor") or that they are simply too incompetent to be employable at all. In the first instance, discrimination contributes to confinement of the group to the low-wage segment of the labor market; in the second, it contributes to its exclusion and hence unemployment.[31]

Positive typification, as opposed to mere neutrality, has been far less common. Preferential hiring of immigrants as workers tends to occur only when employers are of the same nationality. Hence, when a segment of the local labor market is composed of ethnic firms, immigrants of the same origin often gravitate toward them in search of employment opportunities unavailable elsewhere.[32] Positive typification can also occur when members of an ethnic group or immigrant nationality are viewed as more motivated to work and more reliable than their potential competitors. This positive image may grant them preferential access to entry-level jobs, although there is no guarantee that they will be able to rise beyond them.[33]

These various labor market situations interact, of course, with individual skills and resources, leading to a plurality of outcomes. The main difference lies in the ability of different types of immigrants to neutralize labor market discrimination. Lack of resources and information makes discrimination most serious for immigrant laborers who are generally trapped in positions held to be "appropriate" for their group. Even if they receive preferential access to these low-paying menial jobs, these may be dead-end positions that lead nowhere. Professionals and entrepreneurs can escape discrimination by moving to other parts of the country, sometimes by disguising their nationality or ethnicity. In other instances, however, they may emphasize the same traits as a source of solidarity for the construction of ethnically defined employment niches or business enclaves.[34]

The ethnic community itself represents the third and most immediate component of contexts of reception. A first option is that no such community exists, in which case immigrants must confront the host labor market directly. If employers do not discriminate against them, the situation approaches the ideal assumed by individualistic human capital models because, presumably, only the person's education and other resources will affect his or her earnings. Among contemporary immigrants, this situation is most closely approximated by professionals, who frequently accept jobs away from areas of ethnic concentration and who compete primarily on the basis of their scarce skills.[35]

Most common, however, is the arrival of immigrants into places where an ethnic community already exists. As seen in chapter 3, a common sociological observation is that such communities cushion the impact of cultural change and protect immigrants against outside prejudice and initial economic difficulties. As important as this observation is the fact that the process of socioeconomic attainment in this context is largely network driven. Ethnic networks provide sources of information about outside employment, sources of jobs inside the community, and sources of credit and support for entrepreneurial ventures. Because isolating themselves from the influence of kin and friends is quite difficult for newcomers in the early stages of adaptation, the characteristics of the ethnic community acquire decisive importance in molding their entry into the labor market and hence their prospects for future occupational mobility.

Ethnic communities vary widely in a number of dimensions, but, from the perspective of socioeconomic achievement, the central difference is whether they are composed primarily of manual laborers or contain a significant professional or business element. All ethnic groups seek to protect and promote their own, but how they do so varies significantly across these situations. For new immigrants in working-class communities, the natural path is to follow the course traced by earlier arrivals. The assistance that ethnic networks can provide for securing employment in this situation tends to be constrained by the kind of jobs already held by established members of the community. In addition, there is often a collective expectation that new arrivals should not try to surpass, at least at the start, the status achieved by older migrants. In this fashion, individuals of above-average ability and motivation may find themselves restricted to low-status manual jobs and limited in their chances for future mobility. Ethnic network assistance comes at the cost of pressures for conformity, and the latter often reinforce employers' expectations about the "proper" position of the minority in the labor market. These dynamics help explain the self-perpetuating character of working-class immigrant communities and the frequent tendency among their members to receive lower-than-average rewards for their human capital.[36]

The dominant feature of the opposite situation—in which a substantial number of community members hold higher-status occupations—is that the support of ethnic networks is not contingent on acceptance of a working-class lifestyle or outlook. Hence, newcomers, dependent as always on the assistance of kin and friends, may be introduced from the start to the whole range of opportunities available in the host labor market. Within this general pattern, entrepreneurial communities have the additional advantage of being not only sources of information about outside jobs but also sources of employment opportunities themselves. Immigrant firms tend to hire and promote their own, and, as seen previously, they often represent the only segment of the labor market in which newcomers can find preferential employment.

In the past, a common belief held that jobs in coethnic firms were equivalent to those in the lower tier or "secondary" labor market, insofar as both constrained future mobility opportunities. However, more recent research indicates that this is not the case because employment within an ethnic enclave is often the best route for promotion into supervisory and managerial positions and for business ownership. These studies have found that education brought from the home country can have a greater economic payoff, at least initially, in coethnic firms and that a key factor promoting business ownership is prior employment in firms owned by persons of the same nationality. Thus, ethnic enclaves can function as training systems for the acquisition of the requisite business skills by newcomers.[37]

This complex set of factors can be illustrated with data on the differential performance of immigrant groups in the American labor market. Economic models of employment and earnings have focused primarily on individual characteristics such as education and work experience as predictors. As we have seen in this chapter, such variables are important but yield imperfect results that do not fully account for between-group differences. Table 14 illustrates these conclusions with data from a sample of more than two thousand immigrant parents surveyed in 1996 as a part of the Children of Immigrants Longitudinal Study (CILS). Results from that project will be discussed in greater detail in chapter 8. For the moment, our interest is on the incomes of adult immigrant parents and their determinants.[38]

TABLE 14. DETERMINANTS OF ADULT
IMMIGRANT ECONOMIC OUTCOMES[a]

| Predictor | Family monthly earnings[b] | | Individual yearly incomes[b] | |
	I	II	I[c]	II[c]
Sex (male)	562***	429***	2,365***	1,795*
Age	6 n.s.	−1 n.s.	−30 n.s.	−60 n.s.
Years of U.S. residence	10*	16**	135**	165**
Post–high school education	327**	407**	5,425***	5,120***
College graduate	851***	866***	8,680***	7,265***
Postgraduate education	1,565***	1,679***	8,305***	8,450***
Knowledge of English	233.***	275***	2,485***	2,330***
Occupational status	511***	540***	3,605**	3,930***
Self-employment	−49 n.s.	56 n.s.	580 n.s.	1,015 n.s.
Nationality				
Colombian		−454*		−865 n.s.
Cuban		−192 n.s.		1,500 n.s.
Filipino		91 n.s.		4,305**
Haitian		−697*		−5,930**
Laotian/Cambodian		901***		4,960**
Mexican		−401*		−1,910*
Nicaraguan		−583**		−475 n.s.
Vietnamese		324*		1,220 n.s.
West Indian		−441*		−1,015 n.s.
R^2	.248	.313	.311	.354
N	2,010		2,010	

SOURCE: CILS, parental survey.

[a] Ordinary least squares regressions with unlogged dollar figures as dependent variables.
[b] Unstandardized regression coefficients.
[c] Decimals (cents) suppressed. Coefficients evaluated at the mean of each income interval.
*Moderate effect (coefficient exceeds 2.5 times its standard error).
**Strong effect (coefficient exceeds four times its standard error).
***Very strong effect (coefficient exceeds six times its standard error).
n.s. = Nonsignificant effect.

The (CILS) parental survey includes a sizable number of immigrants and refugees who may be considered "emblematic" of different modes of incorporation. Among them, Cubans, Vietnamese, Cambodians, and Laotians—all refugee groups from Communist regimes—received generous governmental resettlement assistance and a generally positive public reception as escapees from governments hostile to the United States during the Cold War. Governmental support for family reunification allowed each of these groups to rebuild families and constitute cohesive communities that became, in turn, a key source of assistance for later arrivals. Such positive context may be expected to have a significant effect on the economic mobility of these minorities.[39]

The survey also contains a sizable number of immigrants who find themselves in the opposite situation. Mexicans, in particular, not only do not receive any governmental aid but have been subject to much official persecution as potential illegal aliens. This treatment is coupled with widespread discrimination and hostility among the native population, who frequently regard Mexicans as the core of the "silent invasion" undermining the linguistic and cultural integrity of the nation. The modest educational qualifications of most Mexicans, combined with negative official and public contexts of reception, have resulted, in turn, in weak and transient communities lacking the material and social resources to support their members effectively.[40] Haitians find themselves in a similar situation in which a federal policy designed to prevent their entry and discourage their stay is combined with widespread public discrimination because of their status as a black minority. As with Mexicans, this hostile environment, coupled with the modest education and economic resources of most Haitians, has given rise to impoverished ethnic communities that function more as traps than as platforms for upward mobility.[41]

The case of Nicaraguan immigrants is also quite telling. This is mostly a population of would-be asylees who came to the United States fleeing the Sandinista regime in their country. They expected a favorable official reception comparable to that received by the early Cuban exile waves, but they were promptly disappointed. By the time of their arrival, U.S. policy had shifted direction, seeking to bottle up discontent inside Nicaragua in support of the Contra insurgency rather than hosting a new Latin refugee community in South Florida. Accordingly, most Nicaraguans were denied asylum, and those who stayed were classified as illegal aliens, thus becoming unable to make use of the considerable human capital resources brought from the home country.[42]

Columns I and III of table 14 show the powerful effects of education, knowledge of English, length of U.S. residence, and gender in the economic attainment of first-generation immigrants. A college degree, for example, yielded a net $850 gain per month in earnings and almost $8,700 in annual income. A postgraduate degree produced even larger monthly earnings. Each additional level in the four-point scale of knowledge of English used in these models yielded almost $2,500 extra in annual incomes, and each additional year of U.S. residence added $135. The human capital equation succeeds in explaining one-fourth of the variance in monthly earnings in this sample. However, with all these variables controlled, between-group differences persist, as indicated by the corresponding national coefficients in Columns II and IV. The direction of these coefficients corresponds to theoretical expectations based on the known modes of incorporation of different groups.

Mexican, Haitian, and Nicaraguan immigrants suffer a significant loss in monthly earnings after controlling for their education, knowledge of English, and occupation. The same is generally true for yearly incomes. For example, Mexicans who are statistically "equal" to the rest of the sample in individual characteristics pay a penalty of almost $2,000 per year; the figure increases to a remarkable $6,000 for Haitians. Since education and other relevant individual traits are controlled, the penalty is directly attributable to the negative modes of incorporation experienced by these groups.

Statistically insignificant nationality effects indicate that initial group differences are fully accounted for by individual human capital, as well as by subsequent work experience in the United States. Thus, for Cubans, an older refugee group with many years of U.S. experience, the advantages of an early favorable mode of incorporation had largely dissipated by 1996 when the survey was conducted. This result also reflects the difference between the favorable context of reception experienced by early Cuban exiles and the increasingly negative reception of Cuban refugees arriving during and after the Mariel exodus of 1980. About 40 percent of Cuban immigrant parents in the sample belong to that second category.[43]

By contrast, Southeast Asian refugees have enjoyed a consistently positive context of reception corresponding to their more recent arrival and continuous governmental assistance. As seen in table 14, these groups enjoy a positive and generally significant net advantage in monthly earnings and yearly incomes, despite their low initial levels of human capital. This is especially true of Laotians and Cambodians, refugee groups of very modest education who nevertheless had a net advantage in yearly incomes of almost $5,000 in the mid-1990s. This remarkable result is directly attributable to governmental assistance, given the low human capital, low labor market participation, and low levels of entrepreneurship of these groups.[44]

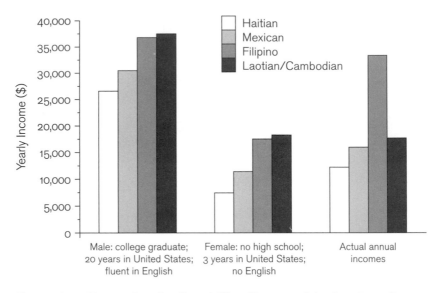

Figure 4. Annual incomes by nationality and different human capital and gender profiles

Figures 4 and 5 graphically illustrate these results by presenting income and earnings data for immigrants of different nationalities possessing two hypothetical individual profiles. The first is a college-educated male who is fluent in English and has lived in the United States for twenty years; the second is a recently arrived female with no English and less than a high school education. The difference in projected earnings based on our models is stark. Yet, in each case, major differences persist across immigrant nationalities. Hence, monthly earnings of our hypothetical male in 1995 dollars would range from $2,950 if he were Haitian to about $4,000 if he were a Southeast Asian refugee. At the opposite end, an uneducated Haitian woman could expect to earn no more than $560 per month, but a Laotian woman in the same situation could receive over $2,100.

Actual earnings of each immigrant nationality, presented in the third panel of the figure, show that they come closer to the profile featuring low human capital. Yet, in all instances but one, they exceed these figures by a considerable margin, indicating higher levels of average education, knowledge of English, and work experience than our hypothetical bottom example. The exception is Laotians/Cambodians, for whom actual earnings come close to those projected on the basis of minimum human capital. This result reflects, once again, the low skill

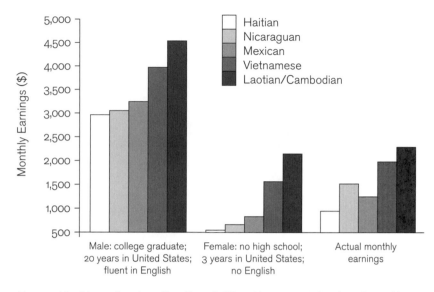

Figure 5. Monthly earnings by nationality and different human capital and gender profiles

endowment of these refugee groups and their almost exclusive reliance on a favorable mode of incorporation.

Similar results (not shown) are found when the effects of education, length of U.S. residence, and other earnings predictors are compared across strategic nationalities. Groups advantaged by an early favorable mode of incorporation, such as Cubans and Vietnamese, enjoy a significant and sizable payoff for their high school or college education and for each year of additional residence in the United States. By contrast, Mexican immigrants and Nicaraguan would-be asylees experienced no gain for spending additional time in the country or for achieving a college degree. Only among the very few who managed to achieve a post-graduate degree does education pay off significantly.

CONCLUSION

Making it in America is a complex process, dependent only partially on immigrants' motivation and abilities. How they use these personal resources often depends on international political factors—over which individuals have no control—and on the history of earlier arrivals and the types of communities they have created—about which newcomers also have little say. These complex structural forces confront immigrants as an objective reality that channels them in different directions. A Nicaraguan or Mexican professional, through no personal fault, may do worse in the U.S. labor market under these external circumstances than a Cuban or Vietnamese worker. Afterward, apologists of successful groups will make necessities out of contingencies and uncover those "unique" traits underlying their achievements; detractors of impoverished minorities will describe those cultural shortcomings or even genetic limitations accounting for their failure. Both are likely to affirm that, in the end, "where there is a will, there is a way."

Greater knowledge of the contexts that immigrants confront negates such assertions because it demonstrates the importance of the modes in which they are incorporated and the resulting material and moral resources made available by governments, society, and their own ethnic communities. The most hardworking individuals may thus end up in poor jobs simply because they perceive no alternatives or none are available; others may rise to the top, riding in the wake of a lucky set of external circumstances. Social context renders individualistic models insufficient because it can alter, in decisive ways, the link between individual skills and motivations and their expected rewards.

Plate 1. First Chinese New Year parade in Monterey Park, California ("the first suburban Chinatown"). Since the 1970s, many Asian-origin newcomers have moved to the San Gabriel Valley of Los Angeles, illustrative of a general trend of immigrants settling in suburban middle-class communities rather than the inner-city locales long associated with immigrant settlements in U.S. urban history. (Photograph by Steve Gold.)

Plate 2. Philippine-American Club of Greater Lansing on parade, Lansing, Michigan. Over the past forty years, only Mexico has sent more immigrants to the United States than the Philippines. (Photograph by Steve Gold.)

Plate 3. Indochinese refugees at the Phanat Nikkom refugee camp in Thailand in the 1980s, saying good-bye to family and friends on "the bus to America" as they leave for a processing center before coming to the United States, not knowing whether they will ever see each other again. (Photograph by Erica Hagen.)

Plate 4. A Hmong refugee woman carries her son while doing her needlework. Her husband was a refugee resettlement worker for Catholic Community Services in San Diego. More than one million refugees from Laos, Cambodia, and Vietnam were resettled in the United States after 1975. (Photograph by Erica Hagen.)

Plate 5. Welcoming the newcomers: Soviet Jews in Chabad program, Los Angeles. (Photograph by Steve Gold.)

Plate 6. Immigrant computer programmers from Hong Kong and Leningrad at the University of California, Berkeley. Labeled "brain drain" in the countries of origin, the immigration of highly trained personnel represents a significant gain for the United States. (Photograph by Steve Gold.)

Plate 7. Trinidadian barbershop, Boston, Massachusetts. On the wall are images of Martin Luther King Jr., Malcom X, and Joe Louis, along with a slogan for the Boston Celtics basketball team. (Photograph by Steve Gold.)

Plate 8. A Mexican restaurant and an Ethiopian restaurant share a wall in Adams Morgan, Washington, D.C. The area has since been gentrified. (Photograph by Luis E. Rumbaut.)

Plate 9. Billboards in Little Saigon, Orange County, California. (Photograph by Steve Gold.)

Plate 10. Along Calle Ocho, Miami, Florida, in the heart of "Little Havana." More than eight hundred thousand Cuban Americans reside in greater Miami. (Photograph by Steve Gold.)

Plate 11. The Grand Central Market in downtown Los Angeles. More than two million Mexican immigrants live in greater Los Angeles; another two million Angelenos were born in the United States of Mexican immigrant parents, including the mayor of Los Angeles, Antonio Villaraigosa. (Photograph by Steve Gold.)

Plate 12. Haitian cabbie, Miami Beach. Most Haitian immigrants in the United States have settled in two metropolitan areas: New York and Miami. (Photograph by Steve Gold.)

Plate 13. View of Cañón Zapata in Tijuana on the U.S.-Mexico border prior to the fencing and militarization of the border in the early 1990s. Each year during the peak summer months, more than a thousand undocumented immigrants crossed nightly into the United States from this point, falling to a low of about two hundred a day during November and December. The same patterns had been observed for many years. (Photograph by Steve Gold.)

Plate 14. Cramped quarters for migrant workers, these crude cavelike shelters are dug into hillsides and covered with cardboard and chaparral in canyons near farms where migrants seek work. The plastic jugs are used to bring water to the site. A typical shelter sleeps three men for eight months of the year. (Photograph by Michael Franklin, *San Diego Union*.)

Plate 15. Mexican migrant farm laborers in northern San Diego County pile on a flatbed truck for a short ride back to camp at the end of a workday. For employers, they are a source of abundant and inexpensive labor. For the migrants themselves, the work is a means of survival and a vehicle of economic mobility. (Photograph by Michael Franklin.)

Plate 16. Two migrant workers pick tomatoes side by side in a field north of San Diego just as they do in their village in Oaxaca, Mexico. Each year they made the two-thousand-mile journey to work in these fields. Growers say the Oaxacans have a gentle way of picking that avoids bruising the fruit. (Photograph by Michael Franklin.)

Plate 17. Pico Union area of Los Angeles, home of a major settlement of Central American immigrants, mostly from El Salvador. (Photograph by Steve Gold.)

Plate 18. Korean shops in Queens, New York. Korean immigrants have settled principally in Los Angeles and New York. (Photograph by Steve Gold.)

Plate 19. First steps in political incorporation: a Vietnamese immigrant runs for Congress in a heavily Vietnamese district in Orange County, California. (Photograph by Steve Gold.)

Plate 20. Civic engagement: a meeting in Little Saigon with the Asian American U.S. secretary of labor.

Plate 21. Voter registration drive at the Arab American festival, Dearborn, Michigan. (Photograph by Steve Gold.)

Plate 22. Palestinian activists at the Dearborn festival. (Photograph by Steve Gold.)

Plate 23. Vermont Avenue in Koreatown, Los Angeles. More than two thousand Korean immigrant shops such as these were burned in the riots of 1992. (Photograph by Steve Gold.)

Plate 24. Striking service workers in San Francisco, 2004. (Photograph by Steve Gold.)

5
From Immigrants to Ethnics
Identity, Citizenship, and Political Participation

IN THE SOCIETY AND NOT OF IT

In 1916, Madison Grant, in a book called *The Passing of the Great Race*, deplored the "mongrelization" of America as the waves of Eastern and Southern European peasant immigrants threatened to overwhelm the great Anglo-Saxon traditions of the past. Grant minced no words: "The immigrant laborers are now breeding out their masters and killing by filth and by crowding as effectively as by the sword."[1]

Exactly eighty-eight years after *The Passing of the Great Race*, the Harvard political scientist Samuel Huntington sounded the same themes with reference to Mexican immigration. In his article "The Hispanic Challenge," Huntington bemoaned the harm that the inferior language and culture of Hispanic immigrants would do to English and the Anglo-Saxon Protestant world. Like Grant before him, Huntington went straight to the point:

> The persistent inflow of Hispanic immigrants threatens to divide the United States into two peoples, two cultures, and two languages. Unlike past immigrant groups, Mexicans and other Latinos have not assimilated into mainstream U.S. culture, forming instead their own political and linguistic enclaves . . . and rejecting the Anglo-Protestant values that built the American dream. The United States ignores this challenge at its peril.[2]

In both 1916 and 2004, the analyses of the distressing influence of immigration on the core fabric of the nation ended up with a call for immediate restrictionism. The noteworthy parallelism between Grant and Huntington is just one of many manifestations of the same underlying motif: a fear of what the "foreign element" can do to America. Interestingly, the fear has taken many and frequently contradictory forms.

In 1903, an act promulgated by the U.S. Congress enabled immigration authorities to look for the many "radicals" allegedly arriving among the masses of European immigrants and deport them expeditiously. Agents of the Immigration Bureau set out to canvass ports of entry and processing stations; working with the Secret Service and local police, they circulated undercover within immigrant communities in search of the centers of rebellion. Few were found. Twenty-three districts out of the thirty or so covered by the campaign reported no "cases" of radicalism at all; in the remainder, agents managed to uncover a handful of anarchists who had lived in the country for a long time.[3]

During the 1980s and 1990s, the U.S. English movement reached nationwide prominence with its campaign for a constitutional amendment to declare English the official language of the country. Headed by S. I. Hayakawa, a senator of Japanese immigrant origin, the movement set out to combat what it saw as the threat of denationalization posed by the new waves of immigrants who speak other languages. Anticipating by two decades the themes sounded by "The Hispanic Challenge," U.S. English set out to suppress the public and, when possible, private use of foreign languages across the land.[4] These efforts took place at the same time that research on language acquisition consistently reported the massive shift to English in the second generation and the equally drastic loss of parental languages. One after another study documented that what was really under threat was the preservation of some fluency in a host of foreign tongues, of use to government and private employers but hopelessly lost among the majority of immigrant children.[5]

Much heated rhetoric and a lot of money have been spent combating these alleged evils; playing on these fears has also proven lucrative for a host of nativist associations, agitators, and pundits. For the most part, the targets of these efforts, the presumed sappers of democracy, linguistic unity, and territorial integrity, have looked at all these activities with a mixture of resignation and puzzlement. One may surmise the attitudes of poor Italian and Polish immigrants who barely knew the language and struggled daily for survival at the sight of Secret Service agents canvassing their neighborhoods in search of political "extremists."

The response of immigrant communities to nativist fears of yesterday and today has been marked more by passive endurance than active opposition. The notion that California and Texas may some day be returned to Mexico, articulated by Huntington and others, is so ludicrous as to preclude any need for a response; the demands of the U.S. English movement have also gone largely unopposed. The view among immigrants who happen to be aware of these demands is that declaring English the official language of the United States is at best a costly redundancy. Immigrants in California and elsewhere overwhelm English classes in the belief that acquisition of the language is the ticket to upward mobility for themselves and their children. Immigrant parents have been known to picket public schools who insisted on teaching their offspring in parental languages, thus delaying English acquisition.[6] No significant movement in favor of the preservation of Spanish or any other foreign language has emerged among immigrant groups. For the most part, U.S. English and similar nativist organizations have been shadowboxing.

To a large extent, nativist fears and the feverish pitch reached by campaigns based on them are due to the peculiar position of immigrant communities that are "in the society, but not yet of it."[7] Their very foreignness provides fertile ground for all sorts of speculations about their traits and intentions. At the same time, immigrants often lack sufficient knowledge of the new language and culture to realize what is happening and explain themselves effectively. For the most part, the first foreign-born generation lacks "voice."[8] It is on this enforced passivity that the nativist fears of many and the active hostility and lucrative demagoguery of a few have flourished.

Campaigns against the first generation have had a peculiar political consequence, however. Because their targets have been largely illusory, they have never visibly succeeded in their declared goals, be they rooting out political extremism or restoring linguistic integrity. What these campaigns have accomplished, above all, is stirring ethnic militancy among subsequent generations. More attuned to American culture and fluent in English, the offspring of immigrants have gained "voice" and have used it to reaffirm identities attacked previously with so much impunity. The resilient ethnic identification of many communities and the solidary ethnic politics based on it can be traced directly to this process of "reactive formation."[9] As Nathan Glazer and others have noted, ethnic resilience is a uniquely American product because it has seldom reflected linear continuity with the immigrants' culture; rather, it has emerged in reaction to the situation, views, and discrimination they faced on arrival. These experiences turned the circumstance of national origin into the primary basis of group solidarity, overwhelming other competing identifications, such as those based on class.

The immigrant world has always been a difficult one, torn between old loyalties and new realities. For the most part, the politics of the first generation—to the extent that such politics have existed—have been characterized by an overriding preoccupation with the home country. Early participation in American politics has been limited to the more educated groups, those prevented from going back to their countries of origin, and those exceptional circumstances in which the very survival of the immigrant community is at stake. Even then, however, old loyalties die hard because individuals socialized in another language and culture have great difficulty giving them up as a primary source of identity.[10]

Throughout the history of immigration, the characteristics of sending countries have also made a significant difference in shaping the politics of the first generation as well as the timing of its shift into American-based concerns. Immigrants in the past or present may have come from (1) stateless nations, divided lands contested by warring factions or occupied by a foreign power; (2) hostile states, dictatorships that oppressed the entire population of their countries or singled out the immigrants' own group for special persecution; (3) consolidated but indifferent nation-states, which neither promoted nor acknowledged the migrants' departure; or (4) states that actually supported and supervised emigration, regarding their nationals abroad as outposts serving their country's interests.

These diverse origins interact with contexts of reception to give rise to a complex geometry of political concerns among the foreign-born that mold, in turn, the politics of later generations. Depending on this variable geometry of places of origin and destination, immigrant communities may be passionately committed to political causes back home, either in support of or in opposition to the existing regime; they may see themselves as representatives of their nation-state abroad; or they may turn away from all things past and concentrate on building a new life in America. Examples of these and other possible outcomes are found both at the turn of the twentieth century and at present. We look first at the earlier period in order to provide a backdrop against which to describe contemporary developments.

IMMIGRANT POLITICS AT THE TURN OF THE CENTURY

THE DOMESTIC IMPACT OF IMMIGRATION

The massive waves of Southern and Eastern Europeans who crossed the Atlantic in the late 1800s and early 1900s and the smaller flows of Asian immigrants who traversed the Pacific about the same time altered in multiple ways the fabric of American society, particularly its political structure. Few could have anticipated at the start that these movements would have such momentous consequences, for they were composed of humble men and women who came to fill the labor needs of an expanding industrial economy. Given the criteria for economic achievement outlined in the previous chapter, turn-of-the century immigrants were in a uniformly disadvantageous position. With some exceptions, their individual educations and occupational skills were modest, and they confronted a generally unfavorable context on arrival: the U.S. government allowed them in but did not assume any responsibility for their well-being; employers hired them but assigned them to the lowest-paying jobs; their own communities helped them but confined them in the process to the same unskilled, dead-end occupations filled by earlier arrivals.

Despite their concentration at the bottom of the economic and social ladders and their political powerlessness, immigrants were the subject of much agitation. A number of alarming traits and political designs were imputed to them, and, on that basis, nativist organizations mobilized for action. As today, the sins attributed to immigrants were quite different and, at times, contradictory; but the ultimate demand was always the same: containment or suppression of the inflow. On the right, the usual accusation was political radicalism. Immigrant workers transported the "virus" of socialistic ideas that threatened to undermine American democratic institutions:

> In 1919, the Socialist Party of the United States had about 110,000 members, over half of whom belonged to non-English-speaking bodies, the autonomous and practically independent language federations. . . . Ultimately, a split was precipitated and the emergence of the new Communist organizations drew predominantly on these federations.[11]

On the political left, immigrants were accused pretty much of the opposite—inertia, organizational incapacity, and docility—which undermined the efforts of the unions and weakened the political organizations of the working class. The central European peasant, "so steeped in deference, so poor, and so desperate for the American dream that . . . he knelt down and kissed the hand of the boss who sent him to work,"[12] was a favorite of employers, who used him to break the power of the unions. Out West, similar accusations were leveled against Asian immigrants. Chinese immigration, for example, was described as "a more abominable slave traffic than the African slave trade," and the immigrants themselves were portrayed as "half-civilized beings" who spread "filth, depravity and epidemic."[13] The Japanese, who arrived subsequently, fared no better:

> Japanese laborers, by reason of race habits, mode of living, disposition, and general characteristics, are undesirable . . . they contribute nothing to the growth of the state [California]. They add nothing to its wealth, and they are a blight on the prosperity of it, and great impending danger to its welfare.[14]

The characterization and denunciation of immigrants as either a radical threat or an inferior stock that undermined the welfare of American workers was based on a stereotypical image of newcomers. Then as now, all immigrants were portrayed as having similar traits. The reality was quite different. Generalizations about political extremism or political docility each had a basis of fact in the characteristics of *some* groups and were contradicted, in turn, by those of others. Most but not all immigrants arriving at the time were peasants or laborers; there were also skilled industrial workers coming from countries with a well-developed working-class movement. Among them were Scandinavian miners and loggers socialized in a strong trade union tradition and artisans and literate merchants from Russia and east-central Europe.

Unlike peasant laborers, who could scarcely go lower, these better-educated groups experienced downward mobility and confronted American capitalism at its harshest. Their response was governed by their European political experience. Skilled German workers, who grew up under the influence of a large and disciplined socialist movement, were notable in this respect. As Fine notes, "It was men trained in such a movement who tried to build up a duplicate in the United States."[15] In the Midwest, Finnish loggers and miners divided between the meek "Church Finns" and the militant "Red Finns." The latter had also learned working-class politics in their native land, and their experience served them well in union organizing in America. Finnish socialists were the backbone of the Socialist Party in many mining and industrial towns, consciously promoting class over ethnic solidarity and proselytizing among the less politically conscious groups, such as Italians and Slavs.[16] Back East, it was the Jewish needle trade workers who formed the core of the union movement. These hardworking immigrants, many refugees from czarist persecution, saw socialism less as a political movement than as a way of life. Their descendants continued this tradition:

> In some neighborhoods, one grew up to be a Socialist, a reader of Cahan's *Jewish Daily Forward* in Yiddish or *The Call* in English, and a member of one of the needle trade unions just as naturally as in some other parts of the country one grew up to be a Republican and a reader of the *Saturday Evening Post.*[17]

In the wake of the Russian Revolution of 1917, membership in the Russian-language Federation of the American Socialist Party trebled, becoming one of the largest ethnic affiliates. After the split that created the new Workers' (Communist) Party, the latter drew most of its membership from workers born in the old czarist empire.[18]

There was, therefore, a factual basis for the view that immigrants participated in and promoted leftist political organizations. The generalization was inaccurate, however, in the majority of cases. Skilled workers and artisans from an urban-industrial background were the minority among turn-of-the-century arrivals. Even less common were those with extensive political socialization. They were present only among certain nationalities, and even within them they did not always represent a majority. German-born farmers, shopkeepers, and laborers outnumbered militant German workers; the views of Church Finns eventually prevailed, and Finnish radicalism faded away; Russian Jewish immigrants became shopkeepers and small entrepreneurs en masse, and their economic progress undermined any support for radical causes.

Most European immigration during this period did not come from the cities but from rural areas, and it was not formed by skilled artisans but by peasants. Past political socialization among these masses had exactly the opposite effect as among the literate minority. Not only were party politics foreign to them, but they sometimes could not even tell what nationality they belonged to. Sicilian peasants identified with their village or at best with the surrounding region; in America, they sought the comfort of fellow villagers. "Thus, in the Italian neighborhoods of New York's Lower East Side in the early 1920s, it was possible to trace, block by block, not only the region of Italy but also the very villages from which the inhabitants had come."[19] Nationality to these immigrants came with their exposure to American society. In Max Ascoli's apt description, "they became Americans before they were ever Italians."[20]

Lack of political consciousness among Italian, Slavic, and Scandinavian peasants proved to be a boon to many American employers, who used them as a valuable tool against domestic labor organizations. By dividing workers along national lines and assigning them different pay and working conditions, employers reinforced ethnic identities over class solidarity. Nowhere was this "divide and rule" strategy more effective than in the Pennsylvania coal mines:

> Beginning in 1875 and for at least a quarter-century thereafter, central, southern, and eastern European laborers flowed steadily into the anthracite coal basin of Pennsylvania. . . . This new wave of immigrants doubled the labor supply, reinforcing competition for jobs with competition between cultures and organizational position. The new immigrants received lower pay, exacerbating cultural and occupational tensions, because mechanization was simultaneously depressing the value of skilled career miners.[21]

The antiunion strategy of Pennsylvania collieries and freight railroads proved highly successful and was adopted by other employers. The difficulty in organizing peasant newcomers into labor unions owed much to the absence of relevant political socialization among these immigrants. The problem was compounded, however, by other factors. First, American workers often displaced their hostility from employers engaged in this union-busting strategy toward the migrants themselves. "Describing new immigrants as probably the offspring of serfs and slaves and . . . as willing to submit to almost any conditions, old labor and its political allies appealed to the free-labor ethos against degradation by the new immigrants."[22]

Second, peasant newcomers were, more often than not, sojourners whose ultimate goals were in their lands of origin. Although many were to settle eventually in America, this final outcome did not preclude their viewing their journey as temporary and instrumental. Commitment to American political causes, especially those of a radical sort, was not particularly attractive to Hungarian, Italian, or Norwegian peasants, whose goal was to save in order to buy land in their home villages. As Rosenblum notes, "Insofar as the late nineteenth and early twentieth century immigration was predominantly economic in orientation, such migrants were, to a large extent, 'target workers' initially seeking the wherewithal to preserve or enhance a position in the society from which they came."[23]

As we saw previously, not all immigrants were sojourners, however. Jews leaving the Pale of Settlement and czarist oppression literally "burned their bridges behind them."[24] Other refugees from turbulent European regions never really intended to return. For these groups, politics in the new land was a more serious matter, and they could have been expected to participate more actively. It is thus not surprising that there was a positive, albeit imperfect, correlation between permanent migration and U.S.-based political participation and militancy: immigrant activists were recruited disproportionately among the settled minorities. This changing combination of personal skills, past political socialization, and return plans helps explain the basic dissimilarity of behaviors among immigrants during this period. Generalizations about immigrant radicalism or docility at the turn of the twentieth century were constantly negated by the actual diversity among the newcomers.

In the end, however, the overall political effect of pre–World War I immigration was to be conservative. Socialist and Communist movements drew large proportions of their members from the foreign-born, but this effect was diluted by the masses of apolitical peasants and laborers arriving during the same period. The question of how these latter groups undermined working-class militance is still a subject of debate. For some authors, it was because domestic trade unions were forced to adopt an increasingly conservative position to defend their privileges against the waves of migrant workers. For others, it was because settled peasant groups themselves rejected political and labor militance in favor of an "instrumental" politics of gradual improvement within the American system. Regardless of the form, the result was the same: a viable labor party never became consolidated, Socialist and Communist ideologies gradually declined, and business unionism under the American Federation of Labor prevailed over the radicalism of the Industrial Workers of the World.[25]

Ethnicity, framed by the experiences of the first arrivals rather than class, was to provide the fundamental matrix of American-based politics for subsequent generations. Ironically, the class consciousness of the more literate immigrants faded away, while ethnic consciousness, forced on the peasant masses by native prejudice, endured. Because turn-of-the-century immigrants had been defined and discriminated against in America according to their imputed national traits, the politics of later generations pivoted around the same traits, seeking their revindication. Hence, ethnic markers, originally used to fragment the working class, were redefined by reactive formation into symbols of pride and rallying points for mass political participation.

OBSCURE IDENTITIES, SPLIT LOYALTIES

The political equation had another side, however: the countries left behind. Because most late nineteenth- and early twentieth-century immigrants intended to return, they paid more attention, at least initially, to events in the sending countries than in the United States. Political leaders and agitators of all sorts came from abroad to canvass immigrant communities in search of support for their causes. In Nathan Glazer's typology, many immigrants came from nations struggling to become states. The early prototypical example had been the Germans. German immigrants started coming to America in the eighteenth century, long before the consolidation of a German state. United by a common language and culture, they proceeded to re-create a nation in the midst of the American republic, just as their ancestors had done under multiple fragmented principalities in Europe.

By the end of the nineteenth century, other immigrant communities from stateless nations had developed: Poles, Lithuanians, Slovaks, Croatians, Slovenians. The larger these communities became, the stronger their influence on home country politics. Educated immigrants from these lands took the lead in promoting the cause of national political independence. Although the masses of rural immigrants proved uninterested in American class politics, they often could be persuaded to support independence movements at home. Nationalist agitation in the United States also had peculiar consequences. According to Glazer, the first newspaper in the Lithuanian language was published in this country, not in Lithuania.[26] The erse revival began in Boston, and the nation of Czechoslovakia was launched at a meeting in Pittsburgh.[27]

Similarly, the cause of Polish liberation was given a powerful impulse by the organization of the Polish Central Relief Committee in the United States, with Paderewski as honorary president, and by the contributions of hundreds of thousands of dollars by Polish Americans.[28]

Examples of the significance of immigration for the cause of independent statehood were not limited to Europe but extended to the New World. The Cuban War of Independence, for instance, was launched from the United States with funds contributed by the émigré communities of New York, Tampa, and Key West. José Martí, leader of the Cuban Revolutionary Party, organized the war against Spanish rule from his New York office. After his death in 1895, the Cuban Revolutionary Committee continued a campaign of agitation through the New York media that contributed, in no small measure, to the entry of the United States into the war on the rebels' side.[29]

The opposite situation, in Glazer's typology, is that of immigrants leaving states that were not yet nations. These immigrants were eventually to describe themselves as Norwegians, Greeks, or Albanians, but such self-definitions were not clear at the start; instead, they worked themselves out in the process of settlement. According to Greeley, "The Norwegians and Swedes came to think of themselves as Norwegians and Swedes only when they banded together to form communities of their fellows, particularly in rural areas."[30]

Southern Italian peasants represented the archetypical example of a group with exclusively local ties that acquired consciousness of their broader identity in America. "Thus the American relatives of Southern Italians (to whom the Ethiopian war meant nothing more than another affliction visited upon them by the alien government of the North) became Italian patriots in America, supporting here the war to which they would have been indifferent at home."[31]

The contribution of immigration to national consciousness was not limited to Europeans but also had its New World counterpart. South of the border, Mexico achieved statehood early in the nineteenth century, but the central government's hold extended precariously into the frontiers of a vast territory. First Central America and then Texas seceded. The rest of the North—today the states of California, Arizona, New Mexico, and Colorado—was lost during the Mexican-American War. Even in its diminished state, governmental authority continued to be a remote presence in most indigenous communities and among rural migrants trekking north.[32] Like Italians and other European groups in the East, Mexican peasant immigrants learned to think of themselves as Mexicans by being defined and treated as such in the American Southwest. The Mexican Revolution of the first decades of the twentieth century increased the size and diversity of this immigrant flow and heightened its sense of identity. Previously apolitical immigrants contributed time and money to a struggle that only a few years before they had been indifferent to.[33]

Finally, flows at the turn of the century were also coming from consolidated nation-states. There was no common pattern within this general category, either, nor did the existence of a strong home government facilitate early return or adaptation to the new country. Immigration under these conditions took three forms. It could be "apolitical" and dictated exclusively by economic conditions; "political" in the sense of escape from an oppressive regime; or "politicized" a posteriori by an interventionist state bent on making use of its nationals abroad.

During most of the nineteenth century, British emigration to America was representative of the first type. British labor flows across the Atlantic took place without much interference from the home government, being governed primarily by supply and demand at different stages of the economic cycle.[34] British subjects abroad may have remained concerned with events at home, but few were intent on revamping either the English or the American political systems.

Russia was also a consolidated nation-state, but migration from this country took place under very different conditions, exemplifying the second situation. The movement was neither free nor temporary because most of those who escaped the czarist autocracy never intended to return. This was especially the case for the two million Jews who left Russia between 1880 and 1914. In the United States, Russian Jews were simultaneously at the forefront of the American Socialist movement and in unanimous opposition to imperial rule back home. Opponents of the autocracy recruited support and funds among this population. Leon Trotsky was in New York at the time of the czar's abdication, and, as seen previously, the Bolshevik triumph led to a rapid rise in Russian affiliations to the American Socialist and Communist parties.[35]

German immigration—previously a stateless flow—became an example of attempted interventionism as the newly minted German state went on to promote its cause abroad. The growth of the pan-German movement in Berlin coincided in time with the consolidation of the German-American Central Alliance in the United States. By 1914, the alliance and related groups had made German Americans "by far the best organized of all foreign elements."[36] However, this impressive organization was not created to support global pan-Germanism but to fight domestic Prohibition. German Americans saw Prohibition as an

Anglo-Puritan threat to their way of life; unfortunately for them, the lines of cleavage in this purely internal matter became entangled with those of the approaching European war. German American organizations were compelled by the force of events to argue strenuously for neutrality and against British efforts to draw the United States into World War I.

When war finally came, German Americans were confronted with one of the most painful choices to be made by any ethnic group. Having re-created their nation in America, they were now forced to choose unequivocally between the two states. In a country at war, attacks against German Americans grew in intensity and focused on "swatting the hyphen" from their self-definition. Theodore Roosevelt made the point in no uncertain terms:

> The men of German blood who have tried to be both Germans and Americans are no Americans at all, but traitors to America and tools and servants of Germany against America. . . . Hereafter we must see that the melting pot really does not melt. There should be but one language in this country—the English.[37]

The outcome was surprising by its unanimity and speed. In April 1918, the German-American Alliance dissolved itself, turning over its funds to the American Red Cross. Other German American organizations changed their names and initiated campaigns for the sale of U.S. war bonds. Men of German ancestry joined the American armed forces by the thousands. After 1918, visible signs of German *Kultur* declined rapidly throughout the country. By their own choice, German Americans had "swatted the hyphen" and acceded to Roosevelt's demand for prompt assimilation.[38]

In summary, the politics of immigration was affected as much by events in the sending countries as by those in the United States. Immigrants differed in their past political socialization, commitment to return, and national situations left behind. The combination of these factors affected not only their stance in American domestic politics but also their orientations and behavior toward the homeland. Depending on the particular mix of factors, some groups struggled for independent statehood for their countries, while others did not know that they had left countries behind. Among immigrants from consolidated nation-states, some regarded the homeland political system as a matter of relative indifference; others left to escape its hold; still others had to contend with its expansionist overtures. This diversity negated any easy generalization during the period and simultaneously established a precedent and point of reference for understanding the political behavior of later arrivals.

IMMIGRANT POLITICS TODAY

LOOKING HOMEWARD

In contrast to pre–World War I immigrants, those bound for America today seldom come from stateless lands or lack well-defined national identities. The gradual consolidation of a global interstate system means that most people today not only belong to a nation-state but are aware of this fact. Consolidated states and strong national identities mean very different things, however, when immigrants see themselves as representatives, in some sense, of their home nations; when they have come fleeing from them; or when their journey has been dictated by purely individual interests and is a matter of official indifference to the sending country. Although, as in the earlier period, these three types are seldom found in pure form, they provide a basic framework for understanding the politics of the first generation.

Early political concerns of the foreign-born today seldom have to do with matters American. Instead, they tend to center on issues and problems back home. This is especially the case for sojourners—those whose stay in the United States is defined as instrumental for attaining goals in their own communities and countries. In such cases, they have every reason to regard U.S. politics with relative indifference. The attachment to home country issues persists, however, even among those who have settled here permanently. For political refugees, barred from returning home, it may be the lingering hope of doing so someday, a feeling of seemingly remarkable persistence. For nonpolitical immigrants, the increasing facility for return trips and ease of communication with family and friends at home serve to keep alive the identifications and loyalties into which they were socialized.

THE ADVENT OF TRANSNATIONALISM

Political ties to the home country have been significantly reinforced in the contemporary period by two novel developments: first, technological innovations in transportation and communications and, second, the strength of sending nation-states and their new attitude toward their respective immigrant diasporas. Cheap air transport and the advent of telephone and electronic communications have greatly facilitated contact across countries and geographic distances. Immigrants today can keep themselves informed, on a daily basis, of events in their home communities and countries and travel there rapidly when conditions require it. They can call their families every day, regardless of distance, and send electronic mail to them as well as to community leaders and government authorities.

The end result of this technological revolution has been the emergence of veritable "transnational communities" suspended, in effect, between two countries. Members frequently keep residences in both and travel back and forth between them for economic as well as social reasons. Politically, this translates into a far greater presence and influence of immigrant diasporas in the affairs of their home nations. They can affect domestic politics through a variety of means, including making financial contributions to parties and candidates, creating philanthropic and political action committees, and influencing the vote of kin and friends at home:

> In many cases, the magnitude, duration, and impact of migration are so strong that migrant social networks mature into transnational social fields spanning the sending and receiving country. . . . [T]hose who live within transnational social fields are exposed to a set of social expectations, cultural values, and patterns of interaction that are shaped by more than one political system.[39]

As we have just seen, earlier European immigrants also engaged in multiple activities concerning the politics of the places they came from, but, no matter how strong their motivation, they could not affect domestic affairs with the intensity and rapidity that contemporary migrants do. To make their voices heard, they depended on the mail or, at best, the telegraph rather than long-distance telephone and the Internet. To be present at key events, they had to travel for days or weeks on boats and trains rather than commute by plane. Today's much more fluid communications decisively affect what influence immigrants can bear on their home communities and nations.

The response of sending-country governments constitutes the second part of the equation. As seen previously, most immigrants do not come today from stateless lands or places where states are a feeble presence. Nor are these states relatively indifferent, as often in the past, to the departure and the lives of their expatriates. The growth of migrant diasporas, the size of the remittances that they send back, and their increasing capacity to support or resist home country authorities mean that the latter must respond actively to the needs and demands of their nationals abroad.[40] For many countries of emigration, remittances have become one of the most sizable and predictable sources of foreign exchange. To these must be added the investments made by expatriates in land, equipment, and business and the impact of the skills and values learned abroad on their home communities, what Levitt calls "social remittances."[41]

Accordingly, sending-country governments have taken an increasingly active role in the affairs of their communities abroad, seeking to rechannel and expand the flow of remittances, stimulate investment, and turn community leaders into representatives for their countries abroad. Some governments harbor the hope that their diasporas would become lobbies for national interests and goals in the United States. Even when diasporas are formed by exiled opponents of the regime in power, efforts have been made to reach out to them. The granting of dual citizenship, voting rights in national elections, tax exemptions, and other privileges have flown from the increasingly proactive stance of sending-country governments toward their nationals abroad.[42] Naturally, these actions interact with the transnational activities and projects initiated by the migrants themselves, creating a highly dynamic back-and-forth traffic of resources, ideas, and outcomes across national borders. The following two examples illustrate the extent and impact of this phenomenon.

TWO TRANSNATIONAL PROJECTS

Salvadorans   The presence of more than a million Salvadorans in the United States is the product of a civil war that tore this small Central American nation apart for more than a decade. Escaping the violence in rural areas, many peasants and small landowners fled abroad, eventually reaching the United States. They were not welcome here, though, since the U.S. government was heavily engaged at that time in buttressing the Salvadoran regime against a Communist insurgency; thus, granting asylum to Salvadoran escapees would represent an admission of that regime's repressive nature. Accordingly, Salvadorans in the United States became, for the most part, illegal aliens.

From these humble beginnings, they struggled to gain a foothold in their new country. Gradually, they regrouped in certain cities, forming sizable concentrations in Los Angeles, Houston, and Washington, D.C., and gained support from churches and other philanthropic organizations to avoid repatriation. Without legal work permits, Salvadorans toiled at the most menial, poorest-paying jobs in the informal economy. From these meager wages, they supported themselves and families left behind, to whom they remained fiercely loyal.[43]

The end of the civil war in El Salvador changed things for the better. The new democratic authorities earnestly petitioned the U.S. government to legalize the situation of the would-be asylees or at least not to deport them. The ruined economy of El Salvador could not absorb them, and the remittances that the expatriates were sending, though individually modest, were becoming in the aggregate a key source of foreign exchange. As seen in chapter 2, the American government refrained from approving most individual asylum requests, but it responded to the entreaties of the Salvadoran government by granting successive temporary stays from deportation for the migrants. The improved legal environment allowed Salvadorans to start organizing socially and politically, primarily to regularize their legal situation in the United States and to help the towns and villages of origin. *Comités de pueblo* proliferated, raising money for public projects in localities hit hard by the civil war. As Landolt puts it:

> Associations have been known to raise up to $50,000 in cash and in kind for their development projects. Life conditions in municipalities that receive "grassroots transnational aid" confirm the economic relevance of this strategy. Towns with a hometown association have paved roads, electricity, and freshly painted public buildings. . . . [T]he quality of life in transnational towns is quite simply better.[44]

Now that travel is safe and legal, an intense back-and-forth movement has ensued, with former asylees returning to create new enterprises and others making use of their home contacts to develop new businesses in Los Angeles and other areas of concentration. The volume of remittances never ceased growing, transforming and modernizing one town after another. As a young Salvadoran sociologist has put it, "Migration and remittances have become the true Adjustment Program of the poor."[45] The new government took note and instructed its diplomats to initiate new programs abroad to court the expatriate community. By 1994, programs based at Salvadoran consulates started to offer

legal services to undocumented Salvadorans and promoted easier chan-
nels for remittance transfers. Subsequently, the Office of Economic
Affairs in the Ministry of Foreign Relations sought to link enterprises in
El Salvador with the migrant market and, from there, with the broader
Latin market in the United States as a specific way of strengthening the
Salvadoran government export-oriented drive.[46]

Governmental attempts to guide or co-opt the organizational projects of its expatriates have not met with much success, however, for two
reasons. First, the elected government came from the political right,
being regarded as the direct successor of the repressive regime that
expelled the migrants in the first place. Second, diplomats and government officials engaged in this effort came from an entirely different
social class than the immigrants. The latter, mostly peasants and workers, regard educated diplomats with a measure of awe and distrust.
Accordingly, Salvadoran expatriate civic organizations have sought to
steer away from national parties and from the government, focusing
instead on their autonomous civic projects.[47] Of the Latin American
groups studied as part of a comparative study on immigrant transnationalism, Salvadorans were the most likely to engage in this type of
civic associations and among the least likely to engage in national party
politics.[48]

Mexicans As seen previously, Mexicans are the largest immigrant
group in the United States today. The 2000 U.S. Census counted 9.2
million Mexican immigrants and indicated that the Mexican-origin
population had reached 20.6 million, or almost two-thirds of all Hispanics, the fastest-growing segment of the U.S. population.[49] As Roberts
et al. have noted, the size of both the sending and receiving countries
and their proximity guarantee that the interaction between these immigrants in the United States and their communities of origin will be very
complex and assume very different forms.[50]

For most of the twentieth century, Mexican migration to the United
States was temporary and fundamentally apolitical. As Massey and
others have stressed, this labor flow was mostly cyclical, involving
young men coming to work in harvests and other agricultural tasks for
part of the year and then returning home. Like any other large-scale
human movement, a sizable "sediment" developed as some temporary
migrants eventually became permanent settlers. Those who did so were
of no concern to Mexican authorities, and, if they acquired U.S. citizenship, they lost their Mexican nationality, including the right to own

land. *Pochos* was the derogatory term used in Mexico to refer at the time to the expatriates and their descendants.[51]

The situation changed dramatically during the last two decades of the twentieth century as a consequence of changes in U.S. immigration law that, first, granted amnesty to formerly unauthorized immigrants and, second, sought to enforce the border by making illegal crossing much more difficult. The first measure, promulgated as part of the 1986 Immigration Reform and Control Act, gave legal residence to more than two million formerly unauthorized migrants, facilitating their free movement across the border and making it possible for them to bring their relatives a few years later. These developments significantly increased the size of the legally settled Mexican population in the United States.[52]

The second measure, heightened border enforcement, did not deter continued illegal immigration across the border, but, as Roberts, Massey, and others have noted, it had the unexpected consequence of encouraging unauthorized immigrants *not* to return to Mexico and to bring their families to the United States instead. This outcome significantly increased the size of the underground Mexican population north of the border.[53] As this newly settled population searched for new sources of employment and sought to avoid detection by the authorities, it started to move eastward, turning what previously had been a regional phenomenon (concentrated in Texas, California, and elsewhere in the Southwest) into a truly national presence.[54]

With roughly one-tenth of its population north of the border, with immigrant remittances becoming the second most important source of foreign exchange, and with immigrant organizations starting to support and make contributions to presidential candidates in Mexico, the Mexican government could not continue to remain indifferent to its millions of expatriates. Beginning with the administration of President Carlos Salinas de Gortari, a drastic change toward Mexicans in the United States took place, aimed at preserving their national loyalty and turning them into an integral part of an imagined, extraterritorial Mexican nation. The change was signaled by the creation of the Program for Mexican Communities Abroad (PCME, in its Spanish acronym), which aimed to strengthen ties with Mexican immigrant communities. This program eventually came to sponsor the *Dos por Uno* plan, in which every dollar raised by immigrant organizations for philanthropic works at home would be matched by two dollars from the Mexican federal and state governments.[55]

Passage of dual nationality legislation enabled Mexican immigrants to acquire U.S. citizenship without losing their Mexican passports or the right to own land in Mexico. In a remarkable policy shift, the Mexican government went from treating those who naturalized in the United States as defectors to encouraging such naturalizations as a way of empowering immigrants and giving them a real voice in North American politics.[56] Recent legislation, passed in 2005, gives immigrants the right to vote in Mexican elections without having to travel back to Mexico. The Institute for Mexicans Abroad (IME, in the Spanish acronym), which replaced the PCME, has taken a still more proactive stance, organizing the election of more than a hundred representatives of immigrant communities to its Consultative Council. As Goldring notes:

> The strategy of fostering ties with Mexicans and people of Mexican origin shifted to become more universalistic, explicitly extraterritorial, and perhaps more rhetorical. This change of orientation began with a redefinition of the Mexican nation to include Mexicans living outside the national territory.[57]

Mexican political transnationalism was not initiated by the actions of the Mexican government; such actions were taken *in response* to the initiatives of the migrants themselves. Migrant transnational initiatives took two principal forms: (1) the organization of hometown committees and (2) campaigns and financial support for candidates in Mexican elections. As soon as a Mexican expatriate community of any size gets settled, one of its first organizational acts is to create a *comité de pueblo* or *club de oriundos* that brings together people of the same locality in an effort to maintain contact with their hometown and support its development. As in the case of Salvadorans, these committees raise money for all kinds of public projects—from repairing the local church to buying a new ambulance for the town's health center.

In Los Angeles alone, 159 such associations were registered with the Mexican consulate in 1994. When the number of these associations from a particular Mexican state reaches ten or more, a state-level federation emerges, generally supported by the respective state government. In Los Angeles, immigrants from the states of Durango, Jalisco, Nayarit, Oaxaca, San Luis Potosí, Sinaloa, Tlaxcala, and Zacatecas have created such federations. Composed of more than forty hometown committees, the Zacatecan Federation is particularly strong. It hosts regular visits from the governor and other state dignitaries and maintains intense year-round contact with the state and municipal governments, focusing on a variety of public works and other projects supported with immigrant funds.[58]

During the Mexican presidential election of 1988, the challenger Cuahtemoc Cárdenas surprised the ruling party by the level of support he garnered among immigrant communities in the United States. That support translated into both substantial campaign contributions and votes in Mexico, as the expatriates influenced the political preferences of kin and friends. More than any other factor, it was the transnational political activism of sizable Mexican communities in Los Angeles, Houston, Chicago, and other areas of concentration during the 1988 election, plus the level of organization achieved by these communities, that prompted the swift shift in orientation by the Mexican government and ruling party.[59]

Using Hirschman's classic trilogy, Roberts and his collaborators have analyzed Mexican political transnationalism as an interplay of "exit," "voice," and "loyalty." Mexicans *exited* their homeland in search of a better life denied to them in their country. As they settled in the United States, their aggregate remittances and organization on behalf of philanthropic and political causes gave them the *voice* in Mexican affairs that they never had before departing. Seeking to maintain and increase remittances, investments, and contributions and to channel them in ways supportive of the regime, the Mexican government launched a number of programs aimed at heightening the *loyalty* of its expatriates.[60] In this manner, an increasingly dense and previously unexpected traffic has developed across the border, with Mexican officials visiting and courting immigrant communities in all major U.S. cities and the migrants, often former peasants and poor unskilled workers, going home in their new role as benefactors of their towns of origin and significant political actors.

ASSIMILATION AND TRANSNATIONALISM

At first glance, the rise in transnational activism among today's immigrants and the numerous programs of sending-country governments aimed at strengthening it appear to undermine the process of assimilation and retard the integration of immigrants into the American body politic. How could immigrants and their children start to turn their interests and attention to political life in their new country when they are still stuck in the affairs and loyalties of the old? As it often happens in social life, reality is more complex. While it is possible that transnational activities may slow the acquisition of new loyalties and identities in some cases, the bulk of the evidence indicates that this is not a zerosum game and that many aspects of transnationalism end up *accelerating* the political integration of immigrants in the United States.

This is so for several reasons. First, political activism is not mutually exclusive, and skills learned in one context frequently "travel" to others. Thus, experience gained in founding hometown committees or lobbying the home country government can be transferred, when the occasion requires, to campaigns to further migrant interests in the American context. For example, the Centro Cívico Colombiano (CCC), one of the principal Colombian organizations in New York, organizes the celebrations of Colombian Independence Day on July 20 by bringing prominent entertainers and political figures from Colombia. The festivities are also well attended by New York City and New York State officials, who use the occasion to lobby for votes and political support. CCC officials and other Colombian immigrant leaders make use of the mass rally, in turn, to highlight the political weight of their community and position themselves favorably for future New York elections.[61]

While some local Dominican leaders in New York have complained that continuing involvement with the political affairs of the island weakens mobilizations in favor of domestic causes, the fact is that transnational activists are commonly involved in both. Thus, representatives of Dominican parties in New York or Providence may support candidates in American elections or take a turn running for local office themselves. Alternatively, a successful ethnic politician may try his or her luck in national elections in the home country. Leonel Fernández, overwhelmingly reelected in 2004 to the presidency of the Dominican Republic, was raised in New York City, where he was active in local community affairs.[62] In general, immigrants who are politically inactive in one setting tend to be inactive in others, whereas those who become involved in transnational political or civic activism are more likely to be interested and involved as well in domestic politics.

Second, the passage of dual nationality and dual citizenship laws by sending nations, far from retarding the acquisition of U.S. citizenship, may instead accelerate it. This happens because immigrants lose the fear of giving up their original nationality and attendant rights and of being perceived as "defectors" at home. The ability to hold on to their identities (and passports) removes a key disincentive against naturalization and often encourages immigrants to acquire U.S. citizenship. Once they do, it is but an easy step to register, vote, and become involved in American politics.[63] As Escobar puts it for Colombian immigrants:

> The concern of Colombian [immigrant] leaders was the lack of U.S. citizenship which was limiting the economic and political development of the Colombian immigrant community. Since Colombians did not want to renounce their nationality, they lacked access to the best financial sources and could not support their own candidates for elected positions in the U.S. . . . Analysis of the rate of naturalization of Colombians in the U.S. following enactment of the new dual nationality law shows that it had the intended effect.[64]

The third reason that assimilation and transnationalism are not necessarily at odds is that many transnational civic and political projects aim precisely at instilling North American values and political practices in the home countries. Pundits who worry about the likelihood that immigrants may act as a "fifth column" here give American institutions too little credit. Writing without knowledge of the facts, Huntington sounds the alarm, for example, about the possibility that the Southwest may one day defect to Mexico because of its large Mexican American population. This concern does not take into account the fact that the bulk of Mexican transnationalism is aimed at improving life in Mexico not only by transferring economic resources but by moralizing and democratizing politics on the basis of U.S.-learned blueprints. The concern is also incompatible with the patriotism repeatedly displayed by Mexican Americans in the nation's wars, which gives the lie, in real terms, to any suspicion about their loyalties.[65]

For Mexican Americans born on this side of the border and fully steeped in American-style civil and political rights, the thought of joining a less developed country just emerging from an authoritarian past is preposterous. Much of the activism stimulated by the new proimmigrant policy of the Mexican government and the "voice" thus gained by expatriate communities has aimed at reducing corruption and repression and increasing the transparency of the political process in Mexico. To judge by these activities, it is more likely that the process and forces unleashed by transnational activism will end by transforming the source country rather than the other way around.[66]

MAKING IT COUNT: CITIZENSHIP ACQUISITION

NATURALIZATION TRENDS

Whether involved in transnational activities or not, immigrants cannot make their voices heard effectively in American politics until they naturalize. As seen previously, transnationalism may actually encourage U.S. citizenship acquisition. However, in the past as in the present, wide differences in naturalization exist among immigrant nationalities, even among those who have become permanent settlers. Some first-generation groups opt for being "in" the society but not "of" it, avoiding naturalization at all costs; others change flags at the first opportunity.

Higher numbers, greater concentration, and higher rates of citizenship acquisition all contribute to the political strength of immigrant communities. As seen in prior chapters, the first two factors vary significantly across immigrant groups; thus, it is not too surprising that the third does, too. The "propensity" of a particular group to naturalize is a composite of two related but different trends: the number who actually acquire U.S. citizenship and the rapidity with which the process takes place. Hence, the political weight of two immigrant groups that exhibit similar rates of naturalization at the end of the first generation will be very different if one completed the change soon after arrival and the other waited until the years of retirement.

Differential propensities for acquiring citizenship combine with the size of eligible pools from each nationality to produce aggregate naturalization trends. Between 1908 and 1990, the number of persons naturalizing each year exceeded three hundred thousand only in 1943 and 1944, in the midst of World War II. Since 1990, in contrast, naturalizations have exceeded that figure every year except 1992.[67] Table 15 presents an overview of naturalization trends between 1993 and 2002. During this period, the regions included in the table accounted for 96 percent of the 6.2 million immigrants who became American citizens. The relative contribution of each region during the decade shifted significantly, however. For example, the "secular" decline in European naturalizations during the 1970s and 1980s slowed and reversed during the 1990s mainly because of new immigrant flows from Eastern Europe and the former Soviet Union. Traditional sources of European immigration (and subsequent naturalizations), such as Great Britain, Germany, and Italy, continued to lose numerical importance, while immigrants from Poland, the Ukraine, and Russia, among others in Eastern Europe, made their presence increasingly felt.

TABLE 15. NATURALIZATIONS FOR SELECTED COUNTRIES AND REGIONS, 1993–2002

Region	1993		1996		1999		2001		2002		Total, 1993–2002	
	N (000s)	%[a]	N (000s)	%[a]	N (000s)	%[a]	N (000s)	%[a]	N (000s)	%[a]	N (000s)	%[a]
Europe	38	12.1	110	10.5	101	12.0	89	14.6	94	16.4	799	12.8
United Kingdom	6	1.9	12	1.1	10	1.3	8	1.3	8	1.4	85	1.4
Poland	6	1.9	14	1.3	13	1.5	12	2.0	13	2.3	103	1.6
Asia	149	47.3	307	29.4	274	32.6	247	40.6	232	40.4	2,272	36.3
China, People's Republic	17	5.4	34	3.3	38	4.5	34	5.6	32	5.6	291	4.7
India	17	5.4	33	3.2	31	3.7	34	6.0	34	5.9	269	4.3
Iran	7	2.2	19	1.8	18	2.1	14	2.3	12	2.1	133	2.1
Korea	10	3.2	28	2.7	18	2.1	18	3.0	17	3.0	169	2.7
Philippines	34	10.8	51	4.8	39	4.6	35	5.8	30	5.8	371	5.9
Vietnam	23	7.3	52	4.9	53	6.3	42	6.9	37	6.4	391	6.3
North America	78	24.8	467	44.7	332	39.5	170	28.0	143	24.9	2,122	33.9
Dominican Republic	12	3.8	29	2.8	23	2.7	15	2.5	16	2.8	174	2.8
Cuba	15	4.8	63	6.0	25	3.0	11	1.8	11	1.9	203	3.2
Mexico	24	7.6	255	24.4	208	24.8	103	17.9	77	13.4	1,240	19.8
Central and South America	28	8.9	161	15.4	108	12.9	73	12.0	70	12.2	815	13.0
Colombia	10	3.2	27	2.6	13	1.5	11	1.8	11	1.9	129	2.1
El Salvador	3	0.9	35	3.3	23	2.7	14	2.3	11	1.9	161	2.7
Total[b]	315		1,045		840		608		574		6,254	

SOURCE: Office of Immigration Statistics 2002 Yearbook, table 35.

[a] Percentage of total number of naturalizations during the year.
[b] Regional percentages do not add up to one hundred because Africa and Oceania have been omitted.

Another noteworthy trend was the partial reversal of the traditional reluctance of Mexican immigrants to acquire U.S. citizenship. As seen in table 15, Mexicans accounted for 20 percent of all naturalizations during the late 1990s, a figure far exceeding that for any other nationality, as well as the corresponding number of Mexicans in the naturalized population during the preceding two decades (7.1 percent).[68] This change was not due to any single factor but to a combination of several forces. First, the change in stance by the Mexican government toward their expatriates and the advent of dual nationality removed a significant disincentive for Mexicans to acquire U.S. citizenship. Second, restrictionist anti-immigrant initiatives, notably Proposition 187 in California, triggered a reactive mobilization of Mexicans in defense of their collective interests during these years. Hispanic and proimmigrant organizations led the way in naturalization and voting registration drives, which, as will be seen in greater detail later, produced notable changes in the electoral weight of the Mexican and Mexican American population.

Third, the Immigration Reform and Control Act of 1986 legalized 2.7 million formerly unauthorized immigrants, the majority of whom were Mexicans. These legalizations increased significantly the pool of persons who became eligible to naturalize in the 1990s. The number of IRCA naturalizations peaked in 1996, when 227,000 such persons acquired U.S. citizenship. This represented a record year, with naturalizations exceeding one million.[69]

A final factor increasing the Mexican naturalization rate was the passage of legislation such as the Personal Responsibility and Work Opportunity Act of 1996 that restricted a number of benefits to U.S. citizens, barring legal residents. Because of their previous reluctance to naturalize, Mexicans were overrepresented among the legal resident population who acquired citizenship during the 1990s in order to avoid the new penalties of this restrictive law.

The one-time IRCA legislation turned North America into the major source of naturalized U.S. citizens during the mid- and late 1990s, but by 2000, Asia had assumed the top spot. In 2001 and again in 2002, 40 percent of all new citizens came from that region. This dominance is a consequence not of higher absolute numbers but of the much greater propensity to acquire citizenship among Asian immigrants and the rapidity with which they undertake the process. As shown in table 16, Asians took an average of seven to eight years after legal arrival to naturalize, as contrasted with nine to ten years for South Americans and

TABLE 16. MEDIAN YEARS OF U.S. RESIDENCE, BY YEAR
OF NATURALIZATION AND REGION OF BIRTH, 1985–2003

Region	Year of naturalization					
	1985	*1990*	*1995*	*2000*	*2001*	*2003*
Totals	8	8	9	10	9	8
Africa	7	7	6	8	10	7
Asia	7	7	7	8	8	8
Europe	9	10	9	8	7	7
North America	13	11	14	11	11	11
Oceania	8	10	11	11	10	9
South America	8	9	10	10	9	8

SOURCE: Office of Immigration Statistics 2004 Yearbook, table I.

eleven to fourteen for those coming from North America (Mexico, Canada, and the Caribbean).

Nonetheless, there were significant shifts in individual nationalities contributing to the regional totals during the last decade. These shifts reflect the dynamic character of both immigration and propensity to naturalize, as some countries' contributions decline to insignificance, while others rise in numbers and visibility. Thus, the Philippines' position as the second major source of immigration and the major source of new citizens during the 1970s and 1980s declined rapidly in the 1990s. The same trend was apparent for South Korea, another major contributor in the past. In their place, the two largest Asian countries, India and the People's Republic of China, became the second and third most important sources of new legal immigrants and of new U.S. citizens.

In the Americas, immigration and naturalization of Colombians, Dominicans, and Salvadorans rose rapidly during the 1990s, easily displacing Cubans, who had been previously the second-largest regional inflow. Given the size of the country of origin, continued instability at home, and their relatively high levels of education, Colombians are slated to become, next to Mexicans, the prime source of U.S. citizens of Latin origin in the years to come.

DETERMINANTS OF NATURALIZATION

European immigrants arriving in the first decades of the twentieth century also registered significant variations in their propensities to acquire

U.S. citizenship. In 1936, sociologist W. S. Bernard proposed that the gap between "old" (northwestern) and "new" (southeastern) Europeans in acquiring citizenship was due to different levels of literacy and education. Among immigrants arriving at the same time, those with better education could be expected to understand the benefits of naturalization faster and to start the process earlier than others. The observed differences between Italian peasants and northern European skilled workers was attributed to this factor.[70]

Bernard's hypothesis has been supported by more recent studies. As seen in chapter 4, Asian and Eastern European immigrants tend to have higher levels of human capital than others, especially those originating in Mexico, Central America, and the Caribbean. The differences in education and skills between these various flows correspond fairly closely with their propensity to naturalize. Table 17 presents additional supportive evidence for the hypothesis by listing the twenty-five major foreign-born nationalities arriving in the United States before 1995 and counted in the 2000 census. The table presents the total rates of naturalization for each group, although these rates are heavily influenced by the different lengths of U.S. residence of different nationalities. For example, Italy has the highest naturalization rate of any country (78.2 percent), but this figures reflects the fact that 90 percent of Italians had been living in the United States for twenty years or more, as compared with 40 percent of all immigrants.

For this reason, countries have been ranked according to the rate of naturalization of immigrants arriving between 1980 and 1984 and, hence, with at least fifteen years of residence in the country. The rankings make apparent two trends. First, *all* national groups that exceeded the average naturalization rate of the 1980–1984 cohort by 10 percent or more came from Asia or Eastern Europe. Taiwan, Russia and other Soviet successor states, and Vietnam had the highest rates of citizenship acquisition, exceeding 80 percent of the respective cohorts. Second, most immigrants who failed to naturalize during this period came from Latin America, in general, and from Mexico, El Salvador, and Guatemala, in particular. As seen previously, these are the countries that represent the major sources of low-skilled, manual labor immigration to the United States at present.

Corresponding to their position as by far the largest immigrant group in the nation, Mexicans had the largest *absolute* number of naturalized citizens, and, as just seen, their contribution to this population increased significantly during the 1990s. Still, the Mexican rate of naturalization

TABLE 17. RATES OF U.S. NATURALIZATION FOR IMMIGRANTS WHO ARRIVED BEFORE 1995 BY NATIONAL ORIGIN, 2000

Country of birth	N	% Naturalized	Year of arrival in the United States		
			Before 1980	*1980–1984*	*1985–1989*
Total immigrants[a]	23,529,292	51.0	73.9	**54.2**	36.8
Above average					
Taiwan	258,957	72.8	94.3	**84.2**	64.0
Former USSR	395,838	64.8	89.9	**83.8**	74.5
Vietnam	841,474	68.4	88.8	**81.3**	68.4
Philippines	1,157,064	70.6	90.0	**78.4**	65.4
China	723,916	60.7	90.3	**73.5**	57.4
Poland	399,942	62.5	86.7	**71.5**	45.4
Iran	244,442	69.0	81.3	**71.5**	61.9
India	655,824	57.0	84.3	**69.4**	52.3
Korea	674,105	62.7	87.2	**65.9**	49.6
Average					
Jamaica	470,170	60.4	77.9	**64.1**	51.4
Peru	208,803	47.6	79.0	**59.8**	38.6
Colombia	357,887	55.4	79.4	**59.4**	42.0
Haiti	335,502	52.0	74.6	**57.0**	47.5
Laos	192,520	47.8	65.9	**55.9**	36.2
Cuba	723,567	71.8	87.9	**53.2**	45.3
Italy	450,376	78.2	82.3	**52.5**	41.3
Below average					
Ecuador	313,088	44.3	70.9	**49.8**	29.3
Honduras	185,638	35.8	73.2	**48.1**	26.1
Dominican Republic	561,119	42.4	66.9	**46.4**	37.6
El Salvador	651,773	30.7	60.4	**41.8**	18.1
Guatemala	348,002	29.3	63.0	**40.9**	17.7
Germany	614,646	73.5	82.1	**40.2**	34.2
United Kingdom	468,420	52.8	68.0	**37.3**	25.7
Canada	661,701	55.2	67.6	**34.5**	28.2
Mexico	6,545,550	29.1	51.8	**33.1**	18.9

SOURCE: 2000 U.S. Census, 5% Public Use Microdata Sample.

[a]Nationalities are ranked according to the rate of naturalization of the 1980–1984 cohort (in bold characters).

remains the lowest of any nationality, reflecting the low average level of education of this population. Immigrants of low human capital not only may take longer to grasp the advantages of citizenship, following Bernard's hypothesis, but also find the process of naturalization much more difficult. Tests of English knowledge and U.S. civics included in this process create an additional and frequently impassable barrier for immigrants of very modest educational backgrounds.[71]

An additional factor contributing to the low relative level of citizenship acquisition among Mexicans is the geographic proximity of their country of origin and hence the "reversibility" of migration. Despite the recent shift in policy by the Mexican government, supporting U.S. citizenship acquisition by their migrants, the fact that their hometowns are often a bus ride away reduces the finality of migration and thus the incentive to initiate the process. The same factor partially accounts for the similarly low propensity to change flags among Canadian immigrants, despite higher average levels of education (see table 17).

Geographic proximity and reversibility of migration weaken commitment to permanent settlement and hence the incentive to naturalize. This situation can be usefully compared with that of Russian and Vietnamese refugees in the early 1980s, coming to escape dire political conditions at home. For these groups, the act of leaving their countries was a momentous, one-time decision with permanent settlement abroad the only alternative. Accordingly, four-fifths of Soviet-era Russians and Vietnamese opted for U.S. citizenship as soon as possible after their arrival.

Reversibility is also behind the low rates of naturalization of British and German immigrants, who come from developed, democratic nations. Persons from these countries may regard the American "green card" more as a convenience than as a permanent commitment to settlement. The cumbersome naturalization process creates an additional disincentive, making U.S. citizenship not a worthwhile prospect for many. Table 17 makes clear a final point: regardless of nationality, the passage of time leads inexorably to higher levels of naturalization. Without exception, and including those groups for which migration is reversible for geographic or economic reasons, longer periods of U.S. residence lead to significantly higher rates of naturalization. The time factor "rounds the picture" as to the principal determinants of citizenship.

Level of education, length of residence in the country, and reversibility of migration jointly provide a powerful model accounting for differences in the probability of naturalization among nationalities. While the most educated and those who come escaping the most harrowing conditions do so first, others eventually follow as part of a time-driven process of integration into American society. Citizenship endows immigrants with the capacity to both contribute and acquire voice in the American political system, a process that naturally culminates with the second generation.

THE FUTURE OF IMMIGRANT POLITICS

RESILIENT ETHNICITIES

Time and the passing of the first generation inevitably turn former immigrant communities into ethnic groups with fundamentally American concerns. Most contemporary immigration is still of recent vintage; hence, the politics of the first generation is still very much in evidence. It is in this situation that transnational activities have flourished. However, despite efforts of immigrant families and sending-country governments to preserve vibrant national loyalties among the second generation, the process of acculturation inexorably turns their members into Americans with primarily domestic views and aspirations.[72] As early transnational concerns fade from view, ethnic politics takes over. The historical record of all immigrant groups, old and new, show that the politics of the second and successive generations pivot less around issues of class than of those tied to a common ethnic origin.

By the early twenty-first century, some contemporary immigrant groups had spent sufficient time in the country for this process to become evident. Mexicans are again the prime example because, as seen previously, they have been coming continuously, with only temporary interruptions, since the nineteenth century. This flow has thus spawned second, third, and even higher generations. Cuban exiles arriving in Miami in the 1960s and 1970s have also become well entrenched after almost half a century in the country. This group has acquired a highly visible political profile, increasingly dominated by its second generation. Despite a common language and religion, these two Latin nationalities are very different in terms of class of origin and contexts of reception representing, respectively, a manual labor inflow versus a displaced entrepreneurial and professional class leaving its country for political reasons. Their experiences can thus illuminate the future of immigrant politics, as other groups consolidate their presence in the American scene.

MEXICAN AMERICAN POLITICS

Although Mexican American political organizing may be dated back to several turn-of-the-century self-help associations known as *mutualistas,* its first real impulse did not occur until World War I and its aftermath. In 1921, returning Mexican American veterans created the Orden de Hijos de Americain San Antonio; in 1923, the League of United Latin American Citizens (LULAC) was formed in Corpus Christi. The Orden, created to protect the veterans and other members of the minority against discrimination, eventually merged with LULAC, which was to become the oldest and largest Spanish-origin political organization in the country.[73] Thus, at a time when the most urbanized European groups back east continued to be involved in socialism and class politics, Mexican American political activism in the Southwest already focused on issues of ethnicity and racial-cultural exclusion.[74]

This orientation was to continue and assume more militant overtones after World War II. Thousands of returning Mexican American veterans, many highly decorated, found that they were still barred from movie theaters, residential neighborhoods, and even cemeteries in their own hometowns. As a result, the GI Forum was organized in 1948 to defend the interests of veterans and campaign against racial barriers. By this time, the process of reactive formation was in full swing: Just as Mexican immigrants had been made aware of a common identity by being discriminated against together, so their descendants recaptured the symbols of that identity and turned them into rallying points of political solidarity. By 1960, the Mexican-American Political Association (MAPA) had been formed. It explained its raison d'être as follows: "MAPA grew out of many and difficult experiences of thousands of Mexican-Americans throughout California who have tried so hard to elect representatives to state and local government. . . . [A]n organization was needed that would be proudly Mexican-American, openly political, necessarily bipartisan."[75]

Ethnic consciousness and mobilization reached their climax during the 1960s and early 1970s, driven by an increasingly vocal U.S.-born generation. Mexican American politics during this period were patterned closely after the black power movement. As with established black groups, older organizations such as LULAC were threatened with displacement by a proliferation of radical youth movements— the United Mexican American Students, the Mexican American Youth Organization, and the Brown Berets. Younger intellectuals went beyond pragmatic demands to articulate a vision of collective identity in which race, language, and culture were paramount. Concepts such as Aztlán (the submerged Indo-Mexican nation of North America) and La Raza (The Race—the racial-cultural community of its inhabitants) were coined and popularized during this period. Like Germans during World War I, Mexican Americans in the 1960s also "swatted the hyphen," but they did so in the direction of ethnic reaffirmation: "Chicano," rather than Mexican American, became the preferred self-designation. By the end of the decade, these symbolic developments had reached political expression in such movements as the Chicano Student Movement of Aztlán (MECHA) and the La Raza Unida Party.[76]

The radical period was short-lived, however. La Raza Unida achieved some notable electoral successes in south Texas, primarily in municipal elections, but by the end of the 1970s, it had effectively disappeared from the political scene. In the 1980s, the older, more moderate LULAC, with branches in forty-one states, and new organizations such as the Mexican-American Legal Defense Fund (MALDEF), staffed by professionals and well financed by private foundations, took the lead in Mexican ethnic politics.[77] In retrospect, the militancy of the 1960s can be interpreted as an inevitable reaction, in the context of the time, to the singularly oppressive conditions Mexican migrants and their descendants had endured for decades. Like African Americans, Mexican Americans saw themselves as a simultaneously exploited and despised minority. Because it was difficult to restore ethnic pride under these circumstances, reactive formation among the younger generation necessarily went beyond mild demands to articulate a radical alternative vision of reality.

Chicano militancy accomplished in a few years what decades of past moderate efforts had not. The doors of high political office opened for the first time to Mexican Americans; citizens of Mexican ancestry finally began registering and voting in high numbers; presidential candidates were increasingly compelled to court the Mexican vote. Because of their concentration in the five southwestern states, Mexican Americans can play a crucial "swing" role in states that heavily influence electoral college outcomes. As table 18 indicates, the Hispanic vote in the Southwest represents a much higher proportion than nationwide. The roughly 15 percent of Mexican voters in the region can, when mobilized as a block, significantly affect elections in states that jointly control one-fifth of the votes needed to elect a new president.

As seen previously, the Mexican American electorate is potentially much higher because of the large number of nonnaturalized legal

TABLE 18. THE SPANISH-ORIGIN VOTE IN THE SOUTHWEST

| | Presidential election, November 2000 | | | | | Registered citizens | | |
Region	Total vote (000s)	Spanish-origin vote (000s)	% Spanish origin	Electoral College votes		Total registered	Spanish-origin registered	% Spanish origin
Arizona	1,644	247	15.0	8		1,879	304	16.2
California	11,489	1,597	13.9	54		13,061	1,919	14.7
Colorado	1,633	158	9.7	8		1,954	199	10.2
New Mexico	647	191	29.5	5		750	239	31.9
Texas	7,005	1,300	18.6	32		8,929	1,905	21.3
Total United States	110,826	5,934	5.4	538		129,549	13,158	10.2

SOURCE: U.S. Bureau of the Census 2002.

immigrants. Between 1990 and 2000, however, the Spanish-origin electorate in the Southwest grew swiftly—from 10 to about 15 percent of the total. As Passel notes, the Hispanic population, composed predominantly of Mexican-origin persons, will become about a quarter of the United States total by midcentury, and its eligibility to vote will increase by about 25 percent. Thus, all indications point to the increasing political weight of this population.[78]

During the late 1970s, 1980s, and 1990s, Mexican Americans were elected to the U.S. House of Representatives, to the governorships of three states, and to mayoralties of major cities such as San Antonio and Denver. In the early 2000s, a Mexican American, Cruz Bustamante, served as lieutenant governor of California and was the runner-up in the 2004 gubernatorial election. Bill Richardson, governor of New Mexico and (despite his name) a second-generation Mexican American, played an increasingly prominent role in Democratic Party politics in preparation for the 2004 presidential elections. By that time, 90 percent of the Hispanic Caucus in Congress was Mexican American. In 2005, Antonio Villaraigosa, a second-generation Mexican American, became mayor of Los Angeles, the first to occupy this post in more than a century.

Proposition 187, an anti-immigrant measure promoted by former governor of California Pete Wilson in a bid to improve his electoral prospects, turned out to be a watershed in Mexican American politics. Interpreted principally as an anti-Mexican measure, it led to a new reactive mobilization of proportions not seen since the 1960s. Mexican American organizations, such as the National Association of Latin Elected Officials (NALEO) and MALDEF, were now sufficiently strong to use the occasion for a massive naturalization and electoral registration campaign. A study of electoral participation among ethnic minorities in the 1990s concludes:

> The evidence from 1994 to 1998 supports our hypothesis regarding anti-immigrant legislation and voting behavior. In 1994, first generation immigrants in California were twice as likely to have voted as their generational counterparts in other states that did not have similar measures. . . . [S]econd generation immigrants in California were 83 percent more likely to have voted as their generational peers elsewhere.[79]

The Mexican American electorate thus turned out in force to punish proponents of 187 and elect their own to office. Congressman Robert Dornan, a conservative Republican from Orange County and a vigorous advocate of the proposition, lost his seat to a young Mexican American Democrat, Loretta Sánchez. Governor Wilson lost the next gubernatorial election and faded from view. Thereafter, no candidate for statewide office in California would dream of antagonizing Mexican American voters; instead, politicians most explicitly courted their support.[80]

The increasing political weight of Mexican Americans is driven both by rising levels of naturalization and electoral registration and by the continuing flow of immigration from Mexico. New immigrants do not vote, but they are counted for purposes of electoral redistricting, increasing political opportunities for coethnic candidates.[81] The Mexican American electorate is pro-Democratic, and this party has increasingly acknowledged its influence. There were up to three Mexican Americans of cabinet-level rank in the Clinton administration. Aware of the fast-rising influence of the Mexican American electorate, Republicans have also been seeking to make inroads in it, with some success. Older, better-established, and wealthier Hispanos from New Mexico have been a prime target, with several prominent Hispanic Republicans coming from their ranks.[82] Under the leadership of President George W. Bush, the Republican Party made considerable strides in this direction, garnering 40 percent of the Hispanic vote in the 2004 presidential elections. This notable success was due, in part, to the perceived rapprochement between the United States and Mexico, punctuated by repeated encounters between Bush and Mexican president Vicente Fox and by the perceived friendly stance of the Republican administration toward Mexican migrants. By the end of 2005, however, these achievements were seriously compromised by passage of a harsh Republican-sponsored bill in the House of Representatives that criminalized undocumented migrants, their employers, and anyone who harbored or assisted them and that proposed building a double fence along the entire southern border.

In response to the crisis created by this bill, both Mexican immigrant and Mexican American organizations—in addition to most other Hispanic civil rights groups, leaders of the Catholic Church, and labor unions such as the Service Employees International Union, whose membership includes a large number of immigrants—mobilized to lead massive civic protests in the streets. The mobilization was helped by Spanish-language radio DJs and other ethnic news media. More than half a million persons marched in protest in Los Angeles on March 25, 2006—the largest protest demonstration in that city's history—and hundreds of thousands more demonstrated in scores of cities throughout the nation, with extraordinarily large crowds in major metropolitan areas such as Chicago, Phoenix, Dallas, and Washington, D.C. The reaction to Proposition 187 in California in the fall of 1994 pales in comparison to what was witnessed in the spring of 2006. HR 4437, the so-called Sensenbrenner-King bill, placed the Bush administration in a very difficult position vis-à-vis Mexico and the Hispanic electorate as a whole, seriously compromising past Republican gains with these voters. It is improbable that this situation can be reversed in the short term. As in the past, preferences for one or another party among Mexican Americans do not reflect consistent class differences but respond instead to the appeal of specific candidates and legislative proposals to the minority as a whole. As with Europeans before them, ethnicity and ethnic issues continue to be the fundamental pivot of Mexican American politics today. The mass mobilizations against HR 4437 reflect again and quite poignantly this pattern.

In the future, it is likely that Mexican politics in the United States will continue to oscillate between the transnational concerns of first-generation immigrants, engaged in an intense dialogue with their communities of origin and Mexican state and federal governments, and the ethnic politics of second and higher generations, seeking an increasing voice in the American political system. Ironically, a migrant group made up mostly of peasants and unskilled laborers has ended up playing an increasingly important role in the politics of both their original and adopted countries.

CUBAN AMERICAN POLITICS

Up to 1980, two decades after the advent of Fidel Castro's revolution in Cuba, Cuban exile politics focused exclusively on seeking the demise of the Communist dictator. That year brought about two events that decisively changed the political orientation of this community, turning it inward. First, the Mariel exodus brought more than 125,000 new refugees in a six-month period. The important characteristic of this exodus is that it was unwelcome, forced on the United States by the decision of the Cuban government to open the Mariel port to all exiles wishing to take their families out of the island. Castro's government deliberately placed aboard the boats common criminals and mental patients with the aim of discrediting both the exodus itself and its enemies in Miami.[83]

This aim was achieved, as the reaction to the Mariel episode among the American public could not have been more negative, casting a pall over the entire Cuban exile community. The native white establishment in Miami viewed the exodus as a cataclysm, thoroughly discrediting the city as an attractive tourist destination. Spearheaded by its mouthpiece, the *Miami Herald*, it organized a vigorous campaign to stop the Mariel flow or at least deflect it from South Florida. Figure 6 presents results of a content analysis of coverage of the episode in the *Herald*. Overwhelmingly, the tone of the articles was negative and denunciatory. On April 24, 1980, for instance, a strong editorial condemned the boatlift, begun three days earlier, calling it humiliating and dangerous and asserting that "would-be rescuers from Florida are pawns in Castro's open diplomatic war." On May 1, a very negative article reported that five thousand refugees had arrived, and "the strident exile community in the United States shows little inclination of winding things down."[84]

This coverage continued for months, tarnishing the Mariel exodus by claiming that "this is not the entrepreneurial class that moved in 15 years ago. . . . A Cuban ghetto might develop."[85] This reception and its effects nationwide also tarnished the "old" exile community, which saw itself demoted from a "model minority" and the "builders of South Florida" to just another undesirable group. Evidence of the arrival of criminals and other misfits rapidly reduced support for the boatlift among older Cubans and led them to take distance from the new arrivals, who started to be called, pejoratively, *marielitos*. But it was too late, and the damage deliberately inflicted by Castro on his Miami adversaries was accomplished.[86]

In the wake of Mariel, a second episode signaled to Cubans how unwelcome they had become. An antibilingual referendum was placed on the ballot in the Miami–Dade County elections of November 1980 and passed overwhelmingly. It directed city and county officials to conduct business exclusively in English and prohibited them from funding activities in other languages. A sponsor of the measure explained his sentiments as follows: "My parents were immigrants and they had to learn English promptly; Cubans should do likewise."[87]

Caught unawares by the hostility of those whom they had perceived so far as allies in the anti-Communist struggle, Cuban exiles reacted by pulling together and reorienting their economic resources and political organization inward. A Cuban American Miami–Dade County official described the situation as follows:

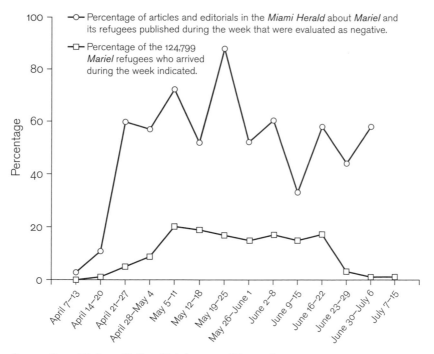

Sources: Camayd-Freixas 1988, III-42; Clark, Lasaga, and Reque 1981, 5.

Figure 6. Weekly *Mariel* arrivals and percentage of *Miami Herald* articles evaluated as negative, April–July 1980

There were four stages to Mariel and its aftermath: In the first, there was great solidarity by Cuban-Americans with the Mariel refugees. . . . In the second, the Feds took over. The campaign against Mariel in the press got tougher. Cuban-Americans began to believe it and abandoned the new arrivals. . . . In the third stage, there was the anti-bilingual referendum which was a slap in our face. People began to feel "more Cuban than anyone." There was anger at the insult, but no organization. In the fourth stage, there is embryonic organization promoted by the business leaders; the plan today is to try to elect a Cuban mayor of the city and perhaps one or two state legislators.[88]

Relative to other immigrant groups, the key difference in the reactive formation process among Cuban exiles in the aftermath of Mariel was the considerable professional and entrepreneurial resources that they brought into play. Following the referendum, Cuban American businessmen began to withdraw from native white ("Anglo") organizations or to combine participation in them with parallel ethnic organizing.

Facts about Cuban Exiles (FACE) and the Cuban-American National Foundation (CANF) were founded at the time. Plans were made to run candidates for local office. More important, a new discourse began to emerge in response to the antibilingual movement. In this alternative discourse, the exile community itself represented the solution to Miami's problems and was the builder of its future. Luis Botifoll, a leading Cuban American banker, became one of the most prominent exponents of this view:

> Before the "Great Change," Miami was a typical southern city, with an important population of retirees and veterans, whose only activity consisted in the exploitation of tourism in the sunny winters. No one thought of transforming Miami into what it is today. It is no exaggeration to say that the motor of this Great Change were the Cuban men and women who elected freedom and came to these shores to rebuild their homes and face with courage an uncertain future. . . . These last decades have witnessed the foundation of a dynamic and multi-faceted Miami over the past of a Miami that was merely provincial and tourist-oriented. Today, the level of progress has reached unanticipated heights, beyond the limits of anyone's imagination.[89]

Instead of complaining about discrimination or arguing for minority rights, Cubans laid claim to the city. Their claim was backed by the considerable economic resources of a business enclave (discussed in chapter 4) and by a very rapid process of naturalization and electoral registration among the early exile waves. Monolithic block voting among Cuban Americans accomplished, in a few years, what would have been unimaginable in 1980. Established native Anglo leaders, including those who had supported the referendum, were voted out of office, to be replaced by former exiles. By mid-decade, the mayors of Miami, Hialeah, West Miami, and other smaller municipalities were Cuban Americans, and ten Cuban Americans held seats in the state legislature.[90] By 2000, the mayoralty of Miami–Dade County itself and three slots in the U.S. Congress were added. Cuban American congresspersons were repeatedly elected, without credible opposition, during the 1990s. In predominantly Hispanic districts of South Florida, it became scarcely worthwhile to run for office if one were not a Cuban American.

Since 1980, this ethnic vote has lined up solidly behind the Republican Party. This support was in response to the abandonment of the Cuban exile brigade in the Bay of Pigs by the Kennedy administration in 1961. Since then, Cuban Americans have seen their best prospects in their perennial struggle with Castro and his regime in aligning themselves with Republican leaders. That view was significantly buttressed by the Elián González episode in 1999. The decision by Democratic attorney general Janet Reno to forcibly remove the child from his Miami Cuban relatives triggered days of rioting in the city. Following Elián's return to Cuba, exile leaders reorganized the community to "punish" the Democrats at election time. Block voting was at its height during the presidential elections of 2000, with over four-fifths of Cuban Americans casting their ballots for George W. Bush.[91]

Though Cubans represent only a small fraction of the Florida electorate, their high voting rates and strong Republican bent were seen as decisive in the highly contested 2000 election in Florida. After his victory, President Bush was compelled to reward his fervent Caribbean allies. He did so by appointing Cuban Americans Mel Martínez to the cabinet and Otto Reich as his personal representative for Latin America, as well as a number of others to important posts. In preparation for the 2004 elections, he further tightened the economic embargo against Cuba by severely limiting trips, remittances, and investments to the island in a bid to please his hard-line allies in Miami.[92] In 2004, Mel Martínez was elected to the U.S. Senate from Florida, further strengthening Cuban American congressional representation. Carlos Gutiérrez, another Cuban American businessman, took Martínez's place as U.S. secretary of commerce.

While quite different in history and ideological orientations, Mexican American and Cuban American politics are similar in two crucial respects. First, in both cases the origins of contemporary mobilizations date back to episodes of reactive formation: for Mexicans, in response to Proposition 187 and a long history of discrimination; for Cubans, in response to Mariel and the antibilingual referendum. Second, for both groups, the consequences of these mobilizations have been long-lasting, with ethnicity easily trumping class as the fundamental determinant of political action. Naturalized first-generation citizens and their offspring seldom vote with their pocketbooks today but rather support those parties and candidates seen as closer to their ethnic self-definition and goals. Nativists of every stripe should take note of these events, for their attempts to put immigrant minorities "in their place" have regularly backfired, producing exactly the opposite consequence.

EMERGENT ETHNICITIES

We have seen previously how "nationalities" were often forged by immigration through the common expedient of lumping together groups that shared only a tenuous bond before arriving in America. The consolidation of nation-states during the twentieth century preempted this function so that, by the time that the doors were reopened in 1965, most immigrants arrived with well-defined national identities. But recent years have witnessed the rise of a higher level of collective identification. Colombian immigrants certainly know that they are Colombian and Mexicans that they are Mexican; what they probably do not know when they arrive in the United States is that they belong to a larger common category called Hispanics.

Colombians, Mexicans, Cubans, and other immigrant groups from Latin America are generally aware that they share common linguistic and cultural roots, but this fact seldom suffices to produce a strong overarching solidarity. National experiences are too divergent and national loyalties too deeply embedded to yield to this supranational logic. In Latin America, patriotism is often sharpened by periodic revivals of conflict with a neighboring Latin nation. Thus, Colombians and Venezuelans, Ecuadoreans and Peruvians, Chileans and Argentines have traditionally reaffirmed their sense of national pride in actual or symbolic confrontations with each other. Upon arrival in the United States, they learn differently. As Sicilian peasants were informed in New York of their being "Italian," contemporary Latin American immigrants are told—in no uncertain terms—that despite their ancestral differences, they are all "Hispanic."

The experience is not an isolated one. Immigrants from the Far East, especially those with common racial features, are lumped together under the label "Asian" or "Oriental." In this instance, the distance between ethnic labeling and actual reality is even more egregious because groups so designated do not even share a common language. Even so, the labels "Asian" and "Asian American" figure prominently as categories under which people are counted, students and workers classified, and journalistic articles written.[93]

Ethnicity has always been a socially constructed product, forged in interaction between individual traits and the surrounding context. It is therefore not impossible that these supranational identities will take hold and come eventually to define groups so labeled to others, as well as to themselves. The history of immigration certainly supports this possibility. Students of ethnic mobilizations, such as Joane Nagel, have argued strongly that receiving nation-states play a crucial role in the rise of ethnicity through their defining and treating various groups differently.[94] According to Nagel, states can actually create ethnic minorities by the simple expedient of acting toward arbitrarily defined aggregates *as if* their internal similarities and external differences with the majority were real.

If this view is accurate, Hispanic Americans and Asian Americans are well on their way toward becoming the new ethnic minorities because they are defined as single entities in numerous official publications, lumped together in affirmative action programs, counted together by the census, and addressed jointly in official rhetoric. Academic researchers and the media have contributed heavily to this process of ethnic construction through the same expedient of addressing disparate nationalities as if they were part of the same collectivity. To the extent that the new labels prevail, the ethnic mobilizations to emerge in the Latin barrios and Asian "towns" of major American cities will not be bound by the original national identities but by the supranational ones initially bestowed on them from the outside.

Evidence indicates that this new process of ethnic formation is taking hold, if not in the first generation at least in the second. Results of the large recent survey of immigrant children and their parents, already described in chapter 4, indicate that parents hold onto their nationalities as their prime self-identifier but that children have learned to describe their ethnicity, and even race, according to pannational labels. Table 19 presents evidence of this trend in cross-generational response to the question "What is your race?" Latin immigrant parents seldom confuse their ethnicity with their race; among children, however, "Hispanic" has taken hold as a *racial* self-designation. Ninety-three percent of first-generation Cubans, for example, identify themselves racially as "white," but only 41 percent of their offspring agree. Fully 36 percent of these adolescents see themselves as Hispanic, a figure that increases to nearly 62 percent among Nicaraguan Americans.

When ethnicity "thickens" into race, important behavioral consequences can be expected to follow. Economic and political entrepreneurs are giving a vigorous push to these emergent ethnicities because of their interests in expanding both the pannational market and the electorate. Even more prominently, nativist tracts, such as the essay penned by Huntington, which attack "Hispanics" as an allegedly uniform category, have the predictable consequence of fostering solidarity

TABLE 19. SELF-REPORTED RACE OF CHILDREN OF IMMIGRANTS AND THEIR PARENTS, BY NATIONAL ORIGIN GROUPS, 1995–1996[a]

National origin[b]	Subject	White (%)	Black (%)	Asian (%)	Multiracial (%)	Hispanic, Latino (%)	National origin[b] (%)	Other (%)
Cuba	Child	41.2	0.8	—	11.5	36.0	5.5	4.9
	Parent	93.1	1.1	0.3	2.5	1.1	0.5	1.4
Mexico	Child	1.5	0.3	—	12.0	25.5	56.2	4.5
	Parent	5.7	—	2.1	21.6	15.9	26.1	28.5
Nicaragua	Child	19.4	—	—	9.7	61.8	2.7	6.5
	Parent	67.7	0.5	1.6	22.0	5.4	0.5	2.2
Other Latin America	Child	22.8	1.9	—	14.7	52.9	4.6	3.1
	Parent	69.5	4.6	0.8	17.8	2.3	1.9	3.1

SOURCE: Portes and Rumbaut 2001, table 7.7.

[a]Figures are raw percentages.
[b]For example, "Mexican."

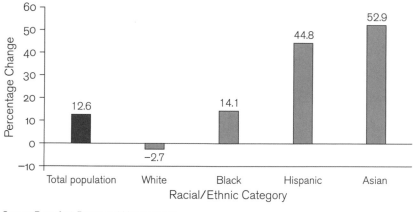

Source: Fasenfest, Booza, and Metzger 2004.

Figure 7. Population change by race/ethnicity, ten largest U.S. metropolitan areas, 1990–2000

among initially dissimilar groups. A late indication of this panethnic reactive formation process is the example of Mel Martínez, a Cuban American U.S. senator taking the lead in the congressional battle against the anti-Mexican Sensenbrenner-King bill. Thus, whatever major differences exist in the historical origins and political orientations of Cuban, Mexican, and Central American immigrants, they are being increasingly swept under a common term. With a different label, the same process is taking place among descendants of Filipino, Korean, Chinese, and Vietnamese immigrants.

To the extent that these panethnic categories take hold as actual ethnicities or even races, the political consequences can be momentous. Figure 7 presents the evolution of four such categories in the ten largest U.S. metropolitan areas between 1990 and 2000. While the white non-Hispanic population declined 3 percent, "Hispanics" increased their numbers by 45 percent and "Asians" by 53 percent. These relative figures translate into a changed ethnic profile in which, by 2000, eleven million, or 20 percent of the U.S. metropolitan population, were Hispanic, surpassing blacks as the nation's largest minority, and an additional 3.6 million, or 6 percent, were Asian.[95]

In reality, the political behavior of contemporary immigrant communities has not yet been completely subsumed under the new panethnic categories. Significant national differences remain, as shown by the prior discussion of Mexican American and Cuban American politics. In addition, transnational activities and the efforts of sending-country governments to strengthen them help keep national identities alive, at least in the first generation. What seems to be happening at present is defined by two trends. First, immigrant nationalities vote their particular interests, but they cooperate panethnically on common issues. Thus, different Latin American nationalities may have specific concerns and even opposite ideological preferences, but they cooperate in defense of bilingualism and in opposition to restrictionist and anti-immigrant policies.[96] Second, leaders and activists from particular nationalities use the pannational categories in order to increase support for specific political goals. Thus, Chinese American political candidates in California and elsewhere regularly appeal to the "Asian" vote. "Hispanic" politics in Florida is quite different from California's: the first is dominated by Cuban American interests and values and the second by those of concern to Mexican Americans. Smaller or more recent Latin groups are prompted, through appeal to the common Hispanic label, to fall in line with the regionally dominant group.

VARIATIONS WITHIN A THEME

Little has been said so far about how the typology of contemporary immigration, outlined in chapter 2, relates to different political activities and orientations. This is so, in part, because the typology is largely based on the different *class* resources that immigrants bring with them, while, as seen in this chapter, ethnicity regularly trumps class as a motive for collective mobilization. Still, major differences exist between types of immigrants in several of the political dimensions discussed previously. Table 20 summarizes these differences by comparing immigrant types along four key dimensions: propensity to naturalize, propensity to engage in transnational political activities, salience of politics, and the character of collective political mobilizations.

It has already been shown that higher levels of human capital lead to higher rates of citizenship acquisition. Thus, with equal lengths of time in the country, immigrant professionals and entrepreneurs can be expected to naturalize faster and more frequently than manual laborers. The factor of reversibility of migration comes into play in the case of asylees and refugees. To the extent that their return option is blocked, higher rates of citizenship acquisition can be expected among these groups. This factor explains the very high rates of naturalization among the early waves of Cuban exiles and among Vietnamese refugees at present. It also partially explains the *low* rates among Salvadoran

TABLE 20. THE POLITICAL ORIENTATIONS
OF CONTEMPORARY IMMIGRANTS

	Immigration type			
Feature	Manual laborers	Professionals	Entrepreneurs	Political refugees
Propensity to naturalize	Low	High	High	High
Transnational activism	Low	High	High	Low
Salience of politics	Low	High	Medium	High
Character of ethnicity	Reactive	Linear	Reactive	Linear

and Guatemalan asylees, groups for whom the return option became open with the end of civil war and the return to democracy in their respective countries.[97]

Recent studies of determinants of political transnationalism have uncovered the fact that higher human capital among first-generation immigrants also leads to increased levels of involvement in the politics of their home nations. Reasons for this trend are twofold. First, higher levels of education translate into more information and concern with political affairs; second, higher human capital also translates into better incomes, which enable immigrant professionals and entrepreneurs to engage in these activities. Table 21 presents evidence of this pattern based on an analysis of factors leading to political transnationalism among first-generation Colombian, Dominican, and Salvadoran immigrants in the United States. The table presents models of both "regular" and "occasional" participation, but, for purposes of discussion, we focus on the first as the more rigorous definition of these activities.[98]

As seen in the table, educated individuals are significantly more likely to take part in political activities across borders. A high school diploma increases the probability of doing so by 173 percent and a college degree by an additional 38 percent relative to the average. The point made previously that there is no zero-sum game between transnationalism and successful integration to American society, including naturalization, is supported by these results. It is further supported by other findings in the table indicating that U.S. citizenship acquisition does not affect the propensity to participate in transnational activities and that length of U.S. residence actually *increases* it. Thus, it is the better established and more educated among these immigrant groups who

TABLE 21. DETERMINANTS OF
POLITICAL TRANSNATIONALISM AMONG
LATIN AMERICAN IMMIGRANTS

Determinants	Regular involvement[a]		Occasional involvement[a]	
	Coefficient	% change[b]	Coefficient	% change[b]
Demographic				
Gender (male)	1.209*	235.3	.710*	103.4
Marital status				
(married)	.118***	12.6	−.056	—
Education[c]				
High school				
graduate	1.003***	172.7	.646***	90.8
College graduate	.324**	38.3	.320**	37.8
Assimilation				
Years in the				
United States	.034***	3.5	.010	—
U.S. citizen	−.041	—	.189	—
Social networks				
Size[d]	.095***	10.0	.078***	8.2
Scope[e]	−.84	—	−.031	—
Likelihood				
ratio	2,331.25***		2,731.87***	
Pseudo R^2	.104		.078	
N (unweighted)	1,202			

SOURCE: Guarnizo, Portes, and Haller 2003.

[a] Negative binomial regression coefficients indicating net effects of each predictor on the count of transnational activities engaged in by Colombian, Dominican, and Salvadoran household heads. The weighted sample is representative of approximately 187,000 first-generation adult immigrants in their principal areas of concentration.
[b] Percentage change in count of transnational activities is computed for significant effects only.
[c] Less than a high school education is the reference category.
[d] Actual number of ties reported by respondents.
[e] Ratio of nonlocal ties to local ties in present city of residence.
*$p < .05$.
**$p < .01$.
***$p < .001$.

are more likely to naturalize *and* be involved in transnational political affairs.

The case of refugees is unique. While the very reasons for their departure makes these groups very "political," salience of politics does not necessarily translate into transnational activism given the relationship of opposition between these groups and the regimes they escaped. As the experiences of Cubans and Vietnamese in the past and of Iranians today illustrate, the situation of political refugees may be referred to as "blocked transnationalism" because the realities on the ground prevent interest and concern with the home country to be translated into an effective presence there. Despite blocked transnationalism, the political orientation of refugee groups tends to be linear, dominated by a continuing opposition to the regime that forced them to escape. This is so unless nativist hostility in the United States triggers a reactive formation process. As seen previously, this was the situation for Cuban exiles whose political orientations were linear until 1980 but became reactive after Mariel.

Contrary to refugees, politics is not a salient issue among immigrant laborers unless sustained discrimination and nativist campaigns against them produce a reactive mobilization. The history of Mexican American politics, especially after Proposition 187, provides a clear example. Professional immigrants are the least likely to experience widespread discrimination. This is so, first, because of their high levels of human capital and, second, because (as seen in chapter 2), they tend to be more dispersed geographically in pursuit of their careers. Professionals seldom create highly visible, culturally distinct concentrations that tend to elicit opposition among the native-born. The politics of first-generation professionals is thus linear and guided by concerns and interests in the home country, to which American ones are gradually added. As just seen, this is the type of immigrant most prone to engage in transnational activism and, simultaneously, to acquire U.S. citizenship.

Immigrant entrepreneurs are in a parallel situation, except that their concentration in visible ethnic enclaves can make them the target of local hostility, thereby leading to reactive mobilization. Korean entrepreneurs in Los Angeles provide a case in point, especially after the riots of 1992, when many of their businesses were torched. The episode elicited a strong, solidary reaction in this community, aimed at both protecting itself and heightening its visibility and significance in local and state politics. Similar attacks against entrepreneurial enclaves created by other nationalities have produced parallel reactions in the past.[99]

CONCLUSION

In *The Immigration Time Bomb: The Fragmenting of America*, former Colorado governor Richard D. Lamm complains:

> Increasingly, the political power of more than fifteen million Hispanics is being used not to support assimilation but to advance "ethnic pride" in belonging to a different culture. The multiplication of outsiders is not a model for a viable society. . . . If immigrants do not feel that they are fully part of this society, as American as everyone else, then we are failing.[100]

Throughout the history of the United States, immigrants have seldom felt "as American as everyone else" because differences of language and culture separated them from the majority and because they were made painfully aware of that fact. Being "in America but not of it," even if they wished to, represents an important aspect of the experience of most foreign groups and a major force promoting ethnic identity in subsequent generations. The rise of ethnic pride among children of recent arrivals is thus not surprising because it is a tale repeated countless times in the history of immigration.

The significant aspect of Lamm's statement is the peril that it outlines and the solution that it proposes. The peril is the "fragmenting of America" by outside cultures, and the solution is rapid assimilation so that immigrants will become "as American as everyone else." As happened at the beginning of the twentieth century, immigration is portrayed as un-American; but whereas before the alleged sins were political radicalism or its opposite, political docility, at present they consist of excessive cultural diversity. Pundits, past and present, have seldom taken the time to examine the evidence, preferring instead to give free rein to their prejudices. Assimilation to America has seldom taken place in the way recommended by nativists. Instead, the reaffirmation of distinct cultural identities—whether actual or invented in the United States—has been the rule among foreign groups and has represented the first effective step in their social and political incorporation. Ethnic solidarity has provided the basis for the pursuit of common goals in the American political system: by mobilizing the collective vote and by electing their own to office, immigrant minorities have learned the rules of the democratic game and absorbed its values in the process.

Assimilation as the immediate transformation of immigrants into people "as American as everyone else" has never happened. Instead, the definition of the foreign-born by their nationality rather than by their class position has meant that the first steps of political apprenticeship consisted of symbolically reaffirming the same national characteristics and organizing along the lines that they demarcated. Italians voted in block for Italian candidates in Boston and New York, just as Mexicans do for their own in Los Angeles and San Antonio today. Socialization into American political institutions has taken place through this process. Before Irish, Italian, or Greek politicians entered the mainstream as interpreters of national values and aspirations, their predecessors had spent much time in ward politics representing their own group's interests.

Ethnic resilience has been the rule among immigrants, old and new, and constitutes simultaneously a central part of their process of political incorporation. Today, "hispanicity" in the Southwest is a synonym of Mexican American cultural reaffirmation, a latter-day manifestation of a familiar process. Despite the growth of transnational ties among first-generation immigrants, the politics of the second and higher generations are overwhelmingly American, as are the values and loyalties of their members. Hence, the perils that so alarm the new self-appointed guardians of national integrity are likely to be as imaginary as those that agitated their forebears. The vain search for political radicals in immigrant neighborhoods, described at the beginning of this chapter, finds its present counterpart in efforts to eradicate nonexisting resistance to English through constitutional reform.

Back in the early 1900s, the United States was receiving a comparable number of immigrants per year as it does today; foreigners represented up to 21 percent of the American labor force and close to half of the urban population. Groups such as the Germans had succeeded in literally transplanting their nations and culture into America. The country was certainly far more "fragmented" then than it is now. What held it together then and continues to do so today was not enforced cultural homogeneity and heightened chauvinism but the strength of its political institutions and the durable framework that they offered for the process of ethnic reaffirmation and mobilization to play itself out. Defense of their own particular interests—defined along ethnic lines—was the school in which many immigrants and their descendants learned to identify with the interests of the nation as a whole. With different actors and in new languages, the process continues today.

6

A Foreign World
Immigration, Mental Health, and Acculturation

TRAVEL AND TRAVAIL

In our old country, whatever we had was made or brought in by our own hands; we never had any doubts that we would not have enough for our mouth. But from now on to the future, that time is over. We are so afraid and worried that there will be one day when we will not have anything for eating or paying the rent, and these days these things are always in our minds. Some nights the sleep hardly comes to me at all. . . . So you see, when you think all of these over, you don't want to live anymore. . . . Talking about this, I want to die right here so I won't see my future. . . . Don't know how to read or write, don't know how to speak the language. My life is only to live day by day until the last day I live, and maybe that is the time when my problems will be solved.

I used to be a real man like any other, but not now any longer. Things I used to do, now I can't do here. I feel like a thing which they say drops in the fire but won't burn and drops in the river but won't flow. So I feel like I have no goal, nothing in the future. . . . We only live day by day, just like the baby birds who are only staying in the nest opening their mouths and waiting for the mother bird to bring the worms. Because we are now like those baby birds who cannot fly yet.

These words could well have been spoken by turn-of-the-century immigrants whose harsh experiences in America were portrayed by William I. Thomas and Florian Znaniecki in *The Polish Peasant in Europe and*

America and later by Oscar Handlin in *The Uprooted.*[1] But they are the words of two middle-aged Hmong refugees from Laos—illiterate and of peasant origins—reflecting on their situation in one of the largest cities in the United States. They arrived on the West Coast with their families in 1980, after spending five years in refugee camps in Thailand. The Hmong are a sizable group among the more than one million Southeast Asian refugees resettled in the United States after the end of the Indo-china War. To be sure, the economic situation of those refugees was dismal, especially in comparison with the successful experiences of other recent immigrants. Still, their emotional response to circumstances in a foreign world, as illustrated in the opening quote, underscores the need to take seriously and to understand the *subjective* experience of immigration.

It is commonplace in the literature on migration, mental health, and mental disorder to observe that long-distance journeys entail a set of engulfing life events (losses, changes, conflicts, and demands) that, although varying widely in kind and degree, severely test the immigrant's emotional resilience. Migration can produce profound psychological distress, even among the best prepared and most motivated and even under the most receptive of circumstances. It is not coincidental, therefore, that the words *travel* and *travail* share an etymology.[2] But some investigators have remarked on the positive drive and the sense of efficacy and "hardiness" certain groups of immigrants exhibit and on how their triumph over adversity promotes increasing self-confidence.[3] Thus, the study of the immigrant experience offers fertile ground to address not merely the pathogenic (what makes people ill) but also the salutogenic (what keeps people healthy) responses of individuals to conditions of personal crisis.[4] Yet the subjective experience of immigration is an area that, compared with the more objective dimensions of the process examined in prior chapters, has been more difficult to study systematically and comparatively.

Although Thomas and Znaniecki as well as Handlin would have found the words of our two Hmong informants uncannily familiar, even regarding these peasant immigrants' almost identical use of agrarian similes to describe their situations, they would have been surprised by the diversity of recent immigrants to the United States. These authors sought, after all, to depict and document not socioeconomic diversity but the unitary theme of adjustment to crisis that they saw underlying the subjective experience of immigration. Thus, Thomas and Znaniecki focused on the "social disorganization" and the struggle for self-esteem of mostly single, young male laborers from Russian

Poland who immigrated to the United States between 1880 and 1910, rather than on immigrants from Austrian or Prussian Poland, who tended to come in entire families.[5] And Handlin, while recognizing that there were differences among the Irish, Germans, and the Poles, nonetheless focused on the common stress of "uprooting" and "arduous transplantation" that constituted the "universality of the migration experience." Thus, his history of immigration became a history of alienation and its consequences:

> The immigrants lived in crisis because they were uprooted. In transplantation, while the old roots were sundered, before the new were established, the immigrants existed in an extreme situation. The shock, and the effects of the shock, persisted for many years. . . . Their most passionate desires were doomed to failure; their lives were those of the feeble little birds which hawks attack, which lose strength from want of food. . . . Sadness was the tone of life. . . . The end of life was an end to hopeless striving, to ceaseless pain, and to the endless succession of disappointment.[6]

The themes of alienation and loneliness permeated the sociological literature on the immigrant experience in America prior to World War I. Although, as with other generalizations, the theme was probably exaggerated, there is no doubt that it reflected an underlying reality. Perhaps more than today, the lot of most turn-of-the-century immigrants was a harsh one, resembling that of our contemporary Hmong refugees more than that of more successful Asian professionals or Caribbean entrepreneurs. Because so much of our understanding of the world of immigrants is molded by ideas and concepts coined during that earlier period, it is important to probe further into it as a prelude to examining subjective aspects of immigration today.

MARGINALITY AND FREEDOM

A step ahead of the stories of unmitigated woe that composed the standard fare of the earlier immigration literature was the concept of marginality. In his essay "Human Migration and the Marginal Man," published in 1928, Robert Park portrayed the immigrant as a personality type, a hybrid on the margin of two worlds. The immigrant was a stranger fully belonging to neither, in whose mind colliding cultures met and fused. Although highly stressful, the situation had its positive aspects. Most important among them was the liberation of the person from the shackles of tradition and the expansion of individual initiative:

Energies that were formerly controlled by custom are released. . . . [Immigrants] become in the process not merely emancipated but enlightened. The emancipated individual becomes in a certain sense and to a certain degree a cosmopolitan. . . . The effect of migration is to secularize relations which were formerly sacred.[7]

To be sure, the experience of transition and crisis also confronts the "marginal man" with such characteristics as inner turmoil, instability, restlessness, and malaise. This counterpoint between newly found enlightenment and the stresses associated with it was to permeate analyses of the phenomenology of immigration for years to come. One of Park's disciples, Everett Stonequist, developed in ample detail the theme of a liberating but contradictory social location. Resorting to French, he labeled immigrants both *déclassé* and *déraciné*, or *uprooted*, a term that was to become standard in the literature on the migration experience:

The conflict of cultures working in the immigrant's mind is more intricate and profound than that expressed by the concept of the déclassé. The idea of the "uprooted" comes nearer to the heart of the problem. The individual undergoes transformation in the social, mental, and emotional aspects of his personality, each reacting upon the other. Some immigrants speak of these changes as constituting a second birth or childhood.[8]

The same author observed that the immigrant's response to the condition of marginality could vary widely, from amusement to despair, from stimulation to depression. At a minimum, however, it entailed a subtle, perhaps indefinable sense of estrangement and malaise.[9] The empirical literature of the time reflected the same theme but gave greater credence to the stressful aspects of marginality. On the whole, immigrants were able to cope, and some may have found removal from their tradition-bound birthplaces exhilarating; but many were not making it, as reflected in that most compelling indicator of distress: suicide.

In 1930, the suicide rate among the foreign-born in Chicago was 38.8 per 100,000, compared with less than one-third that figure (12.4) for the native-born, and the suicide rate for each immigrant group in the United States was found to be two to three times higher than for the same nationality in Europe.[10] Along the same lines, an ecological study of psychopathology in Chicago found that cases of mental disorder showed a regular decrease from the center to the periphery of the city and that rates of schizophrenia and alcoholic psychoses were highest in the neighborhoods of first immigrant settlement with a high proportion of foreign-born residents.[11]

EARLY PSYCHOPATHOLOGY: THE EUGENICS APPROACH TO MENTAL ILLNESS

The association between immigration and mental disturbances was consistently supported by early epidemiological studies, based on rates of hospital admission. Sociologists such as Park, Thomas and Znaniecki, and Stonequist had focused on the whole of the immigrant population or at least on an entire national inflow. For these authors, the higher incidence of mental disturbances among the foreign-born was evidence of the trauma of settlement and marginality, but such outcomes were regarded as exceptional.

Psychiatrists and clinical epidemiologists dealing with an inmate population had a different vision of the problem. In many localities, foreigners made up the bulk of the patient population institutionalized in mental asylums, and this situation encouraged quite a different set of explanations. The first epidemiological study of psychopathology and immigration in the United States was done by Edward Jarvis in 1855. He began by noting the rapid increase in the foreign population of Massachusetts: from an estimated 9,620 in 1830, to 34,818 in 1840, to 230,000 by 1854. But the proportion of lunatics among immigrants was notably larger: Although the insane represented 1 in 445 in the native population, they amounted to 1 in 368 among aliens in the state.[12] Jarvis framed the question of causation in terms that were to become standard in subsequent debates among scientists and policymakers alike: "[E]ither our foreign population is more prone to insanity or their habits and trials, their experiences and privations . . . are more unfavorable to their mental health than to that of the natives."[13]

With considerable analytic acumen, Jarvis noted that 93 percent of foreign lunatics in Massachusetts asylums were paupers and that only one in sixty-six of the whole native population was in this bottom social category, but they represented one in twenty-five among the aliens. Thus, he reasoned, "most of the foreigners are poor . . . and they must, therefore, have a larger proportion of lunatics to their whole number than the Americans."[14] He speculated further on the consequences of stressful life events. Prefiguring by decades the sociological analysis of marginality, he observed how "being in a strange land and among strange men and things," immigrants frequently endeavored to accomplish impractical goals, meeting with repeated, harrowing disappointment and defeat.[15]

This emphasis on the importance of class and context was unfortunately set aside in favor of more simplistic explanations. A growing interest in migration and mental illness reflected underlying policy concerns over the public cost of caring for dependent populations and deeper nativist fears about the impact of increased immigration on American society. As the inflow grew rapidly in the mid–nineteenth century, the foreign-born increasingly made up the inmate population of lunatic asylums as well as of poorhouses, penitentiaries, "houses of refuge" for neglected children, and reformatories. In New York, Massachusetts, Ohio, Minnesota, and Wisconsin, anywhere from half to three-quarters of the inmates in lunatic asylums were immigrants, and similar rates were reported in other custodial institutions, including prisons.[16]

By the early twentieth century, these concerns had fused with those about European immigrant radicalism to become the basis of xenophobic arguments against continuing immigration. Racist theories were given a major impetus by the new vogue of social Darwinism, Mendelian genetics, and the new "science" of eugenics. Advocates of these views raised alarm over the defective biological "stock" of immigrants, adding to the outcries for restriction stemming from the political right.[17] This was the time in which scientific experts wrote about the "remarkable tendency to suicide" among the Japanese in California, "the strong tendency to delusional trends of a persecutory nature" in West Indian Negroes, the frequency of "hidden sexual complexes" among the Hebrews, and "the remarkable prevalence of mutism" among Poles.[18] Hospital superintendents and other officials, blaming the "tremendous increase in mental diseases and defects" on immigrants, declared that states were expending "millions of dollars annually for the care and maintenance of an alien population which should have been excluded by the federal government."[19]

While such campaigns were raging in the media and in public life, researchers were discovering the significance of age in the explanation of differences in rates of mental illness between foreigners and the native-born. Rates of mental disorder varied directly with age, increasing from adolescence to old age. Compared with the native population, there were few children among newly arrived immigrants. Thus, when age-specific rates of mental hospital admission were calculated, the result was to reduce considerably the disproportionately high levels of disorders observed among the foreign-born.[20] A second variable of interest uncovered during the period was the relative spatial distribution of both populations. It turned out that the foreign-born were disproportionately concentrated in northeastern states, where hospitalization of the mentally ill was much more likely to occur than in southeastern states, where native whites predominated but hospitalization was much less common. Hence, immigrants were more likely to be "counted" in epidemiological studies based exclusively on rates of hospital admission.[21]

These healthy cautions on the interpretation of mental disorder differentials between immigrants and natives evaporated, however, in the heat of political agitation for restriction. The most influential arguments, buttressed by the now-prevailing eugenics ideology, brushed aside empirical findings to focus on the gross differences in disturbance rates between the native- and foreign-born. Typical in this regard was the role of Dr. Harry Laughlin, appointed as the "expert eugenics agent" to the House Committee on Immigration and Naturalization.[22] Laughlin's testimony to the committee in 1922 concluded, "In the United States, the foreign-born show an incidence of insanity in the State and Federal hospitals 2.85 times higher than that shown by the whole population, which latter are descended largely from older American stock."[23]

Laughlin did not make any allowances for the roles of socioeconomic status, age differences, or spatial distribution, dismissing such considerations as "special pleading for the alien."[24] The tide was clearly in favor of such explanations, and they were to lead to passage of the most restrictive immigration legislation in U.S. history. The National Origins Act of 1924 not only effectively barred further entries from most countries but did so on the basis of explicitly racial considerations. Asians and southeastern Europeans were the groups most heavily penalized by the new law.[25]

The sharp reduction of immigration after passage of the 1924 act was followed by a corresponding decline in the polemics about mental health and the foreign-born. Still, dominant scholarly views about the psychology of immigration continued to focus on unique traits imputed to certain nationalities or to the migrant contingent among them. Thus, a detailed analysis of the mental health of Norwegian immigrants in Minnesota from 1889 to 1929 found that it was significantly worse than among both the native population of that state and the non-immigrant population of Norway. Upon finding that returnees to Norway exhibited "even more insanity" than was found among settled immigrants in Minnesota, the author—a highly respected psychiatric epidemiologist—concluded that there was something pathological about the immigrant personality:

> If the life situation of the immigrants were the main reason for their high ratio of insanity, we might expect to find a lower ratio among those who "save themselves" and go back to their native country. . . . But instead we find that it is probably even higher. This speaks definitely in favor of the theory that the high incidence of mental diseases in the immigrant population is due to a prevalence of certain psychopathic tendencies in the constitution of those who emigrate.[26]

Alternative explanations, such as the experience of objective failure in the adopted country and the trauma of return after such failure, did not enter at all into these conclusions.

Up to World War II, analyses of the subjective world of immigrants thus featured a peculiar bifurcation. On the one hand, a growing research literature suggested that it was not intrinsic characteristics of the immigrants but rather such objective variables as poverty, age distribution, and spatial concentration that accounted for differential rates in mental disorder. On the other hand, public discourse—including that of most scientific experts—rejected such findings to emphasize, again and again, the inferior psychological makeup of immigrants, especially those of Asian and southeastern European stock. Sociological analyses of the traumas of adaptation and the complex situation of marginality were also swept aside in the enthusiasm to depict the immigrant as an intrinsically pathological figure. That such beliefs were of more than passing consequence is shown by their enactment into law. The National Origins Act of 1924 was to have major consequences for the composition of the American population for decades to come and to pattern the growth of its foreign-born component along explicitly racial lines.

FROM NATIONALITY TO CLASS AND CONTEXT: THE CHANGED ETIOLOGY OF MENTAL ILLNESS

During and after World War II, vast new international population movements brought renewed interest in the social and psychological consequences of emigration, particularly of *forced* emigration. Massive numbers of "displaced persons" in Europe and elsewhere, and the traumatic conditions of their expatriation, led to the formal recognition of "refugees" as a special category of migrant by the United Nations and, beginning with the 1948 Displaced Persons Act, by the United States.[27] The plight of the refugees contributed in no small measure to a momentous change in the public and academic understanding of the subjective world of immigrants. The period saw a significant shift of theoretical interest away from "selection" factors and toward a new emphasis on the effect of environmental stressors and other objective social conditions.

Apart from the vivid experience of the refugees, World War II also contributed to this conceptual shift through repeated clinical observations of "combat stress" among soldiers who had been previously screened for mental disorders. Impairment scales developed during the war permitted analyses of a more complex array of depression and anxiety reactions that went well beyond earlier gross classifications of psychiatric disorders.[28] Clearly, the fact that such impairments affected "American boys" at the front could not be attributed to their intrinsic psychological inferiority, and the new emphasis on environmental stressors was carried to other settings—including those where the foreign-born concentrated.

Beginning in the 1950s, large-scale community surveys based on probability samples of the general population became common, providing a methodological tool superior to earlier studies based on rates of hospital admissions. For the first time, it became possible to obtain psychiatric profiles of various segments of the population unbiased by such factors as the differential availability of hospital care or of knowledge about it. The new methodology was not without its problems, including the difficulty of measuring various types of mental disturbances in "natural" settings.[29] However, it had definitely greater scope and representativeness than the earlier hospitalization approach. Community surveys moved gradually away from the notion of innate psychological shortcomings to focus on contextual and objective factors, particularly on the role of socioeconomic differences in mental health and mental disorders.

The study by Hollingshead and Redlich, conducted during the 1950s, was among the most influential in establishing a causal link between social class and mental illness. A decade later a survey of the research literature reviewed forty-four major studies that confirmed the role of social class as a major predictor of psychological disturbances. Other related research found that the sheer number of reported "life stress" factors most efficiently accounted for mental health risk, but when life stresses were held constant, the risk was highest among those of lowest socioeconomic status.[30]

Community surveys also established a series of robust findings concerning psychological distress and associated disturbances that could be summarized in four basic patterns: the higher the socioeconomic status, the lower the distress; women were more distressed than men; unmarried people were more distressed than married people; and the greater the number of undesirable life events, the greater the distress.[31] These results can be subsumed theoretically under the more general concepts of powerlessness and alienation. Inability to reach one's goals in life and powerlessness to control or affect events—more common among lower-class people, women, and the less socially established—result in greater levels of distress and associated mental disorder. Although most research of the period was not concerned directly with immigration, its implications were obvious: the marginal position of immigrants is one of powerlessness and alienation; like other subordinate groups, they would be expected to exhibit higher rates of psychopathogenic symptoms.

This prediction was tested directly in a large New York City study conducted during the late 1950s and dubbed the Midtown Manhattan Project. Sociologist Leo Srole and his associates divided their large sample by immigrant generation—from the foreign-born to native Americans of native parentage. They found that immigrants had the expected higher prevalence of distress symptoms but that the difference disappeared when controlling for age and social class.[32] Most of the foreign-born in this sample had arrived after the restrictive 1924 legislation and were thus a highly select group who had managed to overcome the "formidable screen" of visa requirements prior to entry. Among this group, mental health impairment was infrequent (18.5 percent) and significantly lower than among pre-1920 arrivals. Over a third of the latter (34.3 percent), a group formed primarily by immigrants of European peasant origin, exhibited significant symptoms of mental pathology. The authors concluded:

> What is decisive among immigrants is *not* transplantation to the American metropolis per se, but resettlement in the American metropolis from a *particular kind* of overseas milieu, namely from the low socioeconomic strata in farm, village, or town. . . . To compress the profound historical changes of a revolutionizing century into a few adult years of an individual life cycle may exact a high price in psychological well-being.[33]

Srole and his associates reached a synthesis of the plausible but until then disjointed themes that had emerged as an alternative to earlier theories of intrinsic racial/cultural differences. Social class and social context were the themes emphasized, respectively, by empirical community surveys and by theoretical elaborations on the earlier concept of marginality. The Midtown Manhattan Project brought both themes together by noting that the trauma of resettlement and marginality was not experienced equally by all immigrants. It was the *social distance* traveled from place of origin to place of destination that accounted for the magnitude of the shock and the ability to cope with it.

For immigrants of urban origin, higher education, and middle-class backgrounds, that distance was less; hence, the difficulties of adaptation—of accomplishing their "sociopsychological vault from one place to the other"—became more manageable. Conversely, a greater sense of powerlessness and alienation was the lot of immigrants of lower status, and with it came the familiar psychopathologies associated with the foreign-born.

The postwar years thus witnessed a remarkable turnaround both in the objective situation of the foreign-born and in the public and academic perceptions of it. The 1924 act reduced immigration to a trickle of highly select individuals and, modified by later legislation after World War II, to contingents of displaced persons who met with considerable public sympathy. With fears of a foreign invasion left behind, research could proceed in a calmer social environment and communicate its results more effectively. The psychological status of immigrants thus ceased to be a uniquely pathogenic condition and became essentially one more manifestation of a general syndrome affecting other relatively powerless segments of the population. Class of origin and context of reception emerged as the key factors molding the content, challenges, and resilience of the immigrants' world.

IMMIGRANTS AND REFUGEES: CONTEMPORARY TRENDS

The contemporary period has seen a rapid diversification in types of immigration and contexts of reception, as seen in prior chapters. This diversity is reflected in the psychological response evident among different categories of immigrants and in their perceptions of American society. Class of origin remains as important as ever in explaining subjective well-being and adaptation, but the diversity of current flows has shifted the locus of the context with which class backgrounds are expected to interact. In Srole's time and earlier, the *context of reception* posed the challenge for newcomers; in recent decades, the *context of exit* has become equally important. The distinction made in chapter 2 between immigrants and refugees becomes crucial at this point because the latter category has emerged as a subject of increasing concern.

Typically, the distinction hinges on the notion of refugees as involuntary and relatively unprepared migrants "pushed out" by coercive political conditions or by an "exposure to disaster," versus immigrants as voluntary and better-prepared movers "pulled in" by perceived opportunities for economic advancement or family reunification.[34] The distinction is actually more elusive than this definition suggests. So-called voluntary migrations are not always as voluntary and planned as described, and there are wide differences in the degree of urgency, suddenness, and "acute flight" experiences of different refugee groups. In addition, as seen in chapter 2, "refugee" is not a self-assigned label but one assigned by the host government. Thus, two groups subject to similar conditions of stressful flight may be defined differently on arrival, one sanctioned and granted the status of bona fide "political" refugees and the other unsanctioned and labeled "clandestine" economic immigrants. Differential labeling by the federal government has marked, for example, the divergent official receptions and subsequent adaptation experiences of Southeast Asian boat people, on the one hand, and Central American escapees, on the other.[35]

Nor is it true that "refugees" did not exist before the contemporary period. What did not exist in earlier times was the appropriate term to identify their situation. Turn-of-the-century "immigrants" such as Russian Jews escaping czarist persecution and pogroms probably experienced conditions of exit as traumatic as many present-day refugees. The advent of the term finally brought attention to different contexts of expulsion and thus introduced an important new variable in our understanding of immigrant mental health, absent from earlier analyses. Thus, the recent research literature has suggested that several features of stressful life events that accompany immigration are associated with subjective distress. Although both refugees and immigrants must cope with a significant amount of life change, many refugees appear to experience more threat, more undesirable change, and less control over the events that define their context of exit.

A study measuring "acculturative stress" among ethnic minorities in Canada found, for example, that Vietnamese refugees had the highest scores, compared with both Korean immigrants and domestic minorities.

Korean immigrants had a psychological profile that was actually quite close to that of the Canadian native-born population. As in other studies in the United States, higher stress was found among females, the elderly, those unable to speak English, the uneducated, and the unemployed. Social support variables—as in the case of newcomers who had sponsors and close coethnic friends—reduced the experience of stress. These objective variables accounted for most, but not all, of the differences between refugees and other ethnic minorities.[36]

More poignant evidence supporting the significance of contexts of exit comes from comparisons between Asian immigrants and Indo-Chinese refugees in California. A study in Santa Clara County (Silicon Valley) compared large samples of Chinese immigrants with Vietnamese, Cambodian, and ethnic Chinese refugees from Southeast Asia along various dimensions of mental health need. As with Koreans in Canada, Chinese immigrants in California exhibited an enviable psychological profile, including much lower indicators of distress than the native-born population. All refugee groups scored worse, but vast differences emerged in their mental health profiles. First-wave Vietnamese refugees approximated the levels of need of the general population, followed in order of distress by the ethnic Chinese, recently arrived Vietnamese, and Cambodians.[37]

Some of these differences were clearly attributable to the effect of social class because the rank order of groups along this variable is identical to that of mental health need: Chinese immigrants had by far the highest levels of education, professional training, and income; Cambodians had the lowest. Still, these and other controls did not entirely account for effects attributable to contexts of exit. Cambodians, in particular, had extraordinarily high levels of distress and dysfunction, with fully three-fourths of the sample requiring some form of mental health assistance. Posttraumatic stress disorders, including recurrent nightmares, intrusive flashbacks of traumatic experiences, depression, and "numbing," were far more common among this refugee minority than in almost any other group for which reliable data were available. This situation corresponds to the depth and intensity of the respective flight experiences. The same study reported an analysis of questions pertaining to contexts of exit that clearly differentiated the Cambodians from other refugee groups along variables reflecting extreme danger and privation, including the death or disappearance of friends and kin.[38]

Similar symptoms of posttraumatic stress disorder have also been reported among Salvadorans and Guatemalans who came to the United

States escaping civil war conditions in their respective countries. Although not recognized as refugees by the U.S. government, many Central Americans endured experiences prior to departure as traumatic as those reported by other sanctioned refugee groups.[39]

Additional evidence that escapees from war-torn contexts constitute a distinct class of immigrants from the point of view of psychological well-being comes from another study of refugees from Vietnam, Laos, and Cambodia resettled in the San Diego metropolitan area. Depressive symptoms among the various Indo-Chinese nationalities were found to be socially patterned, confirming findings from prior research. Significantly higher depression levels were found, for example, among women, respondents over fifty years of age, persons of rural background, the least educated and English proficient, and the unemployed. Lower depression levels were found for those who were married and who had more relatives and friends nearby, underscoring the buffering effects of coethnic social support. However, when all variables were combined in a predictive analysis of depression, reported experiences prior to and during escape emerged as the most powerful predictor. The stressful events that defined the contexts of exit of these refugee groups are summarized in table 22. The study concluded that people of the same social class emerged from the experience of flight in very different mental conditions, depending on what they had to witness and endure.[40]

Contexts of exit accounted, to a large extent, for the considerable differences in depression found among the various groups in the study: highest for Cambodians and Hmong and lowest for ethnic Chinese and first-wave Vietnamese arrivals. Table 23 presents the distribution of depressive symptoms for these refugee samples in 1983 and again in 1984, broken down by gender and education. Aside from national differences, it is worth noting that the level of demoralization, as measured by a widely used screening measure (the General Well-Being Scale) was much higher among the Indo-Chinese as a whole than among the general American population.[41] Twenty-six percent of Americans reported such symptoms; this rate was three times higher (78 percent) for the Indo-Chinese in 1983. A year later there was noticeable psychological improvement for these refugees, especially among men and the better educated, but their rate was still high (66 percent). In 1983, the most educated refugees actually showed higher levels of demoralization than all but those with no education at all, suggesting the psychological impact of status loss. However, by 1984, the best-educated group had made a remarkable turnaround, with the data showing the same linear

TABLE 22. CONTEXTS OF EXIT

Stressful life events in the post-1975 migration of Indochinese refugees resettled in San Diego County

Event	Hmong (N = 109) %	Cambodian (N = 120) %	Chinese (N = 114) %	Vietnamese (N = 157) %	Total (N = 500) %
Reported death of family members	59.6	65.8	32.5	39.5	48.6
Family member in prison in homeland	11.9	5.5	13.6	42.0	20.2
Fled alone, without immediate family	19.3	29.2	11.4	13.4	18.0
Gave bribes to exit	21.3	19.3	71.7	32.7	35.9
Assaulted in escape	25.7	25.2	36.8	30.6	29.6
Feared would be killed during escape	92.7	80.7	73.7	73.2	79.4
Spent over 2 years in refugee camps	72.6	75.9	29.3	22.1	47.7
Cannot communicate with family left behind (unknown whereabouts)	18.4	76.3	16.1	41.0	26.5

SOURCES: Rumbaut 1985, table 1; 1989, table 2.

NOTE: With the exception of the bottom row, which refers to personal situation in 1984, events reported took place after April 1975 and prior to arrival in the United States.

TABLE 23. PREVALENCE OF DEMORALIZATION AMONG INDO-CHINESE REFUGEES
IN SAN DIEGO COUNTY, BY ETHNIC GROUP, GENDER, AND LEVEL OF EDUCATION

| | Year | % Demoralization | | | | |
		Hmong (N = 109)	Cambodia (N = 120)	Chinese (N = 114)	Vietnamese (N = 157)	Total (N = 500)
Gender						
Male	1983	84.0	89.7	58.2	70.6	75.0
	1984	63.3	77.6	60.0	38.8	57.5
Female	1983	89.8	85.2	75.9	73.2	80.7
	1984	65.5	91.9	77.6	62.0	73.9
Education						
0–5 years	1983	89.2	84.9	64.3	70.6	81.0
	1984	69.6	89.2	78.0	70.6	77.2
6–11 years	1983	75.0	90.0	69.4	61.2	71.5
	1984	33.3	83.3	72.0	42.9	60.4
12+ years	1983	—	93.8	68.2	79.5	79.3
	1984	—	68.8	45.5	43.8	47.7
Total	1983	87.2	87.4	67.3	71.8	77.9
	1984	64.5	85.0	69.0	49.4	65.7

SOURCES: Rumbaut 1985, table 6; 1989, table 7.

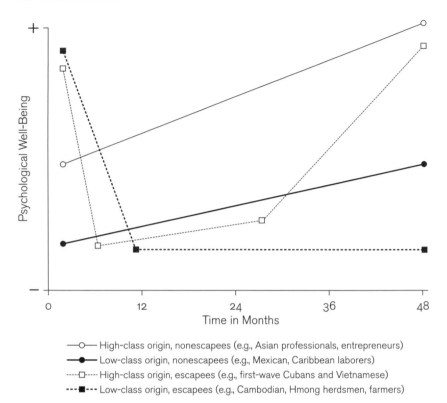

Figure 8. Mental health over time for different immigration categories

relationship between psychological well-being and education found in earlier research on social class and mental illness.[42]

What is the influence of time on the mental outlook of immigrants subject to traumatic departure experiences? The same San Diego study, which followed Indo-Chinese refugees over a twelve-month period, found that effects of such past experiences tend to decline, whereas those associated with their present condition become increasingly important. In other words, contexts of exit gradually lose significance to contexts of reception. However, the relationship between time and mental health is actually curvilinear. The first year in the United States is a relatively euphoric period, and the lowest depression scores and highest levels of well-being are usually reported during this time. By contrast, depression and demoralization hit their highest levels during the second year, a period that may be defined as one of "cultural shock." After the third year, a process of psychological rebounding seems to take place, as indicated by a significant decrease in depressive symptomatology for refugees who had been in the country for more than thirty-six months.[43]

This U-shaped temporal patterning—from elation to depression to recovery—has been observed in several other displaced minorities, such as Hungarians, Czechoslovakians, Lithuanians, Cubans, and Uganda Asians.[44] For each group, high satisfaction with their successful escape was followed by a psychological downturn marked by the renewed salience of past experiences. Time attenuates the severity of these symptoms, although it does not entirely erase differences among groups subject to varying degrees of predeparture stress. Figure 8 summarizes the theoretical relationship between time and mental health for different categories of the foreign-born. For "regular" immigrants, the relationship is expected to be positive and linear, with those of higher class backgrounds making a significantly more rapid psychological adjustment. For escapees from war-torn countries, the relationship is curvilinear, but higher social class again facilitates adjustment once the period of recuperation sets in. Chinese and Korean professional immigrants, on the one hand, and Cambodian and Hmong peasant refugees, on the other, illustrate the polar extremes of this theoretical continuum.

CONTEXTS OF INCORPORATION: MENTAL HEALTH AND HELP SEEKING

Unlike escapees, the subjective world of "regular" immigrants tends to be governed from the start by socioeconomic variables and by the context of reception. As seen in prior chapters, Mexicans in the United States are the prototypical example of manual labor immigration because the majority come from modest educational and social origins. Two large studies of Mexican immigrants in California, conducted by William Vega and his associates, illustrate the effect of diverse conditions in places of destination. The first involved a survey of a rural sample of Mexican farmworkers in the San Joaquin Valley, who numbered more than one million during the peak of the state's agricultural season. These migrant workers were found to be at much higher risk for depression than the general population, resembling other low-status groups in levels of symptomatology. The highest distress scores were observed for young males and for middle-aged farmworkers of both genders. Their rural context and marginality effectively ruled out access to professional help for mental health problems.[45]

A second study surveyed a sample of 1,825 Mexican immigrant women in San Diego. Depressive symptoms in this urban sample were high, with 41 percent of the women meeting the case criteria for depression, as opposed to the usual 16 to 18 percent found in the general U.S. population. Mexican women were not homogeneous in this respect, however; depression scores declined significantly for married respondents and for those with higher family incomes and increased among the poorly educated and the unemployed. As with refugees, time since arrival led to a slow, gradual decline in symptoms, a pattern that supports the theoretical relationship portrayed in figure 8. Presence of friends and kin and perceived difficulty of reuniting with them were also significant predictors of mental health, indicating once again the importance of coethnic networks among immigrants.[46]

The process of incorporation affects not only prospects for psychological well-being but also the probability that those in need will seek and find professional help. This aspect was brought to light in a comparison of Cubans coming to the United States during the 1980 Mariel exodus and Haitians arriving in Florida during the same period. As seen in prior chapters, the U.S. government refused to grant asylum to either group, assigning to them instead the label of "entrant, status pending." Despite this similarity, significant differences between these groups are evident in individual characteristics and in contexts of reception. Table 24 presents results of a large survey of these groups conducted in 1987. Despite comparably low levels of education, Mariel entrants were found to earn significantly higher incomes than Haitians after seven years in the United States, but this economic advantage did not translate into superior psychological well-being among the Cubans. On the contrary, as the bottom rows of table 24 indicate, the Mariel group exhibited consistently higher levels of psychological disorder than the Haitians.

On the surface, differences in indicators of various mental disorders between the two groups can be seen as a classic instance of the "immigrant versus refugee" distinction. However, Haitians in this sample arrived in the United States after eluding a repressive regime and risking a seven-hundred-mile journey aboard barely seaworthy crafts. Their context of exit seems every bit as traumatic as that confronting many Indo-Chinese refugees. Mariel Cubans came as part of an organized flow, in boats chartered in Florida for this purpose and with the consent of the Cuban government. Differences between the two entrant groups can reasonably be attributed less to the trauma of departure than to different levels of selectivity: Haitians were a self-selected group that willingly undertook a perilous journey; Mariel Cubans left because

TABLE 24. SOCIODEMOGRAPHIC AND MENTAL
HEALTH CHARACTERISTICS OF CUBAN AND
HAITIAN ENTRANTS IN MIAMI, 1987

Characteristic	Cubans (N = 452) %	Haitians (N = 500) %
Male	59.3	50.2
Married	42.7	60.2
8 or more years of education	52.6	50.0
No income	26.5	39.7
Income above $8,500	43.1	21.7
Major depressive disorder[a]	7.7	4.0
Anxiety disorder[a]	5.9	4.2
Alcohol disorder[a]	5.4	0.6
Psychotic symptoms[b]	8.4	6.0

SOURCE: Portes, Kyle, and Eaton 1992.

[a] DIS/DSM-III scores based on last six months' symptom prevalence.
[b] Screening items based on last six months' symptom prevalence.

relatives came to take them away or because the Cuban government encouraged their departure.[47]

The positive selectivity of the Haitians did not translate into a more favorable situation in the United States. As shown, their average income level after seven years of U.S. residence was both low and inferior to that of Mariel Cubans. Table 25 indicates that practically no one in the Haitian sample sought professional help to cope with psychological problems of adaptation to the new environment. Almost 13 percent of Cuban entrants sought such help, a figure twelve times higher than that among Haitians and significantly larger than the rate in comparable samples of the native-born population.[48] Need accounts partially for the difference because depression and symptoms of distress were far more common among Mariel Cubans. However, this explanation is insufficient because such symptoms were also present among Haitians without generating commensurate help seeking.

The difference is best explained by the unequal contexts of reception awaiting the two groups. Haitians came to a place where no one spoke their language and where their own group represented a poor and discriminated minority. Mariel Cubans were received into the diversified ethnic community created by earlier arrivals. By the time of their arrival, the Cuban enclave in Miami contained an extensive network of

TABLE 25. HELP SEEKING FOR MENTAL HEALTH
PROBLEMS AND FACILITATIONAL FACTORS
Cuban and Haitian entrants, 1987

	Cubans (N = 452) %	Haitians (N = 500) %
Source of help		
General medical practitioner	3.1	0.2
Psychiatric clinic	7.5	0.2
Social worker or other human service worker	2.0	0.2
Facilitational factors		
Knew where to obtain treatment for a mental or emotional problem	70.0	36.0
Had health insurance or other coverage that pays for treatment of mental health problems	46.0	13.0
Knew someone who was treated by a mental health professional	70.0	15.0

SOURCE: Eaton and Garrison 1988, tables 6 and 7.

clinics and other medical services.[49] Spanish was spoken as a matter of course in these clinics; hence, it was not difficult for new arrivals to obtain both information and assistance. The difference is illustrated in the bottom rows of table 25, which indicate that, in comparison with Haitians, Mariel entrants were twice as knowledgeable about where to seek help for emotional problems, three times more likely to have health insurance or other medical coverage, and almost six times as likely to know others who had received professional mental health assistance in Miami.

ACCULTURATION AND ITS DISCONTENTS

In the past, cultural assimilation or acculturation has frequently been assumed to have beneficial consequences for both economic progress and psychological well-being. Just as better knowledge of the language and relevant occupational skills should propel immigrants and their descendants in the labor market, so should leaving behind the remnants of old cultures and fully embracing the new one eliminate much of their distress.[50] Although these assumptions seem plausible, recent findings not only cast doubt on them but turn them on their head—and focus attention on a question that is often taken for granted: assimilation to what?

GENERATIONAL PATTERNS: ADULTS

A study of Mexican immigrants, native-born Mexican Americans, and non-Hispanic whites in Santa Clara County (Silicon Valley) found the usual positive correlation between immigration and depressive symptomatology. However, although immigrants had a significantly higher prevalence of depression, the density of their "Mexican heritage"— as measured by the number of ties to Mexican-born relatives—did not increase these symptoms. On the contrary, the study found that a pervasive sense of cultural heritage was *positively* related to mental health and social well-being among both immigrants and native Mexican Americans.[51]

An analysis of data from the Epidemiological Catchment Area (ECA) study in Los Angeles examined in greater detail the effects of acculturation on mental health in a sample of 1,243 Mexican immigrants and Mexican Americans. Acculturation was measured by an extensive standardized scale with high levels of reliability.[52] No relationship between acculturation and prevalence of disorder was found for major depression, obsessive-compulsive disorder, or panic disorder. Significant associations were found for four other types of disorder (alcohol and drug abuse or dependence, phobia, and antisocial personality), even after controlling for age and sex. However, the associations ran contrary to conventional expectations. That is, the *higher* the level of acculturation (or "Americanization"), the greater the prevalence of these disorders.[53]

Other results from the same study confirm this surprising finding. Disorders were significantly more prevalent among U.S.-born Mexican Americans than among immigrants, and the latter had a lower prevalence of major depression and dysthymia than natives as a whole, despite the immigrants' lower incomes and educations. In a separate analysis, the only significant difference found within the Mexican-born subsample was for drug abuse/dependence, with higher rates among the "highly acculturated." In attempting to explain this finding, authors of the study noted the ready availability of drugs in Los Angeles, where their recreational use tends to be condoned among large segments of the native population. Less acculturated immigrants were not only less exposed to these practices but also under the influence of the stronger family ties, social controls, and traditional values associated with their cultural heritage.[54]

Similarly, a 1995–1996 survey of adults of Mexican origin, eighteen to fifty-nine years old, in Fresno County, California, used the World Health Organization's Composite International Diagnostic Interview (CIDI) to estimate rates of psychiatric disorders, permitting comparisons of rates found in California with those of the general U.S. population and survey results in Mexico City.[55] The Fresno study reported lower rates of psychiatric disorders for Mexican immigrants than for U.S.-born Mexican Americans; moreover, immigrants with fewer years in the United States had lower rates than those with longer duration of residency. In turn, the lower rates for recent immigrants were similar to those reported in Mexico City, whereas U.S.-born persons of Mexican origin had similar total lifetime rates as the general U.S. population. Such findings reverse the common depiction of the unacculturated immigrant as an intrinsically pathological figure that prevailed for a century before World War II.

In fact, recent research has shown a striking relationship between acculturation and risk behaviors, which in turn are associated with poorer health as well as mental heath outcomes. For example, data from the Hispanic Health and Nutrition Examination Survey (HHANES), with an exceptionally large regional sample, indicated that marijuana use is five to eight times higher among highly acculturated Mexican Americans compared with those who are not, excluding other sociodemographic factors. Studies based on the HHANES and more recent survey data have also documented adverse effects of acculturation among Hispanic groups with respect to cocaine use, alcohol consumption, and, among immigrant women, use of cigarettes and poorer dietary intake.[56]

Recently immigrated Mexican women have very low rates of alcohol abuse or dependence, but the prevalence of any alcohol abuse or dependence among U.S.-born women of Mexican origin is approximately five times greater than that for immigrant women. Among men, the prevalence rate is approximately two times greater for the U.S.-born than that for immigrants. Moreover, whereas in the general U.S. population heavy drinking and alcohol-related social problems tend to peak at ages eighteen to twenty-nine and to decline thereafter, these problems continue among Mexican-origin men in the United States at older ages.[57]

Subsequent research has focused on the co-occurrence (or "comorbidity") of alcohol, drug, and non-substance-use psychiatric disorders meeting established (i.e., *Diagnostic and Statistical Manual*) diagnostic criteria for mood disorder, anxiety disorder, or antisocial personality disorder. One study with a sample of Mexican-origin adults in central California found that the prevalence of substance use disorders, consisting of alcohol or drug abuse or dependence, was highest among U.S.-born males (36 percent), followed by U.S.-born females (18 percent), immigrant males (17 percent), and immigrant females (2 percent). The prevalence of mood disorders ranged from a high of 22 percent among U.S.-born Mexican-origin women, to 15 percent for U.S.-born men, 9 percent for immigrant women, and a low of 7 percent for immigrant men. The study found co-occurring lifetime rates of alcohol or other drug disorder with non-substance-use psychiatric disorder of 12 percent for the U.S.-born and 3 percent for immigrants.[58]

These results suggest that acculturation is not the unqualified good it is commonly believed to be. The complex character of contemporary American society, the stress and obstacles confronted by its poorer classes, and the ready availability of drugs and alcohol as means to cope with these difficulties are arguably responsible for the deteriorating psychosocial and health profile of foreign-origin groups with greater length of U.S. residence. We review next additional evidence supporting the point that acculturation is less than an unmitigated good and will return to it when we examine, in greater detail, the process of adaptation of the second generation in chapter 8.

ACCULTURATION AND THE "EPIDEMIOLOGICAL PARADOX"

Related results from the HHANES had earlier shown that the rate of low-birth-weight infants born to second-generation Mexican American women was two to four times higher than that among comparable first-generation immigrant women, despite the fact that the latter had a lower socioeconomic status, a higher percentage of mothers more than thirty-five years of age, and less adequate prenatal care.[59] Similarly, using data from the Fragile Families and Child Well-Being Study conducted in more than twenty cities across the United States, a recent analysis found that nearly 90 percent of low-income Mexican immigrant mothers breastfed their infants, compared with two-thirds of second-generation and just over half of third-generation women of Mexican origin. The study found that as acculturation (measured using a seven-item scale) increased, the probability of breastfeeding decreased —along with the health benefits associated with it.[60]

This pattern of superior infant health outcomes found among less acculturated immigrants, despite their socioeconomic disadvantages and high-risk profiles, has been referred to as an "epidemiological paradox" because it goes against conventional expectations, but it has now been observed systematically among a wide range of other foreign-born groups from coast to coast.[61]

In Massachusetts, a study of 817 low-income black women delivering at Boston City Hospital found significant differences in health behaviors and birth outcomes between natives and immigrants—the latter mostly from Haiti, Jamaica, and other Caribbean and African countries. Compared with the U.S.-born, immigrant women had better prepregnancy nutrition; were far less likely to use cigarettes, marijuana, alcohol, cocaine, or opiates during pregnancy; and gave birth to healthier babies.[62] In Illinois, foreign-born Mexican and Central American mothers residing in very low-income census tracts were similarly found to have much better pregnancy outcomes than either Puerto Rican or other U.S.-born Hispanics.[63] And in California, a study of all live births (270,000) and infant deaths over the course of a decade in the San Diego metropolitan area revealed that the infant mortality rate was lowest for the Vietnamese (5.5 per 1,000 live births) and Cambodians (5.8), followed by the Chinese, Japanese, and Filipinos (7.0 each), and Mexican Americans (7.3)—mostly immigrant groups—but notably higher for both native whites (8.0) and African Americans (16.3).[64]

Research with national-level data confirms these findings. By 1995, foreign-born mothers accounted for nearly a fifth of all U.S. births (18 percent), but over four-fifths (82 percent) of all Asian-origin babies and nearly two-thirds (62 percent) of all Hispanic-origin babies were born to immigrant women in the United States. In that decade, a comprehensive study used the Linked Birth/Infant Death national data sets to examine the birth outcomes of immigrant versus native-born mothers among ten main groups—including the Chinese, Filipinos, Japanese, Mexicans, Puerto Ricans (island- vs. mainland-born), Cubans, Central and South Americans, and non-Hispanic blacks and whites. The babies of immigrant mothers had lower rates of prematurity, birth weight, and infant mortality than those of U.S.-born mothers. For each of the main groups, native-born mothers were also more likely than foreign-born mothers to be young (less than twenty) and single and to have smoked cigarettes during their pregnancies. In multivariate models, the gap in birth outcomes by nativity and ethnicity was attenuated, but the offspring of immigrant mothers retained a health advantage over those of native-born mothers.[65]

A study in San Diego County sought to unravel the reasons for this epidemiological paradox by examining an in-depth data set drawn from a Comprehensive Perinatal Program (CPP) that provided prenatal care services to low-income pregnant women. Specifically, native-born women (who in this sample were mainly non-Hispanic whites) were significantly more likely than immigrant women (who in this sample were mainly Mexicans and Southeast Asians) to (1) have higher levels of education, employment, and per capita income; (2) be taller, heavier, and gain more weight during their pregnancies; (3) have had fewer live births and more abortions; (4) have diets lower in fruits and cereals and higher in fats and dairy products; (5) report more medical conditions, especially venereal disease and genitourinary problems; (6) smoke, abuse drugs and alcohol, and be at risk for AIDS; (7) have a personal history of significant psychosocial problems, including having been a victim of child abuse and spousal abuse; (8) have generally poorer pregnancy outcomes—which is why infant health outcomes seemed to worsen as the levels of education, English literacy, and general assimilation of the mother increased. Relative to the foreign-born, the comparative socioeconomic advantages of U.S.-born women were trumped by biomedical, nutritional, and psychosocial disadvantages.[66]

GENERATIONAL PATTERNS: ADOLESCENTS

Perhaps at no stage of life are assimilative processes more intensely experienced, or assimilative outcomes more sharply exhibited, than during the formative years of adolescence. A new source of panel data—the National Longitudinal Study of Adolescent Health (Add Health)—has facilitated the investigation of intra- and intergenerational differences in health characteristics and risk behaviors among a nationally representative sample of adolescents. The first wave of the study surveyed more than twenty thousand adolescents enrolled in grades 7 to 12 in 1995. An analysis focusing on three generational groups—first (immigrant children), second (native-born children of immigrant parents), and third or higher (native-born of native-born parents) generations—found that for virtually every empirical indicator, second-generation youth had poorer physical health outcomes and were more prone to engage in risk behavior than foreign-born youth. For example, second-generation youth were more likely than the first generation to have missed school due to a health or emotional problem in the previous month, to be obese, and to have engaged in deviant behaviors (delinquency, violence, and substance abuse). Outcomes for the third or higher generation varied significantly across race and ethnic groups, but in general, native minorities reported the poorest health and the highest levels of risk behaviors.[67]

Among foreign-born youth, the longer their time in and exposure to the United States, the poorer were their health outcomes and the greater was their propensity to engage in each of the risk behaviors measured. A breakdown by national origin for the most sizable groups—from Mexico, Cuba, Puerto Rico (island-born vs. mainland-born), Central and South America, China, the Philippines, Vietnam, other Asian countries, Africa and the Afro-Caribbean, Europe, and Canada—generally confirmed the intergenerational patterns, with outcomes worsening the further removed from the immigrant generation, most strongly seen among Mexicans and Filipinos.

Third-generation youth were the least likely to live in intact families and the most likely to live with a single parent. Controlling in multivariate analyses for socioeconomic status, family structure, degree of parental supervision, and neighborhood contexts actually increased the protective aspects of the immigrant first generation on both health and risk behavior indices. In this analysis, every first-generation nationality had significantly fewer health problems and engaged in fewer risk behaviors than the referent group of native non-Hispanic whites.

This consistent set of findings indicates, once again, the dangers of full acculturation to an increasingly complex and permissive society. A more evenly paced process in which select aspects of the immigrant culture are preserved as assimilation proceeds may offer a better prognosis in terms of health and socioeconomic adaptation than unqualified embracement of what American society has to offer today. We will return to this theme under the label *selective acculturation* when examining the adaptation process of the second generation in a coming chapter.

IMMIGRATION AND INCARCERATION

The present era of mass immigration has coincided with an era of mass imprisonment in the United States. During this period, the number of adults incarcerated in federal or state prisons or local jails has skyrocketed, quadrupling from just over 500,000 in 1980 to more than 2.1 million in 2005.[68] The U.S. incarceration rate has become the highest of any country in the world. The vast majority of those behind bars are young men between eighteen and thirty-nine, and they are overwhelmingly high school dropouts. An estimated 80 percent of them violated drug or alcohol laws, were high at the time they committed their crimes, stole property to buy drugs, or have a history of drug and alcohol abuse and addiction—or some combination of those characteristics.[69] Among some racial minorities, becoming a prisoner has become a modal life event in early adulthood. As Pettit and Western have noted, a black male high school dropout born in the late 1960s had a nearly 60 percent chance of serving time in prison by the end of the 1990s, and recent birth cohorts of black men are more likely to have prison records than military records or bachelor's degrees.[70]

Inasmuch as criminological theories predict higher rates of crime and incarceration for young adult males from minority groups with low educational attainment, it follows that immigrants, particularly poor labor migrants and refugees, should have higher incarceration rates than natives. Those born in Mexico—who comprise fully a third of all immigrant men between eighteen and thirty-nine—could be expected to have the highest rates, given their very low average education. That hypothesis is examined empirically in table 26. Data from the 2000 U.S. Census (5% Public Use Microdata Sample) are used to measure the institutionalization rates of males, eighteen to thirty-nine, among whom the vast majority of the institutionalized are in correctional facilities.[71]

As table 26 shows, 3 percent of the 45.2 million males in this age group were in federal or state prisons or local jails at the time of the 2000 census. However, the incarceration rate of the U.S.-born (3.51 percent) was four times the rate of the foreign-born (0.86 percent). The latter was half the 1.71 percent rate for native white men and thirteen times less than the 11.6 percent incarceration rate for native black men. This pattern is observable among every ethnic group without exception. For every immigrant group, the longer they had resided in the United States, the higher their incarceration rates.

Among Latin American immigrants, the least educated groups had the lowest incarceration rates: Salvadorans and Guatemalans (0.52 percent) and Mexicans (0.70 percent). However, these rates increase significantly for their U.S.-born coethnics. For Mexicans, for example, the incarceration rate increases to 5.9 percent among the U.S.-born. Similar results were found among Asian groups. For the Vietnamese, the incarceration rate increases from 0.46 percent among the foreign-born to 5.6

TABLE 26. RATES OF INCARCERATION FOR MALES EIGHTEEN
TO THIRTY-NINE YEARS OLD IN THE UNITED STATES, 2000

Ethnicity	Total males ages 18–39[a] N	Total incarcerated %	Nativity Foreign-born %	Nativity U.S.-born %	If foreign-born: High school graduate? Yes %	If foreign-born: High school graduate? No %	If U.S.-born: High school graduate? Yes %	If U.S.-born: High school graduate? No %
Total United States	45,200,417	3.04	0.86	3.51	0.57	1.31	2.23	9.76
Asian								
Indian	393,621	0.22	0.11	0.99	0.09	0.29	0.48	6.69
Chinese[b]	439,086	0.28	0.18	0.65	0.07	0.91	0.36	4.71
Korean	184,238	0.38	0.26	0.93	0.24	0.58	0.82	2.05
Filipino	297,011	0.64	0.38	1.22	0.23	1.73	0.81	4.73
Vietnamese	229,735	0.89	0.46	5.60	0.32	0.85	2.85	16.18
Lao, Hmong, Cambodian	89,864	1.65	0.92	7.26	0.52	1.72	5.80	9.11
Latin American								
Salvadoran, Guatemalan	433,828	0.68	0.52	3.01	0.43	0.58	2.16	4.70
Colombian, Ecuadorian, Peruvian	283,599	1.07	0.80	2.37	0.54	1.54	1.58	7.01
Mexican	5,017,431	2.71	0.70	5.90	0.70	0.70	3.95	10.12
Dominican	182,303	2.76	2.51	3.71	1.24	3.99	1.82	8.67
Cuban	213,302	3.01	2.22	4.20	1.78	3.18	2.90	11.32
Puerto Rican[c]	642,106	5.06	4.55	5.37	1.96	9.01	2.66	11.54
Other								
White, non-Hispanic	29,014,261	1.66	0.57	1.71	0.43	1.63	1.23	4.76
Black, non-Hispanic	5,453,546	10.87	2.47	11.61	1.32	7.08	7.64	22.25

SOURCE: 2000 U.S. Census, 5% Public Use Microdata Sample.

percent among the U.S.-born; for Laotians and Cambodians, the rate moves up from 0.92 percent among the foreign-born to 7.26 percent among the U.S.-born, the highest figure for any group, except for native blacks.

For all ethnic groups, as expected, the risk of imprisonment is highest for men who are high school dropouts compared with those who are high school graduates. However, as table 26 shows, the incarceration gap by education is much wider for the native-born. Among them, 9.8 percent of all male dropouts were in jail or prison in 2000, compared with 2.2 percent among those who graduated from high school. But among the foreign-born, the incarceration gap by education is much narrower: only 1.3 percent of immigrant men who were high school dropouts were incarcerated, compared with 0.57 percent of those with at least a high school diploma. The advantage for immigrants holds when broken down by education for every ethnic group. Indeed, native-born high school graduates have a higher rate of incarceration than the foreign-born who are not high school graduates (2.2 percent to 1.3 percent).

These results from the 2000 census confirm an earlier study by Butcher and Piehl based on data from the 1980 and 1990 censuses.[72] Taken together, they provide consistent and compelling evidence over a period of three decades, raising significant questions about conventional theories of acculturation and assimilation. These theories continue to project an overly optimistic outlook of how the acculturation process takes place and often make it a precondition for advancement in American society.[73] The finding that incarceration rates are much lower among immigrant men than the national norm, despite their lower levels of education and greater poverty, but increase significantly among the second generation suggests that the process of "Americanization" can lead to downward mobility and greater risk of involvement with the criminal justice system for a significant segment of this population. In chapter 7, we will turn to an examination of the process of language acculturation, and, in chapter 8, we will focus on the second generation and the process of segmented assimilation to different sectors of American society.

ACCULTURATION AND PERCEPTIONS OF DISCRIMINATION

The fact that rapid acculturation does not necessarily lead to conventionally anticipated outcomes is further illustrated by research on other aspects of the immigrants' subjective world. A comparative study of

TABLE 27. PERCEPTIONS OF DISCRIMINATION AMONG
CUBAN AND MEXICAN IMMIGRANTS, 1973–1979

| | "Is there discrimination against Cubans/Mexicans in the United States?"[a] | | | Total | |
	Yes %	No %	Don't know %	%	N
Cubans					
1973[b]	4.6	69.0	26.5	100.0	590
1976	26.3	67.8	5.9	100.0	426
1979	26.4	62.5	11.2	100.0	413
Mexicans					
1973[b]	21.7	61.5	16.8	100.0	816
1976	40.0	48.3	11.7	100.0	437
1979	36.3	53.8	9.9	100.0	455

SOURCE: Portes and Bach 1985, table 92.

[a] Question phrased according to respondent's nationality.
[b] Year of arrival for legal residence in the United States.

Cuban and Mexican immigrants, described in earlier chapters, collected extensive data on the respondents' perceptions of American society, perceptions of discrimination against their own group, and patterns of social relations within and beyond their respective ethnic communities. Although this study was conducted more than two decades ago, subsequent research has generally confirmed its principal findings. As shown in table 27, perceptions of discrimination increased significantly during the first three years of U.S. residence and remained essentially constant during the next three years. The increase was particularly sharp among Cubans, almost none of whom had reported discrimination at the time of arrival but whose views turned decidedly more negative later on.[74]

The same study developed a scale of perceptions of American society, including perceptions of discrimination, with higher scores indicating a more critical stance toward the new social environment. Items forming this scale and indicators of its reliability are presented in table 28. Conventional theory would lead to the expectation that higher education, knowledge of English, information about U.S. society, and related variables should be negatively associated with scores on this scale: more acculturated immigrants should have more positive views of the host society.[75]

The bottom panel of table 28 presents the relevant correlations for Cuban and Mexican immigrants after three and six years of U.S. residence. The coefficients are small in size, but they run, without exception, in the direction *opposite* to expectations. That is, the more educated, proficient in English, and informed immigrants are, the more critical their views and the greater their perceptions of discrimination. The same is true for those with more modern orientations and with longer periods of U.S. residence. The fact that the same results hold for two independent samples at two different points in time makes them compelling.

The meaning of these findings is not immediately clear. Do they signify that more acculturated immigrants are more alienated and hostile? Table 29 presents results that contradict this conclusion by showing high levels of satisfaction with their present lives and commitment to stay in the United States among both immigrant samples. Moreover, life satisfaction, intentions to remain in the country, and plans to acquire U.S. citizenship all increased over time. Hence, it is not widespread alienation that leads to more critical views. A better conclusion is that the latter represent a more realistic appraisal of the immigrants' new social environment. In other words, the more educated and informed immigrants become, the more they come to understand American society as it actually is, including its various shortcomings and the lingering reality of discrimination. This awareness may not detract from their decision to stay, but it is certainly at variance with the starry-eyed, idealized image often held by new arrivals.

Results of these studies show that acculturation is not a simple solution to the traumas of immigration because it can be a traumatic process itself. Among lower-class immigrants and their children, premature acculturation may lead to a higher incidence of mental illness and drug dependence as they lose their sense of identity and traditional social controls while being exposed to deviant practices in their new environment. For the better educated, acculturation implies shedding idealized perceptions and confronting the host society's complex and sometimes harsh realities. The best way of dealing with the challenge of acculturation is apparently to balance its progress with retention of select elements of the immigrants' culture and a parallel reaffirmation of primary social ties within the ethnic community.[76]

TABLE 28. PERCEPTIONS OF AMERICAN SOCIETY AND ITS CORRELATES
Cuban and Mexican immigrants

Scale components	Mexicans r_{it}^a	Cubans r_{it}
There is racial discrimination in economic opportunities in the United States.	.455	.431
American way of life weakens family ties.	.394	.359
Relations with Anglo-Americans are cold.	.596	.563
Relations with Anglo-Americans are distant.	.572	.587
Relations with Anglo-Americans are hostile.	.528	.533
Anglo-Americans discriminate against Mexicans/Cubans.	.542	.533
In relation to Mexicans/Cubans, Anglo-Americans feel superior.	.485	.495
Scale reliability[b]	.821	.830

Correlation with positive perceptions of U.S. society	Mexicans		Cubans	
	1976	1979	1976	1979
Education on arrival	−.09*	−.10*	−.10*	−.21**
Education in the United States	−.13*	−.14*	−.15**	−.16**
Knowledge of English on arrival[c]	−.10*	−.10*	−.15**	−.15**
Knowledge of English at present[c]	−.12*	−.23**	−.25**	−.22**
Information about U.S. society[d]	−.04	−.19**	−.22**	−.13*
Modernity[e]	−.22**	−.37**	−.13*	−.20**
Length of U.S. residence	−.18**	−.19**	—[f]	—[f]

SOURCE: Portes and Bach 1985, tables 94, 95, and 96.

[a] Correlation between item and total scale corrected for autocorrelation, 1979.

[b] Unit-weighted maximum likelihood omega coefficients, 1979.

[c] Measured by a nine-item objective test of English comprehension. Scale reliabilities (omega) are .90 or above for both samples.

[d] Measured by a nine-item test of factual knowledge about political and economic matters. Scale reliabilities are .673 (Mexicans) and .773 (Cubans).

[e] Scores in Inkeles and Smith's OM-5 Scale of Psycho-social Modernity.

[f] Length of U.S. residence in the Cuban sample is constant.

*Probability of chance relationship is less than .05.

**Probability of chance relationship is less than .01.

TABLE 29. SATISFACTION AND PLANS, CUBAN
AND MEXICAN IMMIGRANTS, 1976 AND 1979

	Mexicans		Cubans	
	1976 (N = 439) %	1979 (N = 454) %	1976 (N = 427) %	1979 (N = 413) %
Dissatisfied with present life in the United States	1.1	0.4	3.0	0.9
Satisfied or very satisfied	79.1	78.8	81.3	93.7
Plans to stay permanently in the United States	85.2	88.3	88.5	95.9
Plans to become U.S. citizen	67.6	71.0	77.2	85.7

SOURCE: Portes and Bach 1985, tables 86 and 87.

CONCLUSION: THE MAJOR DETERMINANTS OF IMMIGRANT PSYCHOLOGY

Contexts of exit have been shown to have a decisive effect on the early adaptation process of certain foreign minorities. However, over time, contexts of reception take over, influencing both the mental health and the perceptual outlooks of immigrants. Acculturation per se is not the decisive variable in this situation because, depending on specific circumstances, it can lead to widely different outcomes. The real question is *what kind* of acculturation do immigrants undergo, and the long-term answer appears to be determined by two main variables: the receptivity found by newcomers in American society and their class of origin.

As seen earlier in the chapter, the pivotal role of social class in immigrants' psychological adjustment has been recognized at least since World War II. What is different at present is the heterogeneous contexts of reception with which social class must interact, far more diversified than at the time Srole and his associates conducted their study. In chapter 4, we saw that this diversity is determined by a variety of factors, including the policies of the U.S. government, the role of employers, and the character of preexisting ethnic communities. For purposes of simplification, the various contexts of reception are summarized as a continuum in figure 9. *Disadvantaged* contexts are those in which governments take a dim view of the newcomers, the native population discriminates them, and the ethnic community either does not exist or is too feeble to generate autonomous employment opportunities. At

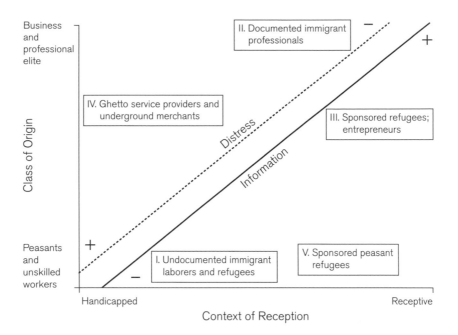

Figure 9. Determinants of immigrant psychological orientations and types

the polar opposite, *receptive* contexts are those in which government takes an active role in facilitating the adaptation of new arrivals, and their own community is sufficiently developed to further their economic prospects.[77]

The conceptual space thus created helps define the objective conditions different immigrant groups confront today, as well as the probable subjective outlook of their individual members. Figure 9 illustrates this range of possibilities on the basis of five ideal-typical instances. Unsanctioned lower-class escapees from war-torn countries and undocumented immigrant laborers tend to approach one extreme in which the depression and distress associated with poverty are compounded by vulnerability and frequent disorientation in a foreign environment. Networks of kin and friends provide the only social shelter under these circumstances, but they are frequently formed by people in the same precarious condition as the recipients themselves. Knowledge of the new social environment is very limited, and there is a good chance for downward assimilation—especially for their U.S.-born or U.S.-reared children—because crime and drugs are a constant presence in the dilapidated neighborhoods where immigrants often settle.

At the other extreme, sanctioned upper-class refugees coming in the initial waves of a political exodus tend to undergo a fairly rapid process of psychosocial adaptation. Theirs is, by comparison, a "golden exile" in which the losses and fears experienced before and during departure are compensated for by a favorable public reception and better chances to rebuild their lives in the United States.[78] Elite refugees, like professional immigrants, tend to develop a highly informed view of American society—including a realistic awareness of its major problems—and, simultaneously, to report high levels of satisfaction. Although their conditions of exit are quite different, the long-term prognosis for upper-class refugees and professional immigrants is similar in the relative scarcity of severe mental symptoms and in their effective adaptation to the new environment.

Less common is the situation of former high-status persons who join an unauthorized refugee or labor flow. Foreign professionals who find themselves in these situations often become ghetto service providers, practicing their careers clandestinely among their own group or other downtrodden minorities. A second common niche is as "middleman" merchants and contractors in underground economic activities. Latin and Asian professionals who arrive in the United States illegally or overstay their visas approximate this situation.[79] Because of their small numbers and clandestine status, little is known about the mental health and subjective outlook of these groups.

More familiar is the case of lower-class persons who arrive at the tail end of a sanctioned refugee flow. Mariel Cubans, Vietnamese boat people, and Cambodian and Laotian arrivals are among the best-known examples. As the quotes at the start of this chapter suggest, legal arrival does not spare these refugees the traumas associated with their past experience. However, they at least have ready access to governmental assistance. Community networks also provide opportunities for employment and entrepreneurship, especially when prior arrivals have developed a viable ethnic economy.[80] The more favorable prognosis for these groups due to a more receptive context is illustrated by the significant differences in mental help seeking and in access to existing facilities between Mariel Cubans and Haitians, despite the apparently worse psychological condition of the former.

The ideal-typical instances represented in figure 9 do not, of course, exhaust the range of possible situations in which immigrants can find themselves today or their psychosocial consequences. Nor do they provide a final statement on the groups that most closely approximate each case because many pieces of factual information are still missing. The typology highlights instead the diversity of contemporary immigration and the principal dimensions along which psychological variation has taken place. For all immigrants, America is a foreign world, but the hues in which this world is painted and the emotional and behavioral reactions that it elicits vary widely under the influence of forces often removed from the knowledge, the will, and the power of newcomers.

7
Learning the Ropes
Language and Education

I n 2005, the U.S. National Spelling Bee champ was a thirteen-year-old boy in a California public school, Anurag Kashyap, who beat 272 spellers from around the country after correctly spelling *appoggiatura*, a type of musical note. The next three finishers—Aliya Deri, Samir Patel, and Rajiv Tarigopula—were, like Anurag, children of Indian immigrants. It has become commonplace for children of immigrants to dominate this national English language competition, in particular those of Indian ancestry, who won the top prize in five of the previous seven years. When Indian-born Chicago schoolboy Balu Natarajan, who spoke Tamil at home, won the 1985 contest, he became an overnight Indian sensation—and twenty years later his name still resonates among Indian Americans, who have tried to emulate his success.[1] The competition is tough—and the toughest competitors are disproportionately drawn from immigrant families.

In 1996, the top prize went to Wendy Guey, twelve, whose family had immigrated from Taiwan and settled in West Palm Beach, Florida. The 1988 winner, Indian-born Rageshree Ramachandran, correctly spelled *elegiacal* to beat out runner-up Victor Wang, a Chinese American. Three years later, she won one of the top ten honors in the national Westinghouse (now Intel) Science Talent Search, the oldest and most prestigious high school science competition in the United States. Seven of the top ten award winners at the 2004 Intel Science Talent Search were immigrant children or children of immigrants. The pattern is evident in other fields as well: a recent winner of the National Geography Bee was Seyi Fayanju, twelve, of Verona, New Jersey, the U.S.-born son of two Nigerian immigrants, who prepared by spending many hours reading his parents' encyclopedias.[2]

Less sanguine than these popular portrayals of success are the findings of investigations that receive less attention in the mainstream media. For example, an affiliate of the National Coalition of Advocates for Students interviewed several hundred immigrant students in public schools in California about their experiences. Some excerpts are presented here:

> A twelfth-grade Lao Mien boy who immigrated at age fourteen told an interviewer: "The school was so big! There was no one who could speak Mien and explain to me. My uncle had told me if I needed any help to go to the Dean. My teacher asked me something and I didn't understand her. So I just said 'Dean, Dean' because I needed help. That is how I got my American name. She was asking me 'What is your name?' Now everybody calls me Dean. Now it is funny, but it is also sad. My name comes from not knowing what was going on."[3]

> A ninth-grade Filipino girl who immigrated with her parents declared: "Our parents don't come [to school functions] because they don't know any English. I don't even tell them when they are supposed to come. They dress so different and I don't want our parents to come because the others will laugh at them and tease us. We are ashamed."[4]

> In an elementary school in San Francisco, a teacher was playing "hangman" with her class as a spelling lesson. One "Limited-English-Proficient" (LEP) student, a Cambodian refugee, bursts into tears and becomes hysterical. Later, through an interpreter, the teacher learns that the student had witnessed the hanging of her father in Cambodia.[5]

> An eleventh-grade Mexican boy who immigrated at age eleven: "I don't have immigration papers and I feel afraid of getting caught. I work at night so it's hard to study. All I want is for my family to stay together and not have problems with la Migra. My uncle says we may not be able to work anymore and may have to go somewhere else. My teacher asks for my mother to sign a paper, but I'm afraid to have her name in the school file. I'm afraid they will deport her."[6]

Learning to live simultaneously in two social worlds is a requisite of "successful" immigrant adaptation. In a world so different from one's native land, much has to be learned initially to cope—especially the new language. With few exceptions, newcomers unable to speak English in the Anglo-American world face enormous obstacles. Learning English is a basic step to enable them to participate in the life of the larger community, get an education, find a job, obtain a driver's license and access to health care or social services, and apply for citizenship. Language has often been cited as the principal initial barrier confronting recent immigrants, from the least educated peasants to the most educated professionals.[7] To be sure, the process of language learning—played out, particularly for the children of the new immigrants, in the institutional context of the public schools—is a complex story of mutual adaptation, of the accommodation of two or more ethnolinguistic groups in diverse structural contexts. It is also, as the vignettes opening this chapter illustrate, a story of considerable diversity, fraught with irony and controversy.

In this chapter, we focus on the process of "learning the ropes" in the domains of language and education, with particular attention to immigrant youth and their adaptation to the world of the American public school. Language shift and language acquisition parallel in many ways the story of immigrant adaptation to the American culture, polity, and economy told in earlier chapters. Yet the process is not simply a reflection of the immigrant experience in these other realms, for language in America has a meaning that transcends its purely instrumental value as means of communication. Unlike many European nations, which are tolerant of linguistic diversity, in the United States the acquisition of nonaccented English and the dropping of foreign languages represent the litmus test of Americanization. Other aspects of immigrant culture (such as cuisine, community celebrations, and religion, which we will examine in a later chapter) often last for several generations, but the home language seldom survives. Linguistic transition, its forms and its implications, is the subject of this chapter. As in previous chapters, we start with the historical record in order to place the analysis of present experience in an appropriate context.

PATTERNS OF ENGLISH LANGUAGE ACQUISITION IN THE UNITED STATES

BILINGUALISM IN COMPARATIVE PERSPECTIVE

"What do you call a person who speaks two languages?"
"Bilingual."
"And one who knows only one?"
"American."[8]

Contrary to what may seem to be true from a purely domestic angle, the use of two languages is not exceptional but normal in the experience of a good part of the world's population. More than six billion people speak an estimated six thousand languages in a world of some two hundred autonomous states. Thus, there are about thirty times as many languages as there are states, and the dominance of certain languages (such as Chinese, Hindi, Russian, Spanish, and English)—combined with global communications and transportation technologies, international trade, and immigration—contributes to the proliferation of bilingualism.[9] Over the past two centuries, the United States has incorporated more bilingual people than any other country in the world. Yet the American experience is remarkable for its nearly mass extinction of non-English languages: in no other country, among thirty-five nations compared in a detailed study by Lieberson and his colleagues, did the mother tongue shift more rapidly toward (English) monolingualism than in the United States. Within the United States, some relatively isolated indigenous groups (such as the Old Spanish, the Navajo and other American Indians, and the Louisiana French) have changed at a much slower rate; but language minority immigrants shifted to English at a rate far in excess of that obtained in all other countries.[10]

Other studies of the languages of European and older Asian immigrant groups in the United States have documented a rapid process of intergenerational "anglicization" that is effectively completed by the third generation. Bilingualism, American style, has been unstable and transitional—at least until recently. The general historical pattern seems clear: those in the first generation learned as much English as they needed to get by but continued to speak their mother tongue at home. The second generation grew up speaking the mother tongue at home but English away from home—perforce in the public schools and then in the wider society, given the institutional pressures for anglicization and the socioeconomic benefits of native fluency in English. The home language of their children, and hence the mother tongue of the third generation, was mostly English. As a classic essay saw it, immigrant families were often transformed "into two linguistic sub-groups segregated along generational lines. . . . [E]thnic heritage, including the ethnic mother tongue, usually ceases to play any viable role in the life of the third generation. . . . [The grandchildren] become literally outsiders to their ancestral heritage."[11]

The remarkable rapidity and completeness of language transition in America are not mere happenstance, for these qualities reflect the operation of strong social forces. In a country lacking centuries-old traditions and culture and simultaneously receiving millions of foreigners from the most diverse lands, language homogeneity came to be seen as the bedrock of nationhood and collective identity. Immigrants were compelled not only to speak English but to speak *only* English as the prerequisite of social acceptance and integration. We showed in chapter 5 how the perfectly bilingual German American community was forced to "swat the hyphen" and abandon German language schools and newspapers shortly after the start of World War I. Under less dramatic circumstances, other immigrant groups were nudged in the same direction. The nemesis of German American biculturalism, Theodore Roosevelt, put the general rule in stark terms: "We have room for but one language here, and that is the English language; for we intend to see that the crucible turns our people out as Americans, and not as dwellers in a polyglot boardinghouse; and we have room for but one sole loyalty, and that is loyalty to the American people."[12]

During the nineteenth and early twentieth centuries, pressures against bilingualism had actually two distinct, albeit related, strands. First, there was the political variant—represented by Roosevelt and others—that saw the continuing use of foreign languages as somehow un-American. Pressure along these lines led to rapid linguistic loss among immigrant minorities and to the subsequent rise of ethnic reactive formation processes, as seen in chapter 5. Second, there was a scientific and educational literature that attempted to show the intellectual limitations associated with lack of English fluency. Paralleling in many ways the evolution of theories about migration and mental health, discussed in chapter 6, these works gave scientific legitimacy to the calls for restriction and linguistic assimilation so common in the political discourse of the time. We turn now to a review of these studies and their conclusions.

LANGUAGE AND ACHIEVEMENT IN THE EARLY TWENTIETH CENTURY

By the early twentieth century, the scientific debate did not revolve around the close relationship between lack of English and lower intelligence—a settled matter at the time—but around the direction of causality: Did the immigrants' lack of intelligence cause their lack of English or vice versa? At about this time, a test of "mental age," developed by Alfred Binet and soon after translated into English by H. H. Goddard, provided a powerful new tool to the eugenics perspective on immigration. In a 1917 study, Goddard administered the English version of the Binet IQ test to thirty newly arrived Jewish immigrants on Ellis Island and found twenty-five of them to be "feeble-minded." Taking the validity of the test for granted, he argued on the basis of their responses to a section of the test measuring word fluency that "such a lack of vocabulary in an adult would probably mean lack of intelligence" and concluded, "[W]e are now getting the poorest of each race."[13]

When World War I broke out, Goddard and his colleagues persuaded the U.S. Army to test some two million draftees, many of whom were foreign-born and illiterate in English. Perhaps the most influential analysis of these data was *A Study of American Intelligence*, published in 1923 by Carl Brigham, who concluded, "The representatives of the Alpine and Mediterranean races in our immigration are intellectually inferior to the representatives of the Nordic race." A confirmed hereditarian, Brigham further insisted that "the underlying cause of the nativity differences we have shown is race, and not language."[14] Along the same lines, in his 1926 volume on *Intelligence and Immigration*, Clifford Kirkpatrick argued against expecting much progress among immigrants through the reform of school programs, because "high grade germplasm often leads to better results than a high per capita school expenditure. Definite limits are set by heredity, and immigrants of low innate ability cannot by any amount of Americanization be made into intelligent American citizens capable of appropriating and advancing a complex culture."[15]

Educational psychologists who shared similar hereditarian views and whose work was shaped by the larger zeitgeist followed with a string of studies seeking to demonstrate that the cause of low IQ among bilingual immigrant schoolchildren was based on genetic factors (nature) rather than on a "language handicap" (nurture). One line of argument claimed that the inferiority of foreign-born children on tests of mental age persisted even after the children had had time to learn English. Another, typified by the influential work of Florence Goodenough, reviewed numerous studies of immigrant children that showed a negative correlation between group intelligence and the extent of foreign language use in the home.

From such correlational evidence, Goodenough argued against a "home environment" theory that would interpret the data to mean that "the use of a foreign language in the home is one of the chief factors in producing mental retardation as measured by intelligence tests" and instead proposed a different causal sequence in favor of innate differences. "A more probable explanation is that those nationality groups whose average intellectual ability is inferior do not readily learn the new language."[16] In other words, for early psychologists of this school, lack of English was not a cause but an effect of inferior intelligence, and the disproportionate presence of feebleminded aliens was blamed on "selective immigration."

Educational psychologists who stressed not heredity but the environment of the bilinguals came to diametrically opposite interpretations regarding causality, but until the early 1960s, most reached equally negative conclusions about immigrant intelligence. From this point of view, low intelligence and poor academic achievement were caused by a learned characteristic: bilingualism itself. Beginning in the early 1920s, in tandem with the flourishing of psychometric tests, the overwhelming majority of these studies consistently reported evidence that bilingual children suffered from a "language handicap." Compared with monolinguals, bilingual children were found to be inferior in intelligence test scores and on a range of verbal and nonverbal linguistic abilities (including vocabulary, grammar, syntax, written composition, and mathematics). Such findings were interpreted as the effects of the "linguistic confusion" or "linguistic interference" supposedly suffered by children who were exposed to two languages at once. That handicap, in turn, was viewed as a negative trait of the bilingual person's mind. Bilingualism in young children particularly was said to be "a hardship and devoid of apparent advantage," bound to produce deficiencies in both languages being learned and to lead to emotional as well as educational maladjustment.[17]

Perhaps most influential in advancing these views was the work of Madorah Smith, whose research on the speech of preschool Chinese, Filipino, Hawaiian, Japanese, Korean, and Portuguese children in Hawaii concluded that the attempt to use two languages was "an important factor in the retardation in speech" found among these youngsters. The bilinguals fared poorly in comparison with a monolingual sample of children from Iowa, based on her method for analyzing proper English usage in speech utterances.[18] This and similar studies reinforced the popular nostrum that bilingualism in children was a serious handicap and that English monolingualism for immigrant youngsters was the proper course to follow.

BILINGUALISM REASSESSED: CURRENT EVIDENCE

This negative view dominated academic circles until the early 1960s, oblivious of the fundamental methodological flaw of the research on which it was based. With few exceptions, none of these studies—whether approached from hereditary or environmental perspectives—had introduced controls for social class. They had also typically failed to assess the immigrant children's actual degree of bilingualism, itself a complex issue (in one study, bilingualism had been determined by looking at the child's name).[19] These and other methodological problems fatally flawed the validity of early research findings purporting to document the negative effects of immigrant bilingualism on intelligence and achievement.

In an influential 1962 study in Montreal, Peal and Lambert pointed out that earlier research often compared high-status English-speaking monolinguals with lower-class foreign-born bilinguals, obviously stacking the results a priori.[20] In their study, Peal and Lambert distinguished between two types of bilinguals: true or "balanced" bilinguals, who master both languages at an early age and can communicate competently in both, and semi- or "pseudo-" bilinguals, who know one language much better than the other and do not use the second language in communication. They carried out a carefully controlled study of ten-year-old children, classified into groups of French monolinguals and French-English balanced bilinguals, finding that the bilingual group had, on the average, a higher socioeconomic level than the monolinguals. Of more consequence, with socioeconomic status controlled, the bilingual group performed significantly better than the monolinguals on a wide range of verbal and nonverbal IQ tests—contradicting four decades of prior research.

In particular, controlling for social class and demographic variables, the bilinguals in this study performed best on the type of nonverbal tests involving concept formation and cognitive or symbolic "flexibility." Peal and Lambert offered several hypotheses to explain the advantages observed for the bilinguals. They suggested, following Leopold's extensive case studies, that people who learn to use two languages have two symbols for every object.[21] Thus, from an early age, they become emancipated from linguistic symbols—from the concreteness, arbitrariness, and "tyranny" of words—developing analytic abilities to focus on essentials and to think in terms of more abstract concepts and relations, independent of the actual word.

In switching from one language to another, the balanced bilingual uses two different perspectives and is exposed to the "enriched environment" of a wider range of experiences stemming from two cultures. By contrast, monolinguals "may be at a disadvantage in that their thought is always subject to language" and "may be more rigid or less flexible than the bilinguals on certain tests."[22] It bears emphasizing, however, that these and subsequent positive evaluations in the literature are built on a considerable body of evidence concerning the performance of fully (or "true") bilingual children. By contrast, little research was done on limited (or "semi-") bilinguals.

A large-scale comparative study of students in the San Diego Unified School District (the nation's eighth largest) provided a unique opportunity to look more closely at this issue. The study collected data for the entire 1986–1987 and 1989–1990 high school cohorts, a combined total of nearly eighty thousand seniors, juniors, and sophomores. Over a third of this sample were classified as Hispanics—overwhelmingly Mexican immigrants and Mexican Americans (20 percent); Filipinos (7 percent); Vietnamese and other Indo-Chinese refugee groups (7 percent); and East Asians—Chinese, Japanese, and Koreans (less than 3 percent). Their growing proportions in the school district are commensurate with the fact that San Diego is a major area of settlement for immigrants from those countries. As table 30 shows, some three-fourths of the Hispanic and Asian students spoke a language other than English at home, usually a good indicator of second-generation status—that is, of children born in the United States of immigrant parents or brought at a young age from abroad. These students were classified by the school district, based on standardized assessments of their English proficiency, as Limited English Proficient (LEP) or Fluent English Proficient (FEP). The significance of the study is that it correlated the students' English language status (English monolingual, FEP, and LEP) with various indicators of school achievement. The FEP-LEP distinction corresponds closely to Peal and Lambert's distinction between "true" and "semi-" bilinguals; hence, their hypotheses concerning differential achievement, untested in the Montreal study, can be examined directly.[23]

In 1986–1987, 30 percent of these students spoke English only at home, with the proportion ranging from almost 60 percent among East Asians to less than 6 percent among the Indo-Chinese. The other 70 percent spoke a language other than English at home: 37 percent were designated as FEP and 33 percent as LEP. Over two-thirds of the

TABLE 30. PERCENTAGE CLASSIFIED AS LEP, FEP, AND ENGLISH-
ONLY AMONG SAN DIEGO HIGH SCHOOL STUDENTS BY
SELECTED ETHNIC GROUPS AND ENGLISH LANGUAGE STATUS

| Ethnolinguistic group | School year | N | English language classification at school | | |
			LEP[a] %	FEP[b] %	English only %
East Asian	1987	826	13.7	26.6	59.7
	1990	1,050	10.7	39.0	50.4
Chinese	1987	166	41.0	59.0	—
	1990	248	21.4	78.6	—
Korean	1987	56	41.1	58.9	—
	1990	99	33.0	67.0	—
Japanese	1987	111	19.8	80.2	—
	1990	156	12.8	87.2	—
Indo-Chinese	1987	2,388	68.7	25.4	5.9
	1990	3,102	52.0	42.5	5.5
Vietnamese	1987	1,184	61.9	38.1	—
	1990	1,618	43.9	56.1	—
Hmong	1987	113	73.5	26.5	—
	1990	170	57.1	42.9	—
Lao	1987	560	83.2	16.8	—
	1990	728	66.5	33.5	—
Cambodian	1987	391	91.8	8.2	—
	1990	415	77.8	22.2	—
Filipino	1987	2,064	11.4	50.1	38.5
	1990	3,311	6.6	56.6	36.8
Hispanic	1987	7,007	29.7	37.5	32.8
	1990	8,193	20.1	54.1	25.8
Totals	1987	12,288	33.1	36.6	30.3
	1990	15,656	22.9	51.3	25.8

SOURCE: Rumbaut 1995, table 2.6.

[a] LEP = "Limited English proficient"; primary home language is other than English.
[b] FEP = "Fluent English proficient"; primary home language is other than English.

Indo-Chinese (and among them, over 90 percent of the Cambodians) were classified as LEP, reflecting the fact that they were the most recently arrived immigrant group. By contrast, less than a third of the Mexican-origin (Hispanic) students and less than 15 percent of the East Asians and Filipinos were LEP. For the 1989–1990 cohort, the proportion of FEPs increased notably, and the proportion of LEPs decreased, for all groups without exception, while the relative rank order of the ethnic groups remained stable.

So that we may examine these students' actual intellectual accomplishments, table 31 presents data on their cumulative grade point averages in high school academic courses since the ninth grade. As a point of reference, the overall GPA in the school district was 2.11; the GPA for white Anglo students (2.24) was above that norm, but it was surpassed by the respective GPAs of all of the Asian nationalities listed in table 31. At the top were Chinese (with GPAs exceeding the norm by a full grade point), Korean, Japanese, and Vietnamese students. Clearly the FEP students did significantly better than their LEP coethnics. More important, in 1986–1987 and again in 1989–1990, fluent bilinguals surpassed English monolinguals by a significant margin—and this applied to their English-only coethnics as well as to white majority students. The gap is greatest among those nationalities with the highest average grades (East and Southeast Asians and Filipinos) and becomes smaller among the low-performing groups.

An analysis of the students' scores on standardized tests of English comprehension and mathematical skills tells a somewhat different story. English monolinguals tended to have the highest scores in reading comprehension, with white Anglo students at the top of the distribution. This result essentially confirms the validity of the linguistic classification of students by saying that those who are supposed to know English best actually do so. The situation changes, however, with math scores. Once again, fluent bilinguals had significantly higher math scores than English monolinguals overall and for every nationality. The exceptions were low-performing groups, for whom the difference is trivial.[24]

In addition, the San Diego study included both "active" (currently enrolled) students as well as "inactive" students who entered their respective high school cohort in the ninth grade but later dropped out of school or left the district. Hence, the data do not suffer from the common bias of selection in favor of those who remain in school; they thus allow an examination of dropout rates as an additional criterion of scholastic achievement. Table 32 presents annual dropout rates for the

TABLE 31. ACADEMIC GRADE POINT AVERAGES
OF TWO COHORTS OF SAN DIEGO HIGH SCHOOL
STUDENTS BY SELECTED ETHNIC GROUPS
AND ENGLISH LANGUAGE STATUS

| Ethnolinguistic group | School year | English language classification | | | Total GPA |
		LEP[a] GPA[c]	FEP[b] GPA	English only GPA	
East Asian	1987	2.83	3.05	2.38	2.62
	1990	2.86	3.02	2.58	2.78
Chinese	1987	2.94	3.40	—	3.21
	1990	2.95	3.26	—	3.19
Korean	1987	2.76	3.00	—	2.90
	1990	2.90	2.81	—	2.84
Japanese	1997	2.56	2.70	—	2.67
	1990	2.69	2.80	—	2.79
Indo-Chinese	1987	2.30	2.88	2.66	2.47
	1990	2.35	2.94	2.72	2.62
Vietnamese	1987	2.38	2.96	—	2.60
	1990	2.47	3.02	—	2.78
Hmong	1987	2.27	2.66	—	2.37
	1990	2.42	2.84	—	2.60
Lao	1987	2.18	2.63	—	2.26
	1990	2.26	2.72	—	2.41
Cambodian	1987	2.30	2.77	—	2.34
	1990	2.21	2.82	—	2.35
Filipino	1987	2.02	2.53	2.33	2.39
	1990	1.94	2.49	2.38	2.41
Hispanic	1987	1.71	1.85	1.81	1.79
	1990	1.74	1.91	2.01	1.90
Totals	1997	2.00	2.21	2.03	2.09
	1990	2.06	2.27	2.23	2.21

SOURCE: Rumbaut 1995, table 2.6.

[a]LEP = "Limited English proficient"; primary home language is other than English.
[b]FEP = "Fluent English proficient"; primary home language is other than English.
[c]GPA = Cumulative grade point average since ninth grade, excluding physical education, in mean scores on a four-point scale, where A = 4, B = 3, C = 2, D = 1, and F = 0.

TABLE 32. ANNUAL DROPOUT RATES[a] FOR
THE 1989–1990 COHORT OF SAN DIEGO
HIGH SCHOOL STUDENTS BY SELECTED ETHNIC
GROUPS AND ENGLISH LANGUAGE STATUS

| Ethnolinguistic group | N | English language classification | | | Total % |
		LEP[b] %	FEP[c] %	English only %	
East Asian	1,050	10.7	2.2	5.3	4.7
Chinese	248	5.7	1.0	—	2.0
Korean	88	17.2	1.7	—	6.8
Japanese	156	15.0	3.7	—	5.1
Filipino	3,311	15.4	4.5	5.5	5.6
Indo-Chinese	3,102	11.0	3.5	7.0	7.6
Vietnamese	1,618	10.7	3.4	—	6.6
Hmong	170	5.2	5.5	—	5.3
Cambodian	415	14.9	5.4	—	12.8
Lao	728	9.9	2.5	—	7.4
Hispanic	8,193	17.9	10.9	9.9	12.1
Totals	15, 656	14.4	7.7	7.8	9.3

SOURCE: Rumbaut 1995, table 2.7.

[a] Percentage of students in grades 10–12 who dropped out of school during a given academic year.
[b] LEP = "Limited English proficient"; primary home language is other than English.
[c] FEP = "Fluent English proficient"; primary home language is other than English.

1989–1990 high school cohort, broken down by ethnic origin and language status. The lowest rate was observed for Chinese language-minority students, who also had the highest GPAs. Dropout rates for the Cambodians actually exceeded the overall rate for Mexican-origin students and were, along with Pacific Islanders', the highest in the school district.

The data show that limited bilinguals were far more at risk to leave school than those fluent in both languages: the overall LEP rate of 14.4 percent doubled the FEP rate of 7.7 percent. The sizable gap between both categories was repeated, virtually without exception, for every immigrant nationality. More important, fluent bilinguals had significantly lower dropout rates than English monolinguals among all Asian groups (Mexican-origin students were the sole exception in the 1989–1990 cohort).

These results lend strong support to Peal and Lambert's hypothesis by showing that nothing in bilingualism as such detracts from scholarly achievement and that, on the contrary, "true" bilingualism is positively associated with the latter. In contrast to decades of psychological research reporting the opposite, these figures indicate that the loss of the mother tongue and a complete shift into English are not necessarily associated with greater ability or performance. The meaning of these findings must be carefully weighed, however: the positive association between fluency in two languages and school test scores does not "prove" that one causes the other. The two may actually be consequences of a third factor not taken into account, such as type of immigration, family socioeconomic status, and family structure. Unfortunately, the San Diego School District collects no information on these or other pertinent variables. Higher-status families and those with both parents present can, for example, increase the proclivity to promote parental language retention *and* scholastic achievement among their offspring. We will return to this point later in this chapter and also pursue it further in chapter 8.

LANGUAGE DIVERSITY AND RESILIENCE IN THE UNITED STATES TODAY

RECENT IMMIGRANTS

Is the United States becoming a polyglot country? The study results just described suggest that multilingualism may not be such a bad idea, at least in terms of the intellectual abilities and skills associated with it. Yet nativists may object to it on the basis of the need for "national identity," "cultural homogeneity," and the like. It is thus important to examine the evidence concerning both the extent of bilingualism in the United States and its resilience over time. The best sources for this purpose continue to be the 1980, 1990, and 2000 U.S. Censuses, which included several relevant questions not included in previous ones.

The first such question asked people age five or older whether they spoke a language other than English at home. In 2000, forty-seven million people, or 18 percent, of the 262.4 million of that age group answered in the affirmative. Those figures were up from 14 percent in 1990 (thirty-two million) and 11 percent in 1980 (twenty-three million). Because the question did not ask whether this was the "usual" language spoken at home or how frequently or well it was used relative to English, it probably elicited an overestimate. Still, the data point to the presence of a substantial and growing minority of those who are not English monolinguals.

Moreover, as figure 10 shows, non-English monolingual households were concentrated in areas of primary immigrant settlement (described in chapter 3)—particularly along the Mexican border from Texas to California and in large cities such as Chicago, Miami, and New York. Among all the 3,141 counties in the United States, the median percentage of the population who spoke a language other than English at home was a mere 4.6 percent. That is, in half of all counties (a vast swath of the United States, shown in white in figure 10), more than 95 percent of the residents were English monolinguals. In other areas, however, bilingualism was prevalent—as was the case in Hialeah and Miami in South Florida; Santa Ana and East Los Angeles in Southern California; Laredo, McAllen, Brownsville, and El Paso along the Texas-Mexico border; and Elizabeth, New Jersey, across the Hudson River from New York City, where between 67 and 93 percent of the residents spoke languages other than English.

In 2000, of the forty-seven million who spoke a foreign language at home, more than twenty-eight million spoke one language: Spanish. The remainder spoke scores of different languages, chiefly reflecting both past and present immigrant flows. These languages included Chinese (two million); French, German, Italian, Tagalog, and Vietnamese (over one million each); and Korean, Russian, Polish, Arabic, and Portuguese (over half a million each). Among all immigrants age five or older who came to the United States between 1990 and 2000, 88 percent spoke a language other than English at home. The figure declines to 74 percent among pre-1980 immigrants and to less than 9 percent among the native-born. The vast majority of the population, more than 215 million, spoke only English.[25]

These results suggest that the United States is far from becoming a multilingual nation. Yet before reaching a final conclusion, we must look at variability within national groups as well as to the evolution of bilingualism over time. Table 33 introduces these features, presenting data on home language use for the largest non-English immigrant cohorts; the total pre-1980, 1980–1989, and post-1990 foreign-born populations; and the native-born.[26] We can derive two main conclusions from these results. First, recently arrived immigrants tend to remain loyal to their native language, regardless of age and education. Although some evidence suggests that nationalities with high proportions of college graduates and professionals shift toward English more

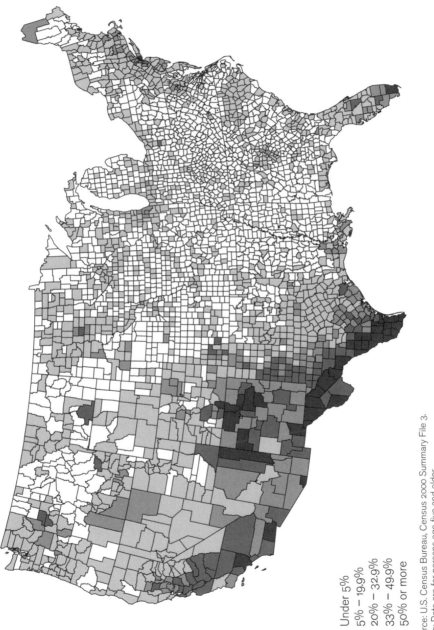

Under 5%
5% – 19.9%
20% – 32.9%
33% – 49.9%
50% or more

Source: U.S. Census Bureau, Census 2000 Summary File 3.
Note: Data are for persons age five and older.

Figure 10. Percentage of persons who spoke a language other than English at home, by county, 2000

TABLE 33. LANGUAGE SPOKEN AT HOME AND RELATED CHARACTERISTICS FOR SELECTED IMMIGRANT GROUPS AND THE NATIVE-BORN, 2000

(ranked by proportion of the foreign-born from non-English-speaking countries who spoke English only)

Country of birth	Persons age 5 or older (N)	Speaks English only at home (%)	Length of residence in United States (years)	College graduate[a] (%)	High-status profession[b] %
Germany	698,651	40	34	27	50
Nigeria	134,041	22	11	58	52
Italy	475,109	21	38	14	36
Japan	339,948	17	17	43	56
Korea	856,488	15	15	43	48
Poland	471,336	13	23	22	31
Philippines	1,367,592	12	17	46	42
Russia	329,907	11	13	52	53
India	1,012,016	9	12	69	68
Arab Middle East	516,370	9	15	39	50
Iran	284,329	8	17	51	59
Colombia	508,482	6	14	22	29
Taiwan	324,228	6	15	67	69
Peru	273,096	6	14	23	29
Cuba	866,649	6	23	19	34
Haiti	418,834	6	15	14	22
Dominican Republic	680,511	6	15	9	19
Mexico	8,996,368	6	14	4	10
Cambodia	136,020	6	16	10	24
Nicaragua	222,690	5	15	14	23
Guatemala	471,744	5	12	6	12
El Salvador	807,555	5	13	5	12
China	976,090	5	14	4	50
Vietnam	984,327	5	14	1	30
Laos	204,414	5	16		18
Foreign-born[c] Arrived 1990–2000	13,240,060	12	5	28	27
Arrived 1980–1989	8,776,740	14	15	21	29
Arrived before 1980	10,290,944	26	34	22	39
U.S.-born	230,067,997	91	NA	25	40

SOURCE: 2000 U.S. Census, 5% Public Use Microdata Sample.

[a] Persons age twenty-five and older.
[b] Employed persons age sixteen and older.
[c] Totals include immigrants from English-speaking countries.

rapidly, the vast majority of recent arrivals retain their own language at home. Second, time has a strong eroding effect on native language retention. As seen in the bottom rows of the table, only one-eighth of recently arrived immigrants use only English at home, but more than one-fourth of immigrants with longer U.S. residence do so. These results align well with those concerning shifting political affiliations and interests with the passage of time, reviewed in the previous chapter.

Language transition among recent immigrants has a second aspect—namely, the extent to which they have learned English. In other words, use of the native language at home does not indicate whether users are non-English monolinguals or limited or fluent bilinguals. The decennial census does not test for English knowledge objectively, but it includes a self-report of ability to speak English (very well, well, not well, or not at all). Table 34 presents the relevant figures, broken down for the largest non-English-origin nationalities and by year of immigration. While self-reported fluent bilinguals (defined here as those who both spoke a foreign language at home and spoke English very well) among 1990–2000 immigrants represented only about one-third of the total, that proportion had grown to nearly one-half of the pre-1980 immigrants. Among the most recent (1990–2000) arrivals, 44 percent reported not being able to speak English well or at all, but that figure had declined to 25 percent of pre-1980 arrivals. Similarly, immigrants in "linguistically isolated" households (defined by the Census Bureau as a household in which no person fourteen or older speaks English only or very well) were found disproportionately among recent arrivals. Over two-fifths of post-1990 immigrants lived in such limited bilingual or non-English monolingual households in 2000, although the proportion among pre-1980 immigrants dropped sharply to less than one-fifth.

A fuller picture of today's linguistic diversity, provided in table 34, can be gleaned by examining the data on English-speaking ability for the largest non-English-origin nationalities. The highest levels of fluent bilingualism are seen for the Germans, Nigerians, Indians, and Filipinos, the latter three coming from countries where English is either the official language or the common language among speakers of different native tongues. Between two-thirds and four-fifths of these immigrants are able to speak English "very well." Most others, however, fall well below those levels of self-reported fluency. Immigrants from Southeast Asia and Central America, China, Mexico, and the

TABLE 34. ENGLISH-SPEAKING ABILITY OF IMMIGRANTS FROM NON-ENGLISH-SPEAKING COUNTRIES, 2000

Country of birth	Immigrants age 5 or older who speak non-English language at home (N)	English proficiency[a]		Linguistically isolated households[b] %
		Speaks English very well (%)	Speaks English not well or at all (%)	
Nigeria	104,952	86	3	5
Germany	416,018	81	3	6
India	918,696	70	10	12
Philippines	1,201,153	64	8	11
Arab Middle East	469,491	58	16	20
Iran	261,928	57	18	19
Italy	376,461	49	19	19
Haiti	393,497	44	2	26
Taiwan	304,686	42	18	32
Poland	408,249	42	23	32
Russia	293,508	42	26	35
Nicaragua	211,142	40	35	27
Peru	256,324	40	31	28
Japan	280,721	36	25	34
Cuba	813,604	36	44	39
Colombia	477,077	35	36	34
Korea	726,950	32	35	36
Laos	194,233	30	39	30
Dominican Republic	641,188	30	45	37
Cambodia	128,499	29	39	28
China	927,634	29	43	44
Vietnam	935,412	27	38	44
El Salvador	767,200	26	48	41
Guatemala	447,920	26	48	44
Mexico	8,488,805	24	53	43
Foreign-born[c]				
Arrived 1990–2000	11,167,607	31	44	44
Arrived 1980–1989	7,181,433	39	33	30
Arrived before 1980	6,804,915	48	25	18

SOURCE: 2000 U.S. Census, 5% Public Use Microdata Sample.

[a] Based on the response to a census question on English-speaking ability asked of persons who spoke a language other than English at home.

[b] Defined as a household in which no person age fourteen or older speaks English only or very well.

[c] Totals exclude immigrants from English-speaking countries and those who speak English only.

Dominican Republic are far more likely to be found in linguistically isolated households.

Even more impressive is the rapidity with which English fluency is acquired by immigrant children, underscoring the importance of age at arrival. As shown in table 35, among immigrants who had arrived in the United States as children under thirteen years of age and who speak another language at home, 64 percent could speak English "very well," compared with 35 percent of those who had immigrated between the ages of thirteen and thirty-five (in adolescence or early adulthood) and only 20 percent of those who were thirty-five or older when they immigrated. In general, age at arrival, time in the United States, and level of education are the most significant predictors of the acquisition of English fluency among immigrants of non-English origin. The effect of each of these three factors is specified in table 36 for the largest immigrant nationalities and illustrated in figure 11 for all Spanish-speaking groups. The power of assimilative forces, already detected on economic achievement and the character of ethnic politics (chapters 4 and 5), is nowhere clearer than in the linguistic shift across generations over time.

GENERATIONAL PATTERNS

Until recently, scarcely any systematic three-generation analyses of language maintenance and shift appeared in the research literature. An exception is the work of David López, who conducted two such studies among Spanish-origin minorities in the United States. The first involved a 1973 survey of a representative sample of 1,129 Mexican-origin couples in Los Angeles. López's findings document a pattern of rapid language transition across the three generations that contradicts the assumption of unshakable Spanish language loyalty among Mexican Americans. Among first-generation women, for example, he found that 84 percent used only Spanish at home, 14 percent used both languages, and just 2 percent used only English. By the third generation, there was almost a complete reversal, with only 4 percent speaking Spanish at home, 12 percent using both, and 84 percent shifting to English only.[27]

Figures for men were similar, except that the shift to English from the first to the second generation was even more marked. The study also attempted to examine the determinants and consequences of language transition. It found that generation had the strongest causal

Characteristics		Speaks English only at home %	If speaks non-English language:		Linguistically isolated[c] %
			How well speaks English[b]		
			Very well (%)	Not well or at all (%)	
Total[a]		10	38	36	33
Age at U.S. arrival	35 or older	7	20	58	41
	13–34	8	35	37	34
	Under 13	17	64	13	23
Decade of U.S. arrival	1990–2000	7	31	44	44
	1980–1989	7	39	33	30
	Before 1980	16	48	25	18
Education[d]	Not high school graduate	7	15	61	43
	High school graduate	11	42	26	27
	College graduate or more	12	64	11	18

SOURCE: 2000 U.S. Census, 5% Public Use Microdata Sample.

[a]Based on the response to a census question on English-speaking ability asked of persons who spoke a language other than English at home.
[b]Defined by the Census Bureau as a household in which no person 14 or older speaks English only or very well.
[c]Persons age five or older from Non-English-speaking countries
[d]Persons age twenty-five or older.

TABLE 36. ABILITY TO SPEAK ENGLISH "VERY WELL" AMONG SELECTED IMMIGRANT
GROUPS WHO SPEAK A LANGUAGE OTHER THAN ENGLISH AT HOME

| | Percentage who speak English "very well" by: | | | | | | | | |
| | Age at U.S. arrival | | | Decade of U.S. arrival | | | Education completed | | |
Country of birth	0–12	13–34	35 and older	Before 1980	1980s	1990s	Not high school graduate	High school graduate	College graduate
Nigeria	80	88	77	92	89	82	48	81	94
Germany	84	82	65	82	86	73	64	83	88
India	81	75	45	78	71	67	20	53	83
Philippines	76	70	45	70	66	58	25	59	79
Arab Middle East	76	61	29	68	65	47	23	56	75
Iran	84	67	22	73	54	37	11	44	73
Italy	82	44	21	48	57	53	30	63	77
Haiti	68	45	20	52	47	37	23	49	69
Taiwan	77	39	13	55	46	30	12	22	48
Poland	80	43	17	47	44	36	22	36	59

Russia	75	50	16	54	47	38	18	27	40
Nicaragua	75	32	15	52	43	27	16	41	54
Peru	76	40	15	52	45	32	15	35	55
Japan	52	37	23	42	47	30	24	33	43
Cuba	83	31	9	46	31	20	12	47	56
Colombia	71	32	11	46	38	26	13	32	49
Korea	70	29	10	41	32	24	14	27	44
Laos	61	19	8	38	30	20	10	36	63
Dominican Republic	63	22	8	34	31	26	12	32	46
Cambodia	63	22	8	37	29	27	9	34	61
China	58	34	10	31	28	28	6	16	48
Vietnam	58	23	7	43	30	17	7	24	56
El Salvador	62	20	8	33	30	19	13	38	48
Guatemala	62	20	11	38	30	19	12	36	52
Mexico	53	15	9	33	27	18	13	37	49
Total[a]	65	35	20	49	40	31	16	43	64

Source: 2000 U.S. Census, 5% Public Use Microdata Sample.

[a]Excluding immigrants from English-speaking countries.

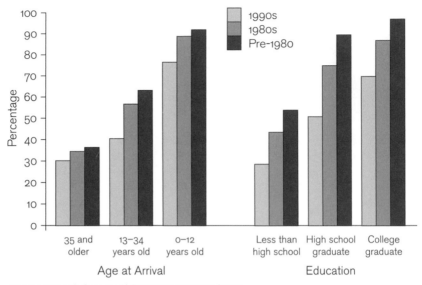

Source: 2000 U.S. Census, 5% Public Use Microdata Survey.
Notes: *English fluency* refers to persons age five or older who speak English only, well, or very well. *Education* refers specifically to the highest level of education completed for persons age twenty-five and older.

Figure 11. English fluency of foreign-born Hispanics in the United States, 2000

effect, exceeding by far those of age, rural origin, and other predictors. Spanish maintenance appears to have some positive occupational advantages—controlling for education and other factors—among the immigrant generation but none for subsequent ones. Among the latter, residual Spanish monolingualism is associated with poor schooling and low socioeconomic status. López concluded that the appearance of high language loyalty among Mexican Americans is due largely to the effect of continuing high immigration from the country of origin.[28]

A second study by the same author assessed language patterns across three generations, this time for different Spanish-origin groups, on the basis of data from the 1979 Current Population Survey. The study confirmed the same negative association between Spanish monolingualism and social class as measured by such variables as education, occupational prestige, and income. For the entire sample, as well as for each national group, adoption of English was positively associated with both higher education and higher socioeconomic status. However, López also uncovered a second trend that differed from both monolingual patterns in which Spanish maintenance was associated with high social class and greater English fluency.[29]

This latter trend was clearer among Spanish-origin groups other than Mexican Americans and may help explain why third-generation bilingualism is relatively higher among Hispanics overall than among other foreign-origin groups. In effect, despite strong pressures toward anglicization, this evidence documents the existence of a small but resilient group of high-achieving bilinguals across generations. Thus, López's findings raise again the issue of "elite" versus "folk" bilingualism or "fluent" versus "limited" use of two languages, discussed earlier. Although the intergenerational trend toward English monolingualism is unmistakable and by far the dominant one for all immigrants, this last intriguing set of results compels us to probe deeper into the relationships among social class, language, and academic achievement.

Before turning to those considerations, however, we highlight briefly the results of three more recent studies of intergenerational language shift that provide convergent and compelling contemporary evidence of the three-generation model of mother tongue erosion from the adult immigrant generation to that of their grandchildren. The first is an innovative analysis of the 2000 census by Richard Alba and his colleagues focusing on school-age children.[30] The second is a national survey of Hispanic adults conducted in 2002 by the Pew Hispanic Center.[31] The third is a 2004 study of immigration and intergenerational mobility in metropolitan Los Angeles.[32]

The first of these studies analyzed the home languages of children age six to fifteen in newcomer families, as reported in the 2000 U.S. Census, linking children to their parents in the same household to permit distinguishing between the second generation (U.S.-born children with at least one foreign-born parent) and the third (or a later) generation (U.S.-born children whose parents are also U.S.-born).[33] Despite group differences in the degree of language shift, for every nationality—without exception—the following patterns hold:

· The vast majority of first-generation immigrants who come to the United States as children speak English well.

· Bilingualism is most common among second-generation children who grow up in immigrant households and speak a foreign language at home but who are almost all proficient in English.

· English-only is the predominant pattern by the third generation.

· What third-generation bilingualism exists is found especially in border communities such as Brownsville and El Paso, Texas, where the maintenance of Spanish has deep historical roots and is affected by proximity to Mexico, or in areas of high ethnic density, such as those among Dominicans in New York and Cubans in Miami. Away from the border, Mexican American children of the third generation are unlikely to be bilingual.

The second study entailed a national telephone survey of a representative sample of adults age eighteen or older in the forty-eight contiguous states, of whom 2,929 self-reported as Hispanic or Latino (with oversamples of Salvadorans, Dominicans, Colombians, and Cubans).[34] Unlike the census (which asks only about spoken proficiency in English), the respondents were asked about their ability to speak and read in both English and Spanish. On the basis of their answers, they were classified as Spanish dominant, bilingual, or English dominant. The breakdown of the results by generation—which parallel uncannily those of López's Los Angeles survey taken three decades earlier—are shown graphically in figure 12. First-generation adults were overwhelmingly Spanish dominant (72 percent), with a fourth classified as bilingual and only 4 percent as English dominant. That pattern was reversed by the third generation, with 78 percent being English dominant and 22 percent still classified as bilingual, but less than 1 percent could be deemed Spanish dominant. Among the second generation, Spanish dominance plummeted to only 7 percent. However, nearly half (47 percent) were classified as bilinguals and nearly as many as English dominant (46 percent) by the second generation.

The final study entailed a comprehensive survey of 4,780 adults twenty to forty years old in metropolitan Los Angeles (the IIMMLA study, which we will discuss again in chapter 9).[35] The sample is representative of 1.5-generation (i.e., those born abroad but brought to the United States while young, generally before age thirteen) and second-generation Mexicans, Salvadorans, Guatemalans, Filipinos, Chinese, Koreans, Vietnamese, and other groups of immigrant origin who have settled in the five-county area, as well as third- and fourth- (and later) generation whites, African Americans, and Mexican Americans. All were asked whether they spoke a language other than English at home growing up; about their speaking, reading, and writing proficiency in the non-English language; and about their current language preferences and use. The results, broken down by detailed generational cohorts from the first to the fourth or greater generations (those with no foreign-born grandparents), are summarized in table 37. They show

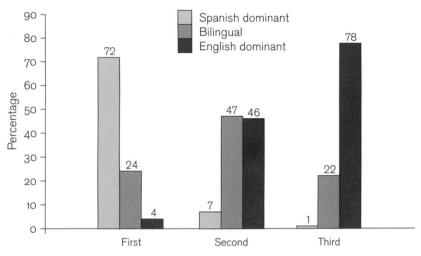

Source: Pew Hispanic Center 2004a, 2004b.

Figure 12. Language shift (Spanish to English) from the first to the third or greater generations among Hispanic adults in the United States, 2002

clearly the generational progression in each of the language measures. For example, while over 90 percent of the foreign-born cohorts and over 80 percent of the U.S.-born with two foreign-born parents grew up speaking a non-English language at home, those proportions dropped to less than half among the U.S.-born with only one foreign-born parent, to between a fifth and a third among the third generation (depending on the number of foreign-born grandparents), and to only a tenth by the fourth generation. However, their preferences for English increased rapidly by the 1.5 and second generations, exceeding 90 percent among the U.S.-born with only one foreign-born parent and becoming virtually universally preferred by the third generation. Those preferences in turn reflect the rapid atrophy of speaking, reading, and writing skills in the foreign language from one generation to the next. These data again provide confirmatory evidence that assimilation forces in American society are strongest in the linguistic area and that they operate most visibly across rather than within generations.

A limitation of all three of these recent studies is that they are cross-sectional; that is, they are snapshots taken at one point in time, but they do not follow specific individuals over time to ascertain the dynamics of acculturation and bilingualism as they take place within a generation. In chapter 8, we will turn to such a longitudinal study.

TABLE 37. NON-ENGLISH LANGUAGE USE,
PROFICIENCY, AND PREFERENCE, BY GENERATION
COHORT, GREATER LOS ANGELES, 2004

Detailed generational cohort	Growing up spoke a non-English language at home (%)	Speaks non-English language very well (%)	Prefers to speak only English at home (%)	N
1.0 generation (arrived age 13 or older)	97.4	86.9	17.7	256
1.5 generation (arrived age 0–12)	92.9	46.6	60.7	1,491
2.0 generation, 2 foreign-born parents	83.5	36.1	73.4	1,390
2.5 generation, 1 foreign-born parent	46.5	17.3	92.5	428
3.0 generation, 3–4 foreign-born grandparents	34.3	11.9	97.0	67
3.5 generation, 1–2 foreign-born grandparents	18.7	3.1	98.3	289
4th+ generation, 0 foreign-born grandparents	10.4	2	99.0	859
Total	65.8	31.5	70.8	4,780

SOURCE: Immigration and Intergenerational Mobility in Metropolitan Los Angeles (IIMMLA) Survey, Rumbaut et al. 2005.

ASSIMILATION AND LINGUISTIC PLURALISM IN THE UNITED STATES

ADDING AND SUBTRACTING

Language learning is only one dimension, though a fundamental one, of the process of acculturation. Until recently, the prevailing notion, derived from the assimilationist perspective, was that of a zero-sum process: acculturation involves shedding the old and assimilating the new and hence making a necessary trade-off between the native language and English. To learn English and become American means, from this point of view, that immigrants should not maintain their mother tongues. In the final analysis, this is the litmus test of Americanization. Bilingualism is regarded as unstable and transitional, for, as Theodore Roosevelt stated, there is no room for two languages and two ethnic

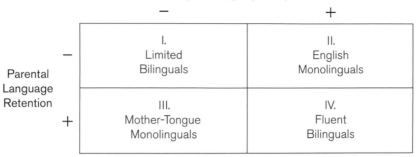

Figure 13. Language retention and acquisition among immigrant groups: A typology

identities under the same national roof. In theory, however, English monolingualism and abandonment of the mother tongue represent only one possible linguistic outcome of the process of immigrant incorporation. As portrayed in figure 13, others include continued mother tongue use, limited bilingualism, and fluency in both languages. Still, assimilationists have continued to emphasize use of English as the proper end result of the process.[36]

The call for prompt linguistic assimilation has not been motivated exclusively by concerns about the inferior intellectual performance of immigrants. Similar concerns have been voiced, albeit in a different tone, when immigrants actually outperform natives. An example comes from a Canadian study conducted in the mid-1920s that departed markedly from the familiar reporting of intellectual inferiority among the foreign-born. Five hundred Japanese and Chinese children attending public schools in Vancouver were tested in the study. The Japanese median IQ score was 114.2, and the Chinese was 107.4, both well above the white norm. The authors found these results "surprising, even startling," and concluded:

> There is every reason for believing that the Japanese are the most intelligent racial group resident in British Columbia, with the Chinese as a more doubtful second. The superiority is undoubtedly due to selection. In the main, it is the Japanese and Chinese possessing the qualities of cleverness, resourcefulness, and courage who emigrate. . . . But the presence of so many clever, industrious, and frugal aliens, capable (as far as mentality is concerned) of competing successfully with the native whites, . . . constitutes a political and economic problem of the greatest importance.[37]

Half a century later, a leader of the U.S. English movement in Miami expressed a similar concern by complaining that "the Latins are coming up fast" and that he and other natives had not come to Miami "to live in a Spanish-speaking province."[38] The meaning of such calls is further clarified when the attempt to compel immigrants to shed their language is contrasted with the efforts of many native-born middle-class youths to acquire a foreign tongue in universities and other institutions of higher learning. There is irony in the comparison between the hundreds of hours and thousands of dollars put into acquiring a halting command of a foreign language and the pressure on fluent foreign-born speakers to abandon its use. These contradictory goals—English monolingualism for the immigrant masses but bilingualism or multilingualism for domestic elites—shed light on the real underpinnings of linguistic nativism.

The pressure for immigrants to learn English can be attributed, reasonably, to the need to maintain a fundamental element of American identity and culture. The pressure to learn English *only*, especially when contrasted with the efforts of many Americans to do exactly the opposite, must be rooted in other factors. The conclusions of Peal and Lambert's study concerning the cognitive advantages accruing to fluent bilinguals are relevant at this point. Knowledge of more than one language represents a resource in terms of both expanding intellectual horizons and facilitating communication across cultures. This resource and its associated advantages can come to represent a serious threat to monolinguals, who must compete in the same labor markets. It is for this reason that nativist calls for subtractive acculturation—not English, but "English only"—find a receptive audience among less educated segments of the domestic population.[39]

Although the sense of threat among those exposed to labor market competition is understandable, we must ask whether virulent campaigns to compel immigrants to abandon their cultural heritage are justified. In chapter 5, we saw how such campaigns leveled against turn-of-the-century immigrants gave rise to processes of reactive formation and ethnic strife later on. Reactive ethnic mobilizations came, however, without the benefit of fluent bilingualism, sacrificed by earlier generations seeking to Americanize as quickly as possible. To the personal suffering inflicted on the first generation by discrimination and xenophobic attacks must be added the net loss of intellectual and economic resources for American society at large. The "Know Nothing" movement has been a perennial tendency in the politics of the nation leading to frequent attacks precisely against those who "know something" or "know more," bilinguals included.

Growing evidence of the significance and positive benefits of speaking more than one language well leads a number of immigrant parents today to seek a balance between learning English among their offspring and preserving their own languages. Such efforts are mostly unsuccessful because of external pressures, but the factors leading to different outcomes deserve additional attention.

THE ROLE OF SOCIAL CLASS

By the mid-1970s, one-fifth of all U.S. physicians were immigrants. By the mid-1980s, foreign-born students were earning more than half of all doctoral degrees in engineering awarded by U.S. universities, most staying to live in America. One in every three engineers with a doctoral degree working in U.S. industry then was an immigrant. It is estimated that well over half of engineering professors in U.S. universities today are foreign-born, including the majority of assistant professors under thirty-five years of age.[40] These successful immigrant professionals and entrepreneurs are, for the most part, fluent bilinguals. There is little reason to suspect that the pattern of native language use at home—found to be predominant among the first generation—does not apply to them. There is also little reason to suspect that they would want their children to become exclusively monolingual.

We have seen earlier how students classified as fluent bilinguals tend to excel in school, surpassing the performance of both English monolinguals and limited bilinguals. This positive association may be due to the effects of bilingualism on cognitive skills, an argument in line with Peal and Lambert's hypothesis; but it may also be due to the effect of other factors, such as family socioeconomic status, which account for *both* language knowledge and academic performance.

The San Diego School District study, described previously, lacked sufficient data to disentangle these causal patterns, but another study of Indo-Chinese refugees in the same city provides the necessary information. The study collected data over time on a probability sample of 340 students from Vietnam, Laos, and Cambodia attending San Diego secondary schools. Complete academic histories for these children were obtained and matched with a comprehensive data set on their parents and households. The characteristics of this sample generally correspond to those reported previously by the larger school district project: 40 percent of respondents were classified as fluent bilinguals (FEP) and 60 percent as limited bilinguals (LEP); the rank order of GPA and standardized test scores among the Indochinese nationalities included in both studies are the same.[41]

Fluent bilingual students were significantly more likely to come from intact families with higher average levels of education, income, and U.S. residence. Along with time in the United States and age, the most significant predictors of fluency in both languages were parental education, occupation, and knowledge of English. Average grade point average in this Indo-Chinese sample was significantly higher than that among white Anglo students. A multivariate analysis indicated that fluent bilinguals had a significantly higher GPA, controlling for other factors. Objective family characteristics did not affect GPA directly, a result suggesting that their influence is mediated by other factors, possibly including language knowledge.[42]

Research findings elsewhere confirm that immigrants from higher class backgrounds are most able to cope with contradictory demands through an "additive" approach that incorporates knowledge of the new language and customs while preserving the old. An example is provided by a 1985 survey of 622 adult Korean immigrants in Chicago. These immigrants, ranging in age from thirty to fifty-nine, had been in the United States for an average of eight years. Their English ability was tested through an objective vocabulary scale drawn from the Wechsler Adult Intelligence Test (WAIS) and through subjective self-reports. English ability and English language use at home decreased with age but increased with time in the United States, as did the proportion of respondents who regularly read American newspapers and magazines —while *also* maintaining fluency and usage of the Korean language, including reading of Korean newspapers. This additive pattern was strongest for college graduates, who maintained more ethnic attachments with Korean friends and organizations. Over time, the more educated the Koreans in this sample, the more they fit the pattern of high-achieving balanced bilingualism noted by López among non-Mexican Hispanics.[43]

Similar results were obtained by the Children of Immigrants Longitudinal Study (CILS), referred to in previous chapters and to be examined in detail in chapter 8. Among this sample of more than 5,200 youths, whose parents come from seventy-seven different countries, it was found that higher parental socioeconomic status (SES) was positively and significantly associated with fluent bilingualism, controlling for other factors. Each additional point in the parental SES index led to a net increase of 3 percent in the probability of fluent bilingualism in

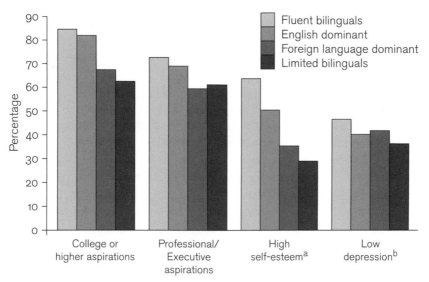

Source: Portes and Rumbaut 2001, 132.
Note: See the text for a description of types of language adaptation.
[a]"High self-esteem" is defined as a mean score of 3.5 or higher on Rosenberg's Self-esteem Scale; the range is 1 (low) to 4.
[b]"Low depression" is defined as a mean score of 1.5 or lower on the Center for Epidemiological Studies—Depression Subscale (CES-D); the range is 1 (low) to 4.

Figure 14. Types of language adaptation and their social psychological correlates

the second generation. Supporting results from the earlier San Diego study, the panel also showed that fluent, but not limited, bilingualism has significant and positive effects on academic achievement, as well as on related dimensions such as educational and occupational aspirations and self-esteem. Controlling for other predictors, fluent bilinguals had significantly higher math and reading scores, as well as grades, in junior high school. Figure 14 depicts the effects of language types on psychosocial correlates of achievement.

Chances for additive acculturation—not English-only, but English-plus—are thus greater in families of professionals and other educated immigrants. Migrant laborers, in contrast, are more likely to swing from foreign-language monolingualism in the first generation to limited bilingualism or English monolingualism in the second. All children of immigrants must contend, however, with the powerful external pressures pushing toward the latter outcome. In the same CILS longitudinal panel, only a minority (28.5 percent) were fully bilingual at about the time of high school graduation; the majority had already shifted toward

English monolingualism, with a significant number (17.8 percent) having become limited bilinguals. As seen in figure 14, the latter pattern is associated with the worst social-psychological adaptation outcomes.[44]

IMMIGRANTS AND THEIR CONTEXTS

The typology of contemporary immigrants that has accompanied us throughout this book—primarily a classification of fundamental differences in social class background and skills—now serves to highlight the principal differences in the process of linguistic adaptation. Before exploring this dimension, however, we must again take into account the social context in which immigrants settle. For our purposes, the basic difference is between immigrants who cluster in ethnic communities and those who become dispersed throughout the country.

The fundamental impact of context in the course of linguistic adaptation has been documented consistently by past research. A large study of bilingualism in Canadian cities, for example, found that French and English usage among urban groups was closely related to the proportion of other-tongue speakers in the same city. In general, the more each group found itself in a linguistic minority, the greater the pressure to become bilingual. Because of the national dominance of English, a greater concentration of French speakers was needed to induce bilingualism in native English speakers than vice versa. The pressure was mainly occupational, resulting in more bilingual men than women, given the higher rate of labor force participation among males. Thus, the greater the occupational demand for one language, the greater the pressure for native speakers of the other to become bilingual.[45]

Labor market pressures in the United States also lead in the direction of prompt English acquisition, but their effect is attenuated by the presence of a large and diversified ethnic community. The latter tends to encourage use of the immigrants' native tongue during off-work hours and results in spin-off commercial and service opportunities that *require* fluent knowledge of the non-English home language. That is why use of these languages tends to flourish in entrepreneurial ethnic enclaves. Linguistic requirements in the outside labor market also vary significantly. For most high-status occupations, fluent and even nonaccented English is required. For many manual-level jobs, however, English may be almost unnecessary. In some extreme cases, employers may actually prefer non-English monolinguals, whom they perceive as more docile sources of labor.[46]

Figure 15 summarizes the interplay among type of immigration, context, and expected social and linguistic outcomes. Working-class immigrants and refugees who become dispersed throughout the country tend to have minimal impact in the communities where they settle. Adult immigrants must perforce learn some English, and their children are likely to become English monolinguals. Working-class immigrants who cluster in certain areas give rise to homogeneous ethnic neighborhoods that help preserve mother-tongue monolingualism among adults. Their children are likely to be limited bilinguals because they are insufficiently exposed to English—as is the case with recent arrivals—or to fully use the mother tongue—as is the case with the U.S.-born.

Entrepreneurial groups that disperse after arrival tend to give rise to middleman-type businesses, as seen in earlier chapters. They must perforce learn some English in order to carry out transactions with their domestic customers. Their children are prone to become English monolinguals because of outside pressures for assimilation and the absence of ethnic supports for using their mother tongue. A different story is that of entrepreneurial groups that give rise to ethnic enclaves. Members of these groups learn English, but adults face less pressure to do so given the possibility of conducting business in their mother tongue. The children of enclave entrepreneurs are likely to become fluent bilinguals because of access to quality English language education, financed by their parents' resources, combined with strong ethnic support for continuing use of the mother tongue. Fluent bilingualism in these contexts is associated with superior economic opportunities. This conclusion is supported by the finding from the CILS study that Cuban American children who attended private schools in the midst of Miami's Cuban enclave were the most likely group in the second generation to preserve bilingual fluency.[47]

As seen in chapter 3, immigrant groups with a strong professional component tend to become dispersed upon arrival. The more dispersed they are, the less impact they have on the communities where they settle. Immigrant professionals become fluent, though not necessarily "accentless," bilinguals by force of circumstance and because of their higher education. Although they may try to transmit full bilingualism to their children, the absence of outside ethnic supports makes this a futile enterprise in most instances. But some professional-level immigrants and many upper-class refugees settle where their own group concentrates. Their presence gives a more diversified educational and occupational character to ethnic enclaves or preexisting ethnic neighborhoods.

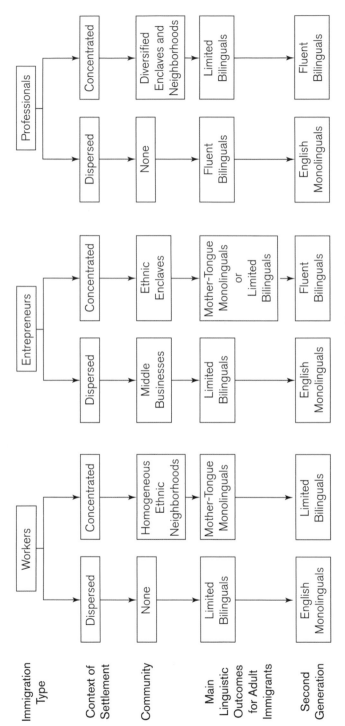

Figure 15. Type of immigration, social context of settlement, and predicted community and linguistic outcomes

Linguistic transition in these contexts is slower because the community tends to attenuate outside pressures for assimilation.[48] Absence of fluent bilingualism among adults is compensated by its presence among children. The mechanism leading to this outcome is exactly the same as in the case of entrepreneurial communities.

Other individual and collective factors affect language use among immigrants and their descendants.[49] Thus, the outcomes summarized in figure 15 must be read as a set of tendencies, based on past experience. The figure highlights the three core findings of the existing research literature on language adaptation—namely, that home-country monolingualism seldom outlasts the first generation; that English monolingualism is the dominant trend among the second generation; and that preservation of fluent bilingualism is an exceptional outcome, dependent on both the intellectual and economic resources of parents and the presence of outside social structural supports.

CONCLUSION

> Wide open and unguarded stand our gates,
> And through them presses a wild motley throng . . .
> Accents of menace alien to our air,
> Voices that once the Tower of Babel knew![50]

The author of these lines, Thomas B. Aldrich, was the eminent editor of the *Atlantic Monthly*, penning his poem in the same period that Emma Lazarus contributed hers to the pedestal of the Statue of Liberty in New York harbor. Although the gates are less "unguarded" today than they were at the turn of the twentieth century, one can only imagine what Aldrich might have written of the far greater linguistic diversity of the newest immigrants to the United States. Yet he might have saved his muse for a better cause. A rapid transition to English has been the lot of the vast majority of foreign groups in the history of American immigration and continues to be so today.

The shift to English is both an empirical fact and a cultural requirement demanded of foreigners who have sought a new life in America. In its most extreme version, the requirement has included both the acquisition of English and the loss of anything else immigrants might have brought with them. Research on intelligence and the psychology of mental ability until midcentury served to buttress this position by documenting the intellectual inferiority of immigrant children and debating whether it caused a lack of English fluency or vice versa. The introduction of controls for social class background after decades of such reports reversed the finding, indicating that fluent or "true" bilingual children actually outperformed monolinguals on a variety of achievement tests. The expansion of intellectual horizons associated with bilingualism must have been suspected earlier by members of the domestic elite, who devoted much effort to acquiring foreign tongues, often the same ones that immigrants were being told to forget.

Calls for subtractive assimilation have persisted and have gained renewed vigor in recent years with the advent of U.S. English and other militant nativist movements.[51] The significant new ingredient brought about by contemporary immigration is, however, the presence of a sizable minority of educated newcomers who are able to both understand the advantages of fluent bilingualism and maintain it. Giving up a foreign language means sacrificing the possibility of looking at things from a different perspective and becoming bound to the symbols and perceptions embedded in a single tongue. Like educated Americans, educated immigrants have sought to avoid these limitations and to transmit this advantage to their children.

Their efforts, however, will have only a limited collective effect. First, the vast majority of immigrants do not belong to this privileged stratum, and their adaptation is likely to follow the time-honored pattern toward English monolingualism in the course of one or two generations. Second, bilingual parents who try to educate their children in their mother tongue confront the immense pressure for cultural conformity from peers, friends, teachers, and the media. In the absence of a sizable and economically potent ethnic community to support language maintenance, fluent bilingualism in the second generation is likely to prove an elusive goal.

These conclusions reverse the usual concerns expressed in popular and journalistic literature, which call attention to the proliferation of foreign languages and to the threat that they pose to English dominance. Fears of linguistic and cultural fragmentation, like fears of ethnic radicalism, play well in the popular press, and harping on them has made the fame and fortune of many a pundit. However, historical and contemporary evidence indicates that English has never been seriously threatened as the dominant language of the United States and that, with well over two hundred million monolingual English speakers, it is certainly not threatened today. The real threat has been to the viability of other languages, which have mostly succumbed in the wake of

American-style assimilation. To the extent that language fluency is an asset and that knowledge of a foreign tongue represents a scarce resource, immigrants' efforts to maintain this part of their cultural heritage and pass it on to their children seem worth supporting. Although in the course of time they, too, may be destined to disappear, the pockets where Chinese, Spanish, Hindi, Korean, French, or Italian continues to flourish enrich American culture and the lives of the native- and foreign-born alike.

8

Growing Up American
The New Second Generation

With the collaboration of
Patricia Fernández-Kelly
and William Haller

Since Oscar Handlin noted that to write the history of immigrants in America is to write American history, the phrase has become de rigueur in any introduction to the subject. In reality, however, American history is not so much the history of its immigrants as of their descendants, for it is they who, as citizens and full participants in the culture, have had the heaviest role in the evolution of American society. In the previous chapters, we have examined the diversity of contemporary immigration, its settlement patterns and modes of incorporation into the American economy and polity, and aspects of the immigrants' psychological, cultural, and linguistic adaptations. It is now time to consider how the children of these immigrants are adapting to their role as American citizens.

During the last four decades, a large new second generation formed by children of immigrants born in the United States or brought at an early age from abroad has emerged. Most of its members are still in school, but many entered adulthood in the 1990s. During this decade, the prior record of twenty-eight million native-born citizens of foreign parentage, reached by descendants of Europeans in the 1940s, was surpassed. Immigrants and their offspring contributed a full 70 percent of the country's population growth between 1990 and 2000. Today, one in five of every American age eighteen and younger is an immigrant or a child of immigrants. Given the continuing flow of immigration for the foreseeable future and the higher fertility of foreign-born women in the United States, that proportion will rapidly increase in the future.[1]

At first glance and based on the experience of the children of earlier European groups, we could anticipate that the adaptation process of the new second generation would be relatively smooth. Children would gradually leave foreign languages and identities behind, embrace American culture, and claim and gain their rightful place in the social mainstream. As we will see, this straight-line vision fits present experience only imperfectly.

Sons and daughters of immigrants from Asia, Latin America, and the Caribbean often encounter obstacles in their path that render their successful adaptation and economic advancement problematic. In today's context, many of these children face the paradox that assimilating to their American surroundings may derail their successful adaptation, while remaining firmly ensconced in their parents' immigrant communities and cultures may strengthen their chances. This paradox stems from the complexities of contemporary American society and the unexpected effects that it has on newcomers. We will examine these dynamics after reviewing what is known about the number, location, and attitudes of this emerging population.

THE NEW SECOND GENERATION AT A GLANCE

The 2000 U.S. Census, like its predecessors in 1980 and 1990, omitted questions about the country of birth of parents, thus preventing a full description of the size and characteristics of today's second generation. As a result, just at the moment when a new era of large-scale immigration made the collection of such data indispensable in the United States, the last three censuses have permitted a detailed examination only of the foreign-born population by country of birth and date of arrival but not of their U.S.-born children.

Fortunately, in 1994 the questions on paternal and maternal nativity were incorporated in the annual Current Population Survey (CPS), a representative survey of American households conducted by the Census Bureau. The March supplement of the CPS contains the necessary questions on ancestry and place of birth to identify members of both the first and second generations (of foreign birth or parentage), as well as the third or higher generations (the native-born of native parentage).

Although the sample size for a given year, while substantial, is not large enough to provide reliable information on smaller immigrant populations or to allow comparative studies by national origin and by generational cohorts, the CPS has since become the main national-level data set in the United States permitting intergenerational analysis.

Results from the 2005 CPS show that more than thirty million second-generation persons—defined as native-born individuals with at least one foreign-born parent—lived at the time in the United States, representing 11 percent of the U.S. civilian population. Added to the more than thirty-seven million foreign-born persons in 2005 (the first generation, accounting for 13 percent of the national population),[2] the foreign-stock population (the first plus second generations) numbered more than sixty-seven million persons and was fast approaching one-fourth of the U.S. total. Of this number, it is possible to distinguish those who belong to the "old" great wave of European immigration of the early twentieth century and those who comprise the "new" post-1960 immigration.

In 2005, about 7.8 million persons had at least one foreign-born parent who had been born in the United States prior to 1960—the rapidly dwindling remnants of the "old second generation," with an average age of sixty-eight years; in contrast, the "new second generation" of children of immigrants born in the United States since 1960 had an average age of sixteen years. In addition, more than one-third of the foreign-born had arrived in the United States as children under the age of thirteen (the "1.5" generation); and of them, the vast majority had come since 1960—also a youthful population, with an average age of twenty-three. Combining those who immigrated as children under thirteen since 1960 with those who were born in the United States after that date (whether of one or two foreign-born parents) yields an estimate of just over thirty million young people who are only now entering adulthood. It is this rapidly growing population that will concern us here.

Table 38 presents data from the 2005 CPS summarizing basic demographic and socioeconomic characteristics of the first, second, and third or higher generations. The table is restricted to the "new" post-1960 immigration and their offspring. The foreign-born are distinguished by their age at arrival (younger or older than thirteen) and the U.S.-born by whether they had one or two foreign-born parents. We see that the foreign-born and foreign-parentage population is much more concentrated in metropolitan areas (over 90 percent) than the native-born of

TABLE 38. THE NEW SECOND GENERATION AT A GLANCE, 2005

Characteristic	New first generation (post-1960) (foreign-born)		New second generation (post-1960) (U.S.-born)			Third generation and higher (self and parents are U.S.-born)
	Arrived 13 or older	Arrived under 13	Two foreign-born parents	One foreign-born parent	Total[a]	
Number[b] (in millions)	26.2	9.1	13.5	7.6	30.3	221.6
Age (mean years)	42.9	23.4	14.3	17.6	17.9	36.5
Metropolitan residence (%)	95.4	93.7	95.7	90.9	93.9	79.2
Both parents present (%)[c]	—	78.0	76.8	69.9	75.2	66.2
Own home (%)	52.1	54.4	59.8	68.2	60.3	75.7
Poverty rate (%)[d]	17.1	18.0	21.1	13.3	18.2	11.8
Education (%)[e]						
Less than high school	34.6	17.3	9.6	5.8	12.1	11.3
High school graduate or more	65.4	82.7	90.4	94.2	87.9	88.7
Bachelor's degree or more	27.1	30.6	39.3	37.8	35.0	27.6
In labor force (%)[f]	68.6	71.4	66.4	73.5	70.2	66.3

a Total of foreign-born persons who arrived after 1960 as children under age thirteen, plus children born in the United States after 1960 of at least one foreign-born parent.
b Estimates based on the March 2005 Current Population Survey. First- and second-generation totals exclude persons born in Puerto Rico or other U.S. territories.
c For children under eighteen years old.
d Below 100 percent of the federal poverty line.
e For persons age twenty-five or older.
f For persons age sixteen or older.

native parentage (under 80 percent). This characteristic has significant consequences for the adaptation process of the second generation, as we will see later in this chapter.

Relative to native-parentage youths, children of immigrants (age eighteen and younger) are more likely to live with both of their parents (75 vs. 66 percent). As we will also see, intact families play an important role in the successful adaptation of these children. On the other hand, the second generation has higher poverty rates than the rest of the U.S. population (18.2 vs. 11.8 percent), especially when both parents are foreign-born, and notably lower homeownership rates than the general population (60 vs. 76 percent).

The educational profile of the second generation is similar to that of the general population (and superior to the first), although a larger proportion of immigrant youths have less than a high school education. Among the U.S.-born second generation, however, the rates of college graduation are also superior to those of the general native-parentage population. The significance of education for occupational and economic success can scarcely be exaggerated, and these figures suggest that immigrant children and children of immigrants exhibit both advantages and disadvantages. As we will see, the disadvantages become much greater among offspring of poorer immigrant nationalities. Despite this result, the labor force status and occupational profile of second-generation persons who are already employed do not differ significantly from those of the rest of the U.S. labor force. Again, however, these average figures conceal significant variations among specific immigrant nationalities, a topic to which we now turn.

PARENTAL HUMAN CAPITAL AND MODES OF INCORPORATION

In chapter 4, we showed how the social context that receives immigrants plays a decisive role in their economic prospects. Combined with the human capital that they bring from abroad, their modes of incorporation determine the paths of occupational and economic mobility followed by different immigrant minorities. It stands to reason that their offspring will be similarly affected, so that their educational performance in school and their career prospects, and even their linguistic habits and self-identities, will reflect the course of adaptation and relative socioeconomic success experienced by their parents.[3]

As we saw in chapters 2 and 4, contemporary immigration is very heterogeneous in terms of human capital and modes of incorporation, featuring, at its core, a basic bimodal pattern between immigrant professionals and entrepreneurs, on the one hand, and labor migrants, on the other. These differences are highlighted again by the data presented in table 39. These results come from two different sources: first, combined CPS surveys for the years 1994–1997;[4] second, the Children of Immigrants Longitudinal Study (CILS), a ten-year panel of 1.5- and second-generation youths in South Florida and Southern California, described in the following section. In 1995–1996, this study conducted face-to-face interviews with more than 2,400 immigrant parents in both regions, obtaining detailed information on their backgrounds, present socioeconomic situation, and outlooks for the future. Table 39 presents information for the principal nationalities represented both in total immigration during the 1990s and in the CILS survey. Jointly these nine nationalities represent over three-fourths of total immigration to the United States during the 1990s.[5]

Although our two data sources differ significantly in sample design, common tendencies emerge in levels of parental human capital, as indexed by years of education. At one extreme, we find Chinese and Filipino adult immigrants and parents with very low proportions of high school dropouts and correspondingly high proportions of college graduates. At the other extreme are Mexican immigrants and Laotian/Cambodian refugees. As seen in chapter 4, modes of incorporation are operationally defined by (1) the availability of official resettlement assistance programs for some groups; (2) legal entry but no assistance and a generally neutral mainstream reception for others; and (3) high levels of racial prejudice against certain immigrants, combined with governmental hostility toward groups regarded as sources of illegal immigration. While actual modes of incorporation vary across families and over time, the relevant column in table 39 provides a summary measure of the actual contexts encountered by different nationalities in the mid-1990s.

Differences in human capital and modes of incorporation are partially reflected, in turn, in monthly earnings, annual incomes, and occupational status. Professional-level occupations were rare among Mexican and Laotian/Cambodian immigrant parents in the mid-1990s, but they were common among Chinese, Cubans, and Filipinos. Despite the disadvantages brought about by racial discrimination, Jamaicans and other West Indian immigrants were also well represented among professionals, on the strength of high levels of human capital. Earnings and incomes follow the same general pattern, with the lowest levels found

TABLE 39. HUMAN CAPITAL, MODES OF INCORPORATION, PRESENT
SITUATION, AND EXPECTATIONS OF IMMIGRANT PARENTS, 1995–1996

| Nationality | % less than high school[a] | % college graduates[a] | | Modes of incorporation[b] | Annual average income[c] ($) | % in professional/ executive occupation | | % intact families[d] | % expects child to graduate college | % expects child to earn a postgraduate degree[e] |
	CPS	CPS	CILS		CILS	CPS	CILS	CILS	CILS	CILS
Chinese	4.4	46.3	41.9	Neutral	58,627	37.9	20.3	76.7	87.8	69.2
Cuban	38.3	19.4	20.9	Positive	48,266	23.3	19.1	58.8	74.3	61.0
Filipino	12.0	44.8	45.5	Neutral	49,007	28.5	16.8	79.4	92.2	33.0
Haitian	35.5	12.6	9.3	Negative	16,394	—	9.3	44.9	76.7	65.2
Jamaican/ West Indian	20.7	18.0	20.0	Negative	39,102	24.7	22.3	43.4	80.8	55.2
Laotian/ Cambodian	45.3	12.3	2.6	Positive	25,696	14.7	1.8	70.8	57.1	38.5
Mexican	69.8	3.7	2.6	Negative	22,442	5.1	2.9	59.5	54.5	39.2
Nicaraguan	39.6	14.1	32.5	Negative	32,376	7.2	17.0	62.8	73.3	55.0
Vietnamese	30.8	15.3	7.6	Positive	26,822	12.9	5.6	73.5	86.9	18.8

[a] For persons age sixteen or older.
[b] Modes of incorporation are defined as follows: positive, refugees and asylees receiving government resettlement assistance; neutral, nonblack immigrants admitted for legal permanent residence; negative, black immigrants and those nationalities with large proportions of unauthorized (illegal) entrants.
[c] Family incomes.
[d] Children living with both biological parents.
[e] Among those parents expecting their child to graduate from college.

among Mexicans and Haitians and the highest among Chinese, Filipinos, and Cubans.

Despite low levels of human capital, Laotian and Cambodian parents are not the most disadvantaged in economic terms, a result that directly reflects their favorable modes of incorporation as legal refugees. However, they, together with Mexican immigrants, had the lowest educational expectations for their offspring. While parental ambition is quite high for all immigrant groups, there are also significant differences in that respect, reflecting wide variations in socioeconomic situations. Practically all Chinese and Filipino parents expect their children to graduate from college, while the proportion among Mexican immigrants is about half.

A third dimension that, together with parental human capital and modes of incorporation, can decisively affect the future of the second generation is family structure. Two-parent families double, by their very character, the scope of available resources to guide and influence the adaptation of children. Clearly, all families are different, and the presence of both biological parents does not guarantee successful results in every case. But, as we will see shortly, intact families can have a strong positive influence on second-generation outcomes, including aspirations, self-esteem, and the likelihood of graduating from high school.

As shown in table 39, the proportion of intact families ranges from 80 percent for Filipinos to slightly above 40 percent for West Indians. There is a clear rank order in this dimension, with Asian immigrants being the most likely to hold families together and Caribbean immigrants the least. Reasons for these differences are multiple and have to do with characteristics of the cultures of origin, the experiences of the group on arrival, and its age and educational composition.[6] We move now to examine how these characteristics of the first generation affect their children as they confront the challenges of adaptation to America.

THE CHILDREN OF IMMIGRANTS LONGITUDINAL STUDY

PAO YANG, A LAOTIAN HMONG FATHER

In 1995, the San Diego home of Pao Yang, age fifty-seven, and his family was in disarray because they were packing to move to Fresno. As refugees, both Pao and his wife Zer Vue received federally supported assistance. Pao complemented this income with some odd jobs, but his options were limited because he spoke little English. The interview was conducted in Hmong. Before starting, the interviewer asked for his eighteen-year-old son, Khae, who had not yet completed the project's schedule. Pao responded that his son had just stepped out of the house, but they could begin the interview. Ten minutes into it, the porch screen door slammed, and Khae stepped in. He wore no shirt and had shaved his head.

The father called, "Khae, come here; you have some questionnaire to fill out." The young man replied, "No, I don't care for it or anybody." He went to his bedroom, slamming the door after him. Fifteen minutes later he came out and was confronted by his mother, who politely asked him to cooperate. Khae answered, "No, all of this is shit." He left the home, again slamming the door. In Hmong, the mother reported, "It was not like this before. He was obedient, well behaved, went to school every day. Two years ago, he joined the Mesa Kings [a local gang], and last year he quit school. He does what he likes, does what he pleases. If you try talking to him, he yells louder and leaves."

Pao added, "We cannot control him; once I hit him, and he pulled a gun on me. He knows English better than us—thinks that he knows everything. If he continues this way, he'll never finish high school; he'll be killed first." By the end of the conversation, it became clear that Khae was the reason why the family was moving to Fresno. There is a larger, more concentrated Hmong population there, and the family had several relatives living in the city. The parents hoped to put Khae back in school and garner the help of the extended family and clan to keep him away from gangs. Zer Vue accompanied the interviewer to the door. "I want to apologize for the bad attitude of my son," she said. "It would not have been like this back home; it is this country that is so hard to understand."[7]

As farmers and herdsmen from the Laotian highlands, most Hmong refugees arrived in the United States with virtually no formal education and skills ill suited for urban life. As political refugees, they received extensive resettlement assistance, but many confronted the challenges awaiting them in America in isolation. For Pao Yang and Zer Vue, leaving San Diego in search of a stronger coethnic community was about the only hope of extracting their son from almost certain tragedy.

This story, one of many that illustrate the challenge and perils of second-generation adaptation, comes from the CILS, a decade-long panel survey designed to accomplish what census or CPS data alone cannot do: to examine in-depth the interaction between immigrant parents and children and the evolution of the young from adolescence into early adulthood. The study is briefly described next as it provides the source for key results reported later on.

STUDYING THE NEW SECOND GENERATION

The CILS focused on a baseline population of mean age fourteen, corresponding to the census estimate of the average for children of Asian and Latin American immigrants in 1990. In addition to this correspondence, there was another powerful reason to concentrate on this age group. At this early age, most children are still in middle school or junior high school, which makes it possible to generate representative samples by tapping the school population. As they get older, an unknown number drop out of school, biasing samples restricted to student cohorts.[8]

The study's original design called for taking large samples of students of foreign parentage in the eighth and ninth grades, ranging in age from thirteen to seventeen, and following them for three to four years until their last year of high school. At this point, a second survey took place of all those students who had remained in school and were about to graduate as well as those who had abandoned their schooling. Through this strategy, it was possible to examine adaptation outcomes at the crucial school-to-work or school-to-college transition and, more important, to unambiguously establish the causal forces determining these outcomes.

In total, 5,262 students took part in the first survey, representing seventy-seven different nationalities. To be eligible for an interview, the student had to be U.S.-born and have at least one foreign-born parent or, if foreign-born, to have lived in the United States for at least five years. The samples were drawn from forty-nine schools in the metropolitan areas of Miami–Fort Lauderdale, Florida, and San Diego, California. Miami receives immigrants mainly from the Caribbean—especially Cubans, Haitians, Dominicans, Jamaicans, and other English-speaking West Indians; from Central America, mostly Nicaraguans; and from South America. San Diego is one of the main entry points and places of settlement for the large inflow from Mexico; it also receives large numbers of Salvadorans and Guatemalans and is one of the cities preferred by immigrants from Asia—such as Filipinos, Vietnamese, Cambodians, and Laotians as well as, to a lesser extent, Chinese, Japanese, and Koreans.

In both cities, the sample design called for inclusion of schools in areas of heavy immigrant concentration as well as those where the native-born predominated. This strategy allows analysis of how various adaptation outcomes are affected by different school contexts. The San Diego school district is sufficiently diverse to contain both types of schools. Miami has been so heavily affected by immigration that most of its schools include large proportions of first- and second-generation students. For this reason, the sample encompassed the schools of Fort Lauderdale (in Broward County), where native-parentage students still predominated. The average age of the sample was fourteen at the time of the first survey, and it was evenly divided by sex and by grade in school. Similarly, about half of the respondents were native-born of foreign parentage (corresponding to a strict definition of second generation), and the remainder were members of the 1.5 generation (born abroad but brought at an early age to the United States). This initial survey was conducted in 1992–1993.

In 1995–1996, three years after the original survey, the first follow-up was launched. Whenever possible, interviews were conducted in school. For students who had dropped out or moved to other areas, questionnaires were completed by mail or through face-to-face interviews. A problem of potential bias exists because the follow-up survey did not retrieve all original respondents; the total follow-up sample is 4,288, or 81.5 percent of the original. The question is whether lost cases were random or whether they overrepresented a particular class of respondents. In the latter case, a sampling bias exists. To test this possibility, we compared retrieved and lost respondents on their characteristics, as measured in the first survey.

Table 40 presents results of this analysis that show the follow-up sample faithfully reproduced the different categories of respondents in the original survey. The follow-up survey retrieved almost identical proportions of boys and girls, of native-born and foreign-born youths, and of U.S. citizens and noncitizens. Similarly, the proportions represented by different nationalities in both surveys are quite close. The same point was demonstrated by a parallel analysis of correlations between characteristics measured in the first survey and presence in the follow-up. With few exceptions, such correlations were nonsignificant.[9] Based on these results, figures from the second CILS survey can be considered representative of the first.

An important limitation of both student surveys is that information on the parents and families was obtained indirectly from teenage respondents. It was obvious that additional and more reliable information on the parents was necessary. For this reason, a survey of immigrant parents was conducted in conjunction with the student follow-up in 1996. Interviews for this supplementary survey were conducted in person and often in the respondent's own language. Because of the complexity of locating and interviewing so many non-English-speaking parents, the survey was conducted with a probability sample representing 50 percent of the student follow-up. Results from this survey have already been used previously (see table 39) and will provide a context to the findings on the adaptation outcomes of the second generation, to be discussed later.

WHERE THEY GROW UP: CHALLENGES TO SECOND-GENERATION ADAPTATION

To a greater extent than at the beginning of the twentieth century, second-generation youths today confront a pluralistic, fragmented environment that offers simultaneously a wealth of opportunities and serious threats to successful adaptation.[10] In this situation, the central question is not whether the second generation will assimilate to American society but *to what segment* of that society it will assimilate. In the present historical context, children of immigrants face three major challenges to educational attainment and career success. The first is the persistence of racial discrimination; the second is the bifurcation of the American labor market and its growing inequality; the third is the consolidation of drug use and street gangs as an alternative lifestyle in American inner cities.

RACE

One of the key features that children inherit from their parents is their race. Defined by contemporary standards, the majority of today's second generation is nonwhite, being formed by children of Asian immigrants, blacks from the West Indies and Africa, and blacks, mulattos, and mestizos from Latin America. The minority of white immigrants also come from Latin America and, in declining numbers, from Europe and Canada. Figure 16 presents the racial self-identities of second-generation youths participating in the CILS during late adolescence, when most were seventeen to eighteen years old. Only a small minority identify themselves as white, the majority seeing themselves as Asian, Hispanic/Latino, black, or multiracial.

Although racial features may appear to be a trait of individuals, in reality they are a contextual feature of the host society. Prejudice is not

TABLE 40. THE CHILDREN OF IMMIGRANTS LONGITUDINAL STUDY
First and follow-up student surveys

| | | Miami/Fort Lauderdale | | | | | | | | San Diego | | | | | | | |
| | | First survey (1992–1993) | | Follow-up survey (1995–1996) | | First survey (1992–1993) | | Follow-up survey (1995–1996) | |
Variables[a]	Values	N	%	N	%	N	%	N	%
Sex	Male	1,366	48.1	1,046	47.0	1,209	50.0	1,023	49.6
	Female	1,467	51.9	1,179	53.0	1,211	50.0	1,040	50.4
Length of U.S. residence	Nine years or less	596	21.0	467	21.0	733	30.3	605	29.3
	Ten years or more	739	26.0	582	26.2	687	28.4	583	28.3
	U.S.-born	1,507	53.0	1,176	52.9	1,000	41.3	875	42.4
U.S. citizen	Yes	1,886	66.4	1,461	65.7	1,449	59.9	1,260	61.1
	No/don't know	956	33.6	764	34.3	971	40.1	803	38.9
Household composition	Father and mother present	1,649	58.0	1,385	62.2	1,689	69.8	1,517	73.5
	Parent and stepparent	450	15.8	306	13.9	242	10.0	182	8.8
	Single parent	658	23.2	478	21.5	403	16.7	310	15.0
	Other	85	3.0	56	2.5	86	3.5	54	2.7
Father's education	Less than high school	1,066	37.5	809	36.4	1,106	45.7	924	44.8
	High school graduate	1,010	35.5	793	35.6	879	36.3	754	36.5
	College graduate or more	766	27.0	623	28.0	435	18.0	385	18.7

	N	%	N	%	N	%	N	%
Mother's education								
Less than high school	891	31.4	676	30.4	1,272	52.6	1,050	50.9
High school graduate	1,319	46.4	1037	46.6	715	29.5	616	29.9
College graduate or more	632	22.2	512	23.0	433	17.9	397	19.2
National origin								
Cuban (public school)	1,042	36.8	820	36.9	2	0.1	2	0.1
Cuban (private school)	183	6.5	146	6.6	0	0.0	0	0.0
Nicaraguan	340	12.0	277	12.4	4	0.2	4	0.2
Colombian	223	8.0	181	8.1	4	0.2	4	0.2
Haitian	177	6.2	134	6.0	1	0.0	1	0.0
West Indian	253	9.0	189	8.5	19	0.8	12	0.6
Mexican	28	1.0	21	0.9	727	30.0	578	28.0
Filipino	11	0.5	8	0.4	808	33.4	716	34.7
Vietnamese	8	0.3	7	0.3	362	15.0	303	14.7
Laotian	1	0.0	1	0.0	154	6.4	143	6.9
Cambodian	1	0.0	1	0.0	94	3.8	88	4.3
Hmong	0	0.0	0	0.0	53	2.2	50	2.4
Other Latin American	411	14.6	317	14.3	58	2.4	41	1.9
Other Asian	22	0.8	40	1.8	118	4.9	107	5.3
Other	120	4.3	83	3.8	16	0.5	14	0.7
Totals	2,842	100.0	2,225	100.0	2420	100.0	2063	100.0

SOURCES: CILS-I and CILS-II.

[a] All variables measured in the original survey.

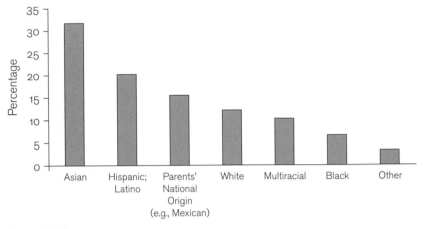

Source: CILS-II, 1995.

Figure 16. The racial identities of children of immigrants, 1996

intrinsic to any particular skin color or racial type, and indeed many immigrants never experienced it in their native lands. It is by virtue of moving to a new country and culture where physical features are assigned great importance that immigrants can become targets and victims of discrimination. Children of Asian, black, mulatto, and mestizo immigrants cannot easily reduce their ethnicity to the level of a voluntary option. Their enduring physical differences from whites and the equally persistent prejudice based on those differences, especially against black persons, throw a barrier in the path of occupational mobility and social acceptance. Immigrant children's ethnic identities, their aspirations, and their academic performance are affected accordingly.[11]

From early adolescence, second-generation youths become very aware of these facts. Thus, 31 percent of respondents in the first CILS survey, when their average age was fourteen, said that they expected to suffer discrimination, "no matter how much education they acquired." The figure, however, climbed to 48 percent among Haitian Americans and 60 percent among West Indians, the two predominantly black minorities in this sample.[12]

LABOR MARKETS

A second barrier to the successful adaptation of the second generation is the deindustrialization and progressive bifurcation of the American labor market. Immigrant workers today form the backbone in what remains of labor-intensive manufacturing as well as in a rapidly growing personal services sector, but these are niches that seldom offer channels for upward mobility. Rapid deindustrialization means that the structure of the American labor market looks today less like a pyramid, where migrants and their descendants can gradually move up along layers of blue-collar and white-collar occupations. Instead, it resembles an "hourglass," where demand exists for minimally paid occupations at the bottom and for those requiring advanced training at the top, but where the middle layers have been thinning.[13]

This process started in the 1960s and accelerated thereafter under the twin influences of technological innovation and foreign competition in industrial goods. Between 1950 and 1996, American manufacturing employment plummeted, from over one-third of the labor force to less than 15 percent. The slack was picked up by service employment, which skyrocketed from 12 percent to close to one-third of all workers. Service employment is, however, bifurcated between menial and casual low-wage jobs commonly associated with personal services and the rapid growth of occupations requiring advanced technical and professional skills. These high-paying service jobs are generated by knowledge-based industries linked to new information technologies and those associated with the command and control functions of a restructured capitalist economy.[14]

From the point of view of new entrants into the labor force, including children of immigrants, these structural changes mean the end of the old industrial ladder of unskilled, semiskilled, and skilled and supervisory occupations and the advent of a growing labor market bifurcation. This changed market implies that, to succeed socially and economically, children of immigrants today must cross, *in one generation*, the educational gap that took their predecessors—descendants of European immigrants—several generations to bridge. They cannot simply improve on their parents' typically modest educational attainment but must sharply increase it by gaining access to an advanced education.

Immigrant parents and their children come to understand this situation early. We saw previously the high educational ambitions that most parents hold for their offspring. By late adolescence, respondents in the CILS sample came to mirror the same lofty aspirations. They realized that without a college degree or higher, chances for fulfilling their career and life dreams would be seriously compromised. Their views are presented in figure 17. Notice, however, the wide differences

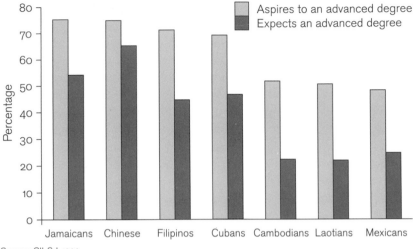

Source: CILS-I, 1992.

Figure 17. Educational aspirations and expectations of children of immigrants, selected nationalities, 1996

among nationalities, similar to those observed among parents, and the wide discrepancies between *aspirations* for an advanced degree and *expectations* of getting one, especially among children of the more disadvantaged immigrant groups.

GANGS AND DRUGS

Why? Why? Why should this country, the richest in the world, have such low educational standards and disruptive behavior? It is sad to see this country's children smoking grass or wearing their hair in spikes. How are these youngsters paying back for the opportunities they receive? . . . You can wear anything to school, you can talk in class—no one can stop you.

Roger, thirty-eight, Nicaraguan father, arrived in Miami in 1987

This is a bad area to live in because of the many homeboys using alcohol and drugs. Every night there is the sound of police sirens and helicopters. My family gets used to it. I am concerned about my younger children. I'm afraid they will join with the homeboys. The reason I'm concerned is because I feel I cannot control the peer pressure; when they step out of the house, it's all over them.

Botum, fifty-one, Cambodian mother of six, arrived in San Diego in 1983

We all live together, children, parents, and grandparents. The grandparents are in charge of discipline here and they are tough—from school to home and back. Kids are taught that our family comes first and that parents must always know where their children are; . . . this is about the only way to survive here. American parents and grandparents do not control their children, and that's why so many turn into bad people.

> Huu Tran, forty-seven, Vietnamese father, arrived in San Diego in 1979[15]

The final challenge confronting children of immigrants is that the social context they encounter, in American schools and neighborhoods, may promote a set of negative outcomes such as dropping out of school, joining a street gang, or participating in the drug subculture.[16] The emergence of deviant lifestyles in American inner cities is partially linked to the transformation of the labor market that did away with the ladder of blue-collar jobs facilitating the upward mobility of earlier children of immigrants. The first victims of this transformation were not members of today's second generation but the children and grandchildren of their predecessors—southern blacks, Mexicans, and Puerto Ricans—brought to fill the labor needs of the American industrial economy during and after World War I.[17]

As descendants of these earlier migrant waves reached working age, they confronted a situation of diminished industrial opportunities and blocked economic mobility. The disappearance of jobs in industry, coupled with racial discrimination, kept second- and third-generation offspring of former labor migrants bottled up in the inner city, while simultaneously preventing them to take advantage of emerging opportunities in the postindustrial economy. The result was the rise of what Wacquant and Wilson called the "hyperghetto"—veritable human warehouses where the disappearance of work and the everyday reality of marginalization led directly to a web of social pathologies. Proliferation of female teenage pregnancy, high involvement of youngsters in crime, and the disappearance of work habits and discipline became common traits in these areas.[18]

Recently arrived immigrants confront these features of life in American cities as a fait accompli conditioning their own and their children's chances for success. As we saw previously, close to 90 percent of all immigrants live in metropolitan areas. Because of low incomes, a third of these families cluster in central city neighborhoods. In that environment, they are exposed to norms of behavior inimical to mobility and to lifestyles and attitudes that reinforce these behaviors. For second-generation

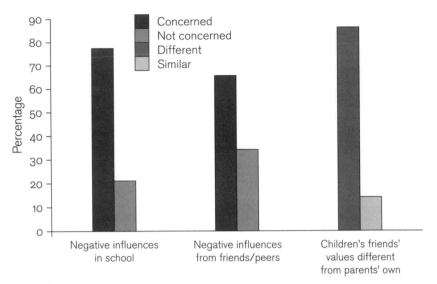

Source: CILS, parental survey.

Figure 18. Immigrant parents' concern with negative influences on their children, 1996

youths, the activities of gangs, sale of drugs, and other elements of "street" culture amount to an alternative path of adaptation, away from school and homework and in direct opposition to their parents' expectations.

Some parents have, in fact, become so distraught at what they see as the permissiveness of American culture and the specific threat posed by inner-city drugs and crime that they have taken to sending their children back home to be educated in the care of grandparents or other kin.[19] The nearly 2,500 immigrant parents interviewed during the second wave of CILS strongly voiced these concerns. As figure 18 shows, vast majorities, over 80 percent, were preoccupied with the negative influences their children receive in school and the gap between their own goals and values and those of their children's friends. These concerns were universal, regardless of nationality or social class.

The interaction between these various challenges and the resources of immigrant families determine the various paths that the process of second-generation adaptation can take. Drawing on a stylized image of the experiences of children of European immigrants in the twentieth century, it was common until recently to speak of "assimilation" as the normal process undergone by immigrants and their descendants on the way toward acceptance and integration into the social mainstream. At present, American society has become so heterogeneous and the contingencies confronting immigrant families so bewildering that it is difficult to sustain the notion of a single "mainstream" or of a normative assimilation path. Instead, the process has become segmented, following divergent courses that depend largely on the ways that family and ethnic community resources are deployed to confront the challenges faced by second-generation youths.

Recent efforts to revise the notion of assimilation, most notably by Alba and Nee,[20] have had to contend with these realities, including an increasingly heterogeneous American society and the presence of multiple alternative options for immigrants and their offspring. As these authors recognize, one such outcome is resistance to assimilation and possible return to the home countries. Most immigrants do not follow this course, however, and instead strive to learn English and incorporate themselves into their new environment. Yet the forms in which they do are so diverse as to render any notion of a uniform assimilation process untenable. In the end, such revivalist attempts express the hope that things will eventually turn out well for most newcomers. These hopes are commendable but also questionable.

Some immigrants today achieve middle-class status in the first generation, drawing on high levels of human capital and a favorable mode of incorporation. Their offspring are thus posed to integrate rapidly into the American middle and upper classes by graduating from college and entering high-status occupations. In the process, they can reduce ethnic distinctions, often turning them into a voluntary option. Other immigrants never manage to rise above the working class, but their families are sufficiently strong and their communities sufficiently cohesive to support parental aspirations and steer children away from pitfalls endangering their progress through the educational system. Such youths can also achieve the necessary credentials, while maintaining strong social ties with their families and communities of origin. Finally, there are those youths for whom ethnicity would be neither a badge of pride nor a social convenience but a mark of subordination. These are usually the offspring of working-class immigrants when a negative mode of incorporation has prevented the development of strong and protective ethnic communities. Such children are at risk of joining the most disadvantaged minorities at the bottom of society. This path is labeled *downward assimilation* because, in this case, learning the cultural ways of the host society does not lead to upward mobility but, instead, to exactly the opposite.

Figure 19 summarizes these alternative paths and serves as a prelude for the presentation of evidence from the third CILS survey. The figure can be read as a set of hypotheses concerning segmented assimilation, which can be compared, in turn, with the actual experiences of second-generation youths, as well as with predictions from conventional assimilation theory.

CONFRONTING THE CHALLENGE

The Entenza family have just come back from helping their son move into his own apartment in Princeton, New Jersey. The Entenzas are being interviewed in their comfortable home in the Miami suburb of Coral Gables. They are first-generation Cubans. Ariel, who is twenty-five, has always lived with his parents, following the custom for unmarried Cuban children. The parents are owners of a medium-sized hardware store catering to a mostly Latin clientele. Ariel's mother, Teresa, came from Cuba with her family in the 1960s, after the Communist government there expropriated the department store they owned in Havana. Scraping together his savings and helped by a Havana friend who had become a loan officer at a small Miami bank, Teresa's father was able to get himself into business. After Teresa married Esteban, whom she met at Miami-Dade College, Esteban went to work in his father-in-law's store. After the father passed away, Esteban took over the business. He and Teresa have always lived in Miami, close to other Cuban families, always worked in the same business, and always attended the same church. They are both devout Catholics.

As a child, Ariel Entenza attended Belén Prep, a Jesuit school transplanted from Havana into Miami. Afterward, he moved to Florida International University, where he completed a degree in finance. He went to work in the same store founded by his grandfather, but his dad encouraged him to move on. "We did not make all these sacrifices for him to be just a small businessman," Esteban says. Ariel first went to work for a local firm and then accepted a well-paying job in the accounting department of a New Jersey corporation. Leaving Miami and his home was a big step, but the career prospects justified it.

Mario, Ariel's brother, joined the U.S. Marines and then went on to work for the sheriff's department of nearby Broward County (Fort

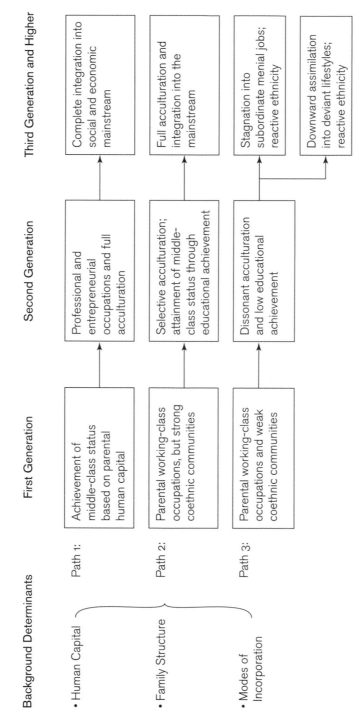

Figure 19. Paths of mobility across generations

Lauderdale), where he is currently a sergeant. He says that he feels "more Cuban than the old-timers." During the protests following the forced removal of the child Elián González to Cuba in 2000, he called in sick and stayed home. "I would do anything for this country, but I could not repress my neighbors," he says. "If I were not a cop, I would have been there protesting with them."[21]

HUMAN CAPITAL AND SOCIAL CAPITAL

Not all families possess the means to promote educational success and ward off the threats posed by discrimination, narrowing labor market options, and street gangs and drugs. Resources necessary to achieve this goal are of two kinds: (1) those that provide access to economic goods and job opportunities and (2) those that reinforce parental normative controls. Parents with high levels of human capital are in a better position to support their children's adaptation for many reasons. Foremost among them are their higher levels of information and the better occupations and higher incomes that they can command. A home in the suburbs, a private school education, and a summer trip back home to reinforce family ties are each an expensive proposition, not within the reach of the average immigrant family. Families able to afford them can confront the many challenges faced by their children with a measure of equanimity.

Yet immigrant parents' human capital and family composition do not exhaust the range of forces determining the path of adaptation followed by their young. The family and the coethnic community supply the other main factors. Social capital, grounded in intact families and community networks, provides a key resource in confronting obstacles to successful adaptation. The two are related as strong ethnic communities commonly enforce norms against divorce and marital disruption, thus helping preserve intact families.

The Entenzas illustrate a situation midway between the first and second paths portrayed in figure 19. Despite modest resources and an education reaching only to junior college for both parents, the family succeeded because of their strong coethnic networks. They lived in that community, drew their customers from it, and educated their children in its schools. The family stayed together, supported by religious conviction and the culture brought from their home country. Growing up in the midst of the middle-class Cuban enclave, Ariel and Mario never had to contend with drugs and never joined a gang. So well ensconced were they in the community where they were born that it was a difficult decision for Ariel to move north in pursuit of his career and an impossible one for Mario, as a police officer, to repress his neighbors. One had to be accompanied by the family to support him while settling in his new abode; the other simply stayed home.

SELECTIVE ACCULTURATION IN ADOLESCENCE

When second-generation children acculturate to American ways without abandoning their parents' language and key elements of their culture, it is easier for parents to guide and support in the children's quest for achievement and success. This pattern, illustrated by the preceding vignette, is labeled *selective acculturation*. It is associated with strong parental social capital in the form of stable families and cohesive communities and commonly, but not always, with fluent bilingualism (English plus the parental language) in the second generation. The opposite pattern is labeled *dissonant acculturation* because children's learning of English and American ways is accompanied by the abandonment of their parents' language and culture. If the latter remain foreign monolinguals, the stage is set for the breakdown of intrafamily communication and the loss of parents' control over their children.

Dissonant acculturation does not necessarily lead to downward assimilation, but it places children at risk because of the absence or weakening of family supports as they confront the external threats and barriers described earlier. It is possible to demonstrate empirically that relative to second-generation youths who become English monolinguals, and who have therefore lost command of the parental language, those who are fluent bilinguals experience superior outcomes in terms of psychosocial adaptation and academic achievement during adolescence. The relevant data come from the CILS-I and CILS-II surveys and were already introduced in the previous chapter (figure 14). Table 41 shows not only that respondents who were fluent bilinguals in early adolescence (at age fourteen, on average) experienced better family relations and personal psychosocial adjustment outcomes than English monolingual but that these effects remain significant after controlling for age, sex, length of U.S. residence, and a number of other variables.[22] Since language adaptation was measured three years earlier than these various outcomes, the causal order of these relationships is clear. Added to

| Outcomes in 1996 | | Language adaptation in 1992 | | |
		Fluent bilinguals	English monolinguals	p^a
Family conflict[b]	Mean score	46.1	53.0	.01
	Net effect[c]	−.171 (−4.1)		.001
Family solidarity[d]	Mean score	30.1	27.6	.01
	Net effect	.223 (5.4)		.001
Self-esteem[e]	Mean score	3.58	3.44	.01
	Net effect	.133 (6.3)		.001
Educational aspirations[f]	Mean score	75.4	69.9	.01
	Net effect	.461 (2.6)		.05
N[g]		1,011	2,065	

SOURCE: Portes and Hao 2002.

[a] p = Statistical significance of reported mean differences or net effect: $p < .001$ = less than one chance in one thousand of observed effect being due to chance; $p < .01$ = less than one chance in one hundred of observed effect being due to chance; $p < .05$ = less than five chances in one hundred of observed effect being due to chance.

[b] Unit-weighted index of five survey items indicating that (1) respondent is embarrassed by parents' ways; (2) respondent gets in trouble with parents because of different ways of doing things; (3) respondent argues with parents because of different goals; (4) parents are indifferent to his or her opinions; (5) parents do not like him or her very much. Reliability of this index, measured by Cronbach's alpha, is moderate to high. Scores are multiplied by 100, with higher scores indicating higher family conflict.

[c] Net effect of fluent bilingualism on the dependent variable, with English monolingualism as the reference category and controls for sex, age, length of U.S. residence, family structure, birthplace of parents, grade point average, family socioeconomic status, and Latin or Asian ethnic background.

[d] Unit-weighted index of three survey items indicating that (1) family members spend their free time with each other; (2) family members feel close to each other; (3) family togetherness is very important. Reliability of this index is moderate to high. Scores are multiplied by 100, with higher scores indicating higher family solidarity.

[e] Scores in the ten-item Rosenberg's Self-esteem Scale. Reliability of this scale in CILS, as measured by Cronbach's alpha, is .81. Higher scores indicate higher self-esteem.

[f] Percentage of respondents aspiring to a postcollege degree.

[g] Foreign monolinguals and limited bilinguals excluded.

the evidence presented in the previous chapter, these results provide support for the role of selective acculturation in adolescence in promoting positive adaptation.

Additional support comes from an analysis of determinants of academic performance in high school. Table 42 presents the effects of selected predictors on standardized math and reading test scores and on grade point averages for students included in the CILS original student sample. Controlling for age, sex, region of the country, and a number of other variables, fluent bilingualism retains a positive and significant association with all indicators of high school academic performance. The evidence in support of the consistent relationship between selective acculturation and positive outcomes of the adaptation process is buttressed by figures in the next row of table 42. They present the effects of the index of family conflict, an indicator of dissonant acculturation, on the three measures of academic performance. As shown by these figures, the more immigrant parents and their children clash because of different views and cultural ways, the lower the academic performance of children, controlling for other factors.[23]

Other evidence in this table highlights the durable influence of the first immigrant generation on the successful adaptation of children, even after controlling for selective acculturation. Parental human capital translates into family socioeconomic status, and this variable has, in turn, a strong positive effect on all measures of educational attainment. Intact families also have positive effects, statistically significant in two of the three performance indicators. Modes of incorporation are indexed by national origin, since most contemporary immigrant groups experience common contexts of reception. The table presents results for six immigrant groups whose reception by federal authorities and by the American public at large were quite different and who, accordingly, gave rise to distinct ethnic communities in the United States.

As noted previously, Chinese and Korean immigrants generally arrive legally and possess high levels of human capital. While they do not receive any extensive governmental assistance, they have benefited from a generally neutral reception. Many Chinese and Korean immigrants enter professional careers, while others become entrepreneurs, commonly in large ethnic enclaves—"Chinatowns" and "Koreatowns."[24] Vietnamese and Cubans are refugees from communist regimes who benefited from extensive governmental assistance and public sympathy in the early stages of their arrival. On that basis, they, too, managed to

TABLE 42. EFFECTS OF SELECTED PREDICTORS
ON THE EARLY EDUCATIONAL ATTAINMENT
OF SECOND-GENERATION STUDENTS

Predictors[a]	Math scores[b]	Reading scores[b]	Grade point average[c]
Acculturation			
Fluent bilingual	1.93*	2.30*	.06*
Parent-child conflict	−3.12***	−2.15**	−.16***
Family			
Parental socioeconomic			
status[d]	5.80***	6.88***	.18***
Intact family[e]	3.45**	.90	.18***
Nationality			
Chinese/Korean	23.22***	12.97**	.76***
Cuban[f]	5.60	7.14*	.25**
Haitian	−7.18*	−8.29**	.00
Mexican	−11.52**	−14.70***	−.25**
Vietnamese	15.79***	−3.20	.51***
Schools			
Inner-city school	−6.21**	−2.07*	.00
Average school SES[g]	.10**	.18**	−.06

SOURCE: Portes and Rumbaut 2001, table 9.2, based on CILS-I.

[a] All regressions control for the following additional predictors: age, sex, geographic region, birthplace, length of U.S. residence, ethnicity of friends, and other nationalities in the CILS sample.

[b] Percentile scores in Stanford standardized tests administered in the eighth and ninth grades and reported by the school systems. Figures in the table are unstandardized regression coefficients indicating the net increase/decrease in percentile test scores per unit change in each predictor, controlling for other variables.

[c] Junior high grade point averages reported by the school systems. Figures in the table are unstandardized regression coefficients indicating the net increase/decrease in grades per unit change of each predictor, controlling for other variables.

[d] Standardized unit-weighted index of father's and mother's education, father's and mother's occupational status, and home ownership.

[e] Both biological parents present.

[f] Results limited to Cuban-origin students attending private schools in Miami whose parents came mostly before the 1980 *Mariel* exodus. Cuban students attending public schools who came mostly after that date are excluded.

[g] One minus the percentage of students in school eligible for the federally subsidized lunch program. This eligibility is used as a proxy for low-status family background.

*p < .05 = less than five chances in a hundred of observed effect due to chance.

**p < .01 = less than one chance in a hundred of observed effect due to chance.

***p < .001 = less than one chance in a thousand of observed effect due to chance.

construct viable ethnic communities and entrepreneurial enclaves. "Little Havana" in Miami and "Little Saigon" in Orange County are the names popularly given to examples of these business concentrations.[25]

In contrast, Haitian and Mexican immigrants have experienced widespread discrimination and have been targets of governmental action as potentially illegal aliens. As a result, their ethnic communities are generally weak and lack the resources to provide entrepreneurial opportunities for adult immigrants or educational training for their children. Table 42 shows that, even after controlling for parental socioeconomic status, family structure, selective acculturation, and other variables, nationality continues to exercise a strong influence on educational attainment. The direction of these effects fits closely with our knowledge of the modes of incorporation of each of these immigrant groups: consistently positive for Chinese, Korean, Cuban, and Vietnamese students and consistently negative for children of Haitian and Mexican immigrants. Since parental status and family structure are controlled, these differences are attributable to the character of the ethnic community created by each immigrant group.

The remaining figures in table 42 illustrate the cumulative character of the process of adaptation. As we saw previously, many immigrant families concentrate in central city areas, where housing is cheaper but where schools are poorer and children are more directly exposed to deviant lifestyles. Even after taking parental status and modes of incorporation into account, we see that attending an inner-city school leads to significantly lower academic test scores among second-generation youths. Not surprisingly, attending schools with students from high-status family backgrounds leads to the opposite result. Children from poorer backgrounds are thus exposed to a triple educational handicap: low-status families, weaker coethnic communities, and poorer schools. In contrast, and illustrating the first two paths in figure 19, offspring of high-status families and cohesive communities are well poised in adolescence to achieve upward mobility. We will see next how the process plays itself out later in life.

SEGMENTED ASSIMILATION IN EARLY ADULTHOOD

A final follow-up of the CILS student sample took place in 2001–2003, ten years after the initial survey. By this time, respondents had reached an average age of twenty-four. This survey retrieved data on 3,564 original respondents, representing 84 percent of the preceding wave. There is evidence of bias in the final sample relative to the original one (but this can be corrected through well-known statistical adjustment methods): the initial runs indicate that the final sample overrepresents students from intact families (both parents present in early adolescence) and those who performed better academically during junior high school. However, this sampling bias exercises only minor effects on statistical estimates of most adaptation outcomes.[26]

During 2002–2003, a qualitative component was added to the survey by conducting detailed interviews with 55 members of our sample living in the Miami–Fort Lauderdale metropolitan area and with 134 respondents living in the San Diego area and elsewhere in California. The story earlier of Ariel Entenza and of others summarized in the following sections come from these interviews. Results from this survey represent the most compelling current evidence of how the adaptation of the second generation actually occurs, by including real-life outcomes of men and women at the start of their adult lives. Such outcomes comprise educational attainment, family incomes, employment and unemployment, marriage and parenthood, and arrests and incarceration.

DANNY GONZALEZ

Danny González lives with his mother and father in a modest house in Hialeah, a working-class suburb of Miami. Like Ariel Entenza, Danny is of Cuban origin. Danny's father is also an entrepreneur but a struggling one. He has never succeeded in rising above a precarious economic situation, and, as a result, the family has been forced to live in poor neighborhoods. The present one is the best they have lived in, in the United States. That poverty had direct consequences for the education of the children, who had to attend, in Danny's words, a string of "really bad schools." It was at Henry A. Fidler Middle School that Danny saw the "dark side of what public school really was." On his first day of the term, he couldn't help but notice the cagelike windows, the security guards in every corner, and all the doors locked and barricaded. "It was mostly gangs and a lot of incidents of kids going around stabbing others. It got to the point where you couldn't go to school anymore . . . going to school meant that you were always afraid."[27]

Despite this terrible education, Danny managed to graduate from high school and is pursuing a degree in graphic arts in junior college. He also holds a job at a store in a local mall. It was his love of art plus his attachment to his family that kept him out of gangs. Most of his friends never finished high school, occupied as they were in "holding down their ground" against rival gangs and crews. They now survive by hustling, meaning "anything you can get your hands on, you turn into money . . . it's a way of life."

Danny did not fall into a gang, but he is not on an upward trajectory, either. Instead, he has turned his love of art and artistic expression in a peculiar direction—toward hip-hop culture and graffiti. To understand his motives, we need to know something about the context where he grew up. The city of Hialeah is commonly held in contempt by middle-class Americans and Cubans alike as a loud, chaotic place where super-stition and ignorance reign. For older, well-established Cuban families, Hialeah is the place that gives Cubans a bad name because of the diffu-sion of voodoo-like Afro-Cuban religious practices and the concentra-tion of newly arrived refugees from the island, politically suspect and viewed as less motivated to work than earlier exiles.

Children growing up in this environment, isolated from the social and economic mainstream and looked down on by members of their own national group, have few chances for occupational advancement or for developing dignified self-definitions. They struggle to hold onto the Cuban identity of their parents but seek to imbue it with meanings quite different from those of the middle-class Cubans who look down on them. Thus, Danny and his crew of six go to "bless" empty walls with their names twisted in spray paint.

> We aim at "murdering the alphabet." It's gonna get to the point where, I'm predicting seven to ten years from now, the elements of hip-hop are goin' to be so untouched by normal day people that they won't be understandable. [The language] will be broken down so intense that it's going to be only for the people who represent.

While holding a day job and going to school, this young rebel is pre-occupied with not "selling out" to conventional society, defending and dignifying what he sees as authentic culture—Cuban hip-hop. This view gets him into difficulties, such as when he applied for a new job and addressed his would-be employer with "Yo! Wassup?" which earned him an instant dismissal. Danny's moral universe is so far away from his hardworking parents that they do not have the slightest idea of what his real life is like, much less how to control it. Nevertheless, Danny has enough respect for them and their sacrifices that he tries hard to reconcile a semideviant lifestyle with their ideals of moving up in the world. The solution? Succeeding as an artist "in his own terms," like Eminem and Puffy Combs. This aspiration would reconcile his world with that of his parents', where social and economic success in America is paramount:

> Tupac Shakur is someone [kids] look up to, meaning you don't have to wear a suit and tie to work because, look at him, he made it and he's representing us. . . . Here we have Cuban graffiti artists, Cuban MCs, Cuban break dancers. Right now the biggest, baddest break dancer is Speedy Legs [Richard Hernández]. He was born in Cuba and grew up in Hialeah.

The story of Danny González serves well to introduce our survey results because they illustrate the complexities of second-generation adaptation on the ground. Quantitative data alone cannot do this. Although Danny lives not three miles away from the house of Ariel Entenza, the two young men's views of themselves and of their life chances are worlds apart. Yet, they both dream of making it on their own terms, they both have devoted families who have stayed together despite all adversities, and they both call themselves Cuban American (although its meaning is altogether different).

The concept of segmented assimilation can be redefined empirically as a set of strategic outcomes in the lives of young children of immigrants. One such outcome is educational attainment, in terms of both completed years of education and whether the person is still in school. A second includes employment, occupation, and income; a third, language use and preferences. Downward assimilation is associated with dropping out of school, bearing children prematurely, and being arrested or incarcerated for a crime. The CILS-III survey contains measures of all these variables. We present these results broken down by major nationalities because of the wide differences among them. These differences, which show remarkable continuity from those observed in the adolescent years, demonstrate the resilient influence of parental human capital and modes of incorporation as they affect the formation of immigrant communities and the lives of the young people living in them.

SURVEY EVIDENCE

The relevant results are presented in table 43. As indicated previously, they have been adjusted for sample selectivity to eliminate that possible

TABLE 43. KEY OUTCOMES OF SECOND-GENERATION ADAPTATION IN EARLY ADULTHOOD, 2002–2003

Nationality	Education		Prefers foreign language %	Prefers English only %	Prefers children bilingual[a] %	Family income		Unemployed[b] %	Has children %	Incarcerated		N
	Average Years	High School or less				Mean $	Median $			Total %	Males %	
South Florida												
Colombian	14.5	17.0	2.0	64.9	82.8	58,339	45,948	2.6	16.6	6.0	10.4	150
Cuban (private school)	15.3	7.5	1.5	72.5	90.3	104,767	70,395	3.0	3.0	2.9	3.4	133
Cuban (public school)	14.3	21.7	1.8	62.7	86.2	60,816	48,598	6.2	17.7	5.6	10.5	670
Haitian	14.4	15.3	5.2	63.5	78.4	34,506	26,974	16.7	24.2	7.1	14.3	95
Nicaraguan	14.2	26.4	2.7	61.8	85.8	54,049	47,054	4.9	20.1	4.4	9.9	222
West Indian	14.6	18.1	0.0	90.8	40.4	40,654	30,326	9.4	24.3	8.5	20.0	148
Other	14.5	20.8			81.4	59,719	40,619	7.3	16.4	4.9	8.3	404
Total	14.5	20.1	2.3	65.0	82.0	59,797	44,185	6.6	17.4	5.4	9.6	1,822
Southern California												
Cambodian/ Laotian	13.3	45.9	3.8	43.2	86.6	34,615	25,179	9.3	25.4	4.3	9.5	186
Chinese	15.4	5.7	0.0	74.3	56.3	57,583	33,611	2.9	0.0	0.0	0.0	35
Filipino	14.5	15.5	0.3	90.2	46.0	64,442	55,323	7.8	19.4	3.9	6.8	586
Mexican	13.4	38.0	6.5	37.9	88.2	38,254	32,585	7.3	41.5	10.8	20.2	408
Vietnamese	14.9	12.6	0.5	56.1	82.9	44,717	34,868	13.9	9.0	7.8	14.6	194
Other (Asian)	15.2	9.1	2.3	86.4	46.3	58,659	40,278	4.5	11.4	6.7	9.5	46
Other (Latin American)	14.4	25.5	4.3	65.2	71.1	43,476	31,500	2.2	15.2	6.4	18.8	47
Total	14.2	24.9	2.6	64.6	68.0	50,657	39,671	8.5	24.0	6.4	11.9	1502

SOURCE: CILS-III.

[a] Among those with children.

[b] Respondents without jobs, whether looking or not looking for employment, except those still enrolled at school.

source of bias. In addition, we divided the large Cuban-origin sample into students who attended public school and those who enrolled in bilingual private high schools in Miami. The latter are mostly the offspring of early middle- and upper-class Cuban exiles who were well received by the American public and government; the former are mostly children of refugees arriving during and after the chaotic Mariel exodus of 1980, whose average human capital is lower and whose context of reception was much more difficult. Cubans are the only major immigrant nationality to experience a significant shift in modes of incorporation in the last decades, and these changes can bear directly on the children's adaptation.[28]

As shown in the first columns of the table, all nationalities in the South Florida CILS sample managed to complete an average of fourteen years of education or two years past high school graduation. Since 50 percent of the sample is still enrolled in school, this average can be expected to increase over time. While variations among nationalities in average education are minor, those pertaining to dropping out of high school or quitting studies after getting a high school diploma are not. Just 5 percent of this sample dropped out of high school, but one-fifth quit after completing it. Those who failed to pursue their studies range from a low of 7.5 percent among children of middle-class Cuban families to a high of 26 percent among Nicaraguans. Cuban children who attended public schools have much lower levels of educational attainment than their more privileged compatriots. Importantly, the two black immigrant minorities in South Florida, Haitians and West Indians, are not particularly disadvantaged in this dimension. Thus, despite below-average academic performance during high school, 85 percent of Haitian children managed to graduate, and their mean educational attainment is only slightly below the sample average.

In Southern California, the greatest educational disadvantage is found among children of Mexican immigrants and Laotian and Cambodian refugees. These groups achieved less than fourteen years of education on average, and close to 40 percent failed to attain more than a high school diploma. These results are far worse than those found among Florida nationalities and reflect the difficulties faced by children coming from poor families with very low levels of human capital. A positive context of reception for Cambodian and Laotian refugees did not suffice to lift their second generation to a position of educational advantage. In the case of Mexican youths, low parental human capital combined with a negative mode of incorporation to produce high rates of school abandonment and low mean levels of academic attainment. However, in this case, the proportion who did not complete high school is only about half the figure among their parents (table 39). This and other results indicate that young Mexican Americans have made considerable progress relative to the adult first generation. However, having started from such a position of disadvantage, they still could not match the educational attainment of other second-generation or native-parentage youths.

At the other end, the combination of high parental human capital and a neutral context of reception led second-generation Chinese and other Asians to extraordinary levels of educational achievement, only matched in South Florida by the offspring of middle-class Cuban exiles. Vietnamese youths also did quite well despite low average levels of parental education. These results reproduce, in all the basics, those observed earlier (see table 42), showing the importance of both early academic performance and national differences in modes of incorporation on educational achievement.

Language, as seen in the previous chapter, is a fundamental part of the adaptation process, and, in this respect, the assimilative power of American society is overwhelming. Majorities of second-generation youths in both California and Florida indicated that they preferred to speak English *only*. The bilingual alternative, speaking English *and* another language, was also endorsed by a substantial number, including children of Mexicans (56 percent), Laotian/Cambodians (53 percent), and Vietnamese (43 percent). The two categories combined (English only and English plus another language) exceed 95 percent, leaving those choosing a foreign language as a tiny minority (less than 3 percent).

A different pattern emerges, however, when respondents are asked in what language they would like to raise their own children. In this case, 68 percent of youths in California and 82 percent of those in Miami indicate a strong preference for bilingualism. Evidently, second-generation adults understand the benefits of bilingualism, even if only a minority have opted to sustain it themselves. Exceptions are children of West Indian and Filipino immigrants, a majority of whom prefer to raise their offspring as English monolinguals. This finding is not surprising since English is the exclusive or predominant language in both countries of origin. (English serves as the common means of communication among speakers of multiple native tongues in the Philippines.)

At more than $59,000 per year, average family incomes in South Florida are high, exceeding the figure for the Miami metropolitan area in 2000 by more than $5,000. The median income is considerably lower than the mean in this CILS sample, reflecting the "pull" of very high incomes.[29] Family incomes only partially reflect respondents' personal earnings since the majority of these youths still live with their parents, so reported figures are the sum of parents' and children's incomes. Still, these figures are important because they indicate that, on average, children of immigrants in South Florida live in relatively comfortable economic circumstances. Since parents generally help their offspring while they become independent, this favorable situation may be expected to continue in the future.[30]

Seen from this perspective, national differences in family income are quite important. At one end of the spectrum are children of middle-class Cuban exiles, who enjoy a median family income of $70,395 per year; at the other end, Haitian American families earn on average only $26,974. These figures can be compared with the median household income for the population of Miami–Fort Lauderdale in 2000: $38,362. All Latin groups in the CILS sample surpass this figure. The two major black groups in the sample, Haitians and West Indians, do not even come close. While 46.5 percent of Cubans who went to private school and 25.2 percent of those who attended public schools have incomes over $75,000, only 11.5 percent of West Indians and just 4.9 percent of Haitians do. These two mostly black groups concentrate in the bottom income categories, with about one-third having annual incomes of less than $20,000. This finding is particularly noteworthy since, as noted earlier, most of these youths did manage to graduate from high school and achieved at least average levels of education.

In California, average second-generation family incomes are lower, but the sample contains the "richest" nationality among all major immigrant groups considered: Filipino Americans, who earn more than $64,000 per year. They are followed by Chinese Americans and other Asians (primarily Korean Americans). At the other end are the same groups that we saw lagging behind in education. The very low incomes of young Mexican Americans reflect again the many handicaps faced by both parents and children. The still-lower figures for Laotian/Cambodians reinforce the conclusion that governmental assistance did not suffice to lift these groups out of poverty. Only 6 percent of Mexicans and only 8 percent of Laotians and Cambodians have family incomes above $75,000, reproducing the situation of the most disadvantaged second-generation youths in South Florida.

Figures on unemployment tell a similar story. They range from 3 percent or less among Chinese, Colombians, and private school Cubans to almost 10 percent among West Indians and Laotian/Cambodians, 14 percent among the Vietnamese, and 17 percent among Haitians. To put these figures into perspective, they can be compared with the unemployment rate among the working-age population of Miami–Fort Lauderdale in 2000, 4.3 percent, and an even lower 3.0 percent in San Diego County in 2000. Again, it is significant that high unemployment rates are found among children of black immigrants in South Florida, despite their relatively high educational achievement.

The dictum that the rich get richer and the poor get children is well supported by figures in the next column of table 43. Only 3 percent of middle-class Cuban Americans have had children by early adulthood. The figure is exactly 0 percent for Chinese Americans. The rate then rises to about 10 percent for second-generation Vietnamese; over 15 percent for Colombians, public school Cubans, and Filipinos; 25 percent for Haitians, West Indians, and Laotian/Cambodians; and a remarkable 41 percent among Mexican Americans. Thus, second-generation groups with the lowest average education and incomes are those most burdened, at an early age, by the need to support children. The overall picture is compelling, pointing toward the cumulative effects of structural disadvantages in the first generation, which in turn raise the probability of downward assimilation in the second.

Still more telling are differences in rates of arrest and incarceration. Compared with an arrest rate of 6.4 percent among persons eighteen and older in Miami–Fort Lauderdale and a crime index of 7.6 percent for this metropolitan area in 2000, only 3 percent of Cubans who attended private schools were incarcerated during the preceding six years. The figure then climbs steadily to 6 percent among public school Cubans and Colombians, 7 percent among Haitians, and 8.5 percent among West Indians. The highest and lowest rates of incarceration are found in California: exactly 0 percent of Chinese Americans experienced incarceration, whereas 11 percent of Mexican Americans did. Second-generation Laotian/Cambodians are not particularly high in these statistics, indicating that their poverty seldom leads to confrontations with the legal system.

Predictably, differences among males are still wider. Those incarcerated for a crime range from 0 percent among the Chinese and just 3 percent among private school Cubans, to about 10 percent of Laotian/ Cambodians and other Latin groups in Miami, and up to 20 percent among second-generation Mexicans and West Indians. To put this last figure in perspective, it can be compared with the nationwide proportion of African American males incarcerated by age forty, 26.6 percent.[31] With an additional sixteen years to go on average, it is quite likely that males from these two groups will catch up to or exceed that figure. Thus, in South Florida, no less than 10 percent and up to 20 percent of black second-generation youths live in poverty, are unemployed, and have already been in jail or on probation. In California, the same fate is suffered by Mexican Americans and, to a lesser extent, by children of Cambodian and Laotian refugees. The fact that Mexican Americans are, by far, the nation's largest second-generation minority adds to the weight carried by these figures.[32]

This is the most tangible evidence of downward assimilation available to date. It clusters, overwhelmingly, among children of nonwhite and poorly educated immigrants, reflecting the structural effects of low parental human capital, racial discrimination, and an overall negative mode of incorporation. Although the figures do show that a majority of the same groups have managed to avoid jail, premature parenthood, and low education, a sizable minority are being left behind. Young adults caught in a cycle of menial jobs, low incomes, early childbearing, and frequent confrontations with the police face immense obstacles for the future, reinforcing the same racial and ethnic stereotypes that contributed to their situation in the first place. The cumulative effects of factors at the family and community levels, along with the different resources available to immigrant parents, are displayed with almost frightening clarity in these divergent paths of adaptation.

CONCLUSION

TWO STORIES

Nghi Van Nguyen managed to escape the inner city to attend a good school in the suburbs of San Diego. He was able to do this because his family pooled resources together to buy a tract house outside the city. "The Vietnamese family is like a corporation," he says. "We all bring our money together—the grandparents, the parents, the children. Everyone works. Vietnamese food is cheap, so we could save for the down payment." Those savings bought the house and also helped Nghi's father open a restaurant specializing in Vietnamese cuisine. At that time, the Vietnamese population of San Diego was fairly small but growing fast. Knowledge of English and his past clerical experience in Vietnam gave Mr. Nguyen a foothold for setting himself up in business. His wife and children provided the requisite labor, at least at the start. "Americans think that big families are a problem, but that's not the Vietnamese way," says Nghi. "Your family is your social security. We know that we need each other to pull ahead." At the time of the interview, Nghi was a medical student at the University of California. His family still owns the restaurant.[33]

Being admitted into the home of Aristide Maillol in the Haitian section of Miami transports the visitor into a new reality. The location is American, but the essence is rural Haiti. Aristide's mother speaks no English. Her eyes drift to the floor when explaining in Creole that her husband is hospitalized and that she had to leave her job as a maid in a local motel to attend to his needs. Both parents came as boat people and were granted only temporary work permits by U.S. authorities. Both have little education, and their earnings are minimal. There is consternation in the woman's demeanor as she contemplates her situation.

In the tiny sitting area adjoining the front door, a large bookcase displays the symbols of family identity in an arrangement suitable for a shrine. On three separate shelves, several photographs show Aristide's brother and three sisters. The boy smiles confidently in the cap and gown of a high school graduate. The girls are displayed individually and in clusters, their attire fit for a celebration. Mixed with the photographs are the familiar trinkets that adorn most Haitian homes. Striking, however, is the inclusion of several trophies earned by the Maillol children in academic competitions.

At seventeen, Aristide's brother has already been recruited by Yale University with a scholarship. Young Aristide, who was fifteen at the time, explains his brother's and his own achievements: "We are immigrants, and immigrants must work harder to overcome hardship. . . . I know that there is discrimination, racism, but you can't let that bother you. . . . God has brought us here, and God will lead us farther." Sitting to his side in her humble dress, the mother nods in agreement. Although her situation looks bleak, her son gives her a firm promise for the future.[34]

A PLACE IN THE SUN

We close this chapter with these two rousing stories to convey the image of today's second generation that we wish readers to keep and hold. By and large, these young people are doing well: performing better academically than their native-parentage peers; graduating from high school and going on to college; working hard at their first jobs and taking the first steps toward independent entrepreneurship. Even children of families with no money and little or no human capital can move forward, riding on their own determination and the support of their families or communities. From the Entenzas to the Maillols, we witnessed in the case of CILS a number of success stories grounded far more in social capital than in the education and economic resources of parents. Even the most alarming statistics—those on incarceration—show that nine-tenths of second-generation males have managed to stay clear of that path.

This overall positive picture and the almost overdetermined success of the scions of immigrant families with high levels of human capital and a positive mode of incorporation should not obscure the challenges faced by many second-generation youths and the anomalies in their process of adaptation. We have discussed the challenges at length in this chapter; among the anomalies, none is more important than the ambiguous role of time. Time spent in the United States increases opportunities for economic progress, although these opportunities vary with individual endowments and contexts of reception. The passage of time also brings about relentless acculturation and, with it, the progressive weakening of the original immigrant drive to succeed in a foreign environment.[35] As already documented at length in chapter 6, acculturation to American society is not an unqualified good, as it often leads to behavioral habits and newfound "freedoms" at variance with the discipline and effort necessary to succeed educationally and economically.

The key questions are how much progress immigrants and their children manage to make by the time that the inevitable consequences of acculturation set in and where in the American social and economic hierarchies do they find themselves at that time. Evidence of a strong immigrant drive to succeed is documented by multiple results in our study. They include the high ambition and optimism of immigrant parents; the equally high educational expectations and efforts of immigrant children, which consistently exceed those of the general student population; and the superior grades and lower dropout rates of second-generation students relative to members of the same ethnic groups in the third and higher generations.[36]

The evidence of a dampening effect with increasing acculturation is equally strong. Congruent with results discussed in chapter 6, it is present in the diminishing school commitment and work effort of students with longer periods of U.S. residence; the negative effect of acculturation on grades and expectations for the future; *and* the fact that members of a particular ethnic group in the third and higher generations generally do worse academically than their second-generation peers. Taken together, these facts suggest that a "race" takes place between acculturation, on the one hand, and the immigrant achievement drive and the individual and social resources supporting it, on the other. The paths of adaptation, described at the start of this chapter (figure 19), may now be reinterpreted as a summary portrayal of the outcomes of that race.

In some cases, the race is won *for* the children by their parents in such a way that they are endowed, from the very start, with the resources needed for educational and economic success; in most cases, the race is won *by* the children drawing on the moral resources of their families and/or the support of strong ethnic communities. For a sizable minority, however, the race can be lost by a juxtaposition of adverse circumstances and the dearth of resources needed to confront them. Once this happens, it is difficult to climb back up again. There is no evidence that groups confined in the past to subordinate positions in the labor market or relegated to permanent poverty in the inner cities have collectively organized to overcome these handicaps. On the contrary, all evidence points to the perpetuation over time of a situation of collective disadvantage and the interlocking set of handicaps that keep it in place.[37]

For this reason, second-generation youths at risk of downward assimilation deserve special attention and support. In our view, expert outside assistance can help young at-risk persons avoid this course. A reservoir of hope and ambition in them can readily be tapped toward that goal. "I'm so close to success, I can almost taste it," remarked one of our respondents in Miami, despite having been in jail twice and having taken only the first fledgling steps toward independent entrepreneurship. We will discuss in the final chapter the question of policies targeted specifically toward that segment of the second generation confronting severe disadvantages. For the moment, it suffices to note that while downward assimilation is a reality, it may still be possible to overcome its worst effects by drawing on external support, a resilient immigrant drive, and the role models provided by those who, like Aristide Maillol, have managed to overcome the challenges of poverty and discrimination to carve a place in the sun for themselves. These examples can be multiplied if we do not turn our backs on the most vulnerable members of this rising population.

Plate 25. All members of this Arab American family are fans of the Detroit Pistons, the local basketball team and NBA champion. The Detroit metropolitan area is home for the largest concentration of Arab Americans in the United States. (Photograph by Steve Gold.)

Plate 26. Children of African immigrants at a school picnic, Okemos, Michigan. (Photograph by Steve Gold.)

Plate 27. Boys at a Chabad (Hassidic) day camp for Soviet Jews, West Hollywood, California. (Photograph by Steve Gold.)

Plate 28. Chinese musicians marching in the St. Patrick's Day Parade, San Francisco. (Photograph by Steve Gold.)

Plate 29. Members of the Young Muslims Association, Dearborn, Michigan. The group was established in 1999. (Photograph by Steve Gold.)

Plate 30. Miss Whittier: Mexican American young women, Los Angeles. (Photograph by Steve Gold.)

Plate 31. Vietnamese New Year (Tet) celebration, Orange County, California. (Photograph by Steve Gold.)

Plate 32. At the annual Tet celebration in Little Saigon, an American beer company offers wishes in Vietnamese for "a new year of happiness and success." (Photograph by Steve Gold.)

Plate 33. A portrait of the pope gazes at homemade *pierogi* and Kellogg's corn flakes at a Polish restaurant in the Detroit metropolitan area. (Photograph by Steve Gold.)

Plate 34. Russian and Hungarian breads—and Polish news—are sold at a Polish bakery in Detroit. (Photograph by Steve Gold.)

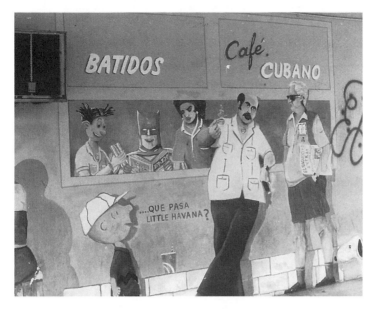

Plate 35. Even Charlie Brown speaks Spanish in Little Havana, Miami, site of the world's largest Cuban community outside Havana itself. (Photograph by Estela R. García.)

Plate 36. Popular Vietnamese music tapes for sale in Little Saigon, Orange County, California. (Photograph by Steve Gold.)

Plate 37. T-shirt sellers (and a post–September 11 message) at the Arab American festival in Dearborn, Michigan. (Photograph by Steve Gold.)

Plate 38. Musical performance at the opening of the Arab American National Museum, 2005. (Photograph by Steve Gold.)

Plate 39. Christian evangelicals proselytize Muslims at the Arab American festival, Dearborn, Michigan. (Photograph by Steve Gold.)

Plate 40. American religious pluralism: the new mosque of the Islamic Center of America, in Dearborn, is adjacent to an Armenian church. (Photograph by Steve Gold.)

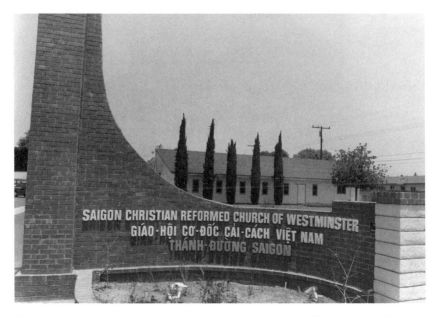

Plate 41. A Vietnamese Protestant Calvinist church in Little Saigon, Orange County, California. (Photograph by Steve Gold.)

Plate 42. Soviet Jewish men at religious services, West Hollywood, California. (Photograph by Steve Gold.)

Plate 43. La Ermita de la Caridad: Catholic church built by Cuban immigrants along Biscayne Bay, Miami. The main entrance faces south toward Cuba. (Photograph by Estela R. García.)

Plate 44. Vietnamese Catholics celebrate the Feast of the Immaculate Conception, St. Mary's Church, Whittier, California. (Photograph by Steve Gold.)

Plate 45. A Mexican church group stages a march in a Los Angeles neighborhood where gang violence had occurred. (Photograph by Steve Gold.)

Plate 46. More than five hundred thousand people marched in downtown Los Angeles on March 25, 2006, in protest against the anti-immigrant Sensenbrenner-King bill passed by the U.S. House of Representatives in December 2005. It was the largest protest march ever in Los Angeles and one of the largest in U.S. history. (Photograph by Rubén G. Rumbaut.)

Plate 47. The 2006 Los Angeles immigrant rights march attracted a mix of young and old of many different national origins, including Salvadorans, Guatemalans, Koreans, Chinese, and, above all, immigrants from Mexico and their children. (Photograph by Rubén G. Rumbaut.)

Plate 48. Bilingual posters at the mass march in Los Angeles opposed the provisions of HR 4437, days before the bill was to be taken up by the U.S. Senate. The bill, sponsored by Rep. F. James Sensenbrenner Jr. (R-Wis.), would make undocumented immigrants and those who assist them felons and erect a seven-hundred-mile fence along the U.S.-Mexico border. The large sign in the background says "We are workers, NOT criminals." (Photograph by Rubén G. Rumbaut.)

Plate 49. The child of an immigrant walks with his mother toward a throng of hundreds of thousands marching down Broadway in downtown Los Angeles. His T-shirt says, "No to Proposition HR 4437," evoking anti-immigrant propositions in California a decade earlier but referring to a bill pending in Congress. (Photograph by Rubén G. Rumbaut.)

9

Religion
The Enduring Presence

With the collaboration of
Patricia Fernández-Kelly
and William Haller

t's 1:00 P.M. on a Sunday in 2005, and the Spanish-language mass in
St. Rose of Lima Catholic Church in Miami is about to begin. The
devout keep arriving in large numbers, delaying the start of the cere-
mony. Despite the church being packed, the choir is feeble, numbering
only five women and no men. Its weakness is more evident because they
sing the chants alone, without the rest of the congregation joining in.
When the time comes for the sermon in Spanish, the young Cuban
American priest, Father Tomás, alludes vaguely to the gospel of the day
but uses it primarily as an allegory for what he really wants to tell his
parishioners. He chides them, in no uncertain terms, for their lateness
and their lack of participation in the mass. He reminds them that,
though that may have been the custom in their countries, now they are
in America where things are done on time and where mass is not an
individual but a collective experience. So strong is his sense of disappointment that a parishioner is moved to speak up, promising in the
name of the congregation that this will not happen again.

Three weeks later, the same church is packed by 1:00 P.M., and mass
begins on time. The few laggards settle in the last pews, timidly. The
choir is now fifteen strong, including five men. Most parishioners join
in their chants or at least pretend to do so. Father Tomás is pleased, and

so he should be, for he has succeeded in instilling a sense of Catholic order and propriety in this congregation mostly made up of recent immigrants. Less obvious but more important, he has given them a powerful lesson in acculturation, one that would inevitably carry to other spheres of life.[1]

What Father Tomás just did at St. Rose of Lima has been done innumerable times before. A rapidly growing literature tells us that religious affiliation and participation have been prime vehicles for many immigrants to cope with the challenges of their new environment and to learn its ways. As Charles Hirschman notes, evoking the classical historical accounts by Handlin and Herberg, many immigrants and their offspring became acculturated and eventually accepted in America not by joining some abstract mainstream but by becoming regular members of religious congregations, Protestant, Catholic, and Jewish.[2] Not all immigrants have followed that path, to be sure, but religion has never ceased to be a crucial presence in the process of incorporation. So long as the likes of Father Tomás continue to preach to packed houses of newcomers coming to church to seek succor and guidance, that presence will not cease.

YESTERDAY AND TODAY

The historical and sociological literature on the interface between religion and immigration has become increasingly abundant of late and has been summarized a number of times before. It would be redundant to do likewise in the following pages. Excellent reviews and syntheses of this literature, as well as comparisons between historical and contemporary experiences, have been published during the last decade by, among others, Alba and Raboteau, Ebaugh and Chafetz, Hirschman, Levitt, Warner and Wittner, and Wuthnow.[3]

Our intention is not to cover the same terrain but to use material from these essays and our own empirical data to explore systematically the interactions between religious affiliation and the other theoretical and practical aspects of immigration examined in prior chapters. These include the modes of incorporation of different immigrant communities, the development of linear and reactive ethnicities, the construction of transnational organizations and communities, the road to citizenship and political participation, and the process of segmented assimilation in the second generation.

A first basic point is that religion seldom causes emigration and seldom determines the structural contexts of reception awaiting immigrants in a new land. There are exceptions to this rule in the experience of some refugee groups escaping religious oppression. But, as seen in chapter 2, the vast majority of immigrants to America belong to other types—labor migrants, professionals and entrepreneurs, and political refugees. More commonly in all these instances, religion has *accompanied* the process of migration, seeking to ameliorate the traumas of departure and early settlement, to protect immigrants against external attacks and discrimination, and to smooth their acculturation to the new environment. The actions and initiatives of religious communities, while not determining the onset of migration or its general mode of incorporation, can affect the influence of these factors, leading to outcomes different from what would otherwise be expected. So important is this mediating and meliorative role that when a church, temple, mosque, or synagogue is not there to receive the newcomers, immigrants have commonly organized in order to build it.[4]

Sociologically, this significance of religion is not difficult to understand. It is compatible with the role of sociability in avoiding the danger of *anomie* and, hence, sustaining moral cohesion and normative controls, as in the classic studies of Émile Durkheim. It also agrees with the prime role of religious conviction and religious charisma in guiding human action and promoting major processes of change, as investigated by Max Weber.[5] The latter author also pioneered in the analysis of the unexpected economic consequences of religious belief at the individual and societal level. This theme has become a staple in sociological analyses of the religious factor to our day.[6]

Yesterday and today, many newcomers in America have felt the need to reaffirm their religious roots or, alternatively, to find new ones, with consequences that have been momentous, both individually and collectively. Individually, Hirschman summarizes the social functions of religion in the "three Rs": refuge, respect, and resources.[7] The first function refers to the early, frequently traumatic stage of arrival and resettlement where a church, temple, or mosque may be a key source of comfort and protection; the second addresses Durkheim's problem of anomie and the associated loss of normative orientation and a sense of self-worth; the third is compatible with Weber's analysis of economic consequences of religious affiliation, as one group of newcomers after another has discovered that, by reaffirming their religious traditions or embracing new ones, they could do well by doing good.

The societal and historical consequences of immigrant religiosity are still more important and are readily evident, among other things, in an American landscape dotted with temples of the most varied sort—from churches to synagogues to mosques; in the institutionalization of the Catholic Church, along with its vast system of schools, universities, and hospitals; and in the entry of Judaism into the social and cultural mainstream, redefined to reflect a "Judeo-Christian" tradition.[8] Relative to the rest of the developed world, the United States remains today a profoundly religious country. This was not always the case, and it is largely due to the interplay between faith and the process of immigrant incorporation.[9]

The historical record shows that, over time, religious convictions have been a source of comfort and protection but also of violent conflict between adherents of various faiths. These include not only the centuries-old confrontation between Christianity and Islam but also the post-Reformation European wars between Catholics and Protestants.[10] Conflicts also arose in Protestant North America with the nineteenth-century arrival of Irish Catholics and, subsequently, of Russian Jews and other non-Protestant foreign groups. However, the freedom of religion and speech enshrined in the U.S. Constitution and Bill of Rights were sufficiently strong to prevent a reenactment of the European religious wars on this side of the Atlantic.[11] While xenophobic attacks were common, as notoriously exemplified by the activities of the Ku Klux Klan, the main story was that enough legal and social space existed for nonhegemonic religions to gain a foothold in North America and then to flourish as institutions. The history of American Catholicism and Judaism and the protective role that they played for their respective immigrant flocks exemplify this central trend.

RELIGION AND MODES OF INCORPORATION

One of the most compelling contemporary stories about religion and immigrant incorporation is that narrated by Zhou, Bankston, and Kim about the construction of a Buddhist temple in the midst of the sugarcane fields of Iberia Parish, Louisiana. The Laotian refugees responsible for this feat began moving to Louisiana in the early 1980s under the sponsorship of the federal government and to take advantage of new occupational opportunities in the area. With funds from the Comprehensive Employment and Training Act (CETA), the men trained as welders and pipe fitters and promptly found employment in the construction of offshore oil platforms in the Gulf of Mexico. The women had brought embroidery skills from Laos, which served many of them well in finding employment in a textile mill north of New Iberia.[12]

With two working-class incomes per family, Laotians were soon able to move out of the housing projects and dangerous neighborhoods where they had initially settled. The problem was where. The majority of these refugees were Theravada Buddhists, and there certainly was not a Buddhist temple in New Iberia around which they could congregate. How they solved the problem is remarkable, although it corresponds well with what other immigrant groups elsewhere have also done: they built the temple out of nowhere and a Laotian village to boot, to which many of the families moved. The struggle to find the funds to buy the land, pay a resident monk, build the temple, and lay out the adjacent streets (named after provinces in Laos) are narrated in elegant detail by Zhou, Bankston, and Kim. The first important lesson to be derived from their story is the significance of modes of incorporation in the course of adaptation of immigrants and refugees. As escapees from a Communist regime, Laotians were the beneficiaries of a generous program of federal resettlement assistance. With that assistance, they were able to rejoin families, move in search of opportunities, and find occupational training that laid the basis for their economic success and the reconstruction of their community.[13]

The colorful and incongruous temple in the midst of the Louisiana cane fields illustrates well the Durkheimian theme of the power of community cohesion against anomie, as well as the Weberian emphasis on the latent economic consequences of religious practice. For the erection of the building not only allowed these refugees to reenact their religious rituals and traditions but also endowed them with a renewed sense of pride and place in a strange land. Not surprisingly, economic consequences flowed out of the temple, in the form of support for members in search of employment and housing loans. In the course of the study, researchers interviewed the human resources director of a company constructing offshore oil drills in the Gulf of Mexico. Upon remarking on how many Laotian workers the company employed, the man responded, "One of our foremen is the financial manager of that Buddhist whatchamacallit. . . . People go to him for a job, and he just refers them here."[14]

In chapter 4, we saw that modes of incorporation—composed of governmental reception, public reaction toward newcomers, and the preexisting coethnic community—represent a fundamental structural factor affecting the long-term adaptation of an immigrant group. As noted previously, religion does not determine by itself any of these contextual elements, but it can interact powerfully with them, generally in the direction of softening their edges. It does not dictate state policy but helps implement it or, alternatively, resist it when seen as inimical to the welfare of its members; it does not create the social context confronted by newcomers, but it seeks to meliorate it by facilitating the integration of immigrants and protecting them from the worse consequences of discrimination. It does not determine the emergence of ethnic communities, but it can be a powerful rallying point for them, to the extent that—as in the case of the Laotian Buddhists—when a religious shrine does not exist, it has to be built. Figure 20 depicts graphically this dynamic interaction between religious institutions and structural modes of incorporation.[15]

Of these interactions, arguably the most important is the role of religion in the development of ethnic communities and the reassertion of national cultures and language. On the whole, religious institutions have been guided in this respect by a logic entirely at variance with dominant stereotypes held by the native population. That logic is well captured in Hirschman's observation that "immigrants became Americans by joining a church and participating in its religious and community life."[16] In other words, the road to successful integration has commonly passed through the creation of ethnic communities and the reenactment of elements of the immigrants' culture, with strong religious undertones. By contrast, a widespread view among the native-born population, and among some government officials as well, is that immigrants' vigorous assertion of distinct ethnic identities and foreign cultures undermines the unity of the nation and the preservation of its cultural integrity.[17]

Thus, as we already saw in chapter 5, a scholar no less famous than Samuel Huntington has raised the banner of xenophobic nationalism, railing against the "Hispanic challenge" posed by new immigrants who, in his view, bring inferior cultures and resist integration into the American mainstream. In their time, Irish and Italian Catholics and Russian Jews were targets of similar hostility, with the "popishness" of the Irish, the superstitions of the Italians, and the Semitic clannishness of the Jews denounced as un-American and as corrosive of national unity and values.[18]

Fortunately, the American constitutional freedoms and the country's legal system were strong enough to prevent xenophobic sentiments

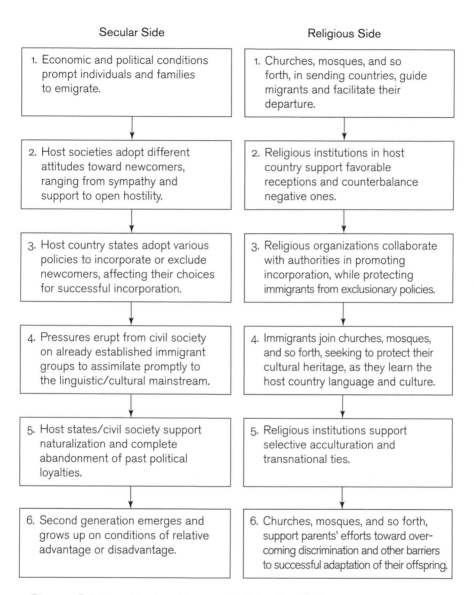

Secular Side	Religious Side
1. Economic and political conditions prompt individuals and families to emigrate.	1. Churches, mosques, and so forth, in sending countries, guide migrants and facilitate their departure.
2. Host societies adopt different attitudes toward newcomers, ranging from sympathy and support to open hostility.	2. Religious institutions in host country support favorable receptions and counterbalance negative ones.
3. Host country states adopt various policies to incorporate or exclude newcomers, affecting their choices for successful incorporation.	3. Religious organizations collaborate with authorities in promoting incorporation, while protecting immigrants from exclusionary policies.
4. Pressures erupt from civil society on already established immigrant groups to assimilate promptly to the linguistic/cultural mainstream.	4. Immigrants join churches, mosques, and so forth, seeking to protect their cultural heritage, as they learn the host country language and culture.
5. Host states/civil society support naturalization and complete abandonment of past political loyalties.	5. Religious institutions support selective acculturation and transnational ties.
6. Second generation emerges and grows up on conditions of relative advantage or disadvantage.	6. Churches, mosques, and so forth, support parents' efforts toward overcoming discrimination and other barriers to successful adaptation of their offspring.

Figure 20. Religion and immigrant incorporation: Interaction effects

from translating themselves into public policy. Instead, the American state allowed immigrant groups to develop their own social and cultural institutions, including their parishes, schools, hospitals, temples, and synagogues. The long-term results of that permissive stance are celebrated today as the "success stories" of European immigrant groups in the United States and of the American ability to assimilate them. That ability was grounded on the state doing rather little, and religious institutions doing a great deal. The lessons of religiously imbued ethnic communities and institutions providing a first leg up on the way to successful integration have somehow been lost by the nativists of yesterday and today, who continue to rally against the "foreign element" and its activities.

These activities, exemplified by the Spanish mass in St. Rose of Lima and the construction of the Buddhist temple in Iberia Parish, are not exceptional but proliferating. According to Warner and Wittner, by the early 1990s, there were 3,500 Catholic parishes where mass was celebrated in Spanish and 7,000 Latin Protestant congregations, most of them Pentecostal or evangelical. There were also upward of 2,600 Korean Christian churches, between 1,500 and 2,000 Buddhist temples, and about 1,000 mosques and Islamic centers. More recently, Wuthnow puts the number of mosques and Islamic centers at 3,000, two-thirds of which had been founded since 1980.[19] According to another recent study, there is one Korean church for every four hundred immigrants of that nationality, an extraordinarily high figure.[20] Given the continuation of immigration, these numbers will grow. Overall, they can be expected to play the same support and integrative functions that religion has always played for migrant newcomers in America.

RELIGIOUS DIVERSITY AND CHANGE

On one recent Sunday, as reported by the *New York Times*, Hindu worshippers paraded down Bowne Street in Flushing, New York, with the bust of Lord Ganesha, an elephant-headed deity who symbolizes auspicious beginnings. The Hindu temple that organizes the annual procession draws $2 million in revenues a year from some three thousand worshippers who come into the sanctuary for prayers, language classes, and lessons in Hindu scripture every weekend. Nearby is another Hindu temple, opposite a once-bustling Orthodox synagogue that now rents its parking lot to members of a Chinese evangelical church. Half a block up, music emerges from a storefront that serves as a Sikh *gurdwara*. Still farther north, English-speaking parishioners of a 150-year-old Protestant church empty out to make room for the Chinese-language service that follows. Just off Bowne Street sits the

3,500-member Korean American Presbyterian Church (one of the largest among the more than one hundred Korean Protestant churches in Flushing alone). At the same time, as older residents have moved out of Flushing, some places of worship have seen their memberships plummet—including the Kissena Jewish Center, no longer what it was in the early 1960s, when Orthodox Jews lived in the neighborhood and could walk to it. The Free Synagogue of Flushing, a Reform temple on nearby Kissena Boulevard, rents out its worship hall to a Korean Presbyterian congregation on Sundays.[21]

That religion has always been a vital part of immigrant life is one of the reasons the United States remains one of the most religious nations in the world. A forty-four-nation survey of more than thirty-eight thousand adults conducted in 2002 by the Pew Global Attitudes Project shows stark global differences in the personal importance of religion. Religion is far more important to Americans than to people living in other wealthy nations. Six out of ten (59 percent) people in the United States say religion plays a "very important" role in their lives—twice the percentage of self-avowed religious people in Canada (30 percent) and an even higher proportion when compared with Japan (12 percent) and Western Europe, including Catholic Italy (27 percent) and France (11 percent).[22]

Americans' views are closer to those of people in developing nations —in some instances more religious than those expressed, for example, in Mexico (57 percent) and Vietnam (24 percent), although less than the very high proportions in predominantly Muslim countries such as Indonesia and Pakistan. Figure 21 plots the national-level data on the importance of religion for the forty-four countries surveyed in the Pew project against their annual per capita income. The negative correlation between religious attitudes and national wealth is very strong (−0.675): the poorer the country, the greater the importance of religion—with the notable exception of the United States.

Despite the new religious diversity and its tradition of religious pluralism, the United States remains an overwhelmingly Christian nation —although one that has changed substantially since the 1950s, when virtually the entire society consisted of Protestants and Catholics, with a proportionately small Jewish population. The U.S. Census Bureau by law does not collect data on religion, but in 1957, it carried out a national survey that provided a snapshot of a population that was over 95 percent Christian.[23] Since 1972, however, the General Social Survey

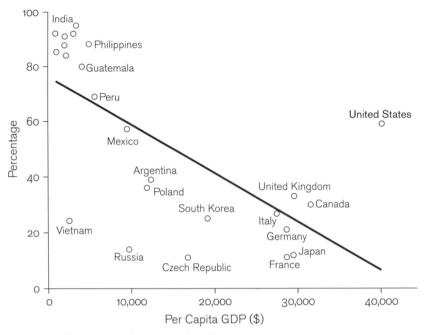

Sources: Pew Global Attitudes Project 2002; Central Intelligence Agency 2004.

Figure 21. Religiosity of forty-four selected countries and per capita gross domestic product, 2002

(GSS) has been conducted annually (or biannually) with nationally representative samples of the adult population, including items on religious identification, participation, and beliefs, which makes it possible to sketch a portrait of religious change in the United States over the thirty-year period from 1972 to 2002—precisely the years encompassing the current wave of immigration.[24]

GSS results are presented in table 44. It provides a breakdown of adults' current religion and the religion they were raised in as a child (about three of four adults adhere to the religion of their childhood), and it shows key correlates of religious identification and change over time, age cohort, generation, and education. Four main trends are discernible:

· The "vanishing Protestant majority": by 2005, the Protestant population of the United States overall fell below 50 percent for the first time—a decline that is sharper still among younger people and among the first and second generations.[25]

TABLE 44. RELIGIOUS IDENTIFICATION IN THE UNITED STATES, 1972–2002
Current religion and religion raised in by period, cohort, generation, and education

	Current religion					Religion raised in					
	Protestant (%)	Catholic (%)	Jewish (%)	Other (%)	None (%)	Protestant (%)	Catholic (%)	Jewish (%)	Other (%)	None (%)	N (total 43,698)
Period of survey											
1972–1978	64.3	25.3	2.4	1.3	6.8	66.8	27.0	2.4	0.9	2.8	10,652
1980–1987	64.7	24.5	2.1	1.7	7.1	66.8	26.7	2.2	1.2	3.1	11,223
1988–1996	61.1	24.5	2.0	3.3	9.0	62.7	28.4	2.1	2.3	4.6	13,409
1998–2002	53.9	24.6	1.9	5.5	14.0	57.5	30.2	2.1	3.5	6.7	8,414
Birth cohort											
Born pre-1930	70.4	22.5	2.6	1.0	3.6	71.5	22.5	2.7	1.0	2.4	12,088
1930–1949	62.8	25.0	2.2	2.2	7.7	65.3	27.4	2.3	1.4	3.5	13,364
1950–1969	55.9	26.1	1.7	4.1	12.2	58.7	32.0	1.8	2.5	5.1	15,426
1970 or after	46.1	25.6	1.8	6.5	19.9	51.7	30.8	1.9	5.2	10.3	2,820
Generation											
First (foreign-born)	27.8	43.8	4.3	13.2	10.9	23.5	51.8	4.1	15.4	5.2	2,290
Second	35.4	44.8	6.5	3.8	9.4	34.0	50.6	7.2	3.5	4.7	3,778
Third	49.0	35.3	3.2	2.5	10.0	50.2	41.1	3.5	1.1	4.1	9,469
Fourth+	75.1	13.4	0.4	2.2	8.9	79.5	14.9	0.3	0.8	4.5	20,115
Education											
0–8 years	70.3	22.6	0.9	1.3	4.9	69.7	24.3	0.8	1.3	3.9	4,732
9–12 years	64.2	25.1	1.0	2.0	7.7	66.3	27.0	1.0	1.3	4.4	20,376
13–16 years	57.1	25.5	2.9	3.8	10.7	60.0	30.3	3.1	2.5	4.0	14,652
17–20 years	51.8	22.5	6.3	5.4	14.0	56.5	28.7	6.5	3.7	4.5	3,799

SOURCE: General Social Survey, 1972–2002.

- Catholics remain stable in their relative national proportion. They have been about a fourth of the population for decades now, but this figure disguises a secular decline over time that is being more than compensated by new influxes of immigrant Catholics from Latin America, as well as from the Philippines and (to a lesser extent) from Vietnam.

- There has been a sharp increase in the proportion of people who indicate "no religion" to the question on religious identification, doubling from 7 to 14 percent over the 1990s. In part, as seen from its correlation with education, this figure reflects a small but growing secularization trend. However, many respondents who no longer identify with organized religion nonetheless profess a belief in God and occasionally attend religious services. Thus, the explanation for this trend is not reducible solely to a secularization thesis.[26]

- Finally, as reflected in the opening *New York Times* story, an increase in non-Christian religions is apparent, notably Buddhism, Hinduism, and Islam. Despite small relative proportions, the GSS trend data show that, excluding Judaism, all other non-Christian religions increased from about 1.5 percent of the adult population in the 1970s and early 1980s, to over 3 percent in the early to mid-1990s, to 5.5 percent in the 1998–2002 period (each 1 percent represents more than two million adults).[27]

Figure 22 summarizes GSS data on frequency of religious attendance by birth cohort, nativity, and gender. These nationally representative figures indicate a monotonic decline in attendance with age, significantly greater participation by females, and insignificant differences between the foreign-born and native-born. Exactly the same trend is shown by GSS data on belief in God, with males and the young being significantly more likely to declare no such belief and the native and foreign-born showing no major differences. These general trends provide a broader framework for examining the role of religion among contemporary immigrants. We focus first on the religious ties linking the foreign-born with their countries of origin, next on religion and adaptation in the second generation and the role of religion in linear and reactive ethnicity, and finally on the specific cases of the Mexican and the Muslim populations. Reasons for selecting these groups for special attention are explained in the respective sections.

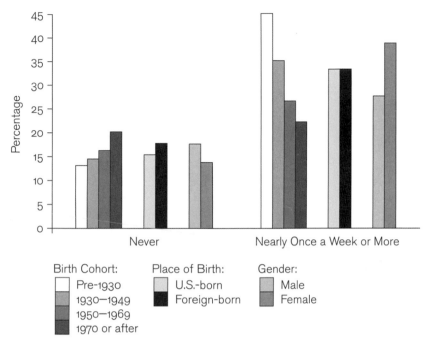

Birth Cohort:
☐ Pre-1930
▨ 1930–1949
▨ 1950–1969
■ 1970 or after

Place of Birth:
▨ U.S.-born
■ Foreign-born

Gender:
▨ Male
▨ Female

Source: General Social Survey, 1972–2002.

Figure 22. Frequency of religious attendance by birth cohort and nativity

RELIGION AND TRANSNATIONALISM

In an impoverished quarter of Bogotá, the capital of Colombia, lies the convent of the Vicentine Sisters of Charity. The modest but ample and comfortable space is the headquarters for a number of projects implemented by the nuns to help the poor in the nearby community and beyond. From it, Sor Irene, a vigorous middle-aged nun, operates a refuge for the homeless of Bogotá, dubbed "inhabitants of the street," mostly mentally disturbed or retarded persons and drug addicts. Every night, Sor Irene and her brave helpers roam the dangerous quarters surrounding the convent in search of the inhabitants of the street. The refuge offers them not only food, shelter, and clothing but also rehabilitation through professional counseling and various occupational therapy programs. All the equipment for learning new work skills—from manufacturing paper out of recycled waste materials to baking bread—has been purchased with donations from Colombian immigrants in the United States.[28]

In the same convent lives Sor Matilde, another nun who has operated an asylum and schools for orphaned children in the nearby city of Tunja for fifteen years. The funds for purchasing the land for the asylum and building the dormitories and the school were donated by the Foundation of the Divine Child (Fundación del Divino Niño), a charity established by a Colombian priest, an immigrant journalist, and a group of immigrant volunteers based in a parish in Passaic, New Jersey. Computers for the school were donated by IBM following a request from the foundation. A new training school for the indigenous population around Tunja is currently being planned.[29]

The examples could multiply. While the literature on religion and immigration has focused overwhelmingly on the adaptation and successful integration of migrants in a new land, the fact is that they seldom forget where they came from and that ties with the homeland, at least in the first generation, remain strong. Most immigrants come from poor nations and communities. As their economic situation abroad improves, it is natural that many feel the impulse of helping those left behind, going beyond their immediate kin. That impulse has a natural affinity with the general charitable orientation of church-led activities and, certainly, with the needs of churches and congregations in the home countries.

The study of transnational participation among Latin American immigrant heads of family, described in chapter 5, found that approximately 10 percent of the 1,842 transnational organizations on which members of this representative sample took part were of a confessional or religious character. A more recent study of the universe of transnational organizations constructed by Colombian, Dominican, and Mexican immigrants on the East Coast found that 3.4 percent were of an explicitly religious character. These figures may not seem like much, except that many of the activities of the most common organizations, such as "civic-cultural" groups and especially "hometown committees" identified in the same study, have clearly religious undertones.[30] These range from repairing and embellishing the hometown church to channeling assistance through the local parish or a religious congregation after a natural disaster.

For example, the municipal president of Xochihuehuetlán in the state of Guerrero, Mexico, whose hometown committee in New York City formed part of the transnational immigrant organizations study, describes this collaboration as follows:

More or less in 1985, works began that benefited our town. . . . [T]hey
were of a religious character to improve the Sanctuary of San Diego de
Alcalá, which is the most respected patron saint around here; then we
bought street lights for the *calzada* leading to the sanctuary, . . . the avenue
where the procession takes place. Today and with the help of migrants
in the U.S., public works are very advanced: the church is in good shape,
redecorated and with gold leaf in the altars; the atrium has new benches
and the avenue is repaved with tile. . . . [N]ow we are looking at rebuilding
the school with support from the municipality and the people that we have
in the United States with whom we always have had good relations.[31]

When a river flood caused the death or disappearance of seven hundred persons in the town of Jimani, Dominican Republic, the Dominican immigrant community in New York and New England quickly
mobilized to provide assistance. Particularly prominent were Alianza
Dominicana, the largest social service organization of this ethnic community in New York, and the hometown committee created by Jimani
immigrants in Boston and environs and known by its acronym ASO-
JIMA. Their aid was directed to the local parish priest, in part out of
fear of corruption among state officials. According to the priest, those
fears were justified:

I had conflicts with the provincial government because the governor wanted
to manage the external aid and was robbing us blind. I denounced him
publicly and, in response, the government removed the military from Jimani
as well as the police protection of our warehouse. On July 11, the provincial
government left and never came back. With very little money, we had to
work out ourselves the logistics of distributing all that foreign assistance.[32]

First-generation immigrants have always looked backward, and
when the economic situation has permitted, they have sought to provide assistance not only to their families but to their communities and
countries of birth. Much of this impulse was religiously inspired or
channeled through religious institutions. In that sense, there are close
parallels between the Irish, Italian, and Polish immigrants of the nineteenth and early twentieth centuries and the Mexicans, Filipinos, Koreans, Vietnamese, Chinese, Indians, and Dominicans today.

Religious transnationalism is not limited to immigrant philanthropic
contributions, however, because it also includes the influence of home
country religious institutions on their expatriates. Thus, if monetary
and other economic resources flow in one direction, moral guidance
and often religious personnel flow in the other. The story of how Irish

clergy literally built the American Catholic Church from the ground up has been recently summarized by Hirschman, drawing on the classic studies by Handlin and Higham, as well as on more recent ones by Larkin, Archdeacon, and others.[33] So abundant were Irish priests and nuns in the late nineteenth and twentieth centuries that they staffed other "ethnic" parishes until the Italian, Polish, and other Catholic migrants could get their own clergy.

Today, the story repeats itself, but with a greater religious diversity. Catholic priests still come from abroad. For instance, the Scalibrini, an Italian order devoted to ministering to migrants, trains priests at its seminaries in Latin America to be sent to Latin migrant congregations in the United States.[34] There they are now joined by Jewish rabbis, Middle Eastern imams, Buddhist monks, and Hindu swamis coming to tend to their various flocks in a foreign land and, in the process, reaffirm community and identity. Thus, Laotian Buddhists in Louisiana and Vietnamese Buddhists in Houston, the first being followers of the Theravada branch of the religion, the second of the Mahayana tradition, had to trek home in search of monks to staff their new temples.[35] In another recent study, Jacob and Thakur relate the construction of the beautiful Jiothi Hindu temple in suburban Houston and of the pilgrimage of well-heeled immigrants from South India to their homeland in search of competent swamis to staff it and conduct its rites in ancient Sanskrit. When a move was afoot to include women in the temple's governing board, word had to be sent back to India requesting authorization from Hindu leaders there.[36]

As with other transnational forms of exchange, what is new at present is not the existence of these activities but their intensity, rooted in innovations in communications and transportation technologies. Today, instant exchanges of information and fast and increasingly accessible air transportation link immigrant communities to their hometowns and countries as never before. For the most part, and despite some downsides, dense transnational ties tend to be beneficial to places of origin as they channel to them an increasing flow of otherwise unavailable information and material resources. The opposite flow of ideas, culture, and even religious personnel from the home country is the one opposed by nativists as underminers of American cultural integrity. As noted earlier, these attacks follow a "secular" logic, according to which immigrants should leave everything behind upon arrival and seek to become indistinguishable from other Americans as quickly as possible.

The alternative "religious" logic sees the reaffirmation of national identities, cultures, and languages as positive insofar as it helps newcomers regain their balance in a foreign land and provides them with information and resources to move ahead in their new social environment. In this sense, transnationalism, religious or otherwise, and successful incorporation to the host society are not at all opposite. The empirical evidence available so far supports this position.[37] In a recent study, Menjívar has shown how both Catholic churches and evangelical ones seek to strengthen a sense of ethnic community among their Latin migrant flocks as a basic step in their adaptation to American society. In this effort, evangelical churches have the upper hand because they are built around immigrants of the same nationality (e.g., Salvadorans) and support their strong concerns and ties with specific localities back home. The pastors themselves take part in this transnational circuit, traveling back and forth between places of origin and of settlement, ministering to congregations in both, and sponsoring projects that bring them together.

In contrast, Catholic churches attract larger but more diverse congregations. Their attempts to merge immigrants of different nationalities into a single panethnic or "Hispanic" flock focused on their present U.S. lives are resisted by migrants, whose thoughts and actions remain oriented to families and communities in their particular countries of origin. For first-generation immigrants, at least, these ties are fundamental as they seek to adapt and move ahead in a different and challenging environment.[38]

RELIGION AND THE SECOND GENERATION

As shown in figure 20, the interplay between religion and immigration does not stop with the first generation but extends to its descendants. If the first of the three Rs—refuge—has been a key function of religious affiliation for recently arrived immigrants, for their offspring, the other two—respect and resources—become paramount as they seek to move ahead in what is now their country. Alba and Raboteau have noted that American society has traditionally pressured immigrants to shed their language and most elements of their culture, but not their religion.[39] The latter takes on different meanings and roles across generations, however.

While fostering transnational ties may be important for first-generation migrants, for their children, issues and concerns tied to their present

American lives become paramount.[40] The same Catholic Church struggling today to integrate new and diverse immigrant flocks from Latin America and Asia did succeed rather well with the earlier European second generation. It did so by offering to children of Irish, Italian, and Polish migrants a wonderful deal: it educated them and their own descendants in good schools, gave them respectability and status as churchgoers, and took care of their health needs through an extensive hospital system. No wonder that these second- and third-generation ethnics whose forebears had been relatively indifferent to religion or practitioners of a folk peasant variety of Catholicism became serious Catholics, well instructed in the canons of the faith.[41]

More generally, as numerous scholars have noted, the American Republic was not a particularly religious country at the time of its foundation. It became increasingly so over the next two centuries, in part out of the interplay between successive waves of immigrants and their religious needs and practices. The strong and widespread religiosity that makes the United States an outlier among developed nations today arose largely out of competition between Christian and then other denominations for the minds and hearts—and souls—of successive migrant waves.[42] Today, Latin and Asian immigrants are spawning a new second generation destined to become a very significant component of America's young population. Like their European forebears, they too need and want the means to move ahead. As seen in chapter 8, however, they face an environment that, while offering multiple opportunities for success, also confronts them with serious challenges. Religion plays a complex role in this environment, isolating and protecting second-generation youths from such threats and, at other times, offering those who have fallen a second chance and a means to rebuild their lives.

As also seen in chapter 8, *selective acculturation*, in which children of immigrants learn the language and culture of the new country while preserving elements of their parents' own culture, offers the best means to fend off challenges to successful adaptation and educational achievement. Naturally, immigrant religions play a central part in this process. When second-generation children continue observing the faith of their parents, certain benefits associated with selective acculturation become apparent: there is a common universe of meanings shared across generations, more open channels of communication between the two generations, and a system of beliefs and norms antithetical to downward assimilation.

In their study of the poor Vietnamese community of the Versailles section of New Orleans, Zhou and Bankston identified the construction of the new Catholic parish, Mary, Queen of Vietnam, as a central element in the high levels of educational achievement of Vietnamese youths, despite the poverty of the area and the modest human capital of most parents. Church attendance and participation in church-sponsored activities effectively insulated these youngsters from neighborhood gangs and helped reinforce parental aspirations for educational achievement and occupational success. In the authors' words:

> The degree of integration into the group is reflected in the behavioral patterns of group members. . . . Because the norm of individual families stem from the ethnic community, the behavior expected by parents and by others around the children are essentially the same, suggesting that young people receive little competition from other desiderata when their social world is restricted . . . to the ethnic group.[43]

To the contrary, Vietnamese American youths who abandoned the church were viewed, for the most part, as undergoing dissonant acculturation and at risk of assimilating downward. As a youth counselor, himself of Vietnamese origin, told the authors about this group of youngsters, "They have become Americans in their own eyes, but they do not have the advantages of white Americans. So they lose the direction that their Vietnamese culture can give them. Since they do not know where they are going, they just drift."[44]

Those Laotian mechanics and welders building a Buddhist temple in the midst of the Louisiana sugarcane fields knew well what they were doing. The temple and its associated rituals were not only for themselves but mainly for the children—a symbol of their origin, a rallying point for their cultural pride, and a springboard for their successful adaptation to schools and society. While these refugees may not have known it, they were reenacting, in a very different time and place, the actions and achievements of millions of immigrants before them. Although the role of religion is not limited to selective acculturation, as we will see shortly, this still represents a dominant path for successful adaptation in early life.

The third wave of the Children of Immigrants Longitudinal Study (CILS), described in chapter 8, collected data on the religious affiliation and participation of young adults at average age twenty-four. Results for the entire sample and for its principal nationalities are presented in figures 23 and 24. Three points are apparent from figure 23: first, all

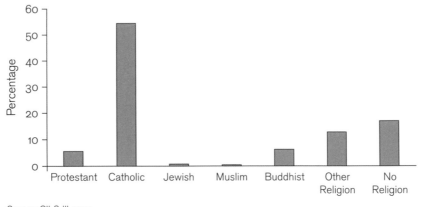

Source: CILS-III, 2002.

Figure 23. Religious affiliation in the second generation

kinds of different religions are represented in this sample, although Catholics are the absolute majority; second, over 80 percent of these young adults are affiliated with a religion; third, a sizable minority have no religious attachment at all.

The dominance of the Catholic faith in these data is partially a consequence of the way that the CILS sample was designed. However, it also reflects a real fact: namely, the large number of Latin American, Filipino, and Vietnamese immigrants that profess this religion and, hence, the preponderant role of Catholicism among the contemporary foreign-born and their offspring. Strong majorities of all second-generation Latin groups profess to be Catholics. The same is the case for Filipinos. While the dominant religion among the Vietnamese is Buddhism, about one-fifth of these youths declared themselves to be Catholics (as are about one-fourth of their parents). This dominant position of the Roman Catholic faith poses both a challenge and an opportunity. The challenge is to provide for this young population a comparable level of support and educational resources as were available to earlier European Catholics. The opportunity lies in that, by doing so, the Catholic Church can consolidate its position as the dominant faith in the United States. As we will see, however, there are indications that Catholicism is not rising up to this challenge—or at least not as much as it did during the period of classic European immigration.

The finding that close to 20 percent of the CILS sample declares no religious belief in early adulthood must be tempered by the fact that

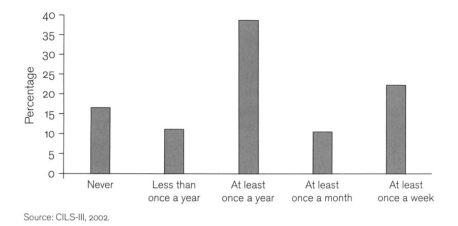

Source: CILS-III, 2002.

Figure 24. Religious attendance in the second generation

this is the dominant position among second-generation Chinese (53.2 percent), and it is endorsed by one-third of other Asians. By and large, these are offspring of families coming from a more secular tradition and whose parents are endowed, on average, with superior levels of human capital. Immigrants from the People's Republic of China were raised in a society where religion is not encouraged, to put it mildly. The absence of strong afterlife beliefs among these immigrants and the fact that they need religion less as a platform for upward mobility partially explain the lack of strong religious convictions among their second generation.

Data on religious attendance, presented in figure 25, confirm this picture. Again, nearly 20 percent do not take part in any religious services, and to them must be added another 10 percent of "nominal" believers who frequent a church or temple less than once a year. They are counterbalanced by about one-third of the sample who are regular churchgoers, with the rest in between. Complete absence of religious participation is most common among the Chinese (41 percent) and other Asians (39 percent), with youths from "other" nationalities (primarily of European and Canadian origin) close behind. Noteworthy is the fact that the most devout groups in this sample are young adults of black Caribbean origin, particularly Haitians. Among them, nonattendance or rare attendance drops to the single digits (3.3 percent), while among Jamaicans and other West Indians, it is less than 15 percent. The rest of second-generation nationalities oscillate between these extremes,

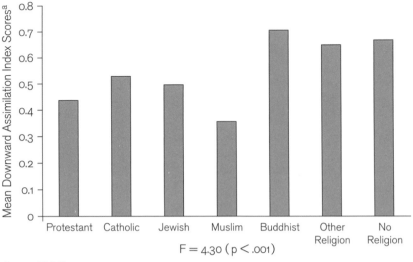

$$F = 4.30 \, (p < .001)$$

Source: CILS-III, 2002.
[a]Higher scores indicate a higher propensity toward downward assimilation. Sample DAI mean score is .579, with a range from 0 to 6.

Figure 25. Downward assimilation by religion in the second generation

with children of middle-class Cuban exiles tending toward the devout pole (13 percent nonattendance) and those of Vietnamese refugees toward a more secular stance (26 percent).

Overall, these data suggest three trends: first, greater religious affiliation and participation among second-generation Latin Americans than Asians, except the (mostly Catholic) Filipinos; second, the predominance of Catholicism (most Catholic groups are more participatory in this sample); third, a tendency among black second-generation youths, often in greater need of external assistance, to be more religiously active (Haitians, West Indians). Part of the explanation for the very high levels of religious affiliation and attendance among second-generation Haitians in Miami has to do with the role of the Catholic Church in promoting the integration of their group, an experience to which we shall return in the conclusion.

Using these data, we can demonstrate an association between religion and adaptation outcomes in the second generation. For this purpose, we first constructed a Downward Assimilation Index (DAI) composed of the sum of six indicators of negative outcomes in early adulthood—from unemployment to arrest and incarceration.[45] Higher

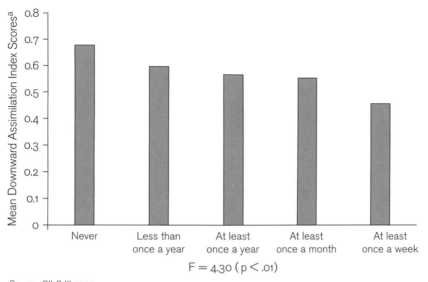

$$F = 4.30 \, (p < .01)$$

Source: CILS-III, 2002.
[a]Higher scores indicate a higher propensity toward downward assimilation. Sample DAI mean score is .579, with a range from 0 to 6.

Figure 26. Downward assimilation by frequency of religious attendance

scores in this index indicate a greater propensity toward downward assimilation. As shown in figure 25, all second-generation youths who profess a religion, with the exception of Buddhists, have lower scores in the DAI than those without any religion. These differences are statistically significant at the .001 level. The exceptional case of Buddhists is due to the poverty and difficulties in the labor market experienced by a relatively large number of Laotian and Cambodian youths. For the CILS sample as a whole, approximately 60 percent register no indicator of downward assimilation at all, while the figure drops to 51 percent among Laotians and Cambodians. To be noted as well is the relatively high DAI score among those professing "other religion." We will return to these points later.

More telling still is the relationship of frequency of religious participation with the DAI. As shown in figure 26, the association is monotonic and inverse, with more religiously active youths showing lower indications of downward assimilation. The association is significant at the .01 level. However, these bivariate relationships do not "prove" that religion prevents negative assimilation because the causal effect can run, at least in some cases, in the opposite direction and because no

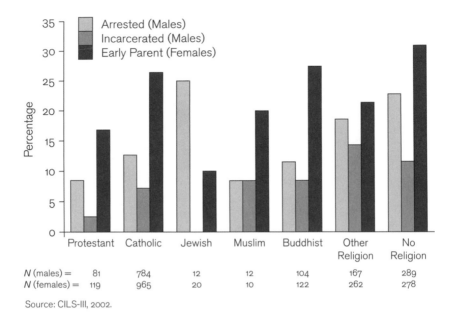

N (males) =   81   784   12   12   104   167   289
N (females) = 119   965   20   10   122   262   278

Source: CILS-III, 2002.

Figure 27. Religious affiliation and indicators of downward assimilation in the second generation

controls have been introduced for other variables. All that the evidence shows at this point is that the two variables correlate in the way that theoretical expectations suggest.

An examination of the individual components of the DAI also indicate a general tendency for religion to be associated with positive adaptation outcomes, but with several notable exceptions. For example, figure 27 shows that youths professing affiliation to a standard religion tend to be arrested or incarcerated less often than those declaring "other religion" or having no religion at all. Similarly, respondents who "never" attend church are significantly more likely to have been arrested and slightly more likely to have been incarcerated than others (figure 28). However, the relationships of frequency of religious attendance with arrest or incarceration are not linear. Similarly, the relationship between early childbearing and religiosity indicates that it is young women professing "other religion" rather than no religion at all who are more likely to have been early mothers.

These anomalies are due to the presence of other factors that also affect and thus confound these bivariate relationships. To clarify what

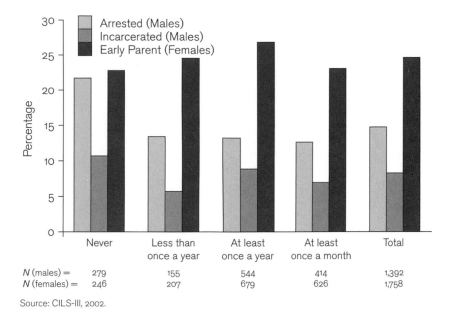

N (males) =   279   155   544   414   1,392
N (females) = 246   207   679   626   1,758

Source: CILS-III, 2002.

Figure 28. Frequency of religious attendance and indicators of downward assimilation in the second generation

is actually taking place, we conducted a series of statistical analyses that control for other possible predictors of adaptation outcomes. These include age, sex, length of U.S. residence, parental socioeconomic status, single- versus two-parent families of origin, and national origin. All of these variables are included in models used in the past to predict major outcomes of second-generation adaptation.[46] With all of them controlled, we find that both religious affiliation and religious participation have resilient and significant effects. For this analysis, we included the DAI as an indicator of downward assimilation and, in addition, educational achievement and occupational status as indicators of the opposite trend. Results are presented in table 45.

With other predictors taken into account, being a member of an established religion is strongly and positively associated with higher educational achievement and higher occupational prestige, and it is significantly and negatively related to incidents of downward assimilation. Based on the scales used to measure each outcome, religious affiliation increases education by a net 0.7 year and occupational prestige by approximately 1.3 percent, and it leads to a 10 percent decline

TABLE 45. NET RELATIONSHIPS OF RELIGIOUS
AFFILIATION AND PARTICIPATION WITH MAJOR
ADAPTATION OUTCOMES IN THE SECOND GENERATION

	Education (years)[a]	Occupational status[b]	Downward assimilation[c]
Religious affiliation[d]			
Major religion	.311 (4.1)***	1.331 (2.3)*	−.099 (2.6)**
Other religion	−.048 n.s.	.121 n.s.	−.045 n.s.
Catholic	.276 (3.4)**	.951 (1.5)##	−.093 (2.3)*
Protestant	.389 (2.9)**	2.548 (2.4)*	−.152 (2.2)*
Jewish	.774 (2.6)**	4.533 (1.8)#	.015 n.s.
Religious participation[e]			
Attends at least once a month	.314 (3.5)***	1.845 (2.7)**	−.081 (1.9)#
Attends at least once a year	.265 (3.03)**	.893 (1.5)##	−.060 (1.5)##
Attends less than once a year	.121 n.s.	.167 n.s.	−.046 n.s.
N	3,293	2,590	3,168

SOURCES: CILS-I–III.

[a] Ordinary least squares regression coefficients controlling for age, sex, length of U.S. residence, parental socioeconomic status, single- versus two-parent families, and national origin.

[b] Ordinary least squares regression coefficients controlling for all the preceding predictors. Dependent variable is measured in Treiman occupational prestige scores.

[c] Negative binomial regression coefficients controlling for all the preceding predictors. Dependent variable is a count of events or conditions indicating downward assimilation (arrest, incarceration, premature childbearing, etc.).

[d] "Major religion" includes Catholic, Protestant, Jewish, Muslim, and Buddhist. "No religion" is the reference category.

[e] "Never attends" is the reference category.

***Probability of a chance relationship is less than one in one thousand.

**Probability of a chance relationship is less than one in one hundred.

*Probability of a chance relationship is less than five in one hundred.

Probability of a chance relationship is less than ten in one hundred.

Probability of a chance relationship is less than fifteen in one hundred.

n.s. = Not significant.

in indicators of downward assimilation. Note that these modest but resilient effects are not associated with affiliation to "other religions," which has no effect whatever on any indicator of adaptation. Additional analyses show that the significant coefficients associated with a "major religion" are due, almost entirely, to Catholic, Protestant, and Jewish affiliations. As shown in table 45, all three religions have strong and positive relationships with educational achievement and, with one exception, more modest but still significant associations with occupational status and the DAI.

The story is quite similar when we consider the net effects of religious attendance on upward or downward assimilation. Relative to youths who "never attend" religious services, those who do have a higher probability of educational and occupational achievement and a lower one of following a downward path. An important finding is that these relationships are strengthened by frequency of religious attendance. Thus, among young adults who go to church but do so less than once a year, the coefficients are of the expected sign, but all are insignificant. On the other hand, stronger and more consistent relationships are found among those who attend religious services at least once a month. Among them, for example, the count of incidents indicative of downward assimilation declines by a net 9 percent.

Because religious affiliation and participation and the various adaptation outcomes were measured during the same survey, it is not possible to say with certainty that one factor always "leads" to another. In some cases, at least, it is possible that the causal relationship runs in the other direction. For example, educational and occupational success may lead to reinforcement of religious convictions, and, alternatively, a downward assimilation path may be accompanied by rejection of the religious traditions inherited from parents. At a more theoretical level, this pattern of mutual influences is compatible with the role of religion outlined in figure 20: just as, at the macrosocial level, religion interacts with other social forces charting the path followed by different immigrant groups, at the individual level, it also interacts with various adaptation outcomes, influencing them at some moments and being influenced by them at others. We examine next the forms that such interactions can take.

RELIGION: LINEAR AND REACTIVE

In chapter 5, we saw that ethnic identities and affiliation could be linear or reactive, representing either a continuation of the cultural traditions learned and brought from the home country or an emergent product, created by the confrontation with different and frequently harsh realities in the host society. As an integral component of immigrants' culture, religion follows a similar course. In the majority of cases, the religious beliefs and affiliations of the foreign-born are *linear*. If immigration is a "theologizing experience"[47] because of the challenges and psychological traumas that it poses, the tendency for most of those who confront them is to hold tight to what they already have—reaffirming traditional beliefs and rituals as a source of comfort and protection. For this reason, immigrants and their children generally stay with the religion of their forebears.[48] This is what the pattern of religious affiliations discussed in the prior section clearly shows.

In some instances, however, religion becomes reactive, signaling a break from the past. In the first generation, this can happen because of the failure of religious traditions brought from the home country to meet immigrants' needs and the presence of more attractive alternatives. As Pierce, Spickard, and Yoo argue for the case of Japanese and Korean immigrants, many embraced Protestant Christianity in part because of its greater cultural affinity to their new environment but also because of its greater capacity to protect and assist those in need than the more passive and distant Buddhism of their ancestors.[49] While pre–World War II Japanese migrants also affiliated with and supported Buddhist "churches" in California, many others turned to Christianity, seeking, in various ways, to merge its beliefs with their strong Japanese identities. Among post-1965 Korean migrants, Pierce et al. estimate that upward of 40 percent converted to Christianity in America, which, added to the significant number of those who were already Christians in Korea, made this tradition—especially Protestantism—the dominant religion of the first generation.[50] Chinese immigrants, raised in a nonreligious environment at home, have also been reported to convert to Protestantism in significant numbers.

Not only Eastern religions, weakly institutionalized in America, have been subject to the challenge of congregational Christianity. Evangelical Protestantism has also made deep inroads among traditionally Catholic Latin immigrants. As López notes, the hierarchical character of Catholicism and the failure of some Catholic churches to actively respond to the emotional and economic needs of poor immigrants in the contemporary period have led them to join evangelical congregations.[51] Charismatic Catholicism emerged, in part, as a movement to counteract the appeal of the more democratic and socially cohesive Protestant churches. But even then, Catholicism failed to retain the allegiance of a significant number of Mexicans and other Latins, especially in the Southwest. According to González, fully 25 percent of Hispanics in New Mexico, both native-born and immigrants, had converted to Protestantism by 1960.[52] More recent data point in the same direction, showing that over 20 percent of Mexican Americans have become Protestant, doubling the average among recent immigrants.[53] The pattern is consistent with the more adaptable role of evangelical churches in response to immigrant transnational concerns and activities, as described earlier.

Reactivity in the second generation is more complex because it may include dissatisfaction with home-country religious affiliations, in the model of some first-generation parents, but also dissatisfaction with the parents themselves and attempts to move away from their traditions. Thus, while first-generation immigrants may or may not have remained loyal to the religion of their forebears, their offspring can still explore other alternatives more consonant with their emotional needs and their attempt to create distance from the parents. The 13 percent of respondents in the CILS sample indicating affiliation with "other" religions are partially representative of this trend since the alternative beliefs that they profess are seldom found in the first generation. They include Rastafarians, Wiccans, and followers of assorted sects and cults, both Christian and non-Christian. The free "marketplace" for religion offered by American society has provided these youngsters with the opportunity to explore alternatives other than those learned at home.

That exploration comes at a cost, because it can sever the young from their family moorings, reducing chances for selective acculturation. In addition, the sects and cults that they join seldom fulfill the traditional functions of religion, as they are accorded little respect and commonly lack the social and economic resources required for upward mobility. Still, for some young people, they offer a chance to escape what they see as a stifling home environment and to gain a better understanding of themselves. Consider the case of Marina Solares López, daughter of a strict working-class Cuban family, reinterviewed in Miami at age twenty-four as part of the CILS sample. During adolescence, she repeatedly clashed with her parents because of their insistence that she be chaperoned on dates. The parents also adhered to the fierce brand of conservative anti-Communism common among their ethnic group. As Marina entered college and started to study social science, she began to see things differently, distancing herself even more from her parents' political views. During the Elián González episode, she publicly defended the right of the child's father to take him back to Cuba. "They almost hung me from a tree," she recalls.

Her deepening sense of difference prompted her to join the Wicca sect, after a visit to Salem at age twenty-one. She defines Wicca as "a neopagan faith very nature oriented. Celebrations take place every six weeks, following cycles of nature, changes of season." As part of her changed identity, she has ceased to see herself as "Cuban," adopting the broader term "Hispanic." Her recent marriage to a Chilean reinforced her views as he also opposes the political ambiance of Miami and, though himself an agnostic, finds her adopted religion "curious and exciting."[54] In cases such as this, parting company with the beliefs and traditions of very strict parents may have liberating effects.

In the prior section, however, we saw how affiliations to "other religion" in the aggregate did not produce the same positive associations with successful adaptation as membership in the major denominations. Part of the reason is that these alternative affiliations are commonly reactive and do not contribute to selective acculturation. There is, however, another social trend contributing to this result. Religious reactivity can also be a way to climb back after a major setback. Among second-generation youths, this reactive variant commonly leads to "finding God" after being thrown into prison for a felony or becoming destitute because of drug addiction or single parenthood. These religious "rebirths" may take the form of reembracing the parents' faith or adopting a new one.

Rastafarianism among West Indians and evangelical Protestantism among Latin Americans are common vehicles for this alternative. Cases of this variant identified in the CILS sample were commonly accompanied by a self-definition as "a new man" or "a new woman" and a serious attempt to rectify the errors that led to the crisis. Thus, Eddie Cifuentes, the twenty-three-year-old son of a Mariel Cuban refugee, culminated a highly successful career as a drug dealer in Miami with a stiff five-year sentence for trafficking. He served three years in an adult correctional facility, where he met Ramón Ruiz, a lifer, who took him under his wing. From Ruiz, Eddie said he learned "family values, then self-respect." He came from prison a deeply changed, religious man. He now works doing electrical work for Artistic Dome Ceilings and brings home $800 a week, a far cry from the $8,000 or more he grossed as a drug dealer. But he says he is now on the right path, guided by his new faith.[55]

The recent Immigration and Intergenerational Mobility in Metropolitan Los Angeles survey (IMMLA), described in chapter 7, yields some revealing results concerning this form of reactive religion.[56] Though the survey is not strictly limited to the 1.5 and second generations, as it also includes native-parentage young adults, the relationship between frequency of religious participation and indicators of downward mobility is telling. For the most part, the association is modestly negative, with greater frequency of participation associated with better outcomes.

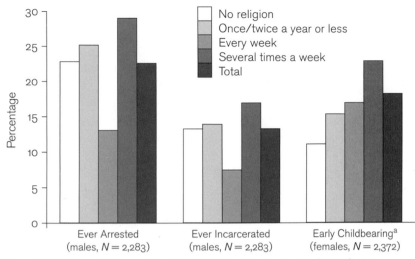

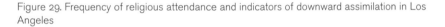

Source: Immigration and Intergenerational Mobility in Metropolitan Los Angeles (IIMMLA), 2004.
[a]Had a child between fourteen and twenty years of age.

Figure 29. Frequency of religious attendance and indicators of downward assimilation in Los Angeles

However, the association reverses dramatically when we consider the most frequent category of attendance—several times a week.

As shown in figure 29, episodes of arrest and incarceration are most frequent for males who go to church or temple several times a week than for those who never attend. The same pattern is true for early childbearing among females. It is implausible that a fervent religious life would lead to early jail or premature parenthood; it is far more likely that such serious setbacks in the path to successful adaptation would lead young people to find solace and guidance in religion. Evangelical Protestantism and, to a lesser extent, charismatic Catholicism plus nonorthodox religions are the favored choices for such reactive conversions. They offer the promise of redemption and a second chance for those who, in one way or another, have deviated from the normative path.

A second anomaly uncovered by the IMMLA survey is that, along with another positive association between dropping out of high school and the most fervent religiosity, the lowest dropout levels and highest levels of college graduation were found among young persons of no religion. The significant presence of Chinese and other Asians in this Los Angeles sample is partially responsible for this finding. Among the

	Linear	Reactive
First Generation	Irish and Italian immigrants before World War I: most Catholic, Buddhist, and Muslim immigrants today	Korean and Chinese converts to mainstream Protestant churches; Mexican and Central American converts to Evangelical sects
Second Generation	Most Cuban, Colombian and other U.S.-born Latin Catholics; Vietnamese, Cambodian, Laotian, and other U.S.-born Asian Buddhists	Converts to Wicca and other exotic cults; converts to Rastafarianism and Evangelical sects after episodes of downward assimilation

Figure 30. Types of religion across generations

Chinese, the proportion of college graduates is a remarkable 71 percent; among other Asians, 46.3 percent. These groups are also heavily represented, as in CILS, in the category declaring no religion.

Linear beliefs and traditions brought from the home country are those more commonly featured in canonical accounts of the functions of religion for immigrant adaptation. However, first-generation reactive affiliations, like those adopted by Korean, Mexican, and Central American Protestant converts, can be every bit as capable of providing the three Rs; indeed, they are commonly embraced for this reason. Second-generation reactive religiosity compromises selective acculturation when it is pitted against the beliefs of the parents, although it may offer to some young people the chance to find the meaning and direction that, for some reason, they lack at home. Lastly, downward assimilation may be *positively* associated with religious beliefs and practices when the latter become a means of salvation for those who have suffered serious reverses early in life. In such cases, the causal order of the relationship between religion and second-generation adaptation is reversed. These variants are the reasons that, in the aggregate, the association between religious affiliation and positive adaptation outcomes in the second generation is modest and registers a number of exceptions. Figure 30 summarizes the various types of situations leading to this conclusion.

In sum, historical and contemporary case studies and our own survey data show that religion continues to be an enduring presence in the lives of most immigrant communities and that its influence persists across generations. However, the evidence warns against a too-uniform or too-celebratory account of the role of religion. Not all migrants or their children follow the traditional path of embracing the beliefs of their ancestors and using them as a means of mutual support and a platform for upward mobility. Alternatives exist, individually and collectively, that undermine the prediction of a uniform process and point to the complexity of the relationship between religion and immigration in the real world.

THE MEXICAN EXPERIENCE

Mexican immigration, as we have noted already, is by far the largest and most enduring flow into the United States. It is also permeated, at every step, by the presence of religion. This is evident in the fervent prayers addressed by migrants from the interior to the Virgin prior to crossing the border. It is equally evident in the high priority assigned by hometown committees to restoring the local church and ensuring that their patron saint is properly dressed and honored at the annual festivities. In the collection of immigrant *retablos*, assembled by Massey and Durand, we find many moving instances of the trek to *El Norte* being indeed a (Catholic) "theologizing" experience. These naive paintings relate the tribulations of migrating peasants upon crossing the border and pay homage to the Virgin or patron saint who saved them. Thus:

> On this date, I dedicate the present *retablo* to the Virgin of San Juan for the clear miracle she granted me on the date June 5, 1986. Re-emigrating to the United States with three friends, the water we were carrying ran out. Traveling in such great heat and with such thirst, and without hope of drinking even a little water, we invoked the Virgin of San Juan and were able to arrive at our destination and return to our homeland in health. In eternal gratitude to the Virgin of San Juan de los Lagos. *Braulio Barrientos.*[57]

> We give thanks to the Virgin of San Juan for having saved us from the People of the Migration (the Border Patrol) on our way to Los Angeles. From León, Guanajuato. *María Esther Tapia Picón.*[58]

Recall also the words of the municipal president of Xochihuehuetlán concerning the projects funded with immigrant contributions from the United States. First and foremost in these migrants' minds was San Diego de Alcalá, the local patron saint, whose church and sanctuary had fallen into bad disrepair. These words find echo in hundreds of similar migrant-sending communities.

However, the Mexican experience simultaneously departs from the canonical "three R" functions of religion for immigrant adaptation. Mexican American sociologist David López minces no words when he concludes:

> The Church may or may not be successful in its attempt to secure the loyalty of its flock but, in contrast to the religious institutions that serve many other contemporary immigrant communities, it is contributing little to the integration and upward mobility of Mexican and other Latino immigrants in the United States.[59]

López contrasts the Italian immigrant experience of a century ago with that of Mexicans today. Despite the initial resistance of the Irish-dominated hierarchy, Italians were eventually incorporated into the Catholic "mobility machine" of elementary and secondary schools, universities, and hospitals. Mexicans, on the other hand, were largely excluded from these vital services and were never sufficiently integrated into the priesthood or the church's hierarchy. Their Catholicism continued to adhere to the traditional practices of processions, masses, and prayers but without connecting effectively to the church-linked secular initiatives that provided a "lift" in the past for successful integration into American society. If anything, services went the other way as the traditional religiosity of migrants in the United States subsidized the upkeep of Catholic parishes and schools in Mexico.[60]

Reasons for this outcome are a complex story that has to do with the historical development of the Catholic Church in the United States and its eventual encounter with masses of migrants coming from an alternative Spanish tradition. The "mobility machine" that the Irish clergy constructed for its own group and, later on, for Southern and Eastern Europeans was centered in the East. It was there, and subsequently in the Midwest around Chicago, that the system of national parishes and parochial schools evolved to counter the hostility and disadvantages of a Protestant-dominated society. While the stern brand of Catholicism preached by the Irish clergy had difficulty absorbing the folk beliefs and superstitions of Italian and Polish peasants, it eventually prevailed by taking advantage of several key factors. These included the diminishing hold of home countries an ocean away, the Irish clergy's own dominance in places of settlement, and the great "bargain" that it offered to the newcomers and their offspring in terms of education and health care.

As the American Catholic Church moved to the Southwest accompanying the displacement of its European ethnic flock, it came face-to-face with a very different religious tradition. The Catholic Church was hegemonic in Mexico and hence did not have to provide a range of services in order to compete effectively with other religions. Mexican Catholicism adhered closely to the Spanish traditions of hierarchy, strict separation between the clergy and the flock, and spirituality. At the popular level, Catholic teachings had mixed thoroughly with pre-Columbian traditions, giving rise to a folk religiosity of quasi-magic rituals, patron saints from whom favors were demanded and repaid, and frequent processions and festivities. In its quest for respectability in a Protestant world, the American Catholic Church could not very well accept the religious traditions of these migrants. In its efforts to absorb them, as it had done previously with Italian and Polish peasants, it ran into two serious barriers.

First, the short distance from places of origin made Mexican migration highly reversible. Without an ocean to cross, Mexicans could go back and forth and, in the process, replenish their traditions. They did not need an accented Irish priest to succor them when they could always return to their reliable hometown *cura*. Second, Mexican migration to the Southwest and later the Midwest never ended. World War I, followed by restrictive laws, the Great Depression, and World War II, effectively terminated mass Italian and Polish migration and thus reduced contact with places of origin, facilitating the acculturation of migrants into American practices. No such things happened to the Mexican flow, which continued uninterrupted for over a century. Not only could migrants return home with relative ease, but those who stayed were constantly receiving fresh arrivals who nourished and reinforced their religious traditions.

The end result of this clash was a stalemate between the two ways of being Catholic in the Southwest. The diocesan system of the region was inherited from Spanish colonial days, and the Mexican church never relinquished its hold on members of its flock "returning" to where they had belonged prior to the American takeover. In turn, the Irish American church regarded its southern counterpart with barely disguised condescension and treated its followers accordingly: "There is a 'Secretariat of Hispanic Affairs' with the U.S. Conference of Catholic Bishops, but its Pastoral Plan, dating from 1987, reads like a missionary plan to evangelize some exotic tribe, not the largest and oldest group in the American Catholic Church."[61]

The stalemate, added to the continuous back-and-forth movement across the border, had a key result: the mass underserving of Mexican

American youths by the Catholic educational system. No precise figures are available about the proportion of Irish American or Italian American children who attended Catholic schools, but, if we are to believe most historical accounts, this path became, at some point, the norm for the second and third generations. No such thing happened to Mexican Americans. The system of parochial schools that so well served Catholic European ethnics was only feebly extended to the Southwest, and then mainly to serve the needs of the Irish and other European-origin Catholics who had migrated to the region. Mexicans were a thing apart. According to López, even today, of the 2.6 million students who attend Catholic elementary and secondary schools nationwide, about two-thirds do so in the East and Great Lake regions. Only about 18 percent are found in the entire "West," which includes all of California and the Southwest.[62]

Thus, the largest immigrant group in the nation and the one that comprises, along with its descendants, the fastest-growing component of the American Catholic population, has not had access, yesterday or today, to the mobility escalator that served other Catholic groups in the past. In the contemporary period, the Mexican experience can be fruitfully contrasted with that of Cuban exiles arriving in South Florida in the 1960s and 1970s. Cuban parishes were promptly established in the archdiocese of Miami, and Cuban priests and bishops quickly found their way into the U.S. Catholic hierarchy. Schools run by such orders as the Jesuits and the Christian and Marist brothers were transplanted from Cuba into Miami to educate the offspring of the middle-class exiled population. As shown in the previous chapter and by a number of prior studies, this education yielded impressive results in terms of both fostering academic excellence and high educational achievement, as well as preserving bilingual fluency among Cuban Americans.[63]

Nationwide, about one-quarter of children of Catholic families attend parochial schools today, while children of Latin American (mostly Mexican) families do so at the rate of only 4 percent. This figure is probably a high estimate for the number of Mexican American children who attend Catholic schools in Los Angeles, the largest archdiocese in the nation, whose membership is now over 50 percent of Mexican origin.[64] Although the archbishop of that city, Cardinal Mahoney, has spoken repeatedly in defense of immigrant rights, and although the American Catholic hierarchy has given unmistakable signs that it is aware of the decisive role of Latin American immigrants and their children for the future of the church, that awareness has translated so far in mostly symbolic gestures. The resources and services made available by other Christian churches to foster the educational success of immigrant groups, such as Koreans, have been largely absent from mostly Mexican Catholic parishes. This absence may have something to do with the loss of close to a quarter of the Mexican American population who have left the church to embrace various Protestant denominations.

The American Catholic Church was built by immigrants and consolidated its institutional strength by promoting their integration and social mobility, as well as those of subsequent migrant waves. Its future may well depend on overcoming the historic stalemate with the Mexican Catholic tradition and becoming, once again, an effective agent in the incorporation of these migrants into American society. The growth and consolidation of churches in the American religious marketplace have been closely linked, yesterday and today, to their success in confronting the needs of the newest members of society and opening doors for their advancement in a foreign land. While masses in Spanish, like the colorful Sunday rituals at St. Rose of Lima, do attract large numbers of Latin immigrants, by themselves they will not suffice to retain their loyalty to the Catholic tradition.

ISLAM

Most contemporary writings on religion and immigration in the United States stop short at the question of what to do with the new player in the religious marketplace—the growing presence of immigrants from Muslim countries. In part, this is because of the still relatively small population of such migrants, who, according to the best estimates, represent well under 1 percent of the adult American population; the dearth of empirical studies about it; and the sheer difficulty of tackling the problem.[65] For unlike the canonical story of linear religious affiliation leading to respectability and eventual upward mobility, the rise of mosques and the presence of a population that prays in them has been viewed with increasing alarm, if not downright hostility, by the surrounding native population.[66]

One could say that the same was true of Catholic churches and Jewish synagogues when they were originally established in America, but there is a vital difference. Neither of these religions had a history of frontal confrontation with Christianity, where the fate of both depended on the outcome of the clash. At least since the ninth century, when the conquest of the Mediterranean by the "saracens" encapsulated the Christian world and emptied its cities, the ups and downs of this confrontation have marked the course of much of world history.[67] No wonder, then that the most conservative of Western intellectuals describe recent events as "the Clash of Civilizations" and that the most radicalized Muslims denounce the Western presence in the Middle East as "the new Crusades."[68]

Public hostility toward Islam reached a climax after the coordinated attacks against the World Trade Center and the Pentagon in September 2001, and it has been kept at a high pitch ever since, in the wake of new bomb attacks in various parts of the Western world and the ever-present threat of new ones in the United States. In the public mind, *Arab*, *Muslim*, and *terrorist* have become almost synonymous, without allowance made for the fact that most of the Arab American population is not Muslim (only about a quarter are; the rest are mostly Christian), not all Muslims are Arabs (the six largest Muslim countries in the world are not Arab; in the United States, more Muslims originate in Asia than in Arab countries), and only a small minority of either group are fundamentalists. Not only society but the federal government has fed this confusion by targeting the Muslim population as a whole for special surveillance and by restricting entries from Arab countries as part of the effort to defend the nation against terrorist attacks.[69]

In the long run, the question is what policies can best address the integration of the Muslim immigrant population into American society. The question is complicated by the global character of this religion and its effects. Like other world religions, Islam is a *multinational* institution that, in turn, supports the *transnational* grassroots activities of its members (see chapter 5). Unfortunately, the latter include not only those of the vast majority of peaceful believers but the conspiracies of a fundamentalist minority bent on radical opposition to the United States and the West. Islamic fundamentalism is driven by a profound sense of *ressentiment* for the historic defeats suffered by this civilization and its relegation to a marginal place in the evolution of the modern world.[70] This trend culminated in the creation of the Israeli state by the summary expedient of subordinating or expelling the Palestinian population from the area. It is safe to say that this historic development triggered the rise of Islamic fundamentalism in the Middle East and that the global threat that it now poses will not disappear until some form of peaceful accommodation is found between the Jewish state and its Arab neighbors.

For the settled Muslim immigrants and Muslim American population, the central issue is whether affiliation with this religion will yield the same benefits as for Catholics and Jews in the past or whether it will be a source of continuous social conflict and marginalization. The typology of linear and reactive religion and its effects, discussed previously, becomes problematic in the case of Islam. Linear adherence to the religion of migrant parents may perpetuate estrangement from the American social mainstream, especially if parents subscribe to the more oppositional and resentful strand of this religious ideology. All evidence indicates that this pattern is exceptional, but, when this is not the case, second-generation Muslims may still react to discrimination and lack of mobility opportunities by embracing the preachings of radicalized imams. This trend has been painfully exemplified by the repeated presence of second-generation British Muslims in terrorist attacks in Great Britain.[71]

Complicating matters is that Islam, unlike Christian denominations, is nonhierarchical and noncongregational. Mosques are autonomous from each other, with each following its own particular brand of the faith. Furthermore, there is no requirement for believers to "go to mosque" (as in "going to church") at set times. As Lin and Jamal note, "Islam is a non-institutional faith. . . . [T]he rituals of faith are lived through daily life and personal practice. . . . For many Muslims, then, mosques do not play the organizing role that churches played for American Catholics . . . nor do other organizations substitute."[72]

This decentralized, fragmented character of the religion makes it difficult for government authorities and mainstream social institutions to engage with Islam and explore alternative means of accommodation and integration. While many imams and individual believers may readily respond to these overtures, there is no hierarchical authority that would enjoin others to follow suit.

On the more positive side, Islam is a monotheistic religion with considerable affinities to Judaism and Christianity. As Alba and Raboteau note, all of these religions partake of the Abrahamic Tree, and they share prophetic traditions, with Jesus Christ being recognized as a prophet by Islam.[73] In addition, there is the encouraging precedent of other non-Christian religions, such as Judaism, that after a difficult start did manage to gain legitimacy and integrate its followers successfully into American society. Read notes that, in the American context, many mosques have reorganized to be more like churches, providing a range of services for Muslims. Thus, the Islamic Society of Greater Houston, founded in 1968, developed the first U.S. zonal service system for Arabs and non-Arabs alike in this metropolitan area.[74] In addition, and unlike the impoverished Muslim population in Great Britain and continental Europe, American Muslims have done rather well economically. According to Baghy, the average mosque-goer in the United States is a married man with children who has a bachelor's degree or higher and earns about $74,000 a year.[75] If this estimate is accurate, it would place the Muslim American population at a considerable distance from the unemployed and angry young men so common in Europe today. As for Arab Americans, the vast majority are secular, and they are also doing rather well. As of 2000, their median household income was $52,000, and they had a very high intermarriage rate with other Americans, which indicates an accelerated process of integration.

As Lin and Jamal point out, organizations such as the Council on Arab American-Islamic Relations (CAIR), the American-Arab Anti-Discrimination Committee (ADC), the Arab American Institute (AAI), and the American Muslim Council (AMC) are already hard at work fostering this process of integration and seeking social legitimacy for their constituents as a whole. As other religious minorities before them, the need to find strength in numbers is ironing out internal differences among different Muslim sects and seems to be homogenizing them into a distinct American identity. Politicians of Arab origin such as James Zogby, leader of the Arab American Institute, and Spencer Abraham, former U.S. senator from Michigan, have sought to speak for the minority as a whole, defending its common interests. The latter include, as a key concern, the creation of a Palestinian state.[76]

All of this does not negate the existence of fundamentalist Islamic pockets or the possibility that some alienated second-generation youths react to their frustrations by joining terrorist cells. It takes the actions of only a few fanatics to tar an entire group, setting back the efforts of the majority. Insofar as its declared target is the Western way of life, Islamic fundamentalism cannot but retard acceptance of the religion and its institutions as legitimate and on a par with other religious traditions. It also makes it impossible to predict with absolute certainty the future of Islam in America.[77]

But American Muslim and Arab organizations are doing their best to show their strong opposition to terror and, by the same token, establish their legitimate place in the American religious mosaic. In July 2005, the Fiqh (religious judisprudence) Council of North America (FCNA) issued a *fatwa*, or religious ruling, against terrorism and extremism that was promptly endorsed by more than 120 U.S. Muslim groups. At a press conference to present the text of the fatwa, the executive director of the CAIR, Nihad Awad, introduced it as follows:

> United, we can confront the terrorists and frustrate their goal of sparking an apocalyptic war between faiths and civilizations. . . . The presence here today of American Muslim leaders indicates the willingness of our community to strengthen national security and to work with policymakers to gain victory over this international menace to humanity.[78]

Along with the necessary governmental surveillance to protect the country against terrorist acts, the best long-term course of action toward Islam is that which has thus far yielded so many instances of success in the incorporation of immigrants to America: respect for the rights of all in the marketplace of ideas and a hands-off policy from all *peaceful* religious institutions and groups, allowing them to seek and find the best course of adaptation for their members. There is no need to tell a young Muslim girl not to wear a head scarf. In due time, that scarf will come off or be replaced by one worn with a distinctive American flair. Despite the very serious challenge posed by the fundamentalists, there is no inevitable "clash of civilizations." Muslim Americans and Arab Americans are becoming part of society, as so many other immigrants before them, in the process contributing to its continuing strength and diversity.

CONCLUSION

In her recent study of the role of the Catholic Church in the adaptation process of Haitian immigrants, Margarita Mooney calls attention to the decisive role of sociopolitical contexts in determining the scope and effects of church action. Haitians come from the poorest country in the Western Hemisphere; being themselves mostly poor and black, they are heavily discriminated against by the native population in the receiving societies and are thus in need of considerable assistance. Since Haitians are overwhelmingly Catholic, the Church is in a privileged position to extend a helping hand and, in the process, reinforce their faith. Yet the extent to which it is able to do so varies greatly with the culture and politics of the host nation.[79]

In France, for example, the national state does not support distinct ethnic cultures and seeks to incorporate immigrants into a uniform French population as soon as possible. The state does attempt to provide education and social services on a universalistic basis, but it opposes channeling this assistance through religious charities because of its secular character and a strict separation between church and state. Accordingly, Catholic support for the Haitian immigrant community is much more restricted in scope, taking the form of celebration of a few masses in Creole at a designated parish, far away from which most migrants live. Since national culture and state policy do not support the emergence of distinct ethnic groups, the church is heavily constrained in promoting the adaptation of Haitians through the creation of vibrant ethnic institutions:

> Even though Haitians in Paris have similar cultural resources as Haitians in other cities, . . . these cultural resources have not encountered much institutional support, either from the Catholic Church or the French state. Although family and social networks support Haitian migrants' initial settlement, several contextual factors make it difficult for Haitians to adapt by relying on ethnic networks and institutions. . . . [F]ew material and financial resources have moved from the Catholic Church in France to Haitians.[80]

On the other hand, the laissez-faire attitude toward most ethnic groups adopted so far by the American state, plus its willingness to channel social assistance through religious charities, creates a much more favorable environment for effective Church action. As we have seen in the case of Mexicans, such action may be compromised by other historical factors, but none of these existed in the case of Haitians. Relative to Mexicans, Haitians are a small minority; the American territories to which they migrate were never part of their nation, and they are cut off from the latter by the sea. In Miami, Catholic leaders saw the need and the opportunity. Strongly supported by the archbishop, they set out to create a wide array of Haitian ethnic institutions that went well beyond those of a purely religious character. A Creole-speaking priest, Father Thomas Wenski, was at the heart of this enterprise, persuading the Archdiocese to cede a ten-acre former Catholic school and convent in the midst of Little Haiti for the creation of what, in fact, became a national parish, Notre Dame d'Haiti:

> For Haitians in Miami who encounter stringent race and language boundaries, Notre Dame has become a cultural resource to recreate their ethnic identity. . . . [E]ven those who regularly attend another church refer to Notre Dame as "the heart of the Haitian community" and "our home in Miami." Beyond its religious functions, Notre Dame has become the

symbol of Haitian culture and a welcoming place for Miami's most discriminated group.[81]

Like Mary, Queen of Vietnam, in New Orleans, Notre Dame d'Haiti in Miami fully meets Hirschman's description of the functions that religion can play in the adaptation of new and poor immigrant groups. Not incidentally, it also shows that, despite the apparent demise of Catholic schools as a mobility vehicle for these minorities, the Catholic Church can still play a vital role in promoting their successful incorporation. The very high levels of Catholic affiliation and church attendance detected among CILS second-generation Haitian youths in Miami (see figure 25) can be traced to the creation of this national parish and its effective promotion of linear religious devotion and cultural pride.

Mooney's comparative study returns us to the theme sounded from the start of this chapter: religion seldom triggers international migrant movements in the contemporary world, and it does not determine their modes of political and social incorporation. However, it interacts with the latter, giving rise to novel and important consequences. The best known of these, described at length in the classic literature on European immigrants and exemplified today by Catholic Vietnamese and Haitians, Laotian Buddhists, and Indian Hindus, is the strengthening of the coethnic community, drawing on the transplantation of the religious traditions brought from home. But other variants exist, as exemplified by Mexican and Central American Protestant converts, by reactive evangelicalism following episodes of downward assimilation, and by the unique and still unfolding experience of Islam.

Because religion has proven to be one of the most resilient elements of immigrants' culture across generations, the beliefs and organized activities carried out by different foreign groups in this realm can be expected to be a trademark of their long-term incorporation into American society and, simultaneously, a key force guiding the character of this process. With a majority Catholic immigrant population, the church faces a challenge that has been met successfully in many instances, including contemporary ones, but that still eludes it in others. Asian Protestants, Buddhists, and Hindus will continue to add diversity to the American religious marketplace, fostering community and socioeconomic mobility in seemingly unproblematic ways. Misguided efforts to stamp out Islam will come to naught, given the resilience of all religions, and will probably encourage the same reactions that they seek to suppress. The only long-term solution, despite present challenges, will be the addition of the small Muslim minority and its institutions to the religious mosaic and their achievement of a measure of legitimacy, based on mutual respect for the interplay of ideas. As evidence cited in this chapter indicates, the process is well on its way and can be expected to continue unless compromised by homegrown believers of the "clash of civilizations" fanatics on the other side.

10
Conclusion
Immigration and Public Policy

There can be no fifty-fifty Americanism in this country.
There is room here only for 100 percent Americanism,
only for those who are American and nothing else.

Theodore Roosevelt (1918)[1]

There can be no question about the average American's
Americanism or his desire to preserve his precious heritage
at all costs. Nevertheless, some insidious foreign ideas have
already wormed into his civilization. . . . Thus dawn finds
the unsuspecting patriot garbed in pajamas, a garment of
East Indian origin. . . . He will begin his day with coffee,
an Abyssinian plant first discovered by the Arabs. . . .
Meanwhile, he reads the news of the day, imprinted in
characters invented by ancient Semites by a process
invented in Germany upon a material invented in China.

As he scans the latest editorial pointing out the dire
results to our institutions of accepting foreign ideas, he
will not fail to thank a Hebrew God in an Indo-European
language that he is one hundred percent (decimal system
invented by the Greeks) American (from Americo Vespucci,
Italian geographer).

Ralph Linton (1937)[2]

P eriods of high immigration are invariably marked by a tide of nativist resistance that characterizes the waves of newcomers as a threat to the integrity of national culture and a source of decay of the qualities of the native population. Such pronouncements are issued both by crusading journalists and politicians and by academics who cloak it in the garb of scientific knowledge. The statement by President Roosevelt is exemplary of the genre. The spoof by anthropologist Ralph Linton is illustrative of how absurd those statements can be.

By the beginning of a new millennium, one would have surmised that the pseudopatriotism and antiforeign hysterics that filled so many tracts in the nineteenth and early twentieth centuries would have gone out of fashion. An expanding process of globalization and the patent reality of living in an interdependent world should have put to rest even the most ardent isolationists. Not so. The correlation between periods of high immigration and heightened xenophobia continues to hold, this time endorsed by well-known intellectuals, as in this excerpt from Samuel Huntington's 2004 book *Who Are We?*:

> Apart from Indian tribes which could be killed off or pushed westward, no society was there, and the seventeenth and eighteenth century settlers came in order to create societies that embodied and would reinforce the culture and values that they brought with them [and] . . . the old European immigrants were absorbed into the core. But the new immigration from Asia and Latin America—above all that from Mexico—is challenging that identity, that core.[3]

Echoing Benjamin Franklin two hundred fifty years earlier and Madison Grant one hundred years ago, the new defenders of national purity express the fear that the foreign element will end up "Germanizing," "Italianizing," and, these days, "Mexicanizing" America. Indeed, good chunks of the country were, in their time, Germanized and Italianized, and these deeds are celebrated today as integral parts of American history and key elements of what makes this a great nation. The fears expressed by Huntington and his followers are likely to go the same way.

There is no small irony in the ambivalent portrayals of immigration to America, past and present: reviled when it is actually taking place and celebrated after a period of time, when the first generation has passed from the scene and its descendants are able to revindicate its achievements. A good part of American literature is made up of nostalgic retrospectives of the trials and accomplishments of immigrants by their children and grandchildren—Jews and Italians earlier on in the century; Chinese, Cubans, and Mexicans today.[4] Based on the record, it is just as predictable that nativist voices will continue to rise against the looming immigration "disaster" as that a revisionist history about current arrivals from Asia and Latin America will be written sometime later.

This cycle of negative and positive stereotyping only skims the surface of the phenomenon of immigration. This is because these successive images emerge in the realm of public opinion where serious understanding of the dynamics underlying the process, including the role of public opinion itself, is lacking. The well-entrenched public view is that immigration is a consequence of the initiative of migrants themselves, who come in search of a better life; they are allowed to settle because of the laxness of government controls and a tolerant attitude among the natives. If such an attitude disappears and the government tightens controls, immigration will certainly go away.[5]

Such views are erroneous. Immigrant flows are initiated not solely by the desires and dreams of people in other lands but by the designs and interests of well-organized groups in the receiving country, primarily employers. Up to a point, public opposition to immigration can play into the hands of these groups by maintaining the newcomers in a vulnerable and dependent position. Similarly, governments are not omnipotent in their regulation of immigration. In particular, governmental attempts at reversing well-established immigrant flows do not generally have the intended effect because of the resistance of social networks linking places of origin and destination.[6]

This final chapter aims at teasing out these complex dynamics in order to lay the basis for a sound understanding of the origins of contemporary immigration and of viable policies toward it. To do so, we must examine the interplay precisely between the two sets of forces just mentioned: first, the surface level of policy debates and shifting currents of public opinion and, second, the underlying realities rooted in the political economy of the nation. The interplay has effects on three key constituencies that must be examined systematically: the immigrants themselves, the ethnic groups created by them, and society at large. We consider each of these forces in turn.

A GAME OF MIRRORS: THE PUBLIC PERCEPTION OF IMMIGRATION

INTRANSIGENT NATIVISM

The general perception of the foreign population among the native-born is not grounded in an understanding of the historical linkages between the United States and the countries of origin or by knowledge of the economic and social forces driving the phenomenon. The public view is guided instead by surface impressions. When foreign accents and faces are few, they are ignored. However, when they grow in number and concentrate in visible spaces, they trigger increasing apprehension. Natives are put on the defensive, fearing that their way of life and their control of the levers of political and economic power will be lost to the newcomers. The sentiment is expressed in familiar outcries such as "the end of white America," the "mongrelization of the race," "the rise of 'Mexifornia,'" and "the Hispanic challenge."[7]

Policies stemming from these fears have followed two basic paths: to exclude the newcomers or to Americanize them as fast as possible. These two positions define the two great ideologies toward immigration among the general public. They have in common that, since neither is rooted in an understanding of the real forces at play, their transformation into policy leads to consequences that are commonly the opposite of those intended. The first ideology, which may be labeled *intransigent nativism*, seeks to stop all or most immigration, expel unauthorized immigrants, and put remaining immigrants on notice that they occupy an inferior position, ineligible for the privileges of citizens.

Supporters of this ideology look mainly to the present. They do not know or care to know about the factors underlying immigration or the history of the process. They give expression instead to the immediate concerns, discomfort, and anxieties of the native population. Accordingly, they lash out not against the true sources of migration but against the migrants themselves. Success for this position consists in rendering the foreign element invisible once again. Intransigent nativism finds expression at a number of levels, ranging from elite intellectuals to xenophobic politicians, such as current Congressmen Tom Tancredo (R-Colorado) and James Sensenbrenner (R-Wisconsin), all the way to radio and television commentators, such as Lou Dobbs.

This ideology has registered some notable successes, such as the passage in 1994 of Proposition 187, the "Save Our State" (SOS) proposal in California (although it was struck down as unconstitutional by the federal courts three years later); the passage in 2004 of Proposition 200 in Arizona, a kindred measure dubbed "Protect Arizona Now" (PAN); the Illegal Immigration Reform and Immigrant Responsibility Act of 1996 (IIRAIRA); and the anti-immigrant provisions attached to the 1996 federal welfare reform bill (the Personal Responsibility and Work Opportunity Reconciliation Act, or PRWORA), which barred immigrants from access to a number of public assistance programs.[8] Most recently, it has found expression in the Border Protection, Antiterrorism, and Illegal Immigration Control Act (HR 4437), a bill sponsored by Representatives James Sensenbrenner and Peter King (R–New York). The *New York Times* called this bill "shameful—a reflection of the power of xenophobic politicians who want to fence in America."[9] Despite extraordinarily expensive and impractical provisions, the bill passed the House of Representatives on December 16, 2005.

As seen in chapter 5, the political campaigns of intransigent nativists frequently produce unintended consequences, such as the mobilization of a powerful and previously dormant ethnic vote and the loss of public office by advocates of such policies. The strong legal system of the United States and its democratic polity guarantees to threatened minorities the right to seek judicial redress and to mobilize in defense of their interests. Reactive mobilizations of this type voted out of office the proponents of Proposition 187 in California, as they did the advocates on the antibilingual referendum in Miami in the 1980s, in both cases to be replaced by representatives of the groups under attack. Ironically, one of the principal functions of nativist campaigns has been to strengthen the legal and collective clout of immigrant minorities, giving them greater voice in the political process, through mobilization in defense of their rights. This process of reactive formation found its clearest expression in the mass mobilizations of immigrants against HR 4437 in the spring of 2006. Millions took to the streets in scores of cities across the nation to protest legislation that would criminalize unauthorized migrants, as well as those who would assist them, and fence the country.[10] Hundreds of thousands of modest laborers who were previously content to labor quietly in the shadows marched loudly in public to revindicate their human and civil rights, often accompanied by their U.S.-born children who, while too young to vote, participated with their parents in historic marches bound to shape their political outlook. In reaction to this latest outburst of intransigent nativism, the "Hispanic" population, which as we saw in chapter 5 is still a disparate and uncertain ethnic minority, came together as never before. If the past is any guide, the Sensenbrenner-King bill may become the catalyst that consolidates the Hispanic electorate as one of the most potent political forces in the future of the nation. Candidates elected by this vote will have the nativists to thank.

FORCED ASSIMILATIONISM

Ronald Unz, the Jewish American millionaire who spearheaded Proposition 227, a California initiative dubbed "English for the Children" in 1998, explained his support for the measure as follows:

> As a strong believer in American assimilationism, I had a long interest in bilingual education. Inspired in part by the example of my own mother who was born in Los Angeles into a Yiddish-speaking immigrant home but had quickly and easily learned English as a young child, I had never understood why children were being kept for years in native-language classes, or why such programs had continued to exist or even expand after decades of obvious failure.[11]

The second mainstream ideology is less irrational than the first. Forced assimilationism does look at the past, but less to find the origins of contemporary immigration than to search for ways in which prior flows were separated from their cultures and integrated into the American mainstream. The nation's success in absorbing so many foreigners in the past is attributed to its relentless hostility to the perpetuation of cultural enclaves and the immersion of foreign children into an English-only environment that made Americans out of them in the course of a single generation. As we saw in chapter 7, the United States is indeed a veritable "cemetery of languages" in which the most varied linguistic backgrounds—from German to Italian; from Chinese to Spanish—have disappeared into a monolingual world in the course of two or three generations.

Assimilationists want the future to mirror this past as a proven way to restore unity and peace. Just as Yiddish-speaking mothers had to leave their culture and language behind, so should Mexican immigrants and Vietnamese refugees today. Though less traumatic than the effects of nativist exclusionary campaigns, forced assimilationism also has important consequences, and they are mostly negative. Policies derived from this ideology delegitimize the culture and language of immigrant parents, thus encouraging the phenomenon described in chapter 8 as dissonant acculturation. By instilling in second-generation youths the sense that their linguistic heritage is inferior and should be abandoned, this ideology drives a wedge across generations, weakening parental authority and efforts of parents to protect children against the dangers confronting them in schools and in the streets. As we saw in chapters 6 and 8, full acculturation to American society is not an unmixed blessing. Bereft of parental guidance, monolinguals and limited bilinguals can succumb to the dangers described at length in these chapters, leading to outcomes inimical to successful integration.

A second consideration is the changing position of the United States in the world economy. By remaining fixed in the past, assimilationists neglect the changes that have been happening all around them in the last half century. One hundred years ago, immigrants came from remote lands to fill the labor needs of a rapidly industrializing country. Few other ties linked sending nations to the United States. At present, sending countries are increasingly part of a single global web, in which the United States plays a central role. In this new world order, in which economic, political, and cultural ties bind nations ever closer, it is not clear that the rapid extinction of foreign languages in America is in the interest of individual citizens or of the country as a whole.[12] The urgent search for fluent Arabic speakers to staff government intelligence services in the wake of the 2001 terrorist attacks stand as the latest example of a commonly repeated saga in which the global communications needs of the United States are sorely served by a uniformly monolingual population.[13]

In an increasingly interdependent global system, the existence of pools of American citizens able to communicate fluently in English plus another language represents not a threat to cultural integration but a resource and a source of enlightenment for individuals and communities alike. Despite being grounded in reflection on the country's past, forced assimilationist policies, such as that championed by Ronald Unz, are ultimately reactionary. They reflect a wish to restore America to its state at the beginning of the last century, not as it must be in the new millennium, after it emerged as the core of the global system. In the process, old-line assimilationism undermines the very forces of parental authority and ambition that can make the difference in guiding the second generation around major obstacles to successful adaptation and productive citizenship.

A THIRD WAY: SELECTIVE ACCULTURATION

These two ideologies—exclude them or assimilate them—are those that resonate with the general population. The fact that they cannot be fully translated into policy has to do with factors that we have discussed in previous chapters and will summarize again here. However, even if advocates of these ideologies remain perennially dissatisfied with their inability to fully put their ideas into practice, this does not mean that they lack real consequences. While nativism may have positive latent functions for the groups so attacked, it also leads to mutual hostility and reactive ethnic identities that unnecessarily divide communities and weaken collective solidarity. While forced assimilationism does not accomplish all its objectives, it leads to generational dissonance, adaptation failures, and isolationism.

The alternative path discussed in chapter 8 under the label selective acculturation offers a much more viable way for successful integration of immigrant minorities and for the utilization of their capabilities. Selective acculturation must not be confused with multiculturalism, a pattern leading to the perpetuation of isolated ethnic enclaves. Instead, it means the acquisition of English fluency and American cultural ways *along with* preservation of certain key elements of the immigrant culture, of which language is paramount.

This pattern contributes to maintaining channels of communication open across generations, keeping youths linked to their community and the material and moral resources that it can provide, and providing a cognitive reference point to guide their successful integration. It is difficult to know where one is going without knowing where one came from. Almost a century ago, a prominent intellectual, Randolph Bourne, railed against the consequences of assimilationism run rampant as follows:

> It means that, letting slip from whatever native culture they had substituted for it only the most rudimentary American—the American culture of the cheap newspaper, the movies, the popular song, the ubiquitous automobile . . . the same moulders [sic] of public opinion whose ideal is to melt the different races into Anglo-Saxon gold hail this poor product as the satisfying result of their alchemy. . . . Those who came to find liberty achieve only license. They become the flotsam and jetsam of American life, the downward undertow of our civilization with its leering cheapness and falseness of taste and spiritual outlook. . . . This is the cultural wreckage of our time.[14]

Absent public support for selective acculturation, it has been left to immigrant groups themselves to implement this pattern. As we saw in chapter 9, religion has played a vital role in this regard. If immigration is a "theologizing experience," it is in part because the traumas and difficulties of coping with an unfamiliar environment have been compounded by the exclusionism or forced assimilationism advocated by leaders of native public opinion. Immigrants have taken refuge in their churches, synagogues, or temples, finding there the resources to maintain their self-respect and often the networks to launch viable careers.

Out of their synagogues, second- and third-generation Russian Jews emerged to claim their rightful place among the professional and business classes of New York and Chicago; from their churches and parish schools, descendants of Irish, Italian, and Polish immigrants came out as well to become full Americans and full-time participants in the country's political and economic systems; in their Buddhist beliefs and temples, Japanese immigrants found the resources to cope with a nativist hostility that culminated in their forced concentration. The *nisei* and *sansei* generations overcame that trauma to become full and highly successful members of society in Los Angeles, San Francisco, Seattle, and elsewhere.[15]

As we also saw in chapter 9, religion is not the only alternative to implement selective acculturation, as more secular immigrant groups find other means to create and maintain protective and productive community ties. However, in the American context, religion retains a preeminent position as the instrument of choice for many immigrants to cope with misguided assimilationist pressures. "Clash of civilizations" tracts to the contrary, the most likely bet is that mosques will play a similar role for the small immigrant Muslim population, protecting it and facilitating the successful integration of its offspring into the American mainstream.

THE REALITY UNDERNEATH: THE POLITICAL ECONOMY OF IMMIGRATION

CHANGING LABOR MARKETS

Underneath the debates about immigrant exclusion and assimilation, there is the hard reality of economic interests and economic survival. There are also real concerns about the growth prospects of the nation, dependent as always on its labor supply. In the postindustrial era, the American labor market has become increasingly bifurcated into an upper tier of professional and technical occupations, requiring advanced educational credentials, and a lower tier of manual occupations, requiring physical strength and few skills in sectors such as agriculture, construction, the food industry, and personal services.[16]

The reality of this new "hourglass" labor market has been documented by a number of studies, as has another important fact: the scarcity of domestic workers to fill the bottom half. A recent report from the Congressional Budget Office summarizes the contemporary situation:

> The U.S. economy faces a demographic challenge to its future growth. Among the native-born population fertility rates are falling, workers are growing older and better educated, and labor force participation rates are flattening. However, the economy continues to create a large number of less-skilled jobs that favor younger and less educated workers. These divergent trends present an obstacle to continued labor force growth which is an essential component of economic growth in general. Barring unlikely increases in productivity growth rates, expansion of the work force is crucial to sustained growth in the labor-intensive industries that generate the greatest number of less-skilled jobs.[17]

Labor immigration provides the answer to these needs. By reason of size, geographic proximity, and history, Mexico has become the real labor reservoir for the American economy. This huge economy, surpassing at present $12 trillion, more than the fifteen largest European economies combined, generates a huge labor demand at both ends of the labor market. Mexico is not really a poor but a middle-income nation, yet its proximity to the United States and the approximate seven-to-one wage gap for manual labor create a continuing incentive for peasants and workers to seek to join their conationals already working in the United States. As will be shown next, it is not individualistic calculations of gain, however, but forces buried deep in the history of the relationships between both nations that actually drive the process. These forces have been intensified, not lessened, by the signing of the North American Free Trade Agreement in 1994 and the ensuing integration of the economies of the two nations. As Douglas S. Massey put it in recent testimony before Congress:

> Two decades of intensive research reveal a fundamental contradiction at the heart of U.S. relations with Mexico. On the one hand, we have joined with that country to create an integrated North American market characterized by the relatively free cross-border movement of capital, goods, services, and information. Since 1986, total trade with Mexico has increased by a factor of eight. On the other hand, we have also sought to block the cross-border movement of workers. The United States criminalized undocumented hiring in 1986 and over the next 15 years tripled the size of the Border Patrol. . . . This contradictory stance has led to continuous immigration under terms that are harmful to the United States, disadvantageous to

Mexico, injurious to American workers, and inhumane to the migrants themselves.[18]

These realities of the American political economy are conveniently swept aside by self-appointed defenders of Americanism and doomsayers about the consequences of immigration. From an academic perch of privilege or a lucrative post at a Washington think tank, it is easy to pontificate about largely illusory threats while ignoring the facts on the ground. For the same Mexican migrant worker so harshly described in nativist tracts is the one for whom thousands of American enterprises—from mom-and-pop businesses to large corporations—are clamoring. As the same Congressional Budget Office report cited previously notes:

> The Bureau of Labor Statistics expects that between 2002 and 2012 the number of U.S. jobs will increase by 21 million and that there will be a total of 56 million job openings after accounting for worker turnover. Many of these jobs will favor workers with age and educational profiles for which the native-born labor force is not well-matched. In 2004, immigrants made up more than a quarter of all 25–34 year old workers with a high school diploma or less and more than half of 25–34 year old workers without a high school diploma. . . . [T]he foreign-born share of workers was highest in less-skilled occupations such as farming, janitorial services, construction, and food preparation where between 20 and 38 percent of workers were immigrants.[19]

HISTORICAL ROOTS OF TODAY'S LABOR SYSTEM

The present system of international migration registers a close association between the history of prior contact, colonization, and influence of powerful nations over weaker "peripheral" ones and the onset of migratory movements out of the latter. The history of contact between the United States and the Latin American countries that supply the major contingents giving rise to today's "Hispanic" communities in the United States provides a suitable example. All of these countries—Mexico, Puerto Rico, and Cuba—were, each in its time, targets of a North American expansionist pattern that remolded their internal economic and social structures to the point that would-be migrants were already presocialized in American ways even before starting their journey.[20]

The concepts of influence in the core-periphery system and of *structural imbalancing* provide an alternative perspective on the origins of migration that moves us away from exclusively individualistic motivations. According to these concepts, the initiation of sizable and durable population flows out of certain peripheral lands is commonly based on a history of prior contact with countries of destination and the consequent growth of a structure of relationships that induces out-migration in various forms. Mexico, the principal source of U.S.-bound labor immigration, is also a prime example of this pattern of external intervention and internal imbalancing.

The Mexican framework of economic and political life constructed under Spanish colonial rule was severely undermined by contact with its more powerful North American neighbor. The Mexican-American War in the 1840s reduced Mexico's territory by almost half and, as Mexican American scholars are wont to repeat, converted a good part of the country's inhabitants into foreigners in their own land. North American expansion did not stop at military conquest, however, because rapid economic growth in what had been the northern provinces of Mexico reclaimed labor from the portion of the country left south of the Rio Grande.[21]

In a pattern typical of the beginning of sizable labor flows elsewhere, Southwest growers and railroad companies started an active recruitment program where paid agents were sent into the interior of Mexico to offer free rail travel and cash advances as incentives for local peasants to come north. The result was to trigger a sizable rural labor outflow that, over time, became self-sustaining. At the time of the early recruitment waves in the nineteenth and early twentieth centuries, the southwestern U.S. border was scarcely enforced. As original settlers of the land, Mexicans came with the territory, and the arrival of new contract laborers and the movement back and forth across the Rio Grande met with little official resistance. Mexicans were thus an integral part of the Southwest population before they became immigrants and long before they became "illegal" immigrants.[22]

Hence, contrary to today's portrayal of Mexican immigration as a movement initiated by individual calculations of gain, the process had its historical origins in U.S. geopolitical and economic expansion that first remolded the neighboring nation and then proceeded to organize dependable labor flows out of it. Such movements across the border of the reduced Mexican republic were a well-established routine in the Southwest before they became redefined as "illegal" immigration.

The process of structural imbalancing of peripheral areas of the world economy, followed by sustained immigration, has taken successive forms during the history of capitalism. Deliberate labor recruitment, such as the employer initiatives that gave rise to U.S.-bound

Mexican migration, represents an intermediate form of a historical process that has ranged from coerced labor extraction (slavery) beginning in the sixteenth century to the present self-initiated labor flows. Migrant labor recruitment saw its height during the second half of the nineteenth century and the first two decades of the twentieth, when it was responsible for the onset of Italian and Polish as well as Mexican labor migrations to the United States and for the growth of sizable Italian and Asian populations in other countries of the Western Hemisphere such as Brazil and Argentina.[23]

Self-initiated migrations are a product of the twentieth century, in which external imbalancing of peripheral societies does not take the form of organized coercion or deliberate recruitment. Instead, mass diffusion of new consumption expectations and the electronic transmission of information about life standards in the developed world suffice to encourage emigration. The gap between modern consumption standards and the economic realities of backward countries, plus increasing information about work opportunities abroad, provides enough incentives to generate an almost limitless supply of would-be migrants.

A key social effect of capitalist globalization is the rise of massive relative deprivation among citizens of nations fully exposed to modern goods and modern consumption but unable to afford them. The dominance of Western culture and consumption patterns thus places the advanced countries in the role of regulators of an inexhaustible flow of foreign workers who are willing to pay their transportation costs and assume all the risks of the journey. This new mode of structural imbalancing via electronic diffusion is less costly than earlier modes and affects a broader cross section of the world's population. Not surprisingly, sources of U.S.-bound migration, as well as migration toward other developed countries, have begun to diversify in terms of both national origins and class composition of newcomers during the last half century.[24]

Despite pervasive absolute and relative deprivation in the global South, the specific historical ties between receiving and sending countries—primarily the impact on the latter of colonial and neocolonial episodes—continue to be clearly reflected in the major immigrant flows today. In the 1980s and 1990s, the top five countries sending legal immigrants to the United States were Mexico, the Philippines, China/Taiwan, South Korea, and Vietnam; the top two sending unauthorized immigrants were Mexico and El Salvador; and the four principal sources of refugees were Vietnam, Laos, Cambodia, and Cuba.[25] A moment's reflection will bring to light the close historical ties between each of these countries and the United States, forged during successive North American interventions—from the Mexican and Spanish-American wars in the nineteenth century to successive anti-Communist struggles after World War II.

By 2005, the global influence of Western standards of living and consumer values had reached farther afield, turning the largest countries in the world—the People's Republic of China and India—into the second- and third-largest sources of U.S.-bound migration. Still, Mexico remained, by far, the largest contributor to U.S.-bound immigration; in line with its historical role, Mexican migration continues to fill demand in the bottom half of the American labor market. Migration from more distant nations, such as China and India, is more diversified, and, as seen in chapters 2 and 4, much of it consists of professionals and technicians meeting labor demand at the high end of the market.[26]

Overall, the close interface among past colonial experiences, the structural imbalancing of peripheral societies—including contemporary global patterns of relative deprivation—and the onset of large-scale migration flows show the limitations of individualistic cost-benefit models and the durable power of historical relations in the world economy. Similarly poor countries have given rise to very different migration patterns in the past, and sizable outflows have originated in more —rather than less—developed regions. The reason is that the beginnings of these movements are rooted in a history of prior economic, political, and cultural contact between sending and receiving nations. Through these processes, social structures are molded that render subsequent calculations of "costs" and "benefits" of migration intelligible to individuals.

SOCIAL NETWORKS: THE MICROSTRUCTURE OF MIGRATION

Not only differences between countries but differences *within* countries in propensities to migration require explanation. Again, an individualistic model proves insufficient at this level since families and communities of similar socioeconomic condition can produce very different migration histories. The main alternative explanation at this level is based on the concept of social networks. Once an external event, such as the presence of labor recruiters or the diffusion of information about economic opportunities abroad, triggers the departure of a few pioneering migrants, the migration process can become self-sustaining through the construction of increasingly dense social ties across space.

The return of successful migrants and the information that they bring facilitate the journey of others. To the extent that migration abroad fulfills the goals of individuals and families, the process continues to the point that it becomes normative. When this happens, going abroad ceases to be an exceptional affair and becomes the "proper thing to do," first for adult males and then for entire families. At some moment, networks across international borders acquire sufficient strength to induce migration for motives other than those that initiated the flow. People then move to join families, care for children and relatives, or avail themselves of social and educational opportunities created by the ethnic community abroad.[27]

The notion that international migration is simultaneously a network-creating and a network-dependent process was established by a string of sociological studies dating back to classics in the field such as Thomas and Znaniecki's *The Polish Peasant in Europe and America*. More recent research has been able to determine the importance of such ties quantitatively. In a study of 822 adult male Mexican immigrants arriving in two Texas ports of entry, Portes and Bach found that over 90 percent of their respondents had obtained legal residence through family and employer connections in the United States. Seventy percent of these men had already traveled to and lived in the North, mostly as unauthorized immigrants. They had been able to secure their legal papers mostly through family and work connections established during this period. The remainder also came, with few exceptions, by making use of the family reunification provisions of the U.S. immigration law.[28]

During the 1980s and 1990s, sociologist Douglas Massey and his associates applied the concept of social networks to account for the differential migration propensities of a large number of Mexican communities. He classified these communities into four stages—from the stage where migration is exceptional to that where it reaches a mass (normative) level. The differentiating factor, in his view, is the timing of the first pioneering trips abroad. Once some adult males had been recruited as laborers or went abroad on their own, their returns led to the gradual consolidation of cross-national networks along the lines described previously.[29]

As Charles Tilly once put it, "Like a honeysuckle vine, the network moved, changed shape, and sent down new roots without entirely severing the old ones. In that sense, networks migrated."[30] Massey, Durand, and Malone have recently summarized more than two decades of research on the origins of migration from Mexico and other Latin American sending countries as follows:

> The first migrants who leave for a new destination have no social ties to draw upon, and for them migration is costly. . . . After the first migrants have left, however, the potential costs of migration are substantially lowered for the friends and relatives left behind. Because of the nature of kinship and friendship structures, each new migrant expands the set of people with social ties to the destination area. . . . [T]he causation of migration becomes cumulative because each act of migration alters the social context within which subsequent migration decisions are made, thus increasing the likelihood of additional movement.[31]

Networks are established not only between migrants and their kin and friends in countries of origin but between migrants and their employers. Every time a building contractor or a restaurant owner approaches one of his migrant workers for a referral, every time the manager of a corporate chain contacts one of his cleaning subcontractors for additional services, they mobilize networks running deep into Mexico, Central America, and other sending nations. As businesses in a number of sectors come to rely more and more on immigrant workers, it is only logical that openings be filled through their networks, as they provide the most efficient and most reliable access to needed labor pools. The fit between the needs of thousands of U.S. firms for manual labor and the motivations of Mexican and Central American workers to take these jobs as a means to fulfill their life aspirations is so strong as to defy any attempt at repression. Build fences at strategic places in the Mexico-U.S. border, and the flow just moves elsewhere, braving the desert and death, if necessary; deport an unauthorized worker with a stable job, and he will find a way to return to it.[32]

THE CLASH OF IDEOLOGY AND REALITY

SELF-DEFEATING POLICIES; SELF-FULFILLING PROPHECIES

The peculiar gap between the history and political economy of immigration and public views of the process is portrayed in figure 31. Restrictionist cries for enforcement of the border have moved Republican and Democratic administrations alike to pour more and more money into

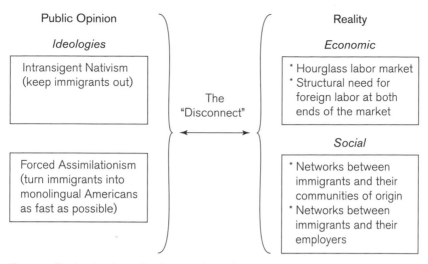

Figure 31. The immigration policy disconnect

the Border Patrol in a vain effort to stem the labor flow. By 2005, the Border Patrol had become the largest arms-bearing branch of the federal government, except for the military itself, with a budget of $1.4 billion.[33]

The country has precious little to show for this massive expenditure in personnel and equipment. The flow from south of the border gives no signs of abating. Every year during the last decade, the Border Patrol has reported about one million apprehensions and deportations—1.7 million in 2000, 1.3 million in 2001, and 955,000 in 2002.[34] All existing studies of unauthorized immigration report that deported migrants at the border try again.

A "repeated trials" model by Espenshade calculates the possibility of apprehension in any one try at 0.32. By the third try, almost every migrant manages to cross successfully. Although Border Patrol apprehension statistics are caseload figures rather than actual individuals, the high probability of successful entry after repeated trials make them a conservative estimate of the size of the unauthorized flow. Espenshade estimates that while the correlation between apprehensions at the border and the actual size of unauthorized immigration was 0.90, the flow exceeded apprehensions by a factor of 2.2.[35] Massey calculates that, despite the massive increase in the size of the Border Patrol, the probability of apprehension in any one entry has declined from its traditional average of about 0.32 to the present rate of 0.10.[36]

The main reason for this decline is that, as border enforcement has increased, unauthorized border crossing has become more professionalized and has shifted to more remote points. What previously was a self-initiated move by migrants crossing in the vicinity of urban areas has now become a highly organized operation by bands of full-time smugglers. This cat-and-mouse game at the border has not had the effects expected by the restrictionists, but it has had two other grave consequences. The first is an increasing number of migrant deaths, as crossing points become more distant and more difficult. Close to five hundred would-be migrants currently lose their lives in the Arizona desert and elsewhere every year.[37] The second consequence is the increasing cost of the journey as migrants are forced to rely more and more on professional smugglers.

As Massey and Durand, Cornelius, Espenshade, and others have noted, the effect of the increasing difficulty and cost of border crossing has not been to deter the flow but to render it more permanent. The previously cyclical pattern in which migrant workers came to harvest crops and engage in other seasonal work prior to returning home have been stopped in its tracks by the militarization of the border.[38] The rise of a permanent unauthorized population has had, in turn, two other important corollaries. The first is the gradual movement east of this population in search of employment opportunities and greater security. This mass demographic movement has transformed what previously was a purely regional phenomenon into a national one. Only fifteen years ago, unauthorized immigrants were found overwhelmingly in the southwestern states, plus Illinois; today they are present in all fifty states and in increasing numbers along the eastern seaboard.[39] Heightened repression, so dear to the self-appointed guardians of national integrity, has had exactly the opposite consequence of that intended.

The second and more serious consequence is what happens to the offspring of this migrant population. As we saw in chapter 8, the decision of unauthorized workers who cannot return to bring their families along is the key factor underlying the emergence of a second generation growing up in conditions of severe disadvantage. Children of these migrants do assimilate to American values and aspirations, but with very limited material and social resources to achieve them. As the evidence presented in chapter 8 showed, these youths are at risk of downward assimilation, compounding the spectacle of poverty and despair in the nation's inner cities. The policies of restrictionism and repressive border enforcement thus can produce what they fear—the continuation of major ethnic and racial inequalities and the reproduction of a marginalized population at the bottom of society.[40]

This self-fulfilling prophecy is the gravest consequence of current policy. Despite its patent failure, others claim for still more repression. In November 2005, Duncan Hunter, a Republican congressman from El Cajon, California, introduced "The TRUE Enforcement and Border Security Act," which proposed building a fence along the entire U.S.-Mexico border, a span of nearly two thousand miles. Congressman Stephen King (R-Iowa) had also come up with his own version of the same project in 2005. In both cases, the idea was to build a sort of Chinese Wall designed to keep out citizens of a friendly nation with which the United States has signed a treaty for free trade and increasingly close economic integration. These proposals actually came to fruition in December 2005 with passage by the House of Representatives of the Sensenbrenner-King bill (HR 4437) which, among other provisions, would criminalize unauthorized workers and build a fence along the southern border at a cost of billions of dollars. Although it gained the approval of a significant segment of the Republican Party, the bill not only triggered massive protest rallies in U.S. cities but provided ample ammunition to opponents and critics of the United States throughout Latin America.[41]

IRCA: A CAUTIONARY TALE

Earlier attempts at restriction have been less irrational than building a nearly two-thousand-mile fence, but they have failed as well because of the same two common flaws: first, their unilateralism or the belief that mass labor migration can be controlled by measures adopted solely by the receiving nation; second, their individualism or the assumption that the move can be controlled by manipulating the "cost-benefit" calculations of would-be migrants. The first assumption neglects the demographic and political characteristics of sending countries; the second neglects the structure of economic interests and the web of social and economic networks sustaining the flow and driving it forward.

Public outcry about the growth of the foreign population and the pressure of influential newspapers and public policy centers led the U.S. Congress in the mid-1980s to consider a series of alternatives to bring unauthorized immigration under control. Following recommendations of the congressionally appointed Select Commission on Immigration and Refugee Policy and after lengthy debate, a series of sweeping measures were passed by both houses. The resulting Immigration Reform and Control Act (IRCA) became law in 1986 and led immediately to a number of important changes in the character and legal treatment of labor immigrants.

As an instrument for immigration control, the new law offered two provisions: first, an amnesty program to regularize the situation of unauthorized immigrants with some period of residence in the United States; second, the civil and criminal sanctioning of employers who engaged in a pattern of repeated hiring of these immigrants. The reasoning behind the law was that the first provision would bring the unauthorized population aboveground and discourage it from further lawbreaking, while the second would change the structure of incentives by making it more difficult for new migrants to find employment.

Supporters of IRCA believed that rewards and sanctions focused on individuals would suffice to bring the flow under control. They did not consider the strength of forces arranged against this goal, which included the organized political resources of growers, ranchers, and a multitude of other employers. Effective lobbying by representatives of these groups succeeded in turning the public outcry against immigration in their favor. This feat was accomplished via two legal devices. First, a provision was inserted into the amnesty program allowing for the legalization of "special agricultural workers," or SAWs, defined as unauthorized immigrants who had worked in U.S. agriculture for at least ninety days between May 1985 and May 1986. Riddled with fraud, this program nonetheless succeeded in legalizing 1.2 million unauthorized immigrants, who, added to the 1.7 million amnestied through the general legalization program, guaranteed to rural and urban employers an ample labor supply for the immediate future.[42]

Second, the same groups succeeded in preventing the employer sanctions provision of the law from including a check for fraudulent documentation. The law provides penalties for engaging in a pattern of "knowingly hiring" illegal aliens. Operationally, this translates into a requirement that employers check prospective employees' documents certifying legal residence. However, firms are not required to verify the authenticity of these documents. Predictably, a counterfeit industry promptly emerged to satisfy the demand for such documentation. Immigrant workers who did not have it were often told by employers to get their papers (false or otherwise) and then return.[43] More generally, employer sanctions did not stop the inflow of unauthorized workers but merely rechanneled it into new forms. As predicted by immigration experts at the time, some of it went further underground, becoming better concealed from the authorities, and the rest found employment in the multitude of firms willing to comply with the letter but not the spirit of the law.[44]

For their part, newly amnestied immigrants did not stay put. The program was conceived with individuals in mind without taking into account that most such immigrants are part of extended networks. Soon, the consequences of this oversight became clear. The question promptly arose as to what to do with the immediate relatives of legalized aliens who themselves were ineligible for amnesty. The Immigration and Naturalization Service was forced to deal with this dilemma through ad hoc administrative measures until the 1990 Immigration Act created a special category of visas for family members of amnestied immigrants.[45]

Legal immigration increased not only through the amnestied immigrants and their immediate relatives but also through the capacity of this newly legalized population to reestablish ties with places of origin. Legalized immigrants could now travel back and forth without fear of deportation. After three years, they became eligible for permanent residence and hence were able to legally petition for other relatives. After another period of three to five years, they could become U.S. citizens—and many did, thus acquiring the right to bring immediate relatives outside quota limits. Through the operation of these networks as well as the effective resistance of labor immigrants and their North American sponsors, a law designed to address the public outcry about immigration ended up *increasing* the flow of both legal and unauthorized immigrants. The experience provides a compelling lesson in the less-than-straightforward effects of ideologies of immigration and the consequences of ignoring the social structures that actually underlie the labor flow.

BETTER POLICIES FOR A BETTER FUTURE

ON BALANCE

In retrospect, the signal failure of IRCA may not have been such a bad thing, as it allowed the continuation of a labor supply needed by multiple sectors of the economy and the fulfillment of many migrants' aspirations. However, the process continued to take place outside the law, leading to the immigration policy "disconnect" and the negative consequences described previously. Any serious attempt to repair immigration policy must be preceded by an assessment of the overall consequences of the process for the receiving nation. Some economists have attempted to answer this question by estimating the tax contributions made by the foreign-born and their cost in terms of schooling and other public services. Depending on assumptions made by the analyst, immigration ends up costing billions of dollars to the public coffers or contributing billions of dollars to them.[46]

This approach is too narrow, however, because it does not take into account the contribution that immigrant labor makes to the nation's economy, nor does it consider the payoff that the schooling of children of immigrants can have in terms of their own successful careers. History shows that every time the United States has initiated a massive public works program, it has turned to immigrants to provide the requisite labor power. It happened with the construction of the Erie Canal, one of the major engineering feats of the nineteenth century, dug up by Irish immigrants paid as little as thirty-eight cents an hour. It happened again after Congress authorized the construction of the transcontinental railroad, with the Central Pacific Railroad turning to China in search for the needed labor. By 1867, over 90 percent of the 13,500 Central Pacific workers were Chinese immigrants paid $26 to $35 for a six-day, twelve-hour work week. And it happened again later on when Italians and other immigrants, paid as little as $1.50 a day, dug up New York City to build its subway system. By the turn of the twentieth century, over 90 percent of public works employees in New York and Chicago were Italians.[47]

The historical examples could be multiplied, but the important point is that the same role and the same contributions continue to be made at present. As the nation prepared to rebuild New Orleans, Biloxi, and other coastal cities devastated by Hurricane Katrina in 2005, it turned again to immigrant labor. Mexicans and Central Americans, many of them without documents, formed the backbone of the reconstruction effort. The federal government has admitted as much by suspending sanctions against construction firms in the region hiring unauthorized workers. The flow of Hispanic workers to take part in the New Orleans reconstruction enterprise is large enough to be able to alter the demographic composition of the city. This possibility finds a precedent in what happened in South Florida after Hurricane Andrew in 1992. The bulk of the reconstruction of Homestead and other devastated communities in the tip of the Florida peninsula was carried out by Mexican and Central American workers who settled there, becoming a major component of the population.[48] In the same vein, a reconstructed New Orleans may yet add to its French Quarter a vibrant Mexican one.

While immigrants today make their most important contributions to the nation by filling demand at the bottom of the American labor market, those who fill a similar need at the top cannot be ignored. As seen in chapters 2 and 4, a sizable flow of foreign-born engineers, software experts, managers, doctors, and nurses make their way to the United States every year, either permanently, under the occupational preferences of the regular immigration system, or temporarily, under the H-1B program. In 2003, the United States admitted close to twenty-five thousand professionals, executives, and "aliens of extraordinary ability" for permanent residence under the first, second, and third occupational preferences of the law. The total number of professionals and executives admitted as regular immigrants under all categories in that year exceeded sixty thousand. Temporary H-1B "specialty occupation" arrivals reached 360,498 in 2003, or more than thrice the number just ten years earlier.[49]

As seen in chapter 8, the majority of today's children of immigrants are moving ahead educationally and occupationally. While children of unauthorized and other low-skilled immigrant laborers are at risk of downward assimilation and hence in need of remedial policies (a topic to be addressed in a following section), the bulk of this population is expected to follow the course of other second generations in the past: it will advance occupationally, economically, and socially and, like earlier children of immigrants, will integrate into the country's social fabric and make a significant contribution to its economy. Descendants of earlier Irish, Italian, Jewish, and Polish immigrants form today the backbone of economic and political life in the regions where they settled. All the empirical evidence points to the children and grandchildren of contemporary immigrants following the same course.

Today, as in the past, the United States is a nation of immigrants. Although there is no denying that the process of integration has met difficulties and challenges, it is equally undeniable that the country would not occupy the paramount position that it has in the world today without the millions of foreigners who have immigrated here and their offspring. Restrictionists and forced assimilationists there have always been, but their dire warnings have always turned to naught. More useful than continuing to pay attention to this lamentable choir is to reflect on what policies can resolve the most important problems confronted by immigration today so as to maximize its contribution to the country and to the communities that it creates.

POLICIES FOR THE FIRST GENERATION

Inocencio Suárez from Xochihuehuetlán, state of Guerrero, came to New Jersey in 1990 after crossing the border without papers in San Isidro, California. He simply sat in the passenger's seat of the car and pretended to sleep. The guards waved them in. In New Brunswick, he counted on the support of a kinsman who had acquired papers and prospered after opening a Mexican restaurant. Inocencio first went to work for an Italian landscaping contractor. He performed so well that, after two years, his boss agreed to support him in launching his own business. Inocencio bought a used truck in cash at a police auction, and Suárez Landscaping Company was born. From Xochihuehuetlán, he imported five reliable young men who crossed the border through various expedients. He also brought his wife and a young son.

In the early-morning hours after a snowstorm, well-to-do clients in New Brunswick and its environs could see the reliable crew of Suárez Landscaping alighting from the old truck to clear their driveways. Inocencio divided his time between working for his Italian boss and protector and working in his own new business. The enterprise prospered. He bought a second truck, and, after the birth of his first U.S.-born child, he took the plunge and made the down payment for a new home.

The company was registered in the name of his legal kinsman, who also arranged a loan for the purchase of the house. As things moved ahead for him and his family, Inocencio's attention focused on legalizing his situation. For this, he hired a lawyer and asked for help from his supportive boss. Things took a very bad turn, however, when, after an attempt to get a legal driver's license (he had been driving with a forged one), the clerk at the Motor Vehicles Administration identified him as a possible illegal and reported him to Immigration Control and Enforcement (ICE). ICE agents promptly rounded him up and, after determining that he was without papers, summarily deported him.

Left behind were the wife, two children (one a U.S. citizen by birth), a home, two trucks, and a car. Fifteen years of ceaseless toil were about to go up in smoke. Fortunately, the Mexican community in and around New Brunswick rallied. They dug up information about the most reliable *coyotes* and the best places to cross the border. They advanced the money for the journey while Inocencio's workers continued to run the business for him. At the moment of this writing, he is still trying to come back to his family, but everyone is confident that he will make it. So sure are they that his kinsmen have already sent a car to an agreed border point so that he can drive himself back to New Jersey.

No doubt Inocencio will make it or perish in the effort, but there is little reason for this tragedy. After fifteen years of working hard, serving others, paying taxes, and raising a model family, Inocencio, one would think, should have justifiable cause for leniency. Present laws do not allow government agents that freedom. Thus, as the cat-and-mouse game continues at the border, people die, families are separated, and children are orphaned.[50]

There is a better way, and it consists in bringing the unauthorized labor flow above ground and regulating it. As seen previously, for reasons of history and geographic location, Mexico has become the de facto low-skilled labor reservoir for the American economy. In collaboration with the government of Mexico, this flow can be managed and controlled. A bipartisan proposal to that effect was advanced in 2005 by Senators Edward Kennedy (D-Massachusetts) and John McCain (R-Arizona), but it became bogged down in the Senate—competing, among others, with Congressmen Sensenbrenner and King's bill that would criminalize unauthorized migrants and those who wish to help them, and Congressman Tancredo's repeated calls to fence in the entire country. For these gentlemen, nothing but an isolationist, claustrophobic America will do. Here is an alternative proposal that takes into account the proactive capacity of the Mexican government and lines it up with the real interests of the United States:

- Set up a temporary labor permit program. Every Mexican with a certifiable work contract in the United States can cross the border legally upon payment of $2,000 (or about two-thirds of the estimated current price to hire a professional smuggler).

- The permit will be valid for three years and renewable for another three. Upon return to Mexico, the migrant gets half of the entry payment as an incentive to go back.

- Migrants who wish to remain in the United States after six years will be able to adjust to permanent residence under a special preference category and after a period of two years of residence in Mexico. Eligibility will be limited to those without a criminal record, with the endorsement of a U.S. employer, and with U.S. bank accounts of $5,000 or more.

- Unauthorized migrants already in the United States can return to Mexico and apply for legal entry permits. They will be given preference over new entrants upon presentation of proof of residence in the United States and a work contract.

- As an incentive for families to remain in the country, the Mexican government will implement special health, education, and job-training programs for the spouses and children of migrants working under the program in the United States. Priority will be given to the families of unauthorized immigrants returning to Mexico.

- The program will be capped at one million entry permits per year (commensurate with a conservative estimate of the annual undocumented flow at present).

- After a trial period of five years, and if it proves successful, the program may be extended to migrant-sending countries in Central America: El Salvador, Guatemala, and Honduras.

The proposed measures will have the following practical advantages:

- By giving migrant laborers legal standing in the country, they will eliminate the worst abuses by unscrupulous employers, some of whom have reduced their workers to a condition of semislavery.

- The measures will allow trade unions to better organize migrant workers, again reducing their vulnerability and, simultaneously, their attractiveness for firms reliant on exploitable labor.

- It will actively involve the government of the sending country, turning unilateral repression into a bilateral labor management program.

- It will create real incentives for migrants to return and to invest in small businesses and other productive activities at home.

- More important, it will motivate them to keep their families and children home, thus avoiding the worst problems associated with a poor and marginalized second generation.

The typology of immigrant workers, professionals, entrepreneurs, and refugees presented in chapter 2 suggests the possibility of other policy changes for other types of migrants. In reality, the rest of the American immigration system is doing generally well, and, with the exception of a refugee policy governed less by geopolitical considerations and more by humanitarian concerns, there is relatively little else to "fix."[51] In particular, the naturalization rules that extend citizenship rights to immigrants in a relatively short period and grant them automatically to children born on U.S. soil have worked so well to facilitate the integration of the foreign-born that there is no point in tinkering with them. In this context, unauthorized immigration is truly the broken part of the system. The preceding measures, based on the best evidence available, should set them right.

POLICIES FOR THE SECOND GENERATION

After accepting a position in a California university, Raúl Amaral, a Brazilian-born psychology professor, set out to enroll his son Luis at a local school. Born in the United States and achievement oriented, little Luis brought excellent grades, along with fluency in two languages—English and his parents' Portuguese. Upon learning about the latter, the school counselor immediately enrolled him in the LEP (Limited English Proficiency) track. To the counselor, the mere fact that a language other than English was spoken in the home sufficed to assign the child to the remedial track, apart from the courses taken by regular students. It took the parents' intervention, all the way to the school's principal and the school board, to overcome the counselor's ignorance and place the child in the mainstream English curriculum.[52]

If this treatment can happen to the son of a university professor, what chance do children of poor immigrants stand? As noted previously, although selective acculturation is the best course for ensuring the proper integration of second-generation youths, it is a policy orientation almost never adopted in U.S. schools. Instead, forced assimilationism, of which Luis's school counselor is a shining example, is the reflex reaction of school personnel to students of foreign origin.

The preceding set of policies toward unauthorized labor migration should significantly reduce the size of the at-risk second generation by encouraging would-be migrants to leave their families behind and even by repatriating those already in the United States. However, a sizable group is likely to remain in the country, and it stands in need of attention. A set of enlightened policies toward children of unauthorized and other low-skilled migrants is likely to make the difference in promoting successful integration and avoiding the worst consequences of downward assimilation. For the most part, these are measures to be taken at the local level, but the U.S. Department of Education and other federal agencies can have a significant influence by providing the right set of incentives:

- Support the creation of *real* dual-language schools that teach the curriculum in English and one major foreign language in areas of immigrant concentration. These schools should be made accessible to both children of immigrants and children of natives as a means of developing sizable groups of fluent bilinguals. As former U.S. secretary of education Richard Riley has noted, this policy would be good for the children and good for the country.[53]

- Create incentives for immigrant parents to come to school and organize to voice their needs and to be informed about the schooling of their children. Lack of information by low-skilled immigrants about American schools and about the means to support their children's education has been shown to be an important factor leading to lower levels of achievement. Schools must be more proactive in giving parents the know-how to help their children.

- Provide incentives for churches and coethnic organizations to create after-school compensatory programs for children of low-skilled immigrants to help them overcome their educational handicap and to teach them about the culture and the language of their parents' country. Such knowledge will help anchor the self-esteem of these children, neutralize the worst effects of discrimination, and foster selective acculturation. Compensatory educational programs are also necessary given the disadvantage that many of these children bring from home.

- Create and make accessible vocational courses for youths who have dropped out of school. Not everyone can go to college, and children of low-skilled immigrants, especially the unauthorized, are particularly unlikely to do so. The vocational route offers an alternative to deviant lifestyles, providing both regular employment and opportunities for entrepreneurship.

The combination of these policies will create a more rational and less traumatic environment for the offspring of manual labor immigrants and give them a better chance for successful integration. Along with the policy measures for the first generation outlined previously, they will endow the United States with the tools to manage needed labor flows, ensure that migrants will be protected against the worst abuses, and turn their offspring into productive members of American society.

CONCLUSION

A recent book by a well-known scholar of immigration, an immigrant himself, begins with a moving retrospective into the travails of his family as it struggled with poverty and the challenges of an unfamiliar culture and language. Like millions of immigrant families before them, the parents managed to cope and move ahead economically, paving the way for the author's college education, a doctorate from a major university, and a subsequent distinguished career. In a remarkable non sequitur, the book proceeds to attack contemporary immigration, arguing that its "quality" has declined and that it poses an increasing burden on the host society.[54]

NIMBY is the acronym coined to refer to those who support construction of public facilities but "not in my backyard." In parallel fashion, we may coin PULLAM to refer to those who, having succeeded in America, wish to "pull the ladder after me." The book just mentioned is a notorious academic version of this syndrome, common among descendants of immigrants. To cite but a few examples, a senator of Japanese origin, S. I. Hayakawa, founded U.S. English out of his preoccupation that foreign languages would undermine the dominance of English; Ronald Unz, a second-generation millionaire, spends his money and time to pressure his most recent counterparts into English monolingualism; and Congressman Tom Tancredo, the fiery xenophobe who advocates fencing not only the Mexican but the Canadian border as well, is the grandson of Italian immigrants.[55]

These examples indicate, in part, how successful the process of assimilation has been in turning descendants of recent immigrants into ardent American patriots. But PULLAM and the policies that follow from it are counterproductive in ensuring the continuation of the process in the future. As repeatedly shown in the preceding chapters, successful integration has never proceeded through pressure, for immigrants are incapable of turning themselves into instant Americans. Instead, with the aid of religious and ethnic institutions, they have carved niches for themselves, preserving their values, language, and customs and using them as platforms to find their way into their new social environment. It is this creative combination of the old and the new that accounts for the success story that immigration to America has been. In its extension to the second generation, what we have called selective acculturation, the nation will find the means to fend off the danger of downward assimilation and ensure the well-being and the productivity of this fast-rising population.[56]

Nativists and forced assimilationists, including PULLAM advocates who extol their own past while attacking those who came after them, will undoubtedly continue to appear. Indeed, they proliferate today, making political hay out of the disconnect between the needs of the economy and the fears of the native population. These fearmongers will be discredited. Immigrants and refugees will continue to give rise to viable communities, infusing new blood in local labor markets, filling positions at different levels of the economy, and adding to the diversity of sounds, sights, and tastes of American cities. The history of this "nation of nations" is, to a large extent, the history of the arrival, struggles, and absorption of its immigrants. Despite the rising chorus of xenophobia and restrictionism as we pen these lines, the evidence points to a future that will mirror this past.

Notes

CHAPTER 1

1. Remedios Díaz-Oliver is a real person, and this short biography was culled from articles published over several years in the Miami press. All other names in these vignettes are pseudonyms, but the stories are true, based on press accounts and field interviews.

CHAPTER 2

1. The amendments passed in 1965 abolished the national-origins quota system and changed the preference system to give greater priority to family reunification over occupational skills. But those changes affected only immigration from the Eastern Hemisphere—notably by the removal of barriers to immigrants from Asian countries who had been previously restricted. Until the 1965 act, Western Hemisphere immigration (notably that from Mexico) had been unrestricted, largely at the behest of American agribusiness. For that matter, the 1965 law had nothing to do with determining the large-scale entry of Cold War refugees—such as the large Cuban exile flows of the early 1960s or the even larger Indochinese refugee flows that would follow much later in the aftermath of the Vietnam War—to say nothing of unauthorized migrants. See Rumbaut, "Ties That Bind."

2. United Nations, Population Division, *International Migration Report 2002*, 2.

3. García, *Desert Immigrants*; Barrera, *Race and Class in the Southwest*.

4. Lamm and Imhoff, *The Immigration Time Bomb*, 226.

5. Ibid.

6. Borjas, "Economic Theory and International Migration"; Borjas, *Friends or Strangers*. For a comprehensive review, see Massey et al., *Worlds in Motion*, chap. 2.

7. Camarota, "Immigrants in the United States—2002."

8. Reichert, "The Migrant Syndrome"; Massey, "Understanding Mexican Migration"; Landolt, "Salvadoran Economic Transnationalism."

9. Alba, "Mexico's International Migration"; Grasmuck and Pessar, *Between Two Islands*; Portes and Ross, "Modernization for Emigration"; Massey and Espinosa, "What's Driving Mexico-U.S. Migration?"

10. Stark, *The Migration of Labour*; Stark, "Migration Decision Making"; Massey et al., *Worlds in Motion*.

11. Piore, *Birds of Passage*.

12. Lebergott, *Manpower in Economic Growth*; Piore, *Birds of Passage*; Barrera, *Race and Class in the Southwest*; Portes and Bach, *Latin Journey*, chap. 3.

13. Landolt, "Salvadoran Economic Transnationalism"; Levitt, "Transnational Migration"; Portes, "From South of the Border"; Alba, "Mexico's International Migration."

14. Stark, *The Migration of Labour*; Massey, "Understanding Mexican Migration"; Portes, "Determinants of the Brain Drain."

15. Ibid.

16. Massey and García España, "The Social Process of International Migration"; Massey and Goldring, "Continuities in Transnational Migration."

17. Tilly, "Transplanted Networks"; Portes and Bach, *Latin Journey*, chap. 2; Roberts, Frank, and Lozano-Asencio, "Transnational Migrant Communities."

18. Sassen, *The Mobility of Labor and Capital*; Portes and Walton, *Labor, Class, and the International System*, chap. 2; Guarnizo and Smith, "The Locations of Transnationalism."

19. Rumbaut, "The Structure of Refuge"; Rumbaut and Ima, *The Adaptation of Southeast Asian Refugee Youth*; Bach and Gordon, "The Economic Adjustment of Southeast Asian Refugees"; Zhou and Bankston, *Growing Up American*.

20. Office of Immigration Statistics, 2002 *Yearbook of Immigration Statistics*, table 39.

21. Portes and Bach, *Latin Journey*; Massey et al., *Return to Aztlán*; Cornelius, "Appearances and Realities."

22. Office of Immigration Statistics, 2002 *Yearbook of Immigration Statistics*, table 8.

23. McCoy, "The Political Economy of Caribbean Workers"; Wood, "Caribbean Cane Cutters."

24. Massey et al., *Beyond Smoke and Mirrors*; Cornelius, "The Structural Embeddedness of Demand."

25. Ibid.; Bean and Stevens, *America's Newcomers*, chap. 3.

26. Ibid.; Smith, "New York in Mixteca."

27. Camarota, "Immigrants in the United States—2002."

28. Office of Immigration Statistics, 2002 *Yearbook of Immigration Statistics*, table 4.

29. Portes, "Determinants of the Brain Drain"; Cariño, "The Philippines and Southeast Asia."

30. Portes and Ross, "Modernization for Emigration"; Glaser and Habers, "The Migration and Return of Professionals"; Stevens, Goodman, and Mick, *The Alien Doctors*.

31. Rumbaut, "Age, Life Stages, and Generational Cohorts"; Espiritu and Wolf, "Paradox of Assimilation."

32. Office of Immigration Statistics, 2002 *Yearbook of Immigration Statistics*, table L, 25.

33. Ibid., table K.

34. Ibid., 135–42.

35. Alarcón, "Recruitment Processes."

36. Zhou, *Chinatown*; Portes and Guarnizo, *Tropical Capitalists*; Pérez, "Cuban Miami."

37. U.S. Bureau of the Census, *1% Public Use Microdata Sample, Summary File*, 3.

38. Light, "Asian Enterprise in America"; Bonacich and Light, "Koreans in Small Business"; Light and Bonacich, *Immigrant Entrepreneurs*; Zhou, *Chinatown*.

39. Portes and Stepick, *City on the Edge*, chap. 6; Pérez, "Cuban Miami"; U.S. Bureau of the Census, *Survey of Minority-Owned Business Enterprises 1997*.

40. Frazier, *The Negro in the United States*. See also Light, *Ethnic Enterprise in America* and "Immigrant and Ethnic Enterprise in North America."

41. Rischin, *The Promised City*; Howe, *World of our Fathers*; Bonacich and Model, *The Economic Basis of Ethnic Solidarity*; Petersen, *Japanese-Americans*, Zhou, *Chinatown*.

42. Min, *Middlemen*; Bonacich et al., "Koreans in Small Business"; Bonacich, "A Theory of Middleman Minorities"; Portes and Manning, "The Immigrant Enclave"; Díaz-Briquets, "Cuban-Owned Businesses."

43. Current Population Survey, March 2002, reported in Camarota, *Immigrants in the United States, 2002*.

44. Portes and Zhou, "Entrepreneurship and Economic Progress in the 1990s."

45. Portes and Rumbaut, *Legacies*, chap. 4; Zhou and Bankston, *Growing Up American*; Zhou, "Straddling Different Worlds."

46. Portes et al., "Transnational Entrepreneurs."

47. Zolberg et al., "International Factors"; Rumbaut, "The Structure of Refuge"; Portes and Bach, *Latin Journey*, chaps. 2 and 3.

48. Office of Immigration Statistics, 2002 *Yearbook of Immigration Statistics*, table 16.

49. Ibid.; Zolberg et al., "International Factors"; Bach and Gordon, "The Economic Adjustment of Southeast Asian Refugees."

50. Menjívar, *Fragmented Ties*; Mahler, *American Dreaming*; Landolt, "Salvadoran Economic Transnationalism"; Guarnizo et al., "Assimilation and Transnationalism."

51. U.S. Immigration and Naturalization Service, *1998 Statistical Yearbook* and *2001 Statistical Yearbook*.

52. Ibid., Portes and Rumbaut, *Legacies*, chap. 4; Rumbaut, "Vietnamese, Laotian, and Cambodian Americans" and "The Structure of Refuge"; Smith-Heffner, *Khmer-Americans*.

53. Borjas, *Heaven's Door* and *Friends or Strangers*; Brimelow, *Alien Nation*. Well-known CNN anchorman Lou Dobbs has been at the forefront of this effort, turning himself into a militant activist in the process.

54. Huntington, *Who Are We?*; Lamm and Imhoff, *The Immigration Time Bomb*.

55. The composition of the contemporary second generation and the principal obstacles to its successful adaptation are examined in chap. 8.

56. As the president of the Catalán government, Jordi Pujol, recently stated, "Europe is on the way of becoming a continent of old people, waited upon hand and foot by immigrants who, on top of this, pay their pensions." *ABC* (Madrid), June 18, 2003, 3.

CHAPTER 3

1. Jerome, *Migration and Business Cycles*, 40.

2. See Handlin, *The Uprooted*; Vecoli, "The Italian Americans"; Alba, *Italian Americans*.

3. Lieberson and Waters, "The Location of Ethnic and Racial Groups," 782.

4. Boswell, "A Split Labor Market Analysis."

5. Kivisto, *Immigrant Socialists*.

6. Wittke, *Refugees of Revolution*; Sowell, *Ethnic America*, chap. 3.

7. U.S. Bureau of the Census, *Ancestry*; http://www.census.gov/prod/2004pubs/c2kbr-35.pdf.

8. Lieberson and Waters, "The Location of Ethnic and Racial Groups," 782, 798–99; U.S. Bureau of the Census, *1990 Ethnic Profiles for States*.

9. Ibid.; Allen and Turner, *We the People*, 84–85.

10. Light, *Ethnic Enterprise in America*, 9.

11. Ibid.; Petersen, *Japanese Americans*.

12. Gardner, Robey, and Smith, "Asian Americans"; Wong and Hirschman, "The New Asian Immigrants"; Nishi, "Japanese Americans."

13. Reichert, "The Migrant Syndrome"; Dinerman, "Patterns of Adaptation"; Massey, "The Settlement Process."

14. On West Indian migration, see Anderson, "Migration and Development"; Dixon, "Emigration and Jamaican Employment"; Levine, *The Caribbean Exodus*. On Dominicans, see Grasmuck and Pessar, *Between Two Islands*; Sassen-Koob, "Formal and Informal Associations." On Haitians, see Stepick and Portes, "Flight into Despair." See also Gardner, Robey, and Smith, "Asian Americans"; Bonacich, "Asian Labor"; Hing, *Making and Remaking Asian America*; Min, *Asian Americans*.

15. Portes and Manning, "The Immigrant Enclave"; Kanjanapan, "The Immigration of Asian Professionals"; Rumbaut, "Origins and Destinies."

16. Korean businesses in Los Angeles are found in the concentrated "Koreatown" enclave and dispersed throughout the metropolitan area. In New York, however, most Korean enterprise appears to be of the "middleman" kind. See Kim, *New Urban Immigrants*; Sassen-Koob, "The New Labor Demand"; Cobas, "Participation in the Ethnic Economy."

17. U.S. Censuses, 1980–2000; Grenier and Pérez, *The Legacy of Exile*; Díaz-Briquets and Pérez, "Cuba"; Rumbaut, "Vietnamese, Laotian, and Cambodian Americans" and "The Structure of Refuge"; Allen and Turner, *We the People*, 163–64, 193.

18. Office of Immigration Statistics, *2002 Yearbook of Immigration Statistics*.

19. Early evidence suggests that Salvadorans—many of whom had to stay in the country illegally after being denied political asylum—settled in Washington, D.C., because they encountered less harassment by Immigration Service personnel in the capital than in West Coast cities. Reasons for the sizable presence of Vietnamese and other legal refugee groups, such as Iranians, Eritreans, and Somalis, in Washington are less clear. On the case of Salvadorans, see Repak, "And They Came."

20. The Cuban enclave is discussed in chap. 4. See also Grenier and Pérez, *The Legacy of Exile*; Díaz-Briquets and Pérez, "Cuba"; Wilson and Martin, "Ethnic Enclaves"; Portes and Stepick, *City on the Edge*.

21. Pessar, "The Role of Households"; Grasmuck and Pessar, *Between Two Islands*.

22. Sassen-Koob, "The New Labor Demand"; Wong and Hirschman, "The New Asian Immigrants." Flushing, New York, and Monterrey Park, California, are examples of new and flourishing "suburban Chinatowns." See Smith and Zhou, *Flushing: Capital and Community*; Fong, *The First Suburban Chinatown*.

23. Hirschman and Wong, "The Extraordinary Educational Attainment"; Sharma, "The Philippines"; Geschwender, "The Portuguese and Haoles."

24. Lack of English proficiency has led many Korean professionals to turn to small business as an avenue of economic advancement. This pattern contrasts significantly with Indians, who arrive proficient in English. The Korean enclave economy is discussed in chap. 4. See also Min, "Ethnic Business" and *Asian Americans*.

25. Rumbaut, "Vietnamese, Laotian, and Cambodian Americans"; Forbes, "Residency Patterns."

26. Cornelius, "Illegal Immigration"; Browning and Rodríguez, "The Migration"; Massey, "The Settlement Process."

27. Grasmuck, "Immigration"; Portes, "Illegal Immigration."

28. Recently arrived refugee groups, such as Ethiopians and Afghans, tend to have high proportions of former professionals—a pattern that reproduces the one found for early refugee nationalities, such as Cubans and Vietnamese. Yet one study found that almost none of these new professionals had achieved comparable employment in the United States during the first three years after arrival. See Cichon, Gozdziak, and Grover, "The Economic and Social Adjustment." See also Stevens, Goodman, and Mick, *The Alien Doctors*; Portes, "Determinants of the Brain Drain"; Rumbaut, "Passages to America"; Kanjanapan, "The Immigration of Asian Professionals."

29. Waldinger, *Still the Promised City?* See also Sassen-Koob, "The New Labor Demand," 149.

30. Sassen-Koob, "The New Labor Demand," 156. See also Waldinger, "Immigration and Industrial."

31. Ibid.; Portes and Sassen-Koob, "Making It Underground."

32. Sassen-Koob, "The New Labor Demand," 158.

33. Waldinger, *Still the Promised City?*

34. Sowell, *Ethnic America*, 277.

35. Lieberson and Waters, "The Location of Ethnic and Racial Groups," 790.

36. Ibid.

37. Ibid. See also Gardner, Robey, and Smith, "Asian Americans"; Bonacich and Modell, *The Economic Basis*.

38. Lieberson and Waters, "The Location of Ethnic and Racial Groups."

39. Baker and North, *The 1975 Refugees*; Forbes, "Residency Patterns"; Rumbaut, "Vietnamese, Laotian, and Cambodian Americans." As seen previously, Vietnamese refugees who have recently adjusted their status to immigrants have significantly reduced their preference for their main area of concentration in Orange County. However, as table 1 shows, they still remain highly concentrated in California. The pattern is congruent with what took place with earlier immigrant groups, as described in the text.

40. Sowell, *Ethnic America*, chap. 11; Alba, *Italian Americans*; Steinberg, *The Ethnic Myth*.

41. Light, *Ethnic Enterprise in America*; Bonacich and Modell, *The Economic Basis*; Portes and Manning, "The Immigrant Enclave"; Cobas, "Participation in the Ethnic Economy."

42. Dahl, *Who Governs?*; Sowell, *Ethnic America*, chap. 2; Glazer and Moynihan, *Beyond the Melting Pot*.

43. Huntington, *Who Are We?*; Lamm and Imhoff, *The Immigration Time Bomb*.

44. Moore and Pachón, *Hispanics in the United States*, chap. 10; Camarillo, *Chicanos in a Changing Society*; Barrera, *Race and Class in the Southwest*.

45. López and Stanton-Salazar, "Mexican-Americans"; Wadestrandt, "Lt. General Ricardo Sánchez named 'Hispanic of the Year'"; Arax et al., "Green Card Marines: Just Looking to Fit In"; Arax et al., "Green Card Marines: Radical Turn for a Rebel."

46. Greeley, *Why Can't They Be Like Us?* 43.

47. Ibid.

CHAPTER 4

1. Piore, *Birds of Passage*, 17.

2. Borjas, "Statement," 219. See also Borjas, *Friends or Strangers*.

3. Portes and Bach, *Latin Journey*; Massey et al., *Beyond Smoke and Mirrors*.

4. Office of Immigration Statistics, *2002 Yearbook of Immigration Statistics*, chaps. 3 and 4.

5. Massey et al., *Return to Aztlán*; Portes and Bach, *Latin Journey*; Cornelius, "The Structural Embeddedness.

6. Office of Immigration Statistics, 2002 *Yearbook of Immigration Statistics*, 94–101.

7. Hirschman and Falcón, "The Educational Attainment."

8. Ibid., 102–4.

9. Portes and Rumbaut, *Legacies*, chap. 9. See also Portes and Hao, "The Schooling of Children of Immigrants."

10. Massey et al., *Beyond Smoke and Mirrors*; Menjívar, *Fragmented Ties*; Portes and Grosfoguel, "Caribbean Diasporas."

11. Alba, "Mexico's International Migration"; Browning and Rodríguez, "The Migration of Mexican 'Indocumentados'"; Grasmuck and Pessar, *Between Two Islands*; Kyle, *Transnational Peasants*.

12. Portes and Rumbaut, *Legacies*, chap. 9; Pérez, "Cuban Miami" and "Growing Up Cuban in Miami."

13. Rumbaut, "Origins and Destinies" and "The Structure of Refuge"; Portes and Stepick, "Unwelcome Immigrants"; Bailey and Waldinger, "Primary, Secondary, and Enclave Labor Markets"; Bean and Stevens, *America's Newcomers*, chap. 6.

14. Light, "Disadvantaged Minorities," 34.

15. Portes and Zhou, "Entrepreneurship and Economic Progress," table 4.2.

16. Ibid.; Raijman and Tienda, "Immigrants' Socio-economic Progress Post-1965."

17. Light, "Immigrant and Ethnic Enterprise."

18. Ibid.; Light and Rosenstein, "Expanding the Interaction Theory of Entrepreneurship"; Portes and Rumbaut, *Legacies*, chap. 4; Portes, "The Social Origins."

19. Bonacich, "A Theory of Middleman Minorities"; Bonacich and Modell, *The Economic Basis*.

20. See Rischin, *The Promised City*; Dinnerstein, "The Last European Jewish Migration"; Rosenblum, *Immigrant Workers*.

21. Piore, *Birds of Passage*.

22. Light, *Ethnic Enterprise in America* and "Disadvantaged Minorities in Self-employment." The same author subsequently moved toward a theory of minority enterprise based on a combination of class and cultural resources that comes very close to our own interpretation. See Light, "Immigrant and Ethnic Enterprise," and Light and Gold, *Ethnic Economies*.

23. Portes and Rumbaut, *Legacies*, chap. 9; Pérez, "Cuban Miami"; Stepick et al., *This Land Is Our Land*.

24. Chiswick, "The Effect of Americanization," 909.

25. Ibid., 914.

26. Reimers, "A Comparative Analysis."

27. Bean and Stevens, *America's Newcomers*, tables 6.2 and 6.3.

28. Barrera, *Race and Class in the Southwest*; Portes and Bach, *Latin Journey*; Massey et al., *Beyond Smoke and Mirrors*; Cornelius, "The Structural Embeddedness."

29. Piore, *Birds of Passage*; Rosenblum, *Immigrant Workers*; Barrera, *Race and Class in the Southwest*.

30. Portes, "The Social Origins"; Rumbaut, "The Structure of Refuge"; Smith-Hefner, *Khmer-Americans*; Zhou and Bankston, *Growing Up American*.

31. Barrera, *Race and Class in the Southwest*; Rosenblum, *Immigrant Workers*; Bonacich, "Advanced Capitalism"; Massey et al., *Return to Aztlán*.

32. Portes and Stepick, *City on the Edge*, chap. 6; Portes, "The Social Origins"; Zhou, *Chinatown*; Bailey and Waldinger, "Primary, Secondary, and Enclave Labor Markets."

33. Waldinger and Lichter, *How the Other Half Works*; Kirchenan and Neckerman, "We Love to Hire Them but . . . ."

34. Portes and Sensenbrenner, "Embeddedness and Immigration"; Light and Rosenstein, "Expanding the Interaction Theory of Entrepreneurship"; Zhou and Bankston, "Entrepreneurship."

35. Alarcón, "Recruitment Process among Foreign-born Engineers and Scientists"; Stevens, Goodman, and Mick, *The Alien Doctors*; Portes, "Determinants of the Brain Drain."

36. Portes and Bach, *Latin Journey*; Portes and Sensenbrenner, "Embeddedness and Immigration"; Menjívar, *Fragmented Ties*; Zhou, "Revisiting Ethnic Entrepreneurship."

37. Portes and Bach, *Latin Journey*, chap. 6; Portes and Zhou, "Self-Employment and the Earnings of Immigrants"; Bailey and Waldinger, "Primary, Secondary, and Enclave Labor Markets."

38. The data come from a face-to-face survey of a random sample of approximately 50 percent of parents of CILS second-generation respondents. Results have been reported previously in Portes and Rumbaut, *Legacies*, chap. 4.

39. Ibid. See also Rumbaut, "The Structure of Refuge," and Portes and Bach, *Latin Journey*.

40. Massey et al., *Return to Aztlán*; Barrera, *Race and Class in the Southwest*; López and Stanton-Salazar, "Mexican-Americans."

41. Stepick, *Pride against Prejudice*; Portes and Stepick, *City on the Edge*, chap. 8.

42. Ibid., chap. 7. Fernández-Kelly and Curran, "Nicaraguans"

43. Portes and Stepick, *City on the Edge*, chap. 6. Pérez, "Growing Up in Cuban Miami."

44. Smith-Hefner, "Khmer-Americans"; Rumbaut, "The Structure of Refuge"; Rumbaut and Ima, *The Adaptation of Southeast Asian Refugee Groups*.

CHAPTER 5

1. Cited in Roth Pierpoint, "The Measure of America," 56.

2. Huntington, "The Hispanic Challenge," 1.

3. Rosenblum, *Immigrant Workers*, 152–53.

4. For examples of this literature, see the regular reports issued during the 1990s by the Federation for American Immigration Reform (FAIR). See also Lamm and Imhoff, *The Immigration Time Bomb*, and Brimelow, *Alien Nation*.

5. López, *Language Maintenance and Shift in the United States*; Lieberson, *Language Diversity and Language Contact*; Lieberson and Hansen, "National

Development, Mother Tongue Diversity"; Hakuta, *Mirror of Language*; Portes and Rumbaut, *Legacies*, chap. 6; Portes and Hao, "The Price of Uniformity."

6. Unz, "California and the End of White America"; Rumbaut, "The New Californians."

7. Glazer, "Ethnic Groups in America." See also Greeley, *Why Can't They Be Like Us?*

8. Hirschman, *Exit, Voice, and Loyalty*.

9. Glazer and Moynihan, *Beyond the Melting Pot*; Rosenblum, *Immigrant Workers*; Vecoli, "The Italian Americans."

10. Glazer, "Ethnic Groups in America"; Higham, *Strangers in the Land*; Handlin, *The Uprooted*; Thomas and Znaniecki, *The Polish Peasant*.

11. Fine, *Labor and Farmer Parties*, cited in Rosenblum, *Immigrant Workers*, 153.

12. Cited in Mink, *Old Labor and New Immigrants*, 61.

13. Cited in Boswell, "A Split Labor Market Analysis," 358.

14. Cited in Daniels, "The Japanese-American Experience, 1890–1940," 257.

15. Fine, *Labor and Farmer Parties*, cited in Rosenblum, *Immigrant Workers*, 152.

16. Gedicks, "Ethnicity, Class Solidarity, and Labor Radicalism."

17. Shannon, *The Socialist Party in America*, cited in Rosenblum, *Immigrant Workers*, 152.

18. Ibid., 154.

19. Greeley, *Why Can't They Be Like Us?* 39.

20. Ascoli, *Group Relations and Groups Antagonisms*, 32.

21. Mink, *Old Labor and New Immigrants*, 63.

22. Ibid., 64.

23. Rosenblum, *Immigrant Workers*, 34.

24. Warner and Srole, *The Social Systems*, 99.

25. Mink, *Old Labor and New Immigrants*, chap. 2; Rosenblum, *Immigrant Workers*, chap. 6; Geschwender, *Racial Stratification in America*.

26. Glazer, "Ethnic Groups in America," 167. Wittke, *Refugees of Revolution*.

27. Glazer, "Ethnic Groups in America," 167; Park, "The Immigrant Press and Its Control," 50.

28. Wittke, *We Who Built America*, 417.

29. Thomas, *Cuba*, 291–309, 339–55.

30. Greeley, *Why Can't They Be Like Us?* 27.

31. Glazer, "Ethnic Groups in America," 167.

32. Barrera, *Race and Class in the Southwest*; Samora, *Los Mojados*; Bustamante, "The Historical Context"; Womack, *Zapata and the Mexican Revolution*.

33. Ibid.; Grebler, Moore, and Guzmán, *The Mexican-American People*; Santitañez, *Ensayo acerca de la Inmigración Mexicana*.

34. The best description of transatlantic labor flows and their relationship to North American development is found in Thomas, *Migration and Economic Growth*.

35. Rosenblum, *Immigrant Workers*, 154.

36. Child, *The German-Americans*, 7.

37. Cited in ibid., 170.

38. Ibid.

39. Levitt, "Transnational Migration," 197.

40. Ibid.; Guarnizo and Smith, "The Location of Transnationalism."

41. Levitt, "Transnationalizing Community Development." See also Landolt, "Salvadoran Economic Transnationalism."

42. Hollifield, "The Emerging Migration State"; Smith, "Diasporic Memberships"; Levitt, *The Transnational Villagers*.

43. Landolt, Autler, and Baires, "From 'Hermano Lejano' to 'Hermano Mayor'"; Menjívar, *Fragmented Ties*.

44. In Portes and Landolt, "Social Capital," 543.

45. Ramos, "Rapporteurs' Comments."

46. Landolt, "Salvadoran Economic Transnationalism."

47. Guarnizo, Portes, and Haller, "Assimilation and Transnationalism," 1235.

48. Ibid.

49. U.S. Bureau of the Census, "The Hispanic Population."

50. Roberts, Frank, and Lozano-Asencio, "Transnational Migrant Communities."

51. Massey, Durand, and Malone, *Beyond Smoke and Mirrors*; Massey et al., *Return to Aztlán*; Barrera, *Race and Class in the Southwest*.

52. Massey et al., *Beyond Smoke and Mirrors*; Guarnizo, "The Rise of Transnational Social Formations"; Massey and Capoferro, "Measuring Undocumented Migration."

53. Ibid.

54. Portes, "The New Latin Nation"; Rumbaut, "The Making of a People."

55. Goldring, "The Mexican State and Transmigrant Organization," 66–67.

56. Guarnizo, "The Rise of Transnational Social Formations"; Roberts et al., "Transnational Migrant Communities."

57. Goldring, "The Mexican State and Transmigrant Organization," 67.

58. Ibid.

59. Ibid.; Guarnizo, "The Rise of Transnational Social Formations."

60. Roberts et al., "Transnational Migrant Communities."

61. Guarnizo, Sánchez, and Roach, "Mistrust, Fragmented Solidarity, and Transnational Migration."

62. Itzigsohn et al., "Mapping Dominican Transnationalism"; Escobar, "Transnational Politics and Dual Citizenship."

63. Portes and Mozo, "The Political Adaptation Process."

64. Escobar, "Transnational Politics," 35, 50.

65. Smith, "Los Ausentes Siempre Presentes"; Fitzgerald, *Negotiating Extraterritorial Citizenship*; Portes and Bach, *Latin Journey*, chap. 3; Wadestrandt, "Lt. General Ricardo Sánchez."

66. Suárez-Orozco, *Crossings*, chap. 1; Guarnizo and Smith, "The Locations of Transnationalism"; Smith, "Mexican Immigrants, the Mexican State."

67. Office of Immigration Statistics, 2002 *Yearbook of Immigration Statistics*, chap. 7.

68. U.S. Immigration and Naturalization Service, *1987 Statistical Yearbook*, 139–41, and *1994 Statistical Yearbook*, 138–39.

69. Office of Immigration Statistics, *2002 Yearbook of Immigration Statistics*, 160–61.

70. Bernard, "Cultural Determinants of Naturalization."

71. García, "Political Integration of Mexican Immigrants"; North, *The Long Grey Welcome*; Portes and Curtis, "Changing Flags."

72. Portes and Rumbaut, *Legacies*, chaps. 6 and 7; Portes, Fernández-Kelly, and Haller, "Segmented Assimilation on the Ground"; Rumbaut, "Origins and Destinies" and "The Crucible Within"; Aleinikoff and Rumbaut, "Terms of Belonging."

73. Gann and Duignan, *The Hispanics in the United States*, 207.

74. Barrera, *Race and Class in the Southwest*; Samora, *Los Mojados*; Grebler, Moore, and Guzmán, *The Mexican-American People*, García and Arce, "Political Orientations and Behavior of Chicanos."

75. Cited in Moore and Pachon, *Hispanics in the United States*, 179.

76. Ibid. 179–84. For examples of scholarly interpretations of the history of Mexican Americans, see Barrera, *Race and Class in the Southwest*; Mirandé, *The Chicano Experience*; Acuña, *Occupied America*.

77. Gann and Duignan, *The Hispanics in the United States*, 217–24.

78. Passel, "The Latino and Asian Vote."

79. Ramakrishnan and Espenshade, "Immigrant Incorporation and Political Participation," 893.

80. Gutiérrez, "Migration, Ethnicity, and the 'Third Space'"; DeSipio and de la Garza, "Forever Seen as New"; Pyle and Romero, "Prop 187 Fuels a New Campus Activism."

81. We are grateful to Louis DeSipio for reminding us of this key point.

82. Prominent among them is Linda Chávez who, for a while, served as chair of U.S. English, a nativist organization, and has been a Republican candidate for prominent offices.

83. Portes and Stepick, *City on the Edge*, chap. 2; Pérez, "Cuban Miami."

84. Ibid., 24, Camayd-Freixas, *Crisis in Miami*, III-27, 39.

85. Portes and Stepick, *City on the Edge*, 25.

86. A Roper Organization survey conducted in 1982 asked respondents whether different ethnic groups had been "good" or "bad" for the United States. Cubans ranked dead last among all groups included, with a disapproval rating of 59 percent, compared with 43 percent for Puerto Ricans, 39 percent for Haitians, and 34 percent for Mexicans. *Roper Reports* (1982) 84-4.

87. Cited in Portes and Stepick, *City on the Edge*, 34.

88. Cited in ibid., 35.

89. Botifoll, "How Miami's New Image Was Created."

90. Portes and Stepick, *City on the Edge*, 37; Pérez, "Cuban Miami"; Stepick and Stepick, "Power and Identity."

91. Stepick and Stepick, "Power and Authority"; Stepick et al., *This Land Is Our Land*, chap. 2.

92. Portes, "La Máquina Política Cubano-Estadounidense"; Schmidt, "Ignored Majority."

93. Rumbaut, "Origins and Destinies"; Zhou and Bankston, *Growing Up American*; Yoon, *On My Own*.

94. Nagel, "The Political Construction of Ethnicity."

95. Passel, "The Asian and Latino Vote"; Fasenfest, Booza, and Metzger, *Living Together*.

96. De la Garza et al., *Latino Voices*; Pierce and Hagstrom, "The Hispanic Community"; Rumbaut, "The Americans"; Gann and Duignan, *The Hispanics in the United States*.

97. Menjívar, *Fragmented Ties*; Booth, "Global Forces and Regime Change"; Jonas and Chase-Dunn, "Guatemalan Development and Democratization."

98. This material is drawn from two previous articles: Guarnizo, Portes, and Haller, "Assimilation and Transnationalism," and Portes, "Theoretical Convergencies and Empirical Evidence."

99. Kim, *New Urban Immigrants*; Yoon, *On My Own*; Zhou, *Chinatown*; Petersen, *Japanese-Americans*.

100. Lamm and Imhoff, *The Immigration Time Bomb*.

CHAPTER 6

1. Thomas and Znaniecki, *The Polish Peasant*; Handlin, *The Uprooted*.

2. Furnham and Bochner, *Culture Shock*, 63. See also Rumbaut, "Life Events."

3. Kuo and Tsai, "Social Networking"; Rumbaut and Rumbaut, "Refugees in the United States"; Richardson, "A Theory and a Method."

4. Antonovsky, *Health, Stress, and Coping*; Rumbaut and Weeks, "Unraveling a Public Health Enigma."

5. Thomas and Znaniecki, *The Polish Peasant*.

6. Handlin, *The Uprooted*, 4, 6, 97. See also Handlin, *Boston's Immigrants*. Handlin's work shaped the later anthropological formulation of the concept of "culture shock." See, for example, Oberg, "Cultural Shock"; Garza-Guerrero, "Culture Shock"; Furnham and Bochner, *Culture Shock*. For contemporary historical scholarship on these themes, see Miller, *Emigrants and Exiles*; Bodnar, *The Transplanted*.

7. Park, "Human Migration," 887–88. On this theme of emancipation, see also Shutz, "The Stranger"; Rumbaut and Rumbaut, "The Family in Exile."

8. Stonequist, *The Marginal Man*, 84, 86, 92.

9. Ibid., 159.

10. Ibid., 203.

11. Faris and Dunham, *Mental Disorders*.

12. Jarvis, *Insanity and Idiocy*, 61–62.

13. Ibid., 59.

14. Ibid., 61.

15. Ibid., 62.

16. Rothman, *The Discovery of the Asylum*; Ranney, "On Insane Foreigners"; Robertson, "Prevalence of Insanity"; Salmon, "The Relation of Immigration."

17. Higham, *Strangers in the Land*; Kraut, *The Huddled Masses*. See also Kraut, *Silent Travelers*.

18. Sanua, "Immigration, Migration, and Mental Illness."

19. Ibid. Virtually identical statements about the fiscal costs of the newest immigration have been made in the 1990s. See, for example, Brimelow, *Alien Nation*. For assessments of recent cost-benefit fiscal analyses, see Fix and Passel, *Immigration and Immigrants*; Clark et al., *Fiscal Impacts of Undocumented Aliens*.

20. Malzberg, "Mental Disease and 'The Melting Pot,'" "Mental Disease in New York State," and *Social and Biological Aspects*; Malzberg and Lee, *Migration and Mental Disease*.

21. Malzberg and Lee, *Migration and Mental Disease*. On this topic, see also the groundbreaking paper by Jarvis, "Influence of Distance."

22. Higham, *Strangers in the Land*, 314.

23. Quoted in Malzberg and Lee, *Migration and Mental Disease*, 7–8.

24. Ibid., 8–9.

25. Portes and Bach, *Latin Journey*, 48.

26. Ødegaard, "Emigration and Insanity," 175–76, and "The Distribution."

27. Murphy, *Flight and Resettlement*; Keller, *Uprooting and Social Change*; Zwingmann and Pfister-Ammende, *Uprooting and After*; Rose, "Some Thoughts"; Haines, *Refugees in the United States*; Williams and Westermeyer, *Refugee Mental Health*.

28. Weissman, Myers, and Ross, *Community Surveys*; Dohrenwend, *Mental Illness*; Schwab and Schwab, *Sociocultural Roots*.

29. Kohn, "Social Class and Schizophrenia."

30. Hollingshead and Redlich, *Social Class and Mental Illness*; Dohrenwend and Dohrenwend, *Social Status and Psychological Disorder* and *Stressful Life Events*; Kohn, "Social Class and Schizophrenia"; Langner and Michael, *Life Stress and Mental Health*. See also Mirowsky and Ross, *Social Causes of Psychological Distress*.

31. Vega and Rumbaut, "Ethnic Minorities and Mental Health"; Mirowsky and Ross, "Social Patterns of Distress"; Seeman, "On the Meaning of Alienation"; Morowsky and Ross, "Paranoia"; Thoits, "Undesirable Life Events" and "Conceptual, Methodological, and Theoretical Problems"; Kessler and Cleary, "Social Class and Psychological Distress."

32. Srole, Langner, and Mitchell, *Mental Health in the Metropolis*.

33. Ibid., 354.

34. Rumbaut, "The Agony of Exile"; Gaertner, "A Comparison of Refugee"; David, "Involuntary International Migration"; Kunz, "The Refugee in Flight" and "Exile and Resettlement"; Stein, "The Experience of Being a Refugee"; Pedraza-Bailey, "Cubans and Mexicans"; Tabori, *The Anatomy of Exile*. For an early critique of this distinction, see Portes and Bach, *Latin Journey*, 72–76.

35. Portes and Bach, *Latin Journey*, 72–76; Haines, *Refugees in the United States*. See also Zolberg, Suhrke, and Aguayo, "International Factors" and *Escape from Violence*.

36. Berry et al., "Comparative Studies of Acculturative Stress." See also Berry, "The Acculturation Process."

37. Meinhardt et al., "Southeast Asian Refugees."

38. Ibid. The social-psychological literature on post-1975 refugees from Indochina is by far the most extensive yet produced on any immigrant group in the United States. See, for example, Mollica and Lavelle, "Southeast Asian Refugees"; Alley, "Life-Threatening Indicators"; Kinzie and Manson, "Five Years' Experience"; Carlin, "The Catastrophically Uprooted Child"; Chan and Loveridge, "Refugees 'in Transit'"; Lin, Tazuma, and Masuda, "Adaptational Problems"; Masuda, Lin, and Tazuma, "Adaptational Problems"; Nicassio, "Psychosocial Correlates"; Simon, "Refugee Families' Adjustment"; Starr and Roberts, "Attitudes toward New Americans"; Rahe et al., "Psychiatric Consultation"; Liu, Lamanna, and Murata, *Transition to Nowhere*; Kinzie and Sack, "Severely Traumatized Cambodian Children."

39. Molesky, "The Exiled"; Vargas, "Recently Arrived"; Espino, "Trauma and Adaptation"; Zamichow, "No Way to Escape the Fear."

40. Rumbaut, "Mental Health," "Portraits, Patterns and Predictors," and "Migration, Adaptation, and Mental Health."

41. Dupuy, "Utility of the National Center." See also Link and Dohrenwend, "Formulation of Hypotheses."

42. Rumbaut, "Portraits, Patterns and Predictors."

43. Ibid.

44. Tyhurst, "Displacement and Migration" and "Psychosocial First Aid"; Mezey, "Psychiatric Illness"; Cohon, "Psychological Adaptation"; Baskauskas, "The Lithuanian Refugee"; Marris, *Loss and Change*; Rumbaut and Rumbaut, "The Family in Exile"; Richardson, "A Theory and a Method." Similar observations of recently arrived immigrant patients in the New York Lunatic Asylum at Blackwell's Island were described as long ago as 1850 by Ranney, "On Insane Foreigners," 54–55.

45. Vega, Warheit, and Palacio, "Psychiatric Symptomatology."

46. Vega et al., "Depressive Symptoms"; Vega, Kolody, and Valle, "Migration and Mental Health." On Mexican immigrants, see also Vega, Warheit, and Meinhardt, "Mental Health Issues"; Mirowsky and Ross, "Mexican Culture"; Martínez, "Mexican-Americans"; Rogler, Malgady, and Rodríguez, *Hispanics and Mental Health*.

47. Portes and Stepick, "Unwelcome Immigrants."

48. Eaton and Garrison, "The Influence of Class." For related analyses of differential access to and utilization of health and mental health care services among other immigrant groups, see Rumbaut et al., "The Politics of Migrant Health Care"; Hough, "Utilization of Health."

49. Camayd-Freixas, *Crisis in Miami*. See also Szapocznik, Cohen, and Hernández, *Coping with Adolescent Refugees*; Bernal and Guitiérrez, "Cubans."

50. Child, *Italian or American?*; Warner and Srole, *The Social Systems*; Sowell, *Ethnic America*; Alba, *Italian Americans*.

51. Vega et al., "The Prevalence of Depressive Symptoms"; Warheit et al., "Mexican-American Immigration."

52. Burnam et al., "Acculturation and Lifetime Prevalence."

53. Ibid. See also Kaplan and Marks, "Adverse Effects of Acculturation"; Moscicki et al., "Depressive Symptoms"; Vega and Rumbaut, "Ethnic Minorities and Mental Health."

54. Ibid. For other pertinent data from the ECA study, see Karno and Hough, "Lifetime Prevalence." See also Febrega, "Social Psychiatric Aspects"; Favazza, "Cultural Change and Mental Health."

55. Alderete et al., "Lifetime Prevalence of and Risk Factors for Psychiatric Disorders."

56. Amaro et al., "Acculturation and Marijuana and Cocaine Use"; Gilbert, "Alcohol Consumption Patterns"; Haynes et al., "Patterns of Cigarette Smoking"; Guendelman and Abrams, "Dietary Intake"; Marks, García, and Solis, "Health Risk Behaviors"; Vega and Amaro, "Latino Outlook"; Gfroerer and Tan, "Substance Use among Foreign-born Youths"; Epstein, Botvin, and Díaz, "Linguistic Acculturation Associated with Higher Marijuana and Polydrug Use."

57. Markides, Kraus, and Mendes de León, "Acculturation and Alcohol Consumption among Mexican Americans"; Caetano and Galván, "Alcohol Use and Alcohol-Related Problems."

58. Vega, Sribney, and Achara-Abrahams, "Co-occurring Alcohol, Drug, and Other Psychiatric Disorders."

59. Guendelman et al., "Generational Differences in Perinatal Health."

60. Kimbro, Lynch, and McLanahan, "The Hispanic Paradox and Breastfeeding."

61. Markides and Coreil, "The Health of Hispanics"; Rumbaut and Weeks, "Unraveling a Public Health Enigma"; Rumbaut, "Assimilation and Its Discontents."

62. Cabral et al., "Foreign-Born and U.S.-Born Black Women."

63. Collins and Shay, "Prevalence of Low Birth Weight."

64. Rumbaut and Weeks, "Infant Health among Indochinese Refugees"; Weeks and Rumbaut, "Infant Mortality."

65. Landale, Oropesa, and Gorman, "Immigration and Infant Health."

66. Rumbaut and Weeks, "Unraveling a Public Health Enigma."

67. Harris, "Health Status and Risk Behavior of Adolescents in Immigrant Families"; Popkin and Udry, "Adolescent Obesity Increases."

68. U.S. Department of Justice, Bureau of Justice Statistics, "Adult Correctional Populations."

69. National Center on Addiction and Substance Abuse, *Behind Bars*.

70. Pettit and Western, "Mass Imprisonment and the Life Course."

71. Rumbaut, "Turning Points in the Transition to Adulthood"; Rumbaut et al., "Immigration and Incarceration."

72. Butcher and Piehl, "Recent Immigrants"; Rumbaut, "Assimilation and Its Discontents."

73. For three different perspectives written decades apart, see Alba and Nee, *Remaking the Mainstream*; Sowell, *Ethnic America*; and Warner and Srole, *The Social Systems*.

74. Portes and Bach, *Latin Journey*, chap. 8. For more recent evidence on determinants of immigrants' perceptions of U.S. society and discrimination, see Zhou and Bankston, *Growing Up American*; Kasinitz et al., "Fade to Black"; Waters, *Black Identities*; Portes and Rumbaut, *Legacies*, chap. 4.

75. For a more detailed presentation of this argument, see Portes, Parker, and Cobas, "Assimilation or Consciousness?"

76. Portes and Bach, *Latin Journey*, 333. See also Portes, "The Rise of Ethnicity"; Rumbaut, "The Agony of Exile."

77. The two events need not occur together. That is, a favorable government reception is not always accompanied by the presence of a strong ethnic community or vice versa. They are combined here for purposes of illustration.

78. See Portes, "Dilemmas of a Golden Exile."

79. Sassen-Koob, "New York City's Informal Economy"; Waldinger, "Ethnic Business in the United States"; Min, *Middlemen in Contemporary America*.

80. See Rumbaut, "The Structure of Refuge"; Portes and Stepick, "Unwelcome Immigrants"; Gold, *Refugee Communities*; Kibria, *Family Tightrope*.

CHAPTER 7

1. Berger, "Striving in America."

2. "Kids Who Know Where It's At"; Powelson, "Florida Girl, 12, Is Top Speller"; Anderson, "The Multiplier Effect"; "'Elegiacal'"; "Immigrants," 29; N "2 in New York"; "The New Whiz Kids," 46; "San Gabriel Student Garners 'Nobel'"; Butterfield, "Why They Excel."

3. Quoted in Olsen, *Crossing the Schoolhouse Border*, 89. See also Suárez-Orozco and Suárez-Orozco, *Children of Immigration*.

4. Olsen, *Crossing the Schoolhouse Border*, 82.

5. Ibid., 66.

6. Ibid., 75. On the case of an illegal immigrant student from Mexico who graduated as valedictorian of his class, see Ibarra, "Looking at Proposition 187."

7. See, for example, Rumbaut, "Passages to America"; Haines, *Refugees as Immigrants*; Strand and Jones, *Indochinese Refugees in America*. See also the research reports of Raul Moncarz on the professional adaptation of Cuban accountants, architects, engineers, lawyers, nurses, optometrists, pharmacists, physicians, pilots, and teachers. His papers are collected in Cortés, *Cuban Exiles in the United States*.

8. Quoted in Görlach, "Comment."

9. Wardhaugh, *Languages in Competition*, 1–22; Mackey, *Bilingualism as a World Problem*, 11; Landry, "Comment." See also Crystal, *Language Death*; and Crystal, *The Cambridge Encyclopedia of Language*.

10. Lieberson, Dalto, and Johnston, "The Course"; Lieberson and Hansen, "National Development." See also Lieberson, *Language Diversity and Language Contact*.

11. Nahirny and Fishman, "American Immigrant Groups"; Fishman, *Language Loyalty in the United States*; Fishman, "Language Maintenance"; Veltman, *Language Shift in the United States* and "Modelling the Language Shift"; López, *Language Maintenance*. See also Bean and Stevens, *America's Newcomers*; Portes and Schauffler, "Language and the Second Generation."

12. Quoted in Brumberg, *Going to America*, 7. See also Schlossman, "Is There an American Tradition?"

13. Quoted in Hakuta, *Mirror of Language*, 17. See also Laponce, *Languages and Their Territories*.

14. Brigham, *A Study of American Intelligence*, 194–97.

15. Kirkpatrick, *Intelligence and Immigration*, 2.

16. Goodenough, "Racial Differences." See also Hakuta, *Mirror of Language*, 28–33.

17. Díaz, "Thought and Two Languages." For an early case study on the question of language and identity, see Child, *Italian or American?*

18. Smith, "Some Light on the Problem."

19. For detailed reviews, see Díaz, "Thought and Two Languages"; Hakuta, *Mirror of Language*; Peal and Lambert, "The Relation of Bilingualism."

20. Peal and Lambert, "The Relation of Bilingualism."

21. Leopold, *Speech Development*.

22. Peal and Lambert, "The Relation of Bilingualism," 5–7, 14–15. See also Reynolds, "Language and Learning."

23. Rumbaut and Ima, *The Adaptation*; Rumbaut, "Immigrant Students." Comparative data from this study on native (English-only) white and black students, as well as Pacific Islanders, American Indians, and other much smaller immigrant groups (Europeans, South Asians, Middle Easterners, and Africans), are not included here for ease of presentation. See also Rumbaut, "The New Californians."

24. Ibid. Chapter 8 presents an analysis of determinants of standardized math and reading scores for a large sample of children of immigrants in secondary schools in San Diego and South Florida.

25. U.S. Bureau of the Census, *Language Use and English-Speaking Ability: 2000*.

26. Excluded from the first group are Great Britain, Canada, and Jamaica, where English is the dominant language. Included are India and the Philippines, where English use is common among the educated classes, but other languages are also spoken.

27. López, *The Maintenance of Spanish*.

28. Ibid.

29. López, *The Maintenance of Spanish*.

30. Alba, "Language Assimilation Today"; Alba et al., "Only English by the Third Generation?"

31. Pew Hispanic Center, "Assimilation and Language" and "Bilingualism."

32. Rumbaut et al., *Immigration and Intergenerational Mobility in Metropolitan Los Angeles*.

33. Alba et al., "Only English by the Third Generation?"

34. Pew Hispanic Center, "Assimilation and Language" and "Bilingualism."

35. Rumbaut et al., *Immigration and Intergenerational Mobility in Metropolitan Los Angeles*.

36. See Marshall, "The Question"; Thernstrom, "Language." For a leading assimilationist statement, see Rodríguez, *Hunger of Memory*.

37. Sandiford and Kerr, "Intelligence."

38. Quoted in Schmalz, "Hispanic Influx." See also Resnick, "Beyond the Ethnic Community."

39. For an example of the argument for forced linguistic assimilation, see Henry, "Against a Confusion of Tongues." See also the journalistic account

of the origins of the U.S. English movement by Crawford, "The Hidden Motives."

40. National Science Foundation, "Human Resource Contributions"; "Wanted"; "Threat to Security"; Cavanagh, "Born to Science." See also Rumbaut, "Passages to America"; National Research Council, *The New Americans*; National Science Board, "Science and Engineering Indicators 2004."

41. For an overview of the parent study, see Rumbaut, "Portraits, Patterns, and Predictors." See also Rumbaut and Ima, *The Adaptation*; Rumbaut, "Immigrant Students."

42. Rumbaut and Ima, "Determinants of Educational Attainment." For a follow-up of this study, see Rumbaut, "The New Californians."

43. Kim and Hurh, "Two Dimensions."

44. Portes and Rumbaut, *Legacies*, chap. 6.

45. Lieberson, *Language and Ethnic Relations*.

46. Sassen-Koob, "Exporting Capital"; Bustamante, "Espaldas Mojadas"; Cornelius, "The United States Demand."

47. Doeringer, Moss, and Terkla, "Capitalism and Kinship"; Min, "Ethnic Business"; Gold, "Refugees and Small Business"; Resnick, "Beyond the Ethnic Community"; Portes and Rumbaut, *Legacies*, chap. 6.

48. Portes and Hao, "The Price of Uniformity"; Zhou, "Straddling Different Worlds"; Alba, "Language Assimilation Today."

49. See, for example, Laponce, *Languages and Their Territories*; Ben-Rafael, *Language, Identity, and Social Division*; Silva-Corvalán, *Language Contact and Change*; Pinker, *The Language Instinct*. For a discussion of the effect of age on accentless second language acquisition, see Lenneberg, *Biological Foundations of Language*. For a statement on the politics of ethnic language use over time in the context of competitive intergroup relations, see Taylor, "Ethnicity and Language." On language and bicultural identities, see Hoffman, *Lost in Translation*; Pérez Firmat, *Life on the Hyphen*.

50. From Aldrich's poem, "Unguarded Gates," quoted in "Immigrants," 31.

51. Crawford, *Hold Your Tongue* and "The Hidden Motives"; Loo, "The 'Biliterate' Ballot Controversy." For a concise argument against the U.S. English movement, see Capen, "Languages Open Opportunity's Door." See also Marshall, "The Question," and the entire special issue of the *International Journal of the Sociology of Language* 60 (1986), in which that article appears; Crawford, *Language Loyalties*; Baron, *The English-Only Question*.

CHAPTER 8

1. Rumbaut, "Coming of Age in Immigrant America"; Jensen, "The Demographic Diversity of Immigrants"; Myers, Pitkin, and Park, "California Demographic Futures."

2. This figure does not include more than 1.5 million persons who were born in Puerto Rico or other U.S. territories, who have birthright citizenship.

3. Portes and Rumbaut, *Legacies*, chap. 3; Portes and Zhou, "The New Second Generation"; Rumbaut, "Ages, Life Stages, and Generational Cohorts" and "Origins and Destinies."

4. Jensen, "The Demographic Diversity."

5. Rumbaut and Portes, *Ethnicities*, chap. 1.

6. Countries of the English-speaking and French-speaking Caribbean have traditionally exhibited high rates of family instability and single parenthood; the opposite has been traditionally the case in the Philippines, China, and Korea and, to a lesser extent, Mexico and Cuba. See Portes and Rumbaut, *Legacies*, chap. 4; Mintz, "The Caribbean."

7. Field interview conducted in the course of the second CILS survey in San Diego, 1995. The names are fictitious.

8. For additional details of sample selection, see Portes and Rumbaut, *Legacies*, chap. 2.

9. Ibid, 28-30.

10. Waters, "Ethnic and Racial Identities"; Suárez-Orozco, "Towards a Psychological Understanding."

11. Waters, "Ethnic and Racial Identities"; Kasinitz, Battle, and Miyares, "Fade to Black?"; Rumbaut, "The Crucible Within"; Portes and MacLeod, "What Should I Call Myself?"

12. The same results were repeated three years later when the CILS sample had reached late adolescence; see Portes and Rumbaut, *Legacies*, 39-40, chap. 7.

13. Bluestone and Harrison, *The Deindustrialization of America*; Sassen, "The New Labor Demand in Global Cities"; Wilson, *The Truly Disadvantaged*; Portes and Zhou, "The New Second Generation."

14. U.S. Bureau of the Census, *U.S. Employment Data, 1950–1997*; Karoly, "The Trend in Inequality among Families, Individuals, and Workers"; Bluestone and Harrison, *The Deindustrialization of America.*

15. From parental interviews conducted by CILS staff in 1995–1996 in conjunction with the study's first follow-up survey. The names are fictitious.

16. Conditions in American inner-city neighborhoods and schools have been described in poignant detail by a number of ethnographers, who have noted the social isolation of these areas, the ready availability of drugs, the proliferation of street gangs, and the social pressure suffered by persons and families seeking to conform to societal norms. See, among others, Anderson, "The Ordeal of Respect"; Fernández-Kelly, "Social and Cultural Capital in the Urban Ghetto"; Bourgois, *In Search of Respect*; Sullivan, *Getting Paid.*

17. Bonacich, "Advanced Capitalism and Black-White Relations"; Massey and Denton, *American Apartheid*; Barrera, *Race and Class in the Southwest*; Mills, *The Puerto Rican Journey.*

18. Wacquant and Wilson, "The Cost of Racial and Class Exclusion in the Inner City"; see also Waters, "West Indian Immigrants, African Americans, and Whites in the Workplace"; and Bourgois, *In Search of Respect.*

19. Matthei, and Smith, "Women, Households, and Transnational Migration Networks"; Landolt, *The Causes and Consequences of Transnational Migration*; Portes, "Global Villagers."

20. Alba and Nee, *Remaking the American Mainstream*; see also Perlmann and Waldinger, "Second Generation Decline?"

21. Interview conducted in Miami as part of the ethnographic module attached to the CILS-III survey, July 2002. Interviews were conducted by a

team under the direction of Patricia Fernández-Kelly, Princeton University. The names are fictitious. The case was reported previously in Portes, Fernández-Kelly, and Haller, "Segmented Assimilation on the Ground."

22. Portes and Hao, "The Price of Uniformity: Language, Family, and Personality Adjustment in the Second Generation"; Portes and Rumbaut, *Legacies*.

23. A valid objection to this argument is that the causal order between selective/dissonant acculturation and academic performance is not well established. It may be that students who do well in school are simply more capable of retaining fluency in two (or more) languages. Similarly, doing poorly in school can lead to clashes between parents and children, rather than the other way around. The data at hand do not permit a definite elucidation of this problem. We note, however, that our measure of fluent bilingualism was constructed in 1992, at the time of the first CILS survey, and that it correlated positively with family solidarity and academic performance (indexed by grades) three years later. The first effect remains significant after controlling for other factors, as shown in table 42 ; the effect on performance remains positive but becomes nonsignificant, showing that much of this relationship is mediated by other variables.

24. Zhou, *New York's Chinatown*; Light and Bonacich, *Immigrant Entrepreneurs*; Portes and Zhou, "Entrepreneurship and Economic Progress in the 1990s."

25. Zhou and Bankston, *Growing Up American*; Portes and Stepick, *City on the Edge*, chap. 6.

26. Heckman corrections for sample selectivity were applied to estimates of central tendency as well as net effects in multivariate analyses of this data set. The correction is based on a predictive equation constructed on the basis of variables measured in the initial survey that have the strongest effects on presence/absence in the third. Without exception, average values in all relevant CILS-III variables were affected minimally by the introduction of this correction. Nevertheless, results presented next are adjusted for sample selectivity. For additional details, see Portes et al., "Segmented Assimilation on the Ground"; and Rumbaut, "Turning Points in the Transition to Adulthood."

27. Like the story of the Entenza family, this account comes from the ethnographic module attached to the CILS-III survey. The interview was conducted in Miami in August 2002. The names are fictitious. This case was reported previously; see Fernández-Kelly and Konczal, "Murdering the Alphabet."

28. The cases of the Entenza and Fernández families partially illustrate these differences. For a fuller analysis of the differences in social origins and context of reception of successive Cuban refugee waves, see Portes and Stepick, *City on the Edge*, and Pérez, "Cuban Miami."

29. The median is preferable as a measure of average income to the mean because it is insensitive to extreme values. It indicates the income level below which 50 percent of the sample falls. On the contrary, the mean can be "pulled" upward or "pushed" downward, relative to the median, by income outliers.

30. Evidence from the ethnographic module attached to CILS-III indicates that high-status parents strongly support the tradition of keeping their children at home until marriage, while low-status parents tend to adopt the more "modern" stance of letting them go or pushing them away from home

because of economic reasons. See Fernández-Kelly and Konczal, "Murdering the Alphabet."

31. Western, "The Impact of Incarceration on Wage Mobility and Inequality."

32. Rumbaut et al., "Immigration and Incarceration."

33. CILS project interview conducted by R. Rumbaut in 1995. Names are fictitious.

34. CILS project interview conducted by P. Fernández-Kelly in 1996. Names are fictitious.

35. Rumbaut, "Assimilation and Its Discontents." Portes and Rumbaut, *Legacies*, chap. 9.

36. Portes and Rumbaut, *Legacies*, 281–82. Results supporting these conclusions and those that follow are presented in various chapters of *Legacies*. See also Feliciano and Rumbaut, "Gendered Paths."

37. The literature on the mutually reinforcing pathologies of poverty in American cities and rural areas is enormous and comprises quantitative and qualitative studies from various social sciences. For some prominent examples, see Wilson, *The Truly Disadvantaged*; Massey and Denton, *American Apartheid*; Sullivan, *Getting Paid*; Dunier, *Slim's Table*; and Bourgois, *In Search of Respect*.

CHAPTER 9

1. Authors' field research in Miami, January 2005.

2. Hirschman, "The Role of Religion"; Handlin, *The Uprooted*; Herberg, *Protestant, Catholic, Jew*.

3. Alba and Raboteau, *The Religious Lives of American Immigrants*; Ebaugh and Chafetz, *Religion and the New Immigrants*; Hirschman, "The Role of Religion"; Levitt, "You Know, Abraham Was Really the First Immigrant"; Warner and Wittner, *Gatherings in Diaspora*; Warner, "Approaching Religious Diversity"; Wuthnow, *America and the Challenges of Religious Diversity*.

4. See the case studies in Ebaugh and Chafetz, "Religion and the New Immigrants." For classic examples, see Handlin, *The Uprooted*; Thomas and Znaniecki, *The Polish Peasant in Europe and America*; Warner and Srole, *The Social Systems of American Ethnic Groups*, chap. 7. For contemporary examples, see also: Crane, *Latino Churches*; Alumkal, *Asian American Evangelical Churches*; Kwon, *Buddhist and Protestant Korean Immigrants*.

5. Durhkeim, *The Elementary Forms of Religious Life* and *Suicide*; Weber, *The Sociology of Religion* and *The Protestant Ethic and the Spirit of Capitalism*.

6. Alba and Orsi, *Passages in Piety*; Min and Kim, *Religions in Asian America*; Zhou and Bankston, *Growing Up American*.

7. Hirschman, "The Role of Religion."

8. Alba and Raboteau, "Comparisons of Migrants and Their Religions"; Glazer, "Ethnic Groups in America."

9. Hirschman, "The Role of Religion"; Hout and Greeley, "The Center Doesn't Hold"; Herberg, *Protestant, Catholic, Jew*.

10. Pirenne, *Medieval Cities*; Weber, *The Sociology of Religion* and *The City*; Mannheim, *Ideology and Utopia*.

11. For classic descriptions of the Catholic-Protestant conflict in America, see Handlin, *The Uprooted*; Thomas and Znaniecki, *The Polish Peasant in Europe and America*; Child, *Italian or American?*; Herberg, *Protestant, Catholic, Jew*. See also Alba and Orsi, "Passages in Piety," and Hirschman, "The Role of Religion."

12. Zhou et al., "Rebuilding Spiritual Lives in the New Land."

13. Ibid.

14. Ibid., 57.

15. This theoretical model was originally presented in Portes and DeWind, "A Cross-Atlantic Dialogue," 844.

16. Hirschman, "The Role of Religion," 1212. The essay is based on the classic statements on the question by Handlin in *The Uprooted* and *Boston's Immigrants* and by Herberg in *Protestant, Catholic, Jew*.

17. For analysis and descriptions of this perspective, as it applied to earlier European immigrants, see Gordon, *Assimilation in American Life*; Warner and Srole, *The Social Systems of American Ethnic Groups*; Alba, *Italian-Americans*; Thomas and Znaniecki, *The Polish Peasant*.

18. In addition to the works cited previously, see Howe, *World of Our Fathers*; Rischin, *The Promised City*; and Dinnerstein, "The East European Jewish Migration."

19. Warner and Wittner, *Gatherings in Diaspora*; Ebaugh and Chafetz, *Religion and the New Immigrants*, 4; Wuthnow, *America and the Challenges of Religious Diversity*, 57.

20. Min, "Korean Americans"; Hurh and Kim, "Religious Participation of Korean Immigrants"; Kim and Kim, "The Ethnic Role of Korean Immigrant Churches."

21. Sengupta, "On One Queens Block, Many Prayers Are Spoken."

22. Pew Global Attitudes Project, "Among Wealthy Nations, U.S. Stands Alone in Its Embrace of Religion."

23. U.S. Bureau of the Census, *Current Population Reports*, P-20, No. 79 (February 2, 1958). See also Gordon, *Assimilation in American Life*, chap. 7.

24. The results reported here are based on an analysis of twenty-five merged GSS surveys conducted from 1972 to 2002 with nationally representative samples of approximately forty-four thousand adults age eighteen to eighty-nine. See http://www.norc.uchicago.edu/projects/gensoc.asp.

25. Smith, "The Vanishing Protestant Majority"; cf. Schneiderman, "The Protestant Establishment."

26. Cf. Groeneman and Tobin, "The Decline of Religious Identity"; Hout and Fischer, "Why More Americans Have No Religious Preference."

27. Smith, "Religious Diversity in America."

28. Field research in Bogotá, Colombia, March 2005. Personal names are fictitious.

29. Ibid.

30. Portes et al., "Immigrant Transnational Organizations and Development."

31. Ibid., 36–37.

32. Field research for the project on Immigrant Transnational Organizations and Development, conducted by Rosario Espinal in Jimani, Dominican Republic, December 2004.

33. Hirschman, "The Role of Religion"; Handlin, *Boston's Immigrants* and *The Uprooted*; Higham, *Strangers in the Land*; Larkin, *The Historical Dimensions of Irish Catholicism*; Archdeacon, *Becoming American*; Dolan, *The Immigrant Church*.

34. Field research in Bogotá, Colombia, March 2005.

35. Zhou et al., "Rebuilding Spiritual Lives"; Huynh, "Center for Vietnamese Buddhism."

36. Jacob and Thakur, "Jyothi Hindu Temple."

37. Guarnizo et al., "Assimilation and Transnationalism"; Portes, "Theoretical Convergencies and Empirical Evidence."

38. Menjívar, "Religious Institutions and Transnationalism." See also Menjívar, "Religion and Immigration in Comparative Perspective."

39. This is a statement drawn directly from the classic works by Handlin, Herberg, and Gordon, cited previously. See Alba and Raboteau, "Comparisons of Migrants and Their Religions"; the statement is restated by Hirschman in "The Role of Religion."

40. Ebaugh and Chafetz, *Religion and the New Immigrants*, chap. 8; Alumkal, *Asian American Evangelical Churches*; Crane, *Latino Churches*; Rumbaut, "Severed or Sustained Attachments?"

41. Hirschman, "The Role of Religion"; Greeley, *Why Can't They Be Like Us?*; Finke and Stark, *The Churching of America*; Greeley and Hout, "Americans' Increasing Belief in Life after Death."

42. Greeley and Hout, "Americans' Increasing Belief in Life after Death"; Hout and Fischer, "Why More Americans Have No Religious Preference."

43. Zhou and Bankston, "Social Capital and the Adaptation of the Second Generation," 207.

44. Ibid., 218.

45. The index is constructed as the unit-weighted sum of six dichotomous indicators and ranges from 0 to 6. Respondents who (1) had dropped out of high school, (2) were unemployed and not attending school, (3) had been arrested, (4) had been incarcerated, (5) had had a child in adolescence, or (6) had very low or no income were coded 1; others were coded 0 in each indicator. For analyses of educational attainment, incarceration (for males) and early childbearing (for females) based on the CILS-III sample, see Portes, Fernández-Kelly, and Haller, "Segmented Assimilation"; and Rumbaut, "Turning Points."

46. Portes and Rumbaut, *Legacies*; Portes and Hao, "The Schooling of Children of Immigrants"; Rumbaut, "Children of Immigrants and Their Achievement."

47. Smith, "Religion and Ethnicity in America."

48. Ibid.; Alba and Orsi, "Passages in Piety"; Thomas and Znaniecki, *The Polish Peasant*.

49. Pierce et al., "Japanese and Korean Migrations."

50. Ibid. See also Hurh and Kim, "Religious Participation of Korean Immigrants"; Kim and Kim, "The Ethnic Role of Korean Immigrant Churches."

51. López, "Whither the Flock?"

52. González, *The Spanish-Americans of New Mexico*. See also Espinosa, Elizondo, and Miranda, *Hispanic Churches in American Public Life*; Sellers, "Hispanic Catholicism."

53. López, "Whither the Flock?"

54. Field interview conducted in Miami, June 2002. The names are fictitious.

55. Field interview conducted in Miami, July 2002. The names are fictitious.

56. Rumbaut et al., *Immigration and Intergenerational Mobility in Metropolitan Los Angeles*.

57. Massey and Durand, *Miracles on the Border*, 135.

58. Ibid., 137. See also: Griffith, *Saints of the Southwest*.

59. López, "Whither the Flock?" 1.

60. Ibid.; Alba and Orsi, "Passages in Piety"; Portes et. al., "Transnational Organizations and Development."

61. López, "Whither the Flock?" 4–5.

62. Ibid.

63. Portes and Stepick, *City on the Edge*; Portes and Rumbaut, *Legacies*, chap. 9; Pérez, "Growing Up in Cuban Miami."

64. López, "Whither the Flock?"

65. Smith, "The Muslim Population of the United States" and "Religious Diversity in America."

66. Stephens and Rago, "Stars, Stripes, Crescent"; Zolberg and Woon, "Why Islam Is Like Spanish."

67. Pirenne, *Medieval Cities*; Dobb, *Studies in the Development of Capitalism*.

68. Huntington, *The Clash of Civilizations*.

69. Alba and Raboteau, "Comparisons of Migrants and Their Religions"; Lim and Jamal, "Muslim, Arab, and American."

70. Pirenne, *Medieval Cities*; Braudel, *The Mediterranean*, vol. 2; Amin, *Unequal Development*; Fanon, *The Wretched of the Earth*.

71. Stephens and Rago, "Stars, Stripes, Crescent"; Lin and Jamal, "Muslim, Arab, and American"; Waldman, "Seething Unease Shaped British Bombers."

72. Lin and Jamal, "Muslim, Arab, and American," 8–9.

73. Alba and Raboteau, "Comparisons of Migrants and Their Religions."

74. Personal communication to authors; see also Read, *Culture, Class, and Work among Arab-American Women*.

75. Cited in Stephens and Rago, "Stars, Stripes, Crescent."

76. Lin and Jamal, "Muslim, Arab, and American."

77. Alba and Raboteau, "Comparisons of Migrants and Their Religions"; Stephens and Rago, "Stars, Stripes, Crescent."

78. "U.S. Muslim Scholars to Forbid Terrorism."

79. Mooney, *Religion in the Haitian Immigrant Communities*.

80. Ibid., 242, 255.

81. Ibid., 153.

CHAPTER 10

1. Roosevelt, "Speech to State Republican Party Convention."

2. Linton, "One Hundred Per-Cent American."

3. Huntington, *Who Are We?*

4. As examples, see Tan, *The Joy Luck Club*, on Chinese Americans; García, *Dreaming in Cuban*, on Cuban Americans; Rodríguez, *Days of Obligation*, on Mexican Americans. See also Portes, "The Longest Migration," on contemporary Mexican American literature.

5. Select Commission on Immigration and Refugee Policy, *U.S. Immigration Policy and the National Interest*, especially xxxi–dxi.

6. This argument will be developed at greater length in later sections. For introductory statements on the role of social networks in international migration, see Tilly, "Transplanted Networks," and Massey and García España, "The Social Process of International Migration."

7. In addition to Huntington's recent writings, see Lamm and Immhoff, *The Immigration Time Bomb*, and Brimelow, *Alien Nation*. Cf. Alba, Rumbaut, and Marotz, "A Distorted Nation."

8. Schuck, "The Message of 187"; Massey et al., *Beyond Smoke and Mirrors*, 95–96.

9. "Cheap Border Politics."

10. Media coverage of the massive rallies of March 25, April 10, and May 1, 2006, staged by immigrants and their supporters, was extensive. For a thoughtful analysis of the consequences of this new round of nativist policy proposals, see Oppenheimer, "Hispanics Should Say Gracias' to Anti-Latin Zealots." See also Watanabe and Gaouette, "Next: Converting the Energy of Protest to Political Clout."

11. Unz, "California and the End of White America," 24.

12. For historical overviews of the forces driving labor immigration to the United States in the nineteenth and early twentieth centuries, see Rosenblum, *Immigrant Workers*; Lebergott, *Manpower in Economic Growth*; and Thomas, *Migration and Economic Growth*. For accounts of contemporary economic globalization and its effects on international migration, see Sassen, *The Mobility of Labor and Capital*; Cohen, *The New Helots*; Smith and Guarnizo, *Transnationalism from Below*.

13. Stephens and Rago, "Stars, Stripes, Crescent"; Lin and Jamal, "Muslim, Arab, and American."

14. Bourne, "Transnational America," 90–91.

15. See chap. 9 for a detailed presentation of this argument.

16. Portes and Zhou, "The New Second Generation"; Massey and Hirst, "From Escalator to Hourglass"; Sassen, *The Mobility of Labor and Capital*.

17. Congressional Budget Office, *Economic Growth and Immigration*, 1.

18. Massey, "Testimony before Immigration Subcommittee," 1–2.

19. Congressional Budget Office, *Economic Growth and Immigration*, 3–4.

20. For a detailed presentation of this argument, see Portes and Walton, *Labor, Class, and the International System*; Portes, "From South of the Border"; Rumbaut, "The Americans" and "The Making of a People"; Sassen, *The Mobility of Labor and Capital*.

21. Barrera, *Race and Class in the Southwest*; Bustamante, "The Historical Context"; Cornelius, "The Structural Embeddedness."

22. Bach, "Mexican Immigration"; Massey et al., *Return to Aztlán*; Portes and Bach, *Latin Journey*, chaps. 1–2; Durand and Arias, *La Experiencia Migrante*.

23. Piore, *Birds of Passage*; de Souza Martins, *Á Immigraçào e a Crise do Brasil Agrario*; Portes and Walton, *Labor, Class, and the International System*, chap. 2.

24. Stark, *The Migration of Labour*; Massey et al., *Worlds in Motion*, chap. 1; Portes and Walton, *Labor, Class, and the International System*, chap. 2; Piore, *Birds of Passage*.

25. U.S. Immigration and Naturalization Service, *2001 Statistical Yearbook*.

26. Office of Immigration Statistics, *2003 Statistical Yearbook*.

27. Tilly, "Transplanted Networks"; Anderson, *Networks of Contact*; Portes and Bach, *Latin Journey*, chaps. 1, 3.

28. Portes and Bach, *Latin Journey*, 92–93, 125–27.

29. Massey, "Understanding Mexican Migration"; Massey et al., "Continuities in Transnational Migration"; Massey et al., *Return to Aztlán*.

30. Tilly, "Transplanted Networks," 85.

31. Massey et al., *Beyond Smoke and Mirrors*, 19–20.

32. Cornelius, "The Structural Embeddedness" and "Appearances and Realities"; Smith, "New York in Mixteca"; Espenshade, "Does the Threat of Border Apprehension Deter Undocumented U.S. Migration?"

33. Massey, "Foolish Fences."

34. Office of Immigration Statistics, *2003 Statistical Yearbook*.

35. Espenshade, "Does the Threat of Border Apprehension Deter Undocumented U.S. Migration?"; Espenshade and Baraka, "Implications of the 1996 Welfare Reform and Immigration Act."

36. Massey, "Foolish Fences."

37. Massey, "Testimony before the Immigration Subcommittee."

38. Ibid.; Cornelius, "Appearances and Realities"; Espenshade and Baraka, "Implications"; Portes, "The New Latin Nation."

39. Massey, "Testimony"; Cornelius, "Death at the Border."

40. Rumbaut and Portes, *Ethnicities*, chap. 1; Portes and Zhou, "The New Second Generation"; Portes et al., "Segmented Assimilation on the Ground"; Rumbaut, "Assimilation and Its Discontents" and "Turning Points."

41. Massey, "Foolish Fences"; Brooks, "La Ley Sensenbrenner."

42. Bach and Brill, *Impact of IRCA*; Fix and Passel, "The Door Remains Open."

43. Bach and Brill, *Impact of IRCA*, 57–64; Cornelius, "The Structural Embeddedness."

44. Cornelius, "Illegal Migration to the United States"; Cornelius and Chávez, *Mexican Immigrants to Southern California*; Portes, "Of Borders and States."

45. Fix and Passel, "The Door Stays Open"; U.S. Immigration and Naturalization Service, *1990 Statistical Yearbook*.

46. Smith and Edmonston, *The Immigration Debate*.

47. Rodríguez, "Once Again, It Will Be Immigrants to the Rescue."

48. Ibid.

49. Office of Immigration Statistics, *2003 Statistical Yearbook*.

50. The story is authentic and has been followed closely by the authors. Names and places are fictitious to protect the participants.

51. See chap. 2 for a description of the evolution of U.S. refugee and asylee policies; see also Rumbaut, "The Structure of Refuge."

52. The story is authentic. The names are fictitious.

53. Riley, "Statement by the Secretary of Education on California Proposition 227."

54. Borjas, *Heaven's Door*.

55. Swarns, "Capitol's Pariah on Immigration Is Now a Power."

56. The mass immigrant demonstrations in the spring of 2006 against the Sensenbrenner bill (HR 4437) added new urgency to the need to put an enlightened policy into place. In late April, the California Senate passed a resolution designating May 1 as "the Great American Boycott of 2006." The show of solidarity with the huge public mobilizations that took place on that day is encouraging, but it does not go far enough. It needs to be followed by concrete measures at the federal level to restore rationality to immigration policy and end the looming prospect of interethnic conflict. The threatened "fragmentation of America" that nativists so often decry is, in the end, their own creation. See Becerra and Blankstein, "L.A. Authorities Brace for Huge Immigration Marches"; Muskal and Williams, "Immigrants Take Economic Impact to the Streets."

References

Acuña, Rodolfo. *Occupied America: A History of Chicanos*. New York: Harper and Row, 1981.

Alarcón, Rafael. "Recruitment Processes among Foreign-Born Engineers and Scientists in Silicon Valley." *American Behavioral Scientist* 42 (June/July 1999): 1381–97.

Alba, Francisco. "Mexico's International Migration as a Manifestation of Its Development Pattern." *International Migration Review* 12 (Winter 1978): 502–51.

Alba, Richard D. *Italian Americans: Into the Twilight of Ethnicity*. Englewood Cliffs, N.J.: Prentice Hall, 1985.

———. "Language Assimilation Today: Bilingualism Persists More Than in the Past, but English Still Dominates." Albany, N.Y.: Lewis Mumford Center for Comparative Urban and Regional Research, University at Albany, December 2004.

Alba, Richard D., John Logan, Amy Lutz, and Brian Stults. "Only English by the Third Generation? Loss and Preservation of the Mother Tongue among the Grandchildren of Contemporary Immigrants." *Demography* 39, no. 3 (2002): 467–84.

Alba, Richard D., and Victor Nee. *Remaking the American Mainstream: Assimilation and Contemporary Immigration*. Cambridge, Mass.: Harvard University Press, 2003.

Alba, Richard D., and Robert Orsi. "Passages of Piety: Generational Transitions and the Social and Religious Incorporation of Italian Americans." In *The Religious Lives of American Immigrants: Past and Present*, ed. R. Alba and A. Raboteau. New York: Russell Sage Foundation, forthcoming.

Alba, Richard D., and Albert Raboteau. "Comparisons of Migrants and Their Religions in the Past and Present." In *The Religious Lives of American Immigrants: Past and Present*, ed. R. Alba and A. Raboteau. New York: Russell Sage Foundation, forthcoming.

Alba, Richard D., Rubén G. Rumbaut, and Karen Marotz. "A Distorted Nation: Perceptions of Racial/Ethnic Group Sizes and Attitudes toward Immigrants and Other Minorities." *Social Forces* 84, no. 2 (2005): 899–917.

Alderete, E., W. A. Vega, B. Kolody, and S. Aguilar-Gaxiola. "Lifetime Prevalence of and Risk Factors for Psychiatric Disorders among Mexican Farm Workers in California." *American Journal of Public Health* 90, no. 4 (2000): 608–14.

Aleinikoff, T. Alexander, and Rubén G. Rumbaut. "Terms of Belonging: Are Models of Membership Self-Fulfilling Prophecies?" *Georgetown Immigration Law Journal* 13 (1998): 1–24.

Allen, James P., and Eugene J. Turner. *We the People: An Atlas of America's Ethnic Diversity*. New York: Macmillan, 1986.

Alley, James Curtis. "Life-Threatening Indicators among the Indochinese Refugees." *Suicide and Life-Threatening Behavior* 12 (Spring 1982): 46–51.

Alumkal, Antony W. *Asian American Evangelical Churches: Race, Ethnicity, and Assimilation in the Second Generation*. New York: LFB Scholarly, 2004.

Amaro, Hortensia, R. Whitaker, J. Coffman, and T. Heeren. "Acculturation and Marijuana and Cocaine Use: Findings from HHANES 1982–84." *American Journal of Public Health*, supplement, 80 (1990): 54–60.

Amir, Samin. *Unequal Development: An Essay on the Social Formations of Peripheral Capitalism*. New York: Monthly Review Press, 1976.

Anderson, Elijah. "The Ordeal of Respect." Unpublished manuscript, Department of Sociology, University of Pennsylvania, 1993.

Anderson, Grace M. *Networks of Contact: The Portuguese and Toronto*. Ontario: Wilfrid Laurier University Press, 1974.

Anderson, Patricia. "Manpower Losses and Employment Adequacy among Skilled Workers in Jamaica, 1976–1985." In *When Borders Don't Divide: Labor Migration and Refugee Movements in the Americas*, ed. Patricia Pessar, 96–128. New York: Center for Migration Studies, 1988.

———. "Migration and Development in Jamaica." In *Migration and Development in the Caribbean*, ed. Robert Pastor, 117–39. Boulder, Colo.: Westview Press, 1988.

Anderson, Stuart. *The Multiplier Effect*. Arlington, Va.: National Foundation for American Policy, 2004.

Antin, Mary. *The Promised Land*. New York: Houghton Mifflin, 1912.

Antonovsky, Aaron. *Health, Stress and Coping*. San Francisco: Jossey-Bass, 1979.

Aponte, Robert. "Urban Unemployment and the Mismatch Theory." Paper presented at the Conference on Urban Poverty, University of Chicago, October 1991.

Arax, Mark, Rich Connell, Daniel Hernández, Robert J. López, and Jennifer Mena. "Green Card Marines: Radical Turn for a Rebel." *Los Angeles Times*, May 28, 2003.

Arax, Mark, Daniel Hernández, Robert J. López, and Jennifer Mena. "Green Card Marines: Just Looking to Fit In." *Los Angeles Times*, May 26, 2003.

Archdeacon, Thomas J. *Becoming American: An Ethnic History.* New York: Free Press, 1983.

Ascoli, Max. Cited in R. M. MacIver, *Group Relations and Group Antagonisms,* 32. New York: Harper, 1944.

Bach, Robert L. "Immigration: Issues of Ethnicity, Class, and Public Policy in the United States." *Annals of the American Academy of Political and Social Science* 485 (May 1986): 139–52.

———. "Mexican Immigration and the American State." *International Migration Review* 12 (Winter 1978): 536–58.

Bach, Robert L., and Howard Brill. *Impact of IRCA on the U.S. Labor Market and Economy.* Report to the U.S. Department of Labor, Institute for Research on International Labor. Binghamton: State University of New York, 1991.

Bach, Robert L., Linda W. Gordon, David W. Haines, and David R. Howell. "The Economic Adjustment of Southeast Asian Refugees in the United States." In *World Refugee Survey, 1983,* 51–55. Geneva: United Nations High Commission for Refugees, 1984.

Bailey, Thomas, and Roger Waldinger. "Primary, Secondary, and Enclave Labor Markets: A Training System Approach." *American Sociological Review* 56 (1991): 432–45.

Baker, Reginald P., and David S. North. *The 1975 Refugees: Their First Five Years in America.* Washington, D.C.: New TransCentury Foundation, 1984.

Barkan, Elliott R. "Race, Religion, and Nationality in American Society: A Model of Ethnicity—from Contact to Assimilation." *Journal of American Ethnic History* (Winter 1995): 38–75.

Baron, D. *The English-Only Question.* New Haven, Conn.: Yale University Press, 1990.

Barrera, Mario. *Race and Class in the Southwest: A Theory of Racial Inequality.* Notre Dame, Ind.: Notre Dame University Press, 1980.

Baskauskas, Luicija. "The Lithuanian Refugee Experience and Grief." *International Migration Review* 15 (1981): 276–91.

Bean, Frank D., Harley L. Browning, and W. Parker Frisbie. "The Sociodemographic Characteristics of Mexican Immigrant Status Groups: Implications for Studying Undocumented Mexicans." *International Migration Review* 18 (Fall 1985): 672–91.

———. "What the 1980 U.S. Census Tells Us about the Characteristics of Illegal and Legal Mexican Immigrants." Mimeograph, Population Research Center, University of Texas, Austin, 1985.

Bean, Frank D., B. Lindsay Lowell, and Lowell J. Taylor. "Undocumented Migration to the United States: Perceptions and Evidence." *Population and Development Review* 13 (December 1987): 671–90.

Bean, Frank D., and Gillian Stevens. *America's Newcomers: Immigrant Incorporation and the Dynamics of Diversity.* New York: Russell Sage Foundation, 2003.

Bean, Frank D., and Marta Tienda. *The Hispanic Population of the United States.* New York: Russell Sage Foundation, 1987.

Becerra, Héctor, and Andrew Blankstein. 2006. "L.A. Authorities Brace for Huge Immigration Marches." *Los Angeles Times*, April 28, A1.

Ben-Rafael, Eliezer. *Language, Identity and Social Division: The Case of Israel.* New York: Oxford University Press, 1994.

Berger, Joseph. "Striving in America, and in the Spelling Bee." *New York Times*, June 5, 2005.

Bernal, Guillermo, and Manuel Gutiérrez. "Cubans." In *Cross-Cultural Mental Health*, ed. Lillian Comas-Díaz and Ezra E. H. Griffith, 233–61. New York: Wiley, 1988.

Bernard, W. S. "Cultural Determinants of Naturalization." *American Sociological Review* 1 (December 1936): 943–53.

Berry, John W. "The Acculturation Process and Refugee Behavior." In *Refugee Mental Health in Resettlement Countries*, ed. Carolyn L. Williams and Joseph Westermeyer, 25–37. New York: Hemisphere, 1986.

Berry, John W., Uichol Kim, Thomas Minde, and Doris Mok. "Comparative Studies of Acculturative Stress." *International Migration Review* 21 (Fall 1987): 491–511.

Bluestone, Barry and Bennett Harrison. *The Deindustrialization of America.* New York: Basic Books, 1982.

Bodnar, John. *The Transplanted: A History of Immigrants in Urban America.* Bloomington: Indiana University Press, 1985.

Bonacich, Edna. "Advanced Capitalism and Black/White Relations: A Split Labor Market Interpretation." *American Sociological Review* 41 (February 1976): 34–51.

———. "Asian Labor in the Development of California and Hawaii." In *Labor Immigration under Capitalism*, ed. Lucie Cheng and Edna Bonacich, 130–85. Berkeley: University of California Press, 1984.

———. "A Theory of Middleman Minorities." *American Sociological Review* 38 (October 1973): 583–94.

Bonacich, Edna, Ivan Light, and Charles Wong. "Koreans in Small Business." *Society* 14 (September–October 1977): 54–59.

Bonacich, Edna, and John Modell. *The Economic Basis of Ethnic Solidarity: Small Business in the Japanese-American Community.* Berkeley: University of California Press, 1980.

Bonilla, Frank A., and Ricardo Campos. "A Wealth of Poor: Puerto Ricans in the New Economic Order." *Daedalus* 110 (Spring 1981): 133–76.

Booth, John A. "Global Forces and Regime Change: Guatemala within the Central American Context." In *Globalization on the Ground: Postbellum Guatemalan Democracy and Development*, eds. C. Chase Dunn, S. Jonas, and N. Amaro, 21–47. Lanham, Md.: Rowman & Littlefield, 2001.

Borjas, George J. "Economic Theory and International Migration." *International Migration Review* 23 (1989): 457–85.

———. *Friends or Strangers: The Impact of Immigrants on the U.S. Economy.* New York: Basic Books, 1990.

———. *Heaven's Door: Immigration Policy and the American Economy.* Princeton, N.J.: Princeton University Press, 2001.

————. "Self-Selection and the Earnings of Immigrants." *American Economic Review* 77 (1987): 531–53.

————. "Statement." Hearings before the Subcommittee on Economic Resources, Competitiveness, and Security Economics, U.S. House of Representatives, 99th Congress. Washington, D.C.: U.S. Government Printing Office, 1987.

Boswell, Terry E. "A Split Labor Market Analysis of Discrimination against Chinese Immigrants, 1850–1882." *American Sociological Review* 51 (June 1986): 352–71.

Boswell, Thomas D., and James R. Curtis. *The Cuban-American Experience.* Totowa, N.J.: Rowman & Allanheld, 1984.

Botifoll, Luis J. "How Miami's New Image Was Created." Occasional Paper 1985-I. Miami: Institute of Interamerican Studies, University of Miami, 1985.

Bourgois, Philippe I. *In Search of Respect: Selling Crack in El Barrio.* Cambridge: Cambridge University Press, 1995.

Bourne, Randolph S. "Trans-National America." *Atlantic Monthly* 118 (1916): 86–97.

Bouvier, Leon F., and Robert W. Gardner. "Immigration to the U.S.: The Unfinished Story." *Population Bulletin* 41 (1986).

Braudel, Fernand. *The Mediterranean and the Mediterranean World in the Age of Philip II*, vol. 2. New York: Harper Colophon Books, [1949] 1973.

Bray, David. "Economic Development: The Middle Class and International Migration in the Dominican Republic." *International Migration Review* 18 (Summer 1984): 217–36.

Briggs, Vernon M. "The Need for a More Restrictive Border Policy." *Social Science Quarterly* 56 (1975): 477–84.

Brigham, Carl C. *A Study of American Intelligence.* Princeton, N.J.: Princeton University Press, 1923.

Brimelow, Peter. *Alien Nation: Common Sense about America's Immigration Disaster.* New York: Random House, 1995.

Brooks, David. 2006. "La Ley Sensenbrenner, Bofetada Que Despertó a los Inmigrantes Mexicanos." *La Jornada* (Mexico City), March 16.

Browning, Harley L., and Nestor Rodríguez. "The Migration of Mexican Indocumentados as a Settlement Process: Implications for Work." In *Hispanics in the U.S. Economy*, ed. George J. Borjas and Marta Tienda, 277–97. Orlando, Fla.: Academic Press, 1985.

Brumberg, Stephen F. *Going to America, Going to School: The Jewish Immigrant Public School Encounter in Turn-of-the-Century New York City.* New York: Praeger, 1986.

Burma, John D. *Mexican-Americans in the United States: A Reader.* New York: Schenkman, 1970.

Burnam, M. Audrey, Richard L. Hough, Marvin Karno, Javier I. Escobar, and Cynthia A. Telles. "Acculturation and Lifetime Prevalence of Psychiatric Disorders among Mexican Americans in Los Angeles." *Journal of Health and Social Behavior* 28 (March 1987): 89–102.

Bustamante, Jorge A. "Espaldas Mojadas: Materia Prima para la Exportación del Capital Norteamericano." *Cuadernos del CES*, 9. El Colegio de México, 1975.

———. "The Historical Context of Undocumented Mexican Immigration to the United States." *Aztlán* 3 (Winter 1973): 257–81.

Bustamante, Jorge A., and Gerónimo Martínez. "Undocumented Immigration from Mexico: Beyond Borders but within Systems." *Journal of International Affairs* 33 (Fall/Winter 1979): 265–84.

Butcher, Kristin F., and Anne Morrison Piehl. "Recent Immigrants: Unexpected Implications for Crime and Incarceration." NBER Working Paper 6067. Cambridge, Mass.: National Bureau of Economic Research, 1997.

Butterfield, Fox. "Why They Excel." *Parade Magazine*, January 21, 1990, 46.

Cabral, H., L. E. Fried, S. Levenson, H. Amaro, and B. Zuckerman. "Foreign-Born and U.S. Born Black Women: Differences in Health Behaviors and Birth Outcomes." *American Journal of Public Health* 80, no. 1 (1990): 70–72.

Caetano, Raúl, and F. H. Galván. "Alcohol Use and Alcohol-Related Problems among Latinos in the United States." In *Health Issues in the Latino Community*, ed. M. Aguirre-Molina, C. W. Molina, and R. E. Zambrana, 383–412. San Francisco: Jossey-Bass, 2001.

Camarillo, Albert. *Chicanos in a Changing Society*. Cambridge, Mass.: Harvard University Press, 1979.

Camarota, Steven A. "Immigrants in the United States—2000." *Backgrounder*. Washington, D.C.: Center for Immigration Studies, November 2002.

Camayd-Freixas, Yohel. *Crisis in Miami: Community Context and Institutional Response in the Adaptation of Mariel Cubans and Undocumented Haitian Entrants in South Florida*. Commissioned report. Boston: Urban Research and Development, 1988.

Capecchi, Vittorio. "The Informal Economy and the Development of Flexible Specialization in Emilia-Romagna." In *The Informal Economy: Studies in Advanced and Less Developed Countries*, ed. A. Portes, M. Castells, and L. A. Benton, 189–215. Baltimore, Md.: Johns Hopkins University Press, 1989.

Capen, Richard. "Languages Open Opportunity's Door." *Miami Herald*, October 30, 1988, 15.

Caplan, Nathan, Marcella H. Choy, and John K. Whitmore. *Children of the Boat People: A Study of Educational Success*. Ann Arbor: University of Michigan Press, 1991.

Cardoso, Lawrence A. *Mexican Emigration to the United States, 1897–1931*. Tucson: University of Arizona Press, 1980.

Cariño, Benjamin V. "The Philippines and Southeast Asia: Historical Roots and Contemporary Linkages." In *Pacific Bridges: The New Immigration from Asia and the Pacific Islands*, ed. J. T. Fawcett and B. V. Cariño, 305–25. Staten Island, N.Y.: Center for Migration Studies, 1987.

Carlin, Jean E. "The Catastrophically Uprooted Child: Southeast Asian Refugee Children." In *Basic Handbook of Child Psychiatry*, vol. 1, ed. Justin D. Call, Joseph D. Noshpitz, Richard L. Cohen, and Irving N. Berlin, 290–300. New York: Basic Books, 1979.

Castles, Stephen. "The Guest-Worker in Western Europe: An Obituary." *International Migration Review* 20 (Winter 1986): 761–78.

Castles, Stephen, Heather Booth, and Tina Wallace. *Here for Good: Western Europe's New Ethnic Minorities*. London: Pluto Press, 1984.

Central Intelligence Agency. *The World Factbook 2003*. http://www.cia.gov/cis/publications/factbook/goes/us.html#econ.

———. *The World Factbook 2004*. http://www.odci.gov/cia/publications/factbook/index.html.

Chan, Kwok B., and David Loveridge. "Refugees 'in Transit': Vietnamese in a Refugee Camp in Hong Kong." *International Migration Review* 21 (Fall 1987): 745–59.

Chávez, Leo R. "Settlers and Sojourners: The Case of Mexicans in the United States." *Human Organization* 47 (Summer 1988): 95–108.

———. *Shadowed Lives: Undocumented Immigrants in American Society*. San Diego: Harcourt Brace Jovanovich, 1992.

Chávez, Leo R., and Estevan T. Flores. "Undocumented Mexicans and Central Americans and the Immigration Reform and Control Act of 1986: A Reflection Based on Empirical Data." In *In Defense of the Alien*, vol. 10: 137–56. New York: Center for Migration Studies, 1988.

"Cheap Border Politics." *New York Times*, December 21, 2005, 38.

Child, Clifton J. *The German-Americans in Politics, 1914–1917*. Madison: University of Wisconsin Press, 1939.

Child, Irving L. *Italian or American? The Second Generation in Conflict*. New Haven, Conn.: Yale University Press, 1943.

Chiswick, Barry R. "The Effect of Americanization on the Earnings of Foreign-Born Men." *Journal of Political Economy* 86 (October 1978): 897–921.

Cichon, Donald J., Elzbieta M. Gozdziak, and Jane G. Grover. "The Economic and Social Adjustment of Non-Southeast Asian Refugees." Mimeographed report to the Office of Refugee Resettlement. Washington, D.C.: Department of Health and Human Services, 1986.

Clark, Juan M., José I. Lasaga, and Rose S. Reque. *The 1980 Mariel Exodus: An Assessment and Prospect*. Washington, D.C.: Council for Inter-American Security, 1981.

Clark, Rebecca L., Jeffrey S. Passel, Wendy N. Zimmerman, and Michael E. Fix. *Fiscal Impacts of Undocumented Aliens: Selective Estimates for Seven States*. Washington, D.C.: Urban Institute, 1994.

Cobas, José. "Participation in the Ethnic Economy, Ethnic Solidarity, and Ambivalence toward the Host Society: The Case of Cuban Emigrés in Puerto Rico." Paper presented at the meetings of the American Sociological Association, San Antonio, 1984.

Cockcroft, James D. *Outlaws in the Promised Land: Mexican Immigrant Workers and America's Future*. New York: Grove Press, 1986.

Cohen, Robin. *The New Helots: Migrants in the International Division of Labor*. Hants, England: Gower House, 1987.

Cohon, J. Donald, Jr. "Psychological Adaptation and Dysfunction among Refugees." *International Migration Review* 15 (Spring–Summer 1981): 255–75.

Collins, J. W., Jr., and D. K. Shay. "Prevalence of Low Birth Weight among Hispanic Infants with United States-Born and Foreign-Born Mothers: The

Effect of Urban Poverty." *American Journal of Epidemiology* 139, no. 2 (1994): 184–92.

Congressional Budget Office. *Economic Growth and Immigration: Bridging the Demographic Divide.* Report Summary (November 15, 2005). Washington, D.C.: U.S. Congress, 2005.

Cornelius, Wayne A. "Appearances and Realities: Controlling Illegal Immigration in the United States." In *Japanese and U.S. Immigration: Refugee and Citizenship Policies,* ed. M. Weiner and T. Hashami, 384–427. New York: New York University Press, 1998.

———. "Death at the Border: Efficacy and Unintended Consequences of U.S. Immigration Control Policy." *Population and Development Review* 27 (December 2001): 661–85.

———. "Illegal Migration to the United States: Recent Research Findings, Policy Implications, and Research Priorities." Mimeograph, discussion paper C/77-11. Cambridge, Mass.: Center for International Studies, MIT, 1977.

———. "Labor Market Impacts of Mexican Immigration: Two Generations of Research." Paper presented at the seminar on the urban informal sector in center and periphery, Johns Hopkins University, Baltimore, June 1984.

———. "Mexican Migration to the United States: Causes, Consequences, and U.S. Responses." Working paper. Cambridge, Mass.: Center for International Studies, MIT, 1977.

———. "Mexican Migration to the United States: The View from Rural Sending Communities." Mimeograph, discussion paper C/76-12. Cambridge, Mass.: Center for International Studies, MIT, 1976.

———. "The Structural Embeddedness of Demand for Mexican Immigrant Labor: New Evidence from California." In *Crossings, Mexican Immigration in Interdisciplinary Perspective,* ed. M. Suárez-Orozco, 115–55. Cambridge, Mass.: Center for Latin American Studies, Harvard University, 1998.

———. "The United States Demand for Mexican Labor." Paper presented at the workshop on migration issues of the Bilateral Commission on the Future of U.S. Mexican Relations, San Diego, August 1987.

Cornelius, Wayne A., Leo R. Chávez, and Jorge G. Castro. *Mexican Immigrants and Southern California: A Summary of Current Knowledge.* Research Report Series 36. La Jolla: Center for U.S.-Mexican Studies, University of California, San Diego, 1982.

Cortés, Carlos E., ed. *Cuban Exiles in the United States.* New York: Arno Press, 1980.

Crane, Ken R. *Latino Churches: Faith, Family, and Ethnicity in the Second Generation.* New York: LFB Scholarly, 2004.

Crawford, James. "The Hidden Motives Stain Official English." *Miami Herald,* November 10, 1988, A13.

———. *Hold Your Tongue: Bilingualism and the Politics of "English Only."* New York: Addison-Wesley, 1992.

———. *Language Loyalties: A Source Book on the Official English Controversy.* Chicago: University of Chicago Press, 1992.

Crystal, David. *Language Death.* New York: Cambridge University Press, 2000.

———. *The Cambridge Encyclopedia of Language.* New York: Cambridge University Press, 1987.

Cumberland, Charles. *Mexico: The Struggle for Modernity.* New York: Oxford University Press, 1968.

Dahl, Robert A. *Who Governs? Democracy and Power in an American City.* New Haven, Conn.: Yale University Press, 1961.

Daniels, Roger. "The Japanese-American Experience, 1890–1940." In *Uncertain Americans: Readings in Ethnic History,* ed. Leonard Dinnerstein and Frederic C. Jaher, 250–76. New York: Oxford University Press, 1977.

David, Henry P. "Involuntary International Migration: Adaptation of Refugees." In *Behavior in New Environments,* ed. Eugene B. Brody, 73–95. Beverly Hills, Calif.: Sage, 1970.

de la Garza, Rodolfo, Louis DeSipio, F. Chris García, John García, and Angelo Falcón. *Latino Voices: Mexican, Cuban, and Puerto Rican Perspectives on American Politics.* Boulder, Colo.: Westview Press, 1992.

DeSipio, Louis, and Rodolfo O. de la Garza. 2002. "Forever Seen as New: Latino Participation in American Elections." In *Latinos, Remaking America,* ed. M. M. Suárez-Orozco and M. M. Paez, 398–409. Berkeley: University of California Press, 2002.

de Souza Martins, José. *Á Immigraçào e a Crise do Brasil Agrario.* São Paulo: Livraría Pioneira, 1973.

DeWind, Josh, Tom Seidl, and Janet Shenk. "Caribbean Migration: Contract Labor in U.S. Agriculture." *NACLA Report on the Americas* 11 (November–December 1977): 437.

Díaz, Rafael M. "Thought and Two Languages: The Impact of Bilingualism on Cognitive Development." *Review of Research in Education* 10 (1983): 23–54.

Díaz-Briquets, Sergio. "Cuban-Owned Business in the United States." *Cuban Studies* 14 (Summer 1985): 57–64.

Díaz-Briquets, Sergio, and Lisandro Pérez. "Cuba: The Demography of Revolution." *Population Bulletin* 36 (April 1981): 2–41.

Dinerman, Ina R. "Patterns of Adaptation among Households of U.S.-Bound Migrants from Michoacán, Mexico." *International Migration Review* 12 (Winter 1978): 485–501.

Dinnerstein, Leonard. "The East European Jewish Migration." In *Uncertain Americans: Readings in Ethnic History,* ed. Leonard Dinnerstein and Frederic C. Jaher, 216–31. New York: Oxford University Press, 1977.

Dixon, Heriberto. "Emigration and Jamaican Employment." *Migration Today* 8 (1980): 24–27.

Dobb, Maurice. *Studies in the Development of Capitalism.* New York: International Publishers [1947] 1963.

Doeringer, Peter B., Philip Moss, and David G. Terkla. "Capitalism and Kinship: Do Institutions Matter in the Labor Market?" *Industrial and Labor Relations Review* 40 (October 1986): 48–59.

Dohrenwend, Barbara S., and Bruce P. Dohrenwend, eds. *Stressful Life Events: Their Nature and Effects.* New York: Wiley, 1974.

Dohrenwend, Bruce P. *Mental Illness in the United States: Epidemiological Estimates.* New York: Praeger, 1980.

Dohrenwend, Bruce P., and Barbara S. Dohrenwend. *Social Status and Psychological Disorder: A Causal Inquiry.* New York: Wiley, 1969.

Dolan, J. P. *The Immigrant Church: New York's Irish and German Catholics.* Baltimore, Md.: Johns Hopkins University Press, 1975.

Duneier, Mitchell. *Slim's Table: Race, Respectability, and Masculinity.* Chicago: University of Chicago Press, 1992.

Durkheim, Emile. *The Elementary Forms of the Religious Life.* New York: Macmillan, 1961.

———. *Suicide: A Study in Sociology.* Trans. J. A. Spaulding and G. Simpson. New York: Free Press, [1897] 1965.

Dupuy, Harold J. "Utility of the National Center for Health Statistics General Well-Being Schedule in the Assessment of Self-Representations of Subjective Well-Being and Distress." National Conference on Education in Alcohol, Drug Abuse, and Mental Health Programs. Washington, D.C.: Department of Health, Education, and Welfare, 1974.

Durand, Jorge, and Patricia Arias. 2000. *La Experiencia Migrante: Iconografía de la Migración México–Estados Unidos.* Guadalajara: Editorial Altexto.

Eaton, William W., and Roberta Garrison. "The Influence of Class and Ethnic Status on Psychopathology and Helpseeking among Two Latin American Refugee Groups." Mimeographed progress report, School of Public Health, Johns Hopkins University, 1988.

Ebaugh, Helen Rose, and Janet Saltzman Chafetz. *Religion and the New Immigrants: Continuities and Adaptations in Immigrant Congregations.* Walnut Creek, Calif.: AltaMira Press, 2000.

Edwards, Richard C. *Contested Terrain: The Transformation of the Workplace in the Twentieth Century.* New York: Harper Torchbooks, 1979.

"'Elegiacal': It Spells Success for Bee Champ." *Los Angeles Times,* June 3, 1988, I1.

Entzinger, Hans B. "Race, Class and the Shaping of a Policy for Immigrants: The Case of the Netherlands." *International Migration Review* 25 (March 1987): 5–20.

Epstein, J. A., G. J. Botvin, and T. Díaz. "Linguistic Acculturation Associated with Higher Marijuana and Polydrug Use among Hispanic Adolescents." *Substance Use and Misuse* 36, no. 4 (2001): 477–99.

Escobar, Cristina. "Transnational Politics and Dual Citizenship: The Colombian Experience in the Latin American Context." Working Paper Series, Center for Migration and Development, Princeton University, 2004.

Espenshade, Thomas J. "Does the Threat of Border Apprehension Deter Undocumented U.S. Migration?" *Population and Development Review* 20 (December 1994): 871–92.

———. "Using INS Border Apprehension Data to Measure the Flow of Undocumented Migrants Crossing the U.S.-Mexico Frontier." *International Migration Review* 29 (Summer 1995): 545–65.

Espenshade, Thomas J., and Jessica L. Baraka. "Implications of the 1996 Welfare and Immigration Reform Acts for US Immigration." *Population and Development Review* 23 (December 1997): 769–801.

Espenshade, Thomas J., and Tracy Ann Goodis. "Are Mexican Immigrant and U.S. Native Workers Substitutes or Complements in Production?" Discussion paper PRIP-UI-3. Washington, D.C.: Urban Institute, 1988.

Espino, Conchita M. "Trauma and Adaptation: The Case of Central American Children." In *Refugee Children: Theory, Research, and Services*, ed. F. L. Ahearn Jr., and J. L. Athey, 106–24. Baltimore, Md.: Johns Hopkins University Press, 1991.

Espinosa, Gastón, Virgilio Elizondo, and Jesse Miranda. *Hispanic Churches in American Public Life: Summary of Findings. Interim Reports*, vol. 2003.2. Notre Dame, Ind.: Institute for Latino Studies, University of Notre Dame, March 2003.

———, eds. *Latino Religions and Civic Activism in the United States*. New York: Oxford University Press, 2005.

Espiritu, Yen Le. *Asian American Panethnicity: Bridging Institutions and Identities*. Philadelphia: Temple University Press, 1992.

Espiritu, Yen Le, and Diane L. Wolf. "The Paradox of Assimilation." In *Ethnicities: Children of Immigrants in America*, ed. Rubén G. Rumbaut and Alejandro Portes, 157–86. Berkeley and New York: University of California Press and Russell Sage Foundation, 2001.

Fabrega, Horacio, Jr. "Social Psychiatric Aspects of Acculturation and Migration: A General Statement." *Comprehensive Psychiatry* 10 (July 1969): 314–29.

Fagen, Patricia W. "Central Americans and U.S. Refugee Asylum Policies." Paper presented at the Conference on Immigration and Refugee Policies sponsored by the Inter-American Dialogue and the University of California, San Diego, 1986.

Fanon, Frantz. *The Wretched of the Earth*. New York: Grove Press, 1968.

Faris, Robert E. L., and H. Warren Dunham. *Mental Disorders in Urban Areas*. Chicago: University of Chicago Press, 1939.

Fasenfest, David, Jason Booza, and Kurt Metzger. *Living Together: A New Look at Racial and Ethnic Integration in Metropolitan Neighborhoods*. Living Cities Census Series. Washington, D.C.: Brookings Institution, 2004.

Favazza, Armando R. "Culture Change and Mental Health." *Journal of Operational Psychiatry* 11 (1980): 101–19.

Feliciano, Cynthia, and Rubén G. Rumbaut. "Gendered Paths: Educational and Occupational Expectations and Outcomes among Adult Children of Immigrants." *Ethnic and Racial Studies* 28, no. 6 (2005): 1087–1118.

Fernández-Kelly, María Patricia. "Social and Cultural Capital in the Urban Ghetto: Implications for the Economic Sociology of Immigration." In *The Economic Sociology of Immigration: Essays in Network, Ethnicity, and Entrepreneurship*, ed. Alejandro Portes, 213–47. New York: Russell Sage Foundation, 1995.

Fernández-Kelly, María Patricia, and Sara Curran. "Nicaraguans: Voices Lost, Voices Found." In *Ethnicities: Children of Immigrants in America*, ed.

Rubén G. Rumbaut and Alejandro Portes. Berkeley and New York: University of California Press and Russell Sage Foundation, 2001.

Fernández-Kelly, María Patricia, and Ana García. "Advanced Technology, Regional Development, and Women's Employment in Southern California." Discussion paper. La Jolla: Center for U.S.-Mexico Studies, University of California, San Diego, 1985.

———. "Informalization at the Core: Hispanic Women, Home Work, and the Advanced Capitalist State." In *The Informal Economy: Studies in Advanced and Less Developed Countries*, ed. Alejandro Portes, Manuel Castells, and Lauren Benton, 247–64. Baltimore, Md.: Johns Hopkins University Press, 1989.

Fernández-Kelly, María Patricia, and Lisa Konczal. "'Murdering the Alphabet': Identity and Entrepreneurship among Second-Generation Cubans, West Indians, and Central Americans." *Ethnic and Racial Studies* 28, no. 6 (2005): 1153–81.

Fernández-Kelly, María Patricia, and Richard Schauffler. "Divided Fates: Immigrant Children in a Restructured U.S. Economy." *International Migration Review* 28 (Winter 1994): 662–89.

Fine, Nathan. *Labor and Farmer Parties in the United States, 1828–1928.* New York: Rand School of Social Science, 1928.

Finke, Roger, and Rodney Stark. *The Churching of America, 1776–1990: Winners and Losers in Our Religious Economy.* New Brunswick, N.J.: Rutgers University Press, 1992.

Fishman, Joshua A., ed. *Language Loyalty in the United States.* The Hague: Mouton, 1966.

———. "Language Maintenance." In *Harvard Encyclopedia of American Ethnic Groups*, ed. Stephan Thernstrom, 629–38. Cambridge, Mass.: Harvard University Press, 1981.

Fitzgerald, David. *Negotiating Extra-Territorial Citizenship: Mexican Migration and the Transnational Politics of Community.* San Diego: Center for Comparative Immigration Studies, University of California, San Diego, 2000.

Fitzpatrick, Joseph. *Puerto Rican Americans: The Meaning of Migration to the Mainland.* 2nd ed. Englewood Cliffs, N.J.: Prentice Hall, 1987.

Fix, Michael E., and Jeffrey S. Passel. "The Door Remains Open: Recent Immigration to the United States and a Preliminary Analysis of the Immigration Act of 1990." Washington, D.C., and Santa Monica, Calif.: Urban Institute and RAND Corporation, 1991.

———. *Immigration and Immigrants: Setting the Record Straight.* Washington, D.C.: Urban Institute, 1994.

Forbes, Susan S. "Residency Patterns and Secondary Migration of Refugees." *Migration News* 34 (January–March 1985): 3–18.

Fordham, Signithia, and John U. Ogbu. "Black Students' School Success: Coping with the Burden of 'Acting White.'" *Urban Review* 18, no. 3 (1987): 176–206.

Frazier, E. Franklin. *The Negro in the United States.* New York: Macmillan, 1949.

Fry, Brian N. 2001. *Responding to Immigration: Perceptions of Promise and Threat*. New York: LFB Scholarly Publishing.

Furnham, Adrian, and Stephen Bochner. *Culture Shock: Psychological Reactions to Unfamiliar Environments*. New York: Methuen, 1986.

Gaertner, Miriam L. "A Comparison of Refugee and Non-Refugee Immigrants to New York City." In *Flight and Resettlement*, ed. H. B. Murphy, 99–112. Lucerne: UNESCO, 1955.

Gamio, Manuel. *Mexican Immigration to the United States*. Chicago: University of Chicago Press, 1930.

Gann, L. H., and Peter J. Duignan. *The Hispanics in the United States: A History*. Boulder, Colo.: Westview Press, 1986.

Gans, Herbert J. "Deconstructing the Underclass." *APA Journal* 56 (Summer 1990): 17.

———. "Second-Generation Decline: Scenarios for the Economic and Ethnic Futures of the Post-1965 American Immigrants." *Ethnic and Racial Studies* 15 (April 1992): 173–92.

García, Cristina. *Dreaming in Cuban*. New York: Ballantine Books, 1992.

García, John A. "Political Integration of Mexican Immigrants: Explorations into the Naturalization Process." *International Migration Review* 15 (1981): 608–25.

García, John A., and Carlos H. Arce. "Political Orientations and Behaviors of Chicanos." In *Latinos and the Political System*, ed. F. C. García, 125–51. Notre Dame, Ind.: Notre Dame University Press, 1988.

García, Mario. *Desert Immigrants: The Mexicans of El Paso, 1880–1920*. New Haven, Conn.: Yale University Press, 1981.

Gardner, Robert W., Bryant Robey, and Peter C. Smith. "Asian Americans: Growth, Change, and Diversity." *Population Bulletin* 40 (October 1985).

Garza-Guerrero, A. C. "Culture Shock: Its Mourning and the Vicissitudes of Identity." *Journal of the American Psychoanalytic Association* 22 (1974): 408–29.

Gedicks, Al. "Ethnicity, Class Solidarity, and Labor Radicalism among Finnish Immigrants in Michigan Copper Country." *Politics and Society* 7 (1977): 127–56.

Geschwender, James A. "The Portuguese and Haoles of Hawaii: Implications for the Origin of Ethnicity." *American Sociological Review* 53 (August 1988): 515–27.

———. *Racial Stratification in America*. Dubuque, Iowa: Brown, 1978.

Gfroerer, J. C., and L. L. Tan. "Substance Use among Foreign-Born Youths in the United States: Does the Length of Residence Matter?" *American Journal of Public Health* 93, no. 11 (2003): 1892–95.

Gibson, Margaret A. *Accommodation without Assimilation: Sikh Immigrants in an American High School*. Ithaca, N.Y.: Cornell University Press, 1989.

———. "Additive Acculturation as a Strategy for School Improvement." In *California's Immigrant Children: Theory, Research, and Implications for Educational Policy*, ed. Rubén G. Rumbaut and Wayne A. Cornelius, 77–105. La Jolla: Center for U.S.-Mexican Studies, University of California, San Diego, 1995.

Gilbert, M. "Alcohol Consumption Patterns in Immigrant and Later Generation Mexican American Women." *Hispanic Journal of Behavioral Sciences* 9 (1989): 299–313.

Glaser, William A., and Christopher Habers. "The Migration and Return of Professionals." *International Migration Review* 8 (Summer 1974): 227–44.

Glazer, Nathan. "Ethnic Groups in America." In *Freedom and Control in Modern Society*, ed. T. A. M. Berger and C. Page, 158–73. New York: Van Nostrand, 1954.

Glazer, Nathan. "Ethnic Groups in America." In *Freedom and Control in Modern Society*, ed. Monroe Berger, Theodore Abel, and Charles Page, 158–73. New York: Van Nostrand, 1954.

Glazer, Nathan, and Daniel P. Moynihan. *Beyond the Melting Pot: The Negroes, Puerto Ricans, Jews, Italians and Irish of New York City.* Cambridge, Mass.: MIT Press, 1970.

Gold, Steven J. *Refugee Communities: A Comparative Field Study.* Newbury Park, Calif.: Sage, 1992.

———. "Refugees and Small Business: The Case of Soviet Jews and Vietnamese." *Ethnic and Racial Studies* 11 (November 1988): 411–38.

Goldring, Luin. "The Mexican State and Transmigrant Organizations: Negotiating the Boundaries of Membership and Participation." *Latin American Research Review* 37 (2002): 55–99.

González, Nancie L. *The Spanish-Americans of New Mexico.* Albuquerque: University of New Mexico Press, 1969.

Goodenough, Florence. "Racial Differences in the Intelligence of Children." *Journal of Experimental Psychology* 9 (October 1926): 392–93.

Gordon, Milton M. *Assimilation in American Life: The Role of Race, Religion, and National Origins.* New York: Oxford University Press, 1964.

Görlach, Mannfred. "Comment." *International Journal of the Sociology of Language* 60 (1986): 97.

Granovetter, Mark. "Economic Action and Social Structure: The Problem of Embeddedness." *American Journal of Sociology* 91 (1985): 481–510.

———. "Small Is Bountiful: Labor Markets and Establishment Size." *American Sociological Review* 49 (June 1984): 323–34.

Grasmuck, Sherri. "Immigration, Ethnic Stratification, and Native Working-Class Discipline: Comparison of Documented and Undocumented Dominicans." *International Migration Review* 18 (Fall 1984): 692–713.

Grasmuck, Sherri, and Patricia Pessar. *Between Two Islands: Dominican International Migration.* Berkeley: University of California Press, 1991.

Grebler, Leo, Joan W. Moore, and Ralph C. Guzmán. *The Mexican-American People: The Nation's Second Largest Minority.* New York: Free Press, 1970.

Greeley, Andrew M. *Why Can't They Be Like Us? America's White Ethnic Groups.* New York: Dutton, 1971.

Greeley, Andrew, and Michael Hout. "American's Increasing Belief in Life after Death: Religious Competition and Acculturation." *American Sociological Review* 64 (December 1999): 813–35.

Grenier, Guillermo, and Lisandro Pérez. *The Legacy of Exile: Cubans in the United States.* Boston: Allyn and Bacon, 2003.

Griffith, Jim. *Saints of the Southwest*. Tucson, Ariz.: Río Nuevo Publishers, 2000.

Groeneman, Sid, and Gary Tobin. *The Decline of Religious Identity in the United States*. San Francisco: Institute for Jewish and Community Research, 2004.

Guarnizo, Luis E. "The Economics of Transnational Living." *International Migration Review* 37 (Fall 2003): 666–99.

———. "The Rise of Transnational Social Formations: Mexican and Dominican State Responses to Transnational Migration." *Political Power and Social Theory* 12 (1998): 45–94.

Guarnizo, Luis E., Alejandro Portes, and William J. Haller. "Assimilation and Transnationalism: Determinants of Transnational Political Action among Contemporary Immigrants." *American Journal of Sociology* 108 (May 2003): 1211–48.

Guarnizo, Luis E., Arturo I. Sánchez, and Elizabeth Roach. "Mistrust, Fragmented Solidarity, and Transnational Migration: Colombians in New York and Los Angeles." *Ethnic and Racial Studies* 22 (March 1999): 367–96.

Guarnizo, Luis E., and Michael P. Smith. "The Locations of Transnationalism." In *Transnationalism from Below*, ed. M. P. Smith and L. E. Guarnizo, 3–34. New Brunswick, N.J.: Transaction Books, 1998.

Guendelman, Silvia, and B. Abrams. "Dietary Intake among Mexican American Women: Generational Differences and a Comparison with White Non-Hispanic Women." *American Journal of Public Health* 85, no. 1 (1995): 20–25.

Guendelman, Silvia, J. Gould, M. Hudes, and B. Eskanazi. "Generational Differences in Perinatal Health among the Mexican American Population: Findings from HHANES 1982–84." *American Journal of Public Health*, supplement, 80 (1990): 61–65.

Gutiérrez, David G. "Migration, Ethnicity, and the 'Third Space': Shifting Politics of Nationalism in Greater Mexico." *Journal of American History* 86 (September 1999): 1–41.

Haines, David W., ed. *Refugees as Immigrants: Cambodians, Laotians and Vietnamese in America*. Totowa, N.J.: Rowman & Littlefield, 1989.

———. *Refugees in the United States: A Reference Handbook*. Westport, Conn.: Greenwood Press, 1985.

Hakuta, Kenji. *Mirror of Language: The Debate on Bilingualism*. New York: Basic Books, 1986.

Hamilton, Denise. "San Gabriel Student Garners 'Nobel' for High School Science." *Los Angeles Times*, March 5, 1991, A1.

Handlin, Oscar. *Boston's Immigrants: A Study of Acculturation*. Cambridge, Mass.: Harvard University Press, 1941.

———. *The Uprooted*. 2nd enlarged ed. Boston: Little, Brown, 1973.

———. *The Uprooted: The Epic Story of the Great Migrations That Made the American People*. Boston: Little, Brown, 1951.

Harris, Kathleen Mullan. "The Health Status and Risk Behavior of Adolescents in Immigrant Families." In *Children of Immigrants: Health, Adjustment, and Public Assistance*, ed. Donald J. Hernández. Washington, D.C.: National Academy of Sciences Press, 1999.

Harrison, Bennett, and Barry Bluestone. *The Great U-Turn*. New York: Basic Books, 1988.

Haynes, S. G., C. Harvey, H. Montes, H. Nicken, and B. H. Cohen. "Patterns of Cigarette Smoking among Hispanics in the United States: Results from the HHANES 1982–84." *American Journal of Public Health*, supplement, 80 (1990): 47–53.

Hechter, Michael. *Internal Colonialism: The Celtic Fringe in British National Development, 1536–1966*. Berkeley: University of California Press, 1977.

Hein, Jeremy. *From Vietnam, Laos, and Cambodia: A Refugee Experience in the United States*. New York: Twayne Publishers, 1995.

Henry, William. "Against a Confusion of Tongues." *Time*, June 13, 1983, 30–31.

Herberg, Will. *Protestant, Catholic, Jew: An Essay in American Religious Sociology*. Rev. ed. Garden City, N.Y.: Anchor Books, 1960.

Higham, John. *Strangers in the Land: Patterns of American Nativism, 1896–1925*. New Brunswick, N.J.: Rutgers University Press, 1955.

Hing, Bill Ong. *Making and Remaking Asian America through Immigration Policy, 1850–1990*. Stanford, Calif.: Stanford University Press, 1993.

Hirschman, Albert O. *Exit, Voice, and Loyalty: Responses to Decline in Firms, Organizations, and States*. Cambridge, Mass.: Harvard University Press, 1970.

———. *Getting Ahead Collectively: Grassroots Experiences in Latin America*. New York: Pergamon Press, 1984.

Hirschman, Charles. "The Role of Religion in the Origins and Adaptation of Immigrant Groups in the United States." *International Migration Review* 38 (Fall 2004): 1206–33.

Hirschman, Charles, and Luis Falcón. "The Educational Attainment of Religio-Ethnic Groups in the United States." *Research in Sociology of Education and Socialization* 5 (1985): 83–120.

Hirschman, Charles, and Morrison G. Wong. "The Extraordinary Educational Attainment of Asian Americans: A Search for Historical Evidence and Explanations." *Social Forces* 65 (September 1986): 127.

Hoffman, Eva. *Lost in Translation: A Life in a New Language*. New York: Penguin Books, 1990.

Hollifield, James. "The Emerging Migration State." *International Migration Review* 38 (Fall 2004): 885–912.

Hollingshead, August B., and F. C. Redlich. *Social Class and Mental Illness: A Community Study*. New York: Wiley, 1958.

Hondagneu-Sotelo, Pierrette. *Gendered Transitions: Mexican Experiences of Immigration*. Berkeley: University of California Press, 1994.

Hough, Richard L. "Utilization of Health and Mental Health Services by Los Angeles Mexican Americans and Non-Hispanic Whites." *Archives of General Psychiatry* 44 (August 1987): 702–9.

Hout, Michael, and Claude Fischer. "Why More Americans Have No Religious Preference: Politics and Generations." *American Sociological Review* 67 (April 2002): 165–90.

Hout, Michael and Andrew Greeley. "The Center Doesn't Hold: Church Attendance in the United States, 1940–1984." *American Sociological Review* 52 (1987): 325–45.

Howe, Irving. *World of Our Fathers*. New York: Harcourt Brace and Jovanovich, 1976.

Huntington, Samuel P. *The Clash of Civilizations and the Remaking of World Order*. New York: Touchstone Books, 1997.

———. "The Hispanic Challenge." *Foreign Policy* (March–April 2004): 30–45.

———. *Who Are We? The Challenges to America's National Identity*. New York: Simon and Schuster, 2004.

Hurh, Won Moo, and Kwang Chung Kim. "Religious Participation of Korean Immigrants in the United States." *Journal for the Scientific Study of Religion* 29 (1990): 19–34.

Huynh, Thuan. "Center for Vietnamese Buddhism: Recreating Home." In *Religion and the New Immigrants*, ed. H. R. Ebaugh and J. S. Chafetz, 163–79. New York: AltaMira Press, 2000.

Ibarra, Rafael. "Looking at Proposition 187 through the Eyes of an Illegal Valedictorian." *Los Angeles Times*, November 6, 1994, M6.

"Immigrants: The Changing Face of America." *Time*, July 8, 1985, 31.

Itzigsohn, Jose, Carlos Dore, Esther Fernández, and Obed Vázquez. "Mapping Dominican Transnationalism: Narrow and Broad Transnational Practices." *Ethnic and Racial Studies* 22 (March 1999): 316–39.

Jacob, Simon, and Pallavi Thakur. "Jyothi Hindu Temple: One Religion, Many Practices." In *Religion and the New Immigrants*, ed. H. R. Ebaugh and J. S. Chafetz, 151–62. New York: AltaMira Press, 2000.

Jarvis, Edward. "Influence of Distance from Nearness to an Insane Hospital on Its Use by the People." *American Journal of Insanity* 22 (January 1866): 361–406.

———. *Insanity and Idiocy in Massachusetts: Report of the Commission on Lunacy, 1855*, intro. Gerald N. Grob. 1855. Reprint, Cambridge, Mass.: Harvard University Press, 1971.

Jasso, Guillermina, and Mark R. Rosenzweig. *The New Chosen People: Immigrants in the United States*. New York: Russell Sage Foundation, 1990.

Jencks, Christopher. *Rethinking Social Policy: Race, Poverty, and the Underclass*. Cambridge, Mass.: Harvard University Press, 1992.

Jensen, Leif. "Children of the New Immigration: A Comparative Analysis of Today's Second Generation." Working paper #1990-32. University Park: Institute for Policy Research and Evaluation, Pennsylvania State University, 1990.

———. "The Demographic Diversity of Immigrants and Their Children." In *Ethnicities: Children of Immigrants in America*, ed. Rubén G. Rumbaut and Alejandro Portes, 21–56. Berkeley and New York: University of California Press and Russell Sage Foundation, 2001.

Jensen, Leif, and Yoshimi Chitose. "Today's Second Generation: Evidence from the 1990 U.S. Census." *International Migration Review* 28 (1994): 714–73.

Jerome, Harry. *Migration and Business Cycles.* New York: National Bureau of Economic Research, 1926.

Jonas, Susanne, and Christopher Chase-Dunn. "Guatemalan Development and Modernization: Past, Present, and Future." In *Globalization on the Ground: Postbellum Guatemalan Democracy and Development*, ed. C. Chase-Dunn, S. Jonas, and N. Amaro, 3–7. Lanham, Md.: Rowman and Littlefield, 2001.

Kanjanapan, Wilawan. "The Immigration of Asian Professionals to the United States, 1988–1990." *International Migration Review* 29, no. 1 (1995): 7–32.

Kao, Grace, and Marta Tienda. "Optimism and Achievement: The Educational Performance of Immigrant Youth." *Social Science Quarterly* 76, no. 1 (1995): 1–19.

Kaplan, M., and G. Marks. "Adverse Effects of Acculturation: Psychological Distress among Mexican American Young Adults." *Social Science and Medicine* 31, no. 12 (1990): 1313–19.

Karno, Marvin, and Richard L. Hough. "Lifetime Prevalence of Specific Psychiatric Disorders among Mexican Americans and Non-Hispanic Whites in Los Angeles." *Archives of General Psychiatry* 44 (August 1987): 695–701.

Karoly, Lynn A. *The Trend in Inequality among Families, Individuals, and Workers in the United States: A Twenty-Five Year Perspective.* Santa Monica, Calif.: RAND Corporation, 1992.

Kasinitz, Philip, Juan Battle, and Inés Miyares. "Fade to Black? The Children of West Indian Immigrants in South Florida." In *Ethnicities: Children of Immigrants in America*, ed. Rubén G. Rumbaut and Alejandro Portes, 267–300. Berkeley and New York: University of California Press and Russell Sage Foundation, 2001.

Keller, S. L. *Uprooting and Social Change: The Role of Refugees in Development.* Delhi: Manohar Book Service, 1975.

Kessler, R. C., and P. D. Cleary. "Social Class and Psychological Distress." *American Sociological Review* 45 (June 1980): 463–78.

Kibria, Nazli. *Family Tightrope: The Changing Lives of Vietnamese Americans.* Princeton, N.J.: Princeton University Press, 1993.

"Kids Who Know Where It's At . . . ." *U.S. News & World Report*, June 10, 1996, 22.

Kim, Illsoo. *New Urban Immigrants: The Korean Community in New York.* Princeton, N.J.: Princeton University Press, 1981.

Kim, Kwang Chung, and Won Moo Hurh. "Two Dimensions of Korean Immigrants' Sociocultural Adaptation: Americanization and Ethnic Attachment." Paper presented at the annual meeting of the American Sociological Association, Atlanta, August 1988.

Kim, Kwang Chung, and Shin Kim. "The Ethnic Roles of Korean Immigrant Churches in the United States. In *Korean Americans and Their Religions: Pilgrims and Missionaries from a Different Shore*, ed. Ho-Youn Kwan, Kwang Chung Kim, and R. Stephen Warner, 71–94. University Park: Pennsylvania State University Press, 2001.

Kimbro, R. T., S. M. Lynch, and S. McLanahan. "The Hispanic Paradox and Breastfeeding: Does Acculturation Matter? Evidence from the Fragile Families Study." Center for Research on Child Wellbeing Working Paper #04-01. Princeton, N.J.: Princeton University, 2004.

Kinzie, J. David, and Spero Manson. "Five Years' Experience with Indochinese Refugee Psychiatric Patients." *Journal of Operational Psychiatry* 14 (1983): 105–11.

Kinzie, J. David, and William Sack. "Severely Traumatized Cambodian Children: Research Findings and Clinical Implications." In *Refugee Children: Theory, Research, and Services*, ed. F. L. Ahearn Jr. and J. L. Athey, 92–105. Baltimore, Md.: Johns Hopkins University Press, 1991.

Kircheman, Joleen, and Kathryn M. Neckerman. "We Love to Hire Them but . . . : The Meaning of Race to Employers." In *The Urban Underclass*, ed. C. Jencks and P. E. Peterson. Washington, D.C.: Brookings Institution, 1991.

Kirkpatrick, Clifford. *Intelligence and Immigration*. Baltimore, Md.: Williams and Wilkins, 1926.

Kivisto, Peter. *Immigrant Socialists in the United States: The Case of Finns and the Left*. Rutherford, N.J.: Farleigh Dickinson University Press, 1984.

Kohn, Melvin L. "Social Class and Schizophrenia: A Critical Review and Reformulation." *Schizophrenia Bulletin* 7 (Winter 1973): 60–79.

Kraut, Alan M. *The Huddled Masses: The Immigrant in American Society, 1880–1921*. Arlington Heights, Ill.: Harlan Davidson, 1982.

———. *Silent Travelers: Germs, Genes, and the "Immigrant Menace."* New York: Basic Books, 1994.

Kunz, Egon F. "Exile and Resettlement: Refugee Theory." *International Migration Review* 15 (Spring–Summer 1981): 42–51.

———. "The Refugee in Flight: Kinetic Models and Forms of Displacement." *International Migration Review* 7 (Summer 1973): 125–46.

Kuo, Wen H., and Yung-Mei Tsai. "Social Networking, Hardiness and Immigrants' Mental Health." *Journal of Health and Social Behavior* 27 (June 1986): 133–49.

Kwon, Okyun. *Buddhist and Protestant Korean Immigrants: Religious Beliefs and Socioeconomic Aspects of Life*. New York: LFB Scholarly, 2004.

Kyle, David. "The Transnational Peasant: The Social Structures of Economic Migration from the Ecuadoran Andes." Ph.D. diss., Johns Hopkins University, 1995.

Lamm, Richard D., and Gary Imhoff. *The Immigration Time Bomb: The Fragmenting of America*. New York: Dutton, 1985.

Landale, Nancy S., and R. S. Oropesa. "Immigrant Children and the Children of Immigrants: Inter- and Intra-Ethnic Group Differences in the United States." Population Research Group (PRG) Research Paper 95-2. East Lansing: Institute for Public Policy and Social Research, Michigan State University, 1995.

Landale, Nancy S., R. S. Oropesa, and B. K. Gorman. "Immigration and Infant Health: Birth Outcomes of Immigrant and Native Women." In *Children of Immigrants: Health, Adjustment, and Public Assistance*, ed. Donald J. Hernández, 244–85. Washington, D.C.: National Academy Press, 1999.

Landolt, Patricia. "The Causes and Consequences of Transnational Migration: Salvadorans in Los Angeles and Washington DC." Ph.D. diss., Johns Hopkins University, 2000.

———. "Salvadoran Economic Transnationalism: Embedded Strategies for Household Maintenance, Immigrant Incorporation, and Entrepreneurial Expansion." *Global Networks* 1 (2001): 217–42.

Landolt, Patricia, Lilian Autler, and Sonia Baires. "From '*Hermano Lejano*' to '*Hermano Mayor*': The Dialectics of Salvadoran Transnationalism." *Ethnic and Racial Studies* 22 (1999): 290–315.

Landry, Walter. "Comment." *International Journal of the Sociology of Language* 60 (1986): 129–38.

Langner, Thomas S., and Stanley T. Michael. *Life Stress and Mental Health: The Midtown Manhattan Study*, vol. 2. London: Collier-Macmillan, 1963.

Laponce, J. A. *Languages and Their Territories*. Trans. Anthony Martin-Sperry. Toronto: University of Toronto Press, 1987.

Larkin, E. *The Historical Dimensions of Irish Catholicism*. Washington, D.C.: Catholic University of America Press, 1984.

Lebergott, Stanley. *Manpower in Economic Growth: The American Record Since 1800*. New York: McGraw-Hill, 1964.

LeMay, Michael C. *Anatomy of a Public Policy: The Reform of Contemporary American Immigration Law*. Westport, Conn.: Praeger, 1994.

Lenneberg, Eric H. *Biological Foundations of Language*. New York: Wiley, 1967.

Leopold, Werner F. *Speech Development of a Bilingual Child*. Evanston, Ill.: Northwestern University Press, 1939, 1947, 1949.

Levine, Barry. *The Caribbean Exodus*. New York: Praeger, 1987.

Levitt, Peggy. "Transnational Migration: Taking Stock and Future Directions." *Global Networks* 1 (2001): 195–216.

———. *The Transnational Villagers*. Berkeley: University of California Press, 2001.

———. "Transnationalizing Community Development: The Case of Migration between Boston and the Dominican Republic." *Voluntary Sector Quarterly* 26 (1997): 509–26.

Lieberson, Stanley. *Language and Ethnic Relations in Canada*. New York: Wiley, 1970.

———. *Language Diversity and Language Contact*. Stanford, Calif.: Stanford University Press, 1981.

———. *A Piece of the Pie: Blacks and White Immigrants since 1880*. Berkeley: University of California Press, 1980.

———. "You Know, Abraham Was Really the First Immigrant: Religion and Transnational Migration." *International Migration Review* 37 (Fall 2003): 847–73.

Lieberson, Stanley, Guy Dalto, and Mary Ellen Johnston. "The Course of Mother Tongue Diversity in Nations." *American Journal of Sociology* 81 (July 1975): 34–61.

Lieberson, Stanley, and Lynn K. Hansen. "National Development, Mother Tongue Diversity, and the Comparative Study of Nations." *American Sociological Review* 39 (August 1974): 523–41.

Lieberson, Stanley, and Mary C. Waters. "The Location of Ethnic and Racial Groups in the United States." *Sociological Forum* 2 (Fall 1987): 780–810.

Light, Ivan. "Asian Enterprise in America: Chinese, Japanese, and Koreans in Small Business." In *Self-Help in Urban America*, ed. Scott Cummings, 33–57. New York: Kennikat Press, 1980.

———. "Disadvantaged Minorities in Self-Employment." *International Journal of Comparative Sociology* 20 (March–June 1979): 31–45.

———. *Ethnic Enterprise in America: Business and Welfare among Chinese, Japanese, and Blacks.* Berkeley: University of California Press, 1972.

———. "Immigrant and Ethnic Enterprise in North America." *Ethnic and Racial Studies* 7 (April 1984): 195–216.

Light, Ivan, and Edna Bonacich. *Immigrant Entrepreneurs: Koreans in Los Angeles, 1965–1982.* Berkeley: University of California Press, 1988.

Light, Ivan, and Steven J. Gold. *Ethnic Economies.* San Francisco: Academic Press, 2000.

Light, Ivan, and Carolyn Rosenstein. "Expanding the Interaction Theory of Entrepreneurship." In *The Economic Sociology of Immigration*, ed. A. Portes. New York: Russell Sage Foundation, 1995.

Lin, Ann Chich, and Amaney Jamal. "Muslim, Arab, and American: The Adaptation of Muslim Arab Immigrant to American Society." In *The Religious Lives of American Immigrants: Past and Present*, ed. R. Alba and A. Raboteau. New York: Russell Sage Foundation, forthcoming.

Lin, Keh-Ming, Laurie Tazuma, and Minoru Masuda. "Adaptational Problems of Vietnamese Refugees: I. Health and Mental Health Status." *Archives of General Psychiatry* 36 (August 1979): 955–61.

Link, Bruce, and Bruce P. Dohrenwend. "Formulation of Hypotheses about the True Prevalence of Demoralization." In *Mental Illness in the United States: Epidemiological Estimates*, ed. Bruce P. Dohrenwend, 114–32. New York: Praeger, 1980.

Linton, Ralph. "One Hundred Per-Cent American." *American Mercury* 40 (1937): 427–29.

Lipset, Seymour M., and Reinhard Bendix. *Social Mobility in Industrial Society.* Berkeley: University of California Press, 1959.

Liu, William T., Maryanne Lamanna, and Alicia Murata. *Transition to Nowhere: Vietnamese Refugees in America.* Nashville, Tenn.: Charter House, 1979.

Loo, Chalsa M. "The 'Biliterate' Ballot Controversy: Language Acquisition and Cultural Shift among Immigrants." *International Migration Review* 19 (Fall 1985): 493–515.

López, David E. "Chicano Language Loyalty in an Urban Setting." *Sociology and Social Research* 62 (1978): 267–78.

———. *Language Maintenance and Shift in the United States Today: The Basic Patterns and Their Social Implications.* 4 vols. Los Alamitos, Calif.: National Center for Bilingual Research, 1982.

———. *The Maintenance of Spanish over Three Generations in the United States.* Los Alamitos, Calif.: National Center for Bilingual Research, 1982.

———. "Whither the Flock? The Catholic Church and the Success of Mexicans in America." In *The Religious Lives of American Immigrants: Past and*

Present, ed. R. Alba and A. Raboteau. New York: Russell Sage Foundation, forthcoming.

López, David E., and Ricardo Stanton-Salazar. "Mexican-Americans: A Second Generation at Risk." In *Ethnicities: Children of Immigrants in America*, ed. Rubén G. Rumbaut and Alejandro Portes, 57–90. Berkeley and New York: University of California Press and Russell Sage Foundation, 2001.

Mackey, William F. *Bilingualism as a World Problem*. Montreal: Harvest House, 1967.

Madhavan, M. C. "Indian Emigrants: Numbers, Characteristics, and Economic Impact." *Population and Development Review* 11 (September 1985): 457–81.

———. "Migration of Skilled People from Developing to Developed Countries: Characteristics, Consequences, and Policies." Paper presented at the United Nations Development Program Conference on Transfer of Knowledge through Expatriate Nations, New Delhi, India, February 1988.

Mahler, Sarah J. *American Dreaming: Immigrant Life at the Margins*. Princeton, N.J.: Princeton University Press, 1995.

Mailman, Stanley, and Stephen Yalel-Loehr. "Immigration Reform: Restrictionists Win in the House." *New York Law Journal*, December 28, 2005, 1–6.

Maldonado, Edwin. "Contract Labor and the Origin of Puerto Rican Communities in the United States." *International Migration Review* 13 (Spring 1979): 103–21.

Malzberg, Benjamin. "Mental Disease and 'the Melting Pot.'" *Journal of Nervous and Mental Disease* 72 (October 1930): 379–95.

———. "Mental Disease in New York State According to Nativity and Parentage." *Mental Hygiene* 19 (October 1935): 635–60.

———. *Social and Biological Aspects of Mental Disease*. Utica, N.Y.: State Hospitals Press, 1940.

Malzberg, Benjamin, and Everett S. Lee. *Migration and Mental Disease: A Study of First Admissions to Hospitals for Mental Disease, New York, 1939–1941*. New York: Social Science Research Council, 1956.

Mannheim, Karl. *Ideology and Utopia*. New York: Harcourt, Brace, and World, 1936.

Margolis, Maxine L. *Little Brazil: An Ethnography of Brazilian Immigrants in New York City*. Princeton, N.J.: Princeton University Press, 1994.

Markides, K. S., and J. Coreil. "The Health of Hispanics in the Southwestern United States: An Epidemiological Paradox." *Public Health Reports* 101 (1986): 253–65.

Markides, K. S., N. Krause, and C. F. Mendes de León. "Acculturation and Alcohol Consumption among Mexican Americans." *American Journal of Public Health* 78 (1998): 1178–81.

Marks, G., M. García, and J. Solis. "Health Risk Behaviors in Hispanics in the United States: Findings from HHANES 1982–84." *American Journal of Public Health*, supplement, 80 (1990): 20–26.

Marris, Peter. *Loss and Change*. Garden City, N.Y.: Doubleday, 1975.

Marshall, David F. "The Question of an Official Language: Language Rights and the English Language Amendment." *International Journal of the Sociology of Language* 60 (1986): 7–75.

Martínez, Cervando, Jr. "Mexican-Americans." In *Cross-Cultural Mental Health*, ed. Lillian Comas-Díaz and Ezra E. H. Griffith, 262–302. New York: Wiley, 1988.

Massey, Douglas S. "Do Undocumented Immigrants Earn Lower Wages Than Legal Immigrants? New Evidence from Mexico." *International Migration Review* 21 (Summer 1987): 236–74.

———. "Foolish Fences." *Washington Post*, November 29, 2005, A23. http://www.washingtonpost.com/wp-dyn/content/article/2005/11/29/AR2005112901101.html.

———. "Latinos, Poverty, and the Underclass: A New Agenda for Research." *Hispanic Journal of Behavioral Sciences* 15 (November 1993): 449–75.

———. "The Settlement Process among Mexican Immigrants to the United States." *American Sociological Review* 51 (October 1986): 670–84.

———. "Social Structure, Household Strategies, and the Cumulative Causation of Migration." *Population Index* 56 (1990): 3–26.

———. "Testimony before Immigration Subcommittee." Senate Committee on the Judiciary, Washington, D.C.: U.S. Senate, May 26, 2005.

———. "Understanding Mexican Migration to the United States." *American Journal of Sociology* 92 (May 1987): 1372–1403.

Massey, Douglas S., Rafael Alarcón, Jorge Durand, and Humberto González. *Return to Atzlán: The Social Process of International Migration from Western Mexico*. Berkeley: University of California Press, 1987.

Massey, Douglas S., Joaquín Arango, Graeme Hugo, Ali Kouaouci, Adela Pellegrino, and J. Edward Taylor. *Worlds in Motion: Understanding International Migration at the End of the Millennium*. New York: Oxford University Press, 1998.

Massey, Douglas S., and Chiara Capoferro. "Measuring Undocumented Migration." *International Migration Review* 38 (Fall 2004): 1075–1102.

Massey, Douglas S., and Jorge Durand. *Miracles on the Border: Retablos of Mexican Migrants to the United States*. Tucson: University of Arizona Press, 1995.

Massey, Douglas S., Jorge Durand, and Nolan J. Malone. *Beyond Smoke and Mirrors*. New York: Russell Sage Foundation, 2003.

Massey, Douglas S., and Kristin E. Espinosa, "What's Driving Mexico-U.S. Migration? A Theoretical, Empirical and Policy Analysis." *American Journal of Sociology* 102, no. 4 (1997): 939–99.

Massey, Douglas S., and Felipe García España. "The Social Process of International Migration." *Science* 237 (1987): 733–38.

Massey, Douglas S., and L. Goldring. "Continuities in Transnational Migration: An Analysis of Nineteen Mexican Communities." *American Journal of Sociology* 99 (May 1994): 1492–1533.

Massey, Douglas S., and Deborah Hirst. "From Escalator to Hourglass: Changes in the U.S. Occupational Structure: 1949-1989." *Social Science Research* 27 (1998): 51–71.

Masuda, Minoru, Keh-Ming Lin, and Laurie Tazuma. "Adaptational Problems of Vietnamese Refugees: II. Life Changes and Perceptions of Life Events." *Archives of General Psychiatry* 37 (April 1980): 447–50.

Matthei, Linda M., and David A. Smith. "Women, Households, and Transnational Migration Networks: The Garifuna and Global Economic Restructuring." In *Latin America in the World Economy*, ed. R. P. Korzeniewicz and W. C. Smith, 133–49. Westport, Conn.: Greenwood Press, 1996.

Matute-Bianchi, María Eugenia. "Ethnic Identities and Patterns of School Success and Failure among Mexican-Descent and Japanese-American Students in a California High School." *American Journal of Education* 95 (November 1986): 233–55.

———. "Situational Ethnicity and Patterns of School Performance among Immigrant and Nonimmigrant Mexican-Descent Students." In *Minority Status and Schooling: A Comparative Study of Immigrant and Involuntary Minorities*, ed. Margaret A. Gibson and John U. Ogbu, 205–47. New York: Garland, 1991.

McCoy, Terry L. "The Political Economy of Caribbean Workers in the Florida Sugar Industry." Mimeograph, paper presented at the fifth annual meeting of the Caribbean Studies Association, Willemstad, Curaçao, May 1980.

Meinhardt, Kenneth, Soleng Tom, Philip Tse, and Connie Young Yu. "Southeast Asian Refugees in the 'Silicon Valley': The Asian Health Assessment Project." *Amerasia* 12 (1985–1986): 43–65.

Menjívar, Cecilia. *Fragmented Ties: Salvadoran Immigrant Networks in America*. Berkeley: University of California Press, 2000.

———. "Religion and Immigration in Comparative Perspective: Salvadorans in Catholic and Evangelical Communities in San Francisco, Phoenix, and Washington D.C." *Sociology of Religion* 64, no. 1 (2003): 21–45.

———. "Religious Institutions and Transnationalism: A Case Study of Catholic and Evangelical Salvadoran Immigrants." *International Journal of Politics, Culture and Society* 12, no. 4 (1999): 589–612.

Mezey, A. G. "Psychiatric Illness in Hungarian Refugees." *Journal of Mental Science* 106 (April 1960): 628–37.

Miller, Jake C. *The Plight of Haitian Refugees*. New York: Praeger, 1984.

Miller, Kerby A. *Emigrants and Exiles: Ireland and the Irish Exodus to North America*. New York: Oxford University Press, 1985.

Min, Pyong Gap, ed. *Asian Americans: Contemporary Trends and Issues*. 2nd ed. Thousand Oaks, Calif.: Sage, 2005.

———. "Ethnic Business and Economic Mobility: Korean Immigrants in Los Angeles." Paper presented at the meetings of the American Sociological Association, Atlanta, August 1988.

———. "Korean Americans." In *Asian Americans: Contemporary Trends and Issues*, ed. Pyong Gap Min, 230–59. Thousand Oaks, Calif.: Sage, 2005.

———. *Middlemen in Contemporary America: Koreans in New York and Los Angeles, 1970–1994*. Berkeley: University of California Press, 1996.

Min, Pyong Gap, and Jung Ha Kim. *Religions in Asian America: Building Faith Communities*. New York: AltaMira Press, 2002.

Mink, Gwendolyn. *Old Labor and New Immigrants in American Political Development*. Ithaca, N.Y.: Cornell University Press, 1986.

Mirande, Alfredo. *The Chicano Experience*. Notre Dame, Ind.: Notre Dame University Press, 1985.

Mirowsky, John, and Catherine E. Ross. "Mexican Culture and Its Emotional Contradictions." *Journal of Health and Social Behavior* 25 (March 1984): 2–13.

———. "Paranoia and the Structure of Powerlessness." *American Sociological Review* 48 (April 1983): 228–39.

———. *Social Causes of Psychological Distress*. New York: Aldine de Gruyter, 1989.

———. "Social Patterns of Distress." *Annual Review of Sociology* 12 (1986): 23–45.

Molesky, Jean. "The Exiled: Pathology of Central American Refugees." *Migration World* 14 (1986): 19–23.

Mollica, Richard F., and James P. Lavelle. "Southeast Asian Refugees." In *Clinical Guidelines in Cross-Cultural Mental Health*, ed. Lillian Comas-Díaz and Ezra E. H. Griffith, 262–302. New York: Wiley, 1988.

Mooney, Margarita. *Religion in the Haitian Communities of Miami, Montreal, and Paris*. Ph.D. diss., Princeton University, 2005.

Moore, Joan, and Harry Pachón. *Hispanics in the United States*. Englewood Cliffs, N.J.: Prentice Hall, 1985.

Morales, Rick, and Richard Mines. "San Diego's Full-Service Restaurants: A View from the Back of the House." La Jolla: Center for U.S.-Mexico Studies, University of California, San Diego, 1985.

Moscicki, E. K., B. Z. Locke, D. S. Rae, et al. "Depressive Symptoms among Mexican Americans: The Hispanic Health and Nutrition Examination Survey." *American Journal of Epidemiology* 130 (1989): 348–60.

Moynihan, Daniel P. *Maximum Feasible Misunderstanding*. New York: Random House, 1969.

Muller, Thomas, and Thomas J. Espenshade. *The Fourth Wave: California's Newest Immigrants*. Washington, D.C.: Urban Institute, 1985.

Murphy, H. B. M., ed. *Flight and Resettlement*. Geneva: UNESCO, 1955.

Muskal, Michael, and Carol J. Williams. "Immigrants Take Economic Impact to the Streets." *Los Angeles Times*, May 1, 2006, A1.

Myers, Dowell, Joel Pitkin, and Julie Park. "California Demographic Futures: Projections to 2030, by Immigrant Generations, Nativity, and Time of Arrival in U.S." Report of the Population Dynamics Research Group. Los Angeles: University of Southern California, 2005.

Nagel, Joane. "The Political Construction of Ethnicity." In *Competitive Ethnic Relations*, ed. Joane Nagel and Susan Olzak, 93–112. Orlando, Fla.: Academic Press, 1986.

Nahirny, Vladimir C., and Joshua A. Fishman. "American Immigrant Groups: Ethnic Identification and the Problem of Generations." *Sociological Review* NS13 (1965): 311–26.

National Center on Addiction and Substance Abuse (CASA). *Behind Bars: Substance Abuse and America's Prison Population*. New York: CASA, Columbia University, 1998.

Nee, Victor, and Jimy Sanders. "The Road to Parity: Determinants of the Socio-Economic Achievement of Asian Americans." *Ethnic and Racial Studies* 8 (January 1985): 75–93.

Nelson, Candace, and Marta Tienda. "The Structuring of Hispanic Ethnicity: Historical and Contemporary Perspectives." *Ethnic and Racial Studies* 8 (January 1985): 49–74.

"The New Whiz Kids." *Time*, August 31, 1987, 42, 44, 46.

Nicassio, Perry M. "Psychosocial Correlates of Alienation: Study of a Sample of Indochinese Refugees." *Journal of Cross-Cultural Psychology* 14 (September 1983): 337–51.

Nishi, Setsuko Matsunaga. "Japanese Americans." In *Asian Americans: Contemporary Trends and Issues*, ed. Pyong Gap Min, 95–133. Thousand Oaks, Calif.: Sage, 1995.

North American Congress on Latin America (NACLA). "Undocumented Immigrant Workers in New York City." *Latin American and Empire Report* 12 (November–December 1979), special issue.

North, David S. *The Log Gray Welcome: A Study of the American Naturalization Program*. Washington, D.C.: Report to the National Association of Latino Elected Officials (NALEO), 1985.

North, David S., and Marion F. Houstoun. "The Characteristics and Role of Illegal Aliens in the U.S. Labor Market." Mimeograph. Washington, D.C.: Linton, 1976.

Oberg, K. "Cultural Shock: Adjustment to New Cultural Environments." *Practical Anthropology* 7 (1960): 177–82.

Ødegaard, Ørnulv. "The Distribution of Mental Diseases in Norway." *Acta Psychiatrica et Neurologica* 20 (1945): 247–84.

———. "Emigration and Insanity: A Study of Mental Disease among the Norwegian-Born Population of Minnesota." *Acta Psychiatrica et Neurologica*, supplement, 4 (1932): 1–206.

Office of Immigration Statistics. *2002 Yearbook of Immigration Statistics* Washington, D.C.: U.S. Department of Homeland Security, 2003.

———. *2003 Yearbook of Immigration Statistics*, Washington, D.C.: U.S. Department of Homeland Security, 2004.

Ogbu, John U. "Variability in Minority School Performance: A Problem in Search of an Explanation." *Anthropology of Education Quarterly* 18 (December 1987): 312–34.

Olsen, Laurie. "Crossing the Schoolhouse Border: Immigrant Children in California." *Phi Delta Kappan* 70 (November 1988): 2–11.

———. *Crossing the Schoolhouse Border: Immigrant Students and the California Public Schools*. San Francisco: California Tomorrow, 1988.

Olson, James S., and Judith E. Olson. *Cuban Americans: From Trauma to Triumph*. New York: Twayne Publishers, 1995.

Oppenheimer, Andrés. "Los Tres Amigos: Hispanics Should Say 'Gracias' to Anti-Latin Zealots." *Miami Herald*, April 18, 2006.

Ortiz, Vilma. "Changes in the Characteristics of Puerto Rican Migrants from 1955 to 1980." *International Migration Review* 20 (Fall 1986): 612–28.

Park, Robert E. "Human Migration and the Marginal Man." *American Journal of Sociology* 33 (May 1928): 881–93.

———. *The Immigrant Press and Its Control*. New York: Harper, 1922.

Passel, Jeffrey S. "Election 2004: The Latino and Asian Vote." Washington, D.C.: Urban Institute, July 27, 2004. http://www.urban.org/UploadedPDF/900723.pdf#search='passel%20The%20Latino%20and%20Asian%20Vote.

Passel, Jeffrey S., and Barry Edmonston. "Immigration and Race: Recent Trends in Immigration to the United States." Paper PRIP-UI-22. Washington, D.C.: Urban Institute, 1992.

Passel, Jeffrey S., and Karen A. Woodrow. "Geographic Distribution of Undocumented Immigrants: Estimates of Undocumented Aliens Counted in the 1980 Census by State." *International Migration Review* 18 (Fall 1984): 642–71.

Pastor, Robert. *Migration and Development in the Caribbean.* Boulder, Colo.: Westview Press, 1985.

Peal, Elizabeth, and Wallace E. Lambert. "The Relation of Bilingualism to Intelligence." *Psychological Monographs: General and Applied* 76 (1962): 1–23.

Pedraza-Bailey, Silvia. "Cubans and Mexicans in the United States: The Functions of Political and Economic Migration." *Cuban Studies* 11 (July 1979): 79–97.

———. "Cuba's Exiles: Portrait of a Refugee Migration." *International Migration Review* 19 (Spring 1985): 4–34.

Pérez, Lisandro. "Cuban Miami." In *Miami Now!* ed. Guillermo J. Grenier and Alex Stepick, 83–108. Gainesville: University Press of Florida, 1992.

———. "Growing Up in Cuban Miami: Immigration, the Enclave, and New Generations." In *Ethnicities: Children of Immigrants in America*, ed. Rubén G. Rumbaut and Alejandro Portes, 91–126. Berkeley and New York: University of California Press and Russell Sage Foundation, 2001.

Pérez Firmat, Gustavo. *Life on the Hyphen: The Cuban-American Way.* Austin: University of Texas Press, 1994.

Pérez-Sainz, Juan Pablo. *El Dilema del Nahual.* San José: FLACSO Editores, 1994.

Perlmann, Joel, and Roger Waldinger. "Second Generation Decline? Immigrant Children Past and Present—A Reconsideration." *International Migration Review* 31 (1997): 893–922.

Pessar, Patricia R. "The Role of Households in International Migration and the Case of the U.S.-Bound Migration from the Dominican Republic." *International Migration Review* 16 (Summer 1982): 342–64.

Petersen, William. *Japanese Americans: Oppression and Success.* New York: Random House, 1971.

Pettit, Becky, and Bruce Western. "Mass Imprisonment and the Life Course." *American Sociological Review* 69 (2004): 151–69.

Pew Global Attitudes Project. *Among Wealthy Nations, U.S. Stands Alone in Its Embrace of Religion.* Washington, D.C.: Pew Research Center, December 2002.

Pew Hispanic Center. "Assimilation and Language." Survey Brief. March 2004a. http://pewhispanic.org/files/reports/15.10.pdf.

———. "Bilingualism." Survey Brief. March 2004b. http://pewhispanic.org/files/factsheets/12.pdf

Pierce, Lori, Paul Spickard, and David Yoo. "Japanese and Korean Migrations: Buddhist and Christian Communities in America, 1885–1945." In *The Religious Lives of American Immigrants: Past and Present*, ed. R. Alba and A. Raboteau. New York: Russell Sage Foundation, forthcoming.

Pierce, Neal R., and Jerry Hagstrom. 1988. "The Hispanic Community." In *Latinos and the Political System*, ed. F. Chris García, 11–27. Notre Dame, Ind.: Notre Dame University Press, 1988.

Pinker, Steven. *The Language Instinct*. New York: Morrow, 1994.

Piore, Michael. *Birds of Passage*. Cambridge, Mass.: Cambridge University Press, 1979.

Pirenne, Henri. *Medieval Cities: Their Origins and the Revival of Trade*. Princeton, N.J.: Princeton University Press, 1970.

Pujol, Jordi. "La Inmigración Hará de Cataluña un Revoltijo." *ABC* (Madrid), June 18, 2003, 3.

Popkin, B. M., and J. R. Udry. "Adolescent Obesity Increases Significantly in Second and Third Generation U.S. Immigrants." *Journal of Nutrition* 128, no. 4 (1998): 701–6.

Portes, Alejandro. "Children of Immigrants: Segmented Assimilation and Its Determinants." In *The Economic Sociology of Immigration: Essays on Networks, Ethnicity, and Entrepreneurship*, ed. Alejandro Portes, 248–79. New York: Russell Sage Foundation, 1995.

———. "Determinants of the Brain Drain." *International Migration Review* 10 (Winter 1976): 489–508.

———. "Dilemmas of a Golden Exile: Integration of Cuban Refugee Families in Milwaukee." *American Sociological Review* 34 (August 1969): 505–18.

———. "From South of the Border: Hispanic Minorities in the United States." In *Immigration Reconsidered: History, Sociology, and Politics*, ed. V. Yans-McLaughlin, 160–84. New York: Oxford University Press, 1990.

———. "Global Villagers: The Rise of Transnational Communities." *American Prospect* 25 (1996): 74–77.

———. "Illegal Immigration and the International System: Lessons from Recent Legal Mexican Immigrants to the United States." *Social Problems* 26 (April 1979): 425–38.

———. "Immigration Reform: The Theory and the Realities." *Baltimore Sun*, January 2, 1987, 15A.

———. "La Máquina Política Cubano-Estadounidense: Reflexiones sobre su Origen y Permanencia." *Foro Internacional* 43 (July–September 2003): 608–26.

———. "The Longest Migration." *New Republic*, April 26, 1993.

———. "Migration and Underdevelopment." *Politics and Society* 8 (1978): 148.

———. "The New Latin Nation: Immigration and the Hispanic Population of the United States." Paper presented at the Conference on the Hispanic Population Today, organized by the Tomás Rivera Policy Institute, Los Angeles, January 2004.

———. "Of Borders and States: A Skeptical Note on the Legislative Control of Immigration." In *America's New Immigration Law: Origins, Rationales, and Potential Consequences*, ed. W. A. Cornelius and R. Anzaldina Montoya, 17–30. La Jolla: Center for U.S.-Mexican Studies, University of California, San Diego, 1983.

———. "The Rise of Ethnicity." *American Sociological Review* 49 (June 1984): 383–97.

———. "The Social Origins of the Cuban Enclave Economy of Miami." *Sociological Perspectives* 30 (October 1987): 340–72.

———. "Theoretical Convergencies and Empirical Evidence in the Study of Immigrant Transnationalism." *International Migration Review* 37 (Fall 2003): 874–92.

———. "When More Can Be Less: Labor Standards, Development, and the Informal Economy." In *Labor Standards and Development in the Global Economy*, ed. S. Herzenberg and J. Pérez-López, 219–37. Washington, D.C.: Bureau of International Labor Affairs, U.S. Department of Labor, 1990.

Portes, Alejandro, and Robert L. Bach. *Latin Journey: Cuban and Mexican Immigrants in the United States*. Berkeley: University of California Press, 1985.

Portes, Alejandro, and József Böröcz. "Contemporary Immigration: Theoretical Perspectives on Its Determinants and Modes of Incorporation." *International Migration Review* 23 (Fall 1989): 606–30.

Portes, Alejandro, and Juan M. Clark. "Mariel Refugees: Six Years Later." *Migration World* 15 (Fall 1987): 14–18.

Portes, Alejandro, Juan M. Clark, and Manuel M. López. "Six Years Later: The Process of Incorporation of Cuban Exiles in the United States." *Cuban Studies* 11/12 (January 1982): 1–24.

Portes, Alejandro, and John Curtis. "Changing Flags: Naturalization and Its Determinants among Mexican Immigrants." *International Migration Review* 21 (Summer 1987): 352–71.

Portes, Alejandro, and Josh DeWind. "A Cross-Atlantic Dialogue: The Progress of Research and Theory in the Study of International Migration." *International Migration Review* 38 (Fall 2004): 828–51.

Portes, Alejandro, Cristina Escobar, and Alexandria Walton. "Transnational Organizations and Development: A Comparative Study." Working paper, Center for Migration and Development, Princeton University, 2005. http://cmd.princeton.edu/papers.shtml.

Portes, Alejandro, Patricia Fernández-Kelly, and William Haller. "Segmented Assimilation on the Ground: The New Second Generation in Early Adulthood. *Ethnic and Racial Studies* 28, no. 6 (2005): 1000–1040.

Portes, Alejandro, and Ramón Grosfoguel. "Caribbean Diasporas: Migration and the Emergence of Ethnic Communities in the U.S. Mainland." *Annals of the American Academy of Political and Social Sciences* 533 (May 1994): 48–69.

Portes, Alejandro, and Luis E. Guarnizo. "Tropical Capitalists: U.S.-Bound Immigration and Small Enterprise Development in the Dominican Republic." In *Migration, Remittances, and Small Business Development: Mexico and Caribbean Basin Countries*, ed. S. Díaz-Briquets and S. Weintraub, 101–31. Boulder, Colo.: Westview Press, 1991.

Portes, Alejandro, William Haller, and Luis E. Guarnizo. "Transnational Entrepreneurs: An Alternative Form of Immigrant Adaptation." *American Sociological Review* 67 (April 2002): 278–98.

Portes, Alejandro, and Lingxin Hao. "The Price of Uniformity: Language, Family, and Personality Adjustment in the Immigrant Second Generation." *Ethnic and Racial Studies* 25 (November 2002): 889–912.

———. "The Schooling of Children of Immigrants: Contextual Effects on the Educational Attainment of the Second Generation." *Proceedings of the National Academy of Sciences* 101 (2004): 11920–27.

Portes, Alejandro, and Patricia Landolt. "Social Capital: Promise and Pitfalls of Its Role in Development." *Journal of Latin American Studies* 32 (2000): 529–47.

Portes, Alejandro, and Dag MacLeod. "What Should I Call Myself? Hispanic Identity Formation in the Second Generation." *Ethnic and Racial Studies* 19, no. 4 (1996): 523–47.

Portes, Alejandro, and Robert D. Manning. "The Immigrant Enclave: Theory and Empirical Examples." In *Competitive Ethnic Relations*, ed. Joane Nagel and Susan Olzak, 47–68. Orlando, Fla.: Academic Press, 1986.

Portes, Alejandro, and Rafael Mozo. "The Political Adaptation Process of Cubans and Other Ethnic Minorities in the United States." *International Migration Review* 19 (Spring 1985): 35–63.

Portes, Alejandro, Robert N. Parker, and José A. Cobas. "Assimilation or Consciousness?" *Social Forces* 59 (September 1980): 200–224.

Portes, Alejandro, and Adreain R. Ross. "Modernization for Emigration: Medical Brain-Drain from Argentina." *Journal of Inter-American Studies and World Affairs* 13 (November 1976): 395–422.

Portes, Alejandro, and Rubén G. Rumbaut. 2001. *Legacies: The Story of the Immigrant Second Generation*. Berkeley and New York: University of California Press and Russell Sage Foundation.

Portes, Alejandro, and Saskia Sassen-Koob. "Making It Underground: Comparative Materials on the Informal Sector in Western Market Economies." *American Journal of Sociology* 93 (1987): 30–61.

Portes, Alejandro, and Richard Schauffler. "Language and the Second Generation: Bilingualism Yesterday and Today." *International Migration Review* 28, 4 (1994): 640–61.

Portes, Alejandro, and Julia Sensenbrenner. "Embeddedness and Immigration: Notes on the Social Determinants of Economic Action." *American Journal of Sociology* 98 (1993): 1320–50.

Portes, Alejandro, and Alex Stepick. *City on the Edge: The Transformation of Miami*. Berkeley: University of California Press, 1993.

———. "Unwelcome Immigrants: The Labor Market Experiences of 1980 (Mariel) Cuban and Haitian Refugees in South Florida." *American Sociological Review* 50 (August 1985): 493–514.

Portes, Alejandro, and Cynthia Truelove. "Making Sense of Diversity: Recent Research on Hispanic Minorities in the United States." *Annual Review of Sociology* 13 (1987): 359–85.

Portes, Alejandro, and John Walton. *Labor, Class, and the International System*. New York: Academic Press, 1981.

Portes, Alejandro, and Min Zhou. "Divergent Destinies: Immigration, Poverty, and Entrepreneurship in the United States." In *Poverty, Inequality, and the Future of Social Policy*, ed. K. McFate, R. Lawson, and W. J. Wilson, 489–520. New York: Russell Sage Foundation, 1995.

———. "Entrepreneurship and Economic Progress in the 1990s: A Comparative Analysis of Immigrants and African Americans." In *Immigration and Ethnicity in the United States*, ed. F. Bean and S. Bell-Rose, 143–71. New York: Russell Sage Foundation, 1999.

———. "The New Second Generation: Segmented Assimilation and its Variants." *Annals of the American Academy of Political and Social Sciences* 530 (November 1993): 74–96.

———. "Self-Employment and the Earnings of Immigrants." *American Sociological Review* 61 (1996): 219–30.

Powelson, Richard. "Florida Girl, 12, Is Top Speller." *Washington Times*, May 31, 1996, A6.

Pyle, Amy, and Simon Romero. "Prop 187 Fuels a New Campus Activism." *Los Angeles Times*, October 15, 1994, B1.

Rahe, Richard H., John G. Looney, Harold W. Ward, Tran M. Tung, and William T. Liu. "Psychiatric Consultation in a Vietnamese Refugee Camp." *American Journal of Psychiatry* 135 (February 1978): 185–90.

Raijman, Rebecca, and Marta Tienda. "Immigrants' Socio-Economic Progress Post-1965: Forging Mobility or Survival?" In *The Handbook of International Migration*, ed. P. K. C. Hirschman and J. DeWind, 239–56. New York: Russell Sage Foundation, 1999.

Ramakrishnan, S. Karthick, and Thomas J. Espenshade. "Immigrant Incorporation and Political Participation in the United States." *International Migration Review* 35 (Fall 2001): 870–909.

Ramos, Carlos Guillermo. "Rapporteurs' Comments." Paper presented at the "Conference on Immigrant Transnationalism and Its Impact on Sending Nations," Center for Migration and Development, Princeton University and Latin American School of Social Science (FLACSO), Santo Domingo, Dominican Republic, January 2002.

Ranney, M. H. "On Insane Foreigners." *American Journal of Insanity* 7 (July 1850): 53–63.

Read, Jen'nan Ghazal. *Culture, Class, and Work among Arab-American Women*. New York: LFB Scholarly, 2004.

Reichert, Joshua S. "The Migrant Syndrome: Seasonal U.S. Wage Labor and Rural Development in Central Mexico." *Human Organization* 40 (Spring 1981): 59–66.

Reimers, Cordelia W. "A Comparative Analysis of the Wages of Hispanics, Blacks, and Non-Hispanic Whites." In *Hispanics in the U.S. Economy*, ed. George J. Borjas and Marta Tienda, 27–75. Orlando, Fla.: Academic Press, 1985.

Reimers, David M. *Still the Golden Door: The Third World Comes to America*. New York: Columbia University Press, 1985.

Repak, Terry A. "And They Come on Behalf of Their Children: Central American Families in Washington, D.C." Report prepared for the Conference on Immigration, U.S. Department of Labor, September 1988.

Resnick, Melvin C. "Beyond the Ethnic Community: Spanish Language Roles and Maintenance in Miami." *International Journal of the Sociology of Language* 69 (1988): 89–104.

Reynolds, Maura. "Language and Learning: Lessons from Canada." *San Diego Union-Tribune*, May 30, 1993, A1.

Richardson, Alan. "A Theory and a Method for the Psychological Study of Assimilation." *International Migration Review* 2 (Fall 1967): 3–29.

Riley, Richard W. "Statement by the Secretary of Education Richard W. Riley on California Proposition 227." Washington, D.C.: U.S. Department of Education, April 27, 1998.

Rischin, Moses. *The Promised City: New York Jews, 1870–1914*. Cambridge, Mass.: Harvard University Press, 1962.

Rist, Ray. "Guestworkers in Germany: Public Policies as the Legitimation of Marginality." *Ethnic and Racial Studies* 2 (October 1979): 401–15.

Roberts, Bryan R. "Employment Structure, Life Cycle, and Life Chances: Formal and Informal Sectors in Guadalajara." In *The Informal Economy: Studies in Advanced and Less Developed Countries*, ed. Alejandro Portes, Manuel Castells, and Lauren Benton, 41–59. Baltimore, Md.: Johns Hopkins University Press, 1989.

———. "Socially Expected Durations and the Economic Adjustment of Immigrants." In *The Economic Sociology of Immigration*, ed. Alejandro Portes, 42–86. New York: Russell Sage Foundation, 1995.

Roberts, Bryan R., Reanne Frank, and Fernando Lozano-Asencio. 1999. "Transnational Migrant Communities and Mexican Migration to the United States." *Ethnic and Racial Studies* 22 (March 1999): 238–66.

Robertson, John W. "Prevalence of Insanity in California." *American Journal of Insanity* 60 (July 1903): 81–82.

Rodríguez, Clara. *The Ethnic Queue in the U.S.: The Case of Puerto Ricans*. San Francisco: R and E Research Associates, 1976.

Rodríguez, Gregory. "Once Again, It Will Be Immigrants to the Rescue." *Los Angeles Times*, October 9, 2005, A13.

Rodríguez, Nestor P. "Undocumented Central Americans in Houston: Diverse Populations." *International Migration Review* 21 (Spring 1987): 4–26.

Rodríguez, Richard. *Days of Obligation: An Argument with My Mexican Father*. New York: Viking, 1992.

———. *Hunger of Memory*. Boston: Godline, 1982.

Rogler, Lloyd H., Robert G. Malgady, and Orlando Rodríguez. *Hispanics and Mental Health: A Framework for Research*. Malabar, Fla.: Krieger, 1989.

Roosevelt, Theodore. "Speech to State Republican Party Convention, Saratoga, New York, July 19, 1918."

Roper Organization. 1982. *Roper Reports* 84-4: 2–27.

Rose, Peter I. "Some Thoughts about Refugees and the Descendants of Theseus." *International Migration Review* 15 (Spring–Summer 1981): 8–15.

Rosenblum, Gerald. *Immigrant Workers: Their Impact on American Radicalism*. New York: Basic Books, 1973.

Roth Pierpont, Claudia. "The Measure of America." *New Yorker*, March 8, 2004, 48–63.

Rothman, David J. *The Discovery of the Asylum*. Boston: Little, Brown, 1971.

Rubenstein, Hyzine. "Remittances and Rural Underdevelopment in the English-Speaking Caribbean." *Human Organization* 42 (Winter 1983): 295–306.

Rumbaut, Rubén D. "Life Events, Change, Migration, and Depression." In *Phenomenology and Treatment of Depression*, ed. William E. Fann, Ismet Karacan, Alex D. Pokorny, and Robert L. Williams, 115–26. New York: Plenum, 1977.

Rumbaut, Rubén D., and Rubén G. Rumbaut. "The Family in Exile: Cuban Expatriates in the United States." *American Journal of Psychiatry* 133 (April 1976): 395–99.

———. "Refugees in the United States: A Mental Health Research Challenge." Paper presented to the Karl Menninger School of Psychiatry, Topeka, Kansas, June 1986.

———. "Self and Circumstance: Journeys and Visions of Exile." In *The Dispossessed: An Anatomy of Exile*, ed. Peter I. Rose, 331–55. Amherst: University of Massachusetts Press, 2005.

Rumbaut, Rubén G. "Ages, Life Stages, and Generational Cohorts: Decomposing the Immigrant First and Second Generations in the United States." *International Migration Review* 38, no. 3 (2004): 1160–1205.

———. "The Agony of Exile: A Study of Indochinese Refugee Adults and Children." In *Refugee Children: Theory, Research, and Services*, ed. F. L. Ahearn Jr. and J. L. Athey, 53–91. Baltimore, Md.: Johns Hopkins University Press, 1991.

———. "The Americans: Latin American and Caribbean Peoples in the United States." In *Americas: New Interpretive Essays*, ed. Alfred Stepan, 275–307. New York: Oxford University Press, 1992.

———. "Assimilation and Its Discontents: Between Rhetoric and Reality." *International Migration Review* 31, no. 4 (1997): 923–60.

———. "Assimilation and Its Discontents: Ironies and Paradoxes." In *The Handbook of International Migration: The American Experience*, ed. Charles Hirschman, Josh DeWind, and Philip Kasinitz, 172–95. New York: Russell Sage Foundation, 1999.

———. "Coming of Age in Immigrant America." *Research Perspectives on Migration* 1, no. 6 (1998): 1–14.

———. "The Crucible Within: Ethnic Identity, Self-Esteem, and Segmented Assimilation among Children of Immigrants." *International Migration Review* 28, no. 4 (Winter 1994): 748–94.

———. *Immigrant Students in California Public Schools: A Summary of Current Knowledge*. Center for Research on Effective Schooling for Disadvantaged Children, Report No. 11. Baltimore, Md.: Johns Hopkins University, 1990.

———. "The Making of a People." In *Hispanics and the Future of America*, ed. Marta Tienda and Faith Mitchell, 16–65. Washington, D.C.: National Academies Press, 2006.

———. "The Melting and the Pot: Assimilation and Variety in American Life." In *Incorporating Diversity: Rethinking Assimilation in a Multicultural Age*, ed. Peter Kivisto, 154–73. Boulder, Colo.: Paradigm Publishers, 2005.

———. "Mental Health and the Refugee Experience: A Comparative Study of Southeast Asian Refugees." In *Southeast Asian Mental Health*, ed. Tom C. Owan, 433–86. Rockville, Md.: National Institute of Mental Health, 1985.

———. "Migration, Adaptation, and Mental Health: The Experience of Southeast Asian Refugees in the United States." In *Refugee Policy: Canada and the United States*, ed. Howard Adelman, 383–427. Toronto: York Lanes Press, 1991.

———. "The New Californians: Comparative Research Findings on the Educational Progress of Immigrant Children." In *California's Immigrant Children: Theory, Research, and Implications for Educational Policy*, ed. R. G. Rumbaut and W. A. Cornelius, 17–70. La Jolla: Center for U.S.-Mexican Studies, University of California, San Diego, 1995.

———. "Origins and Destinies: Immigration to the United States since World War II." *Sociological Forum* 9 (1994): 583–621.

———. "Passages to America: Perspectives on the New Immigration." In *America at Century's End*, ed. Alan Wolfe, 208–44. Berkeley: University of California Press, 1991.

———. "Portraits, Patterns, and Predictors of the Refugee Adaptation Process." In *Refugees as Immigrants: Cambodians, Laotians and Vietnamese in America*, ed. David W. Haines, 138–82. Totowa, N.J.: Rowman & Littlefield, 1989.

———. "Severed or Sustained Attachments? Language, Identity, and Imagined Communities in the Post-Immigrant Generation." In *The Changing Face of Home: The Transnational Lives of the Second Generation*, ed. Peggy Levitt and Mary C. Waters, 43–95. New York: Russell Sage Foundation, 2002.

———. "The Structure of Refuge: Southeast Asian Refugees in the United States." *International Review of Comparative Public Policy* 1 (Winter 1989): 97–129.

———. "Ties That Bind: Immigration and Immigrant Families in the United States." In *Immigration and the Family: Research and Policy on U.S. Immigrants*, ed. Alan Booth, Ann C. Crouter, and Nancy S. Landale, 3–46. Mahwah, N.J.: Erlbaum, 1997.

———. "Turning Points in the Transition to Adulthood: Determinants of Educational Attainment, Incarceration, and Early Childbearing among Children of Immigrants." *Ethnic and Racial Studies* 28, no. 6 (2005): 1041–86.

———. "Vietnamese, Laotian, and Cambodian Americans." In *Asian Americans: Contemporary Trends and Issues*, 2nd ed., ed. Pyong Gap Min, 262–89. Thousand Oaks, Calif.: Sage, 2005.

Rumbaut, Rubén G., Frank D. Bean, Susan K. Brown, Leo R. Chávez, Louis DeSipio, Jennifer Lee, and Min Zhou. *Immigration and Intergenerational*

Mobility in Metropolitan Los Angeles. Report to the Russell Sage Foundation. Irvine: University of California, 2005.

Rumbaut, Rubén G., Leo R. Chávez, Robert J. Moser, Sheila Pickwell, and Samuel Wishik. "The Politics of Migrant Health Care: A Comparative Study of Mexican Immigrants and Indochinese Refugees." *Research in the Sociology of Health Care* 7 (1988): 143–202.

Rumbaut, Rubén G., and Wayne A. Cornelius, eds. *California's Immigrant Children: Theory, Research, and Implications for Educational Policy.* La Jolla: Center for U.S.-Mexican Studies, University of California, San Diego, 1995.

Rumbaut, Rubén G., Roberto G. Gonzales, Golnaz Komaie, Charlie V. Morgan, and Rosaura Tafoya-Estrada. "Immigration and Incarceration: Patterns and Predictors of Imprisonment among First- and Second-Generation Young Adults." In *Immigration and Crime: Race, Ethnicity, and Violence,* ed. Ramiro Martínez Jr. and Abel Valenzuela Jr. New York: New York University Press, 2006.

Rumbaut, Rubén G., and Kenji Ima. *The Adaptation of Southeast Asian Refugee Youth: A Comparative Study.* Washington, D.C.: U.S. Office of Refugee Resettlement, 1988.

———. "Determinants of Educational Attainment among Indochinese Refugees and Other Immigrant Students." Paper presented at the annual meeting of the American Sociological Association, Atlanta, August 1988.

Rumbaut, Rubén G., and Alejandro Portes, eds. *Ethnicities: Children of Immigrants in America.* Berkeley and New York: University of California Press and Russell Sage Foundation, 2001.

Rumbaut, Rubén G., and John R. Weeks. "Fertility and Adaptation: Indochinese Refugees in the United States." *International Migration Review* 20 (1986): 428–66.

———. "Infant Health among Indochinese Refugees: Patterns of Infant Mortality, Birthweight and Prenatal Care in Comparative Perspective." *Research in the Sociology of Health Care* 8 (1989): 371–96.

———. "Unraveling a Public Health Enigma: Why Do Immigrants Experience Superior Perinatal Health Outcomes?" *Research in the Sociology of Health Care* 13 (1996): 335–88.

Sabel, Charles F. "Changing Modes of Economic Efficiency and Their Implications for Industrialization in the Third World." In *Development, Democracy, and Trespassing: Essays in Honor of Albert O. Hirschman,* ed. M. S. McPherson, A. Foxley, and G. O'Donnell, 27–55. Notre Dame, Ind.: Notre Dame University Press, 1986.

Salmon, T. W. "The Relation of Immigration to the Prevalence of Insanity." *American Journal of Insanity* 64 (July 1907): 53–71.

Samora, Julián. Los Mojados: *The Wetback Story.* Notre Dame, Ind.: Notre Dame University Press, 1971.

Sánchez-Korrol, Victoria. *From Colonia to Community.* Westport, Conn.: Greenwood Press, 1983.

Sandiford, Peter, and Ruby Kerr. "Intelligence of Chinese and Japanese Children." *Journal of Educational Psychology* 17 (September 1926): 366–67.

Santibáñez, Enrique. *Ensayo Acerca de la Inmigración Mexicana en los Estados Unidos*. San Antonio, Tex.: Clegg, 1930.

Santoli, Al. *New Americans: An Oral History*. New York: Viking, 1988.

Sanua, Victor D. "Immigration, Migration, and Mental Illness." In *Behavior in New Environments: Adaptation of Migrant Populations*, ed. Eugene B. Brody, 291.–352. Beverly Hills, Calif.: Sage, 1970.

Sassen, Saskia. "Changing Composition and Labor Market Location of Hispanic Immigrants in New York City, 1960–1980." In *Hispanics in the U.S. Economy*, ed. George J. Borjas and Marta Tienda, 299–322. New York: Academic Press, 1985.

———. "Exporting Capital and Importing Labor: The Role of Caribbean Migration to New York." Occasional Paper no. 28. Center for Latin American and Caribbean Studies, New York University, 1981.

———. "Formal and Informal Associations: Dominicans and Colombians in New York." *International Migration Review* 13 (Summer 1979): 314–32.

———. "Immigrant and Minority Workers in the Organization of the Labor Process." *Journal of Ethnic Studies* (Spring 1981): 134.

———. *The Mobility of Labor and Capital: A Study in International Investment and Labor Flow*. New York: Cambridge University Press, 1988.

———. "The New Labor Demand in Global Cities." In *Cities in Transformation*, ed. Michael P. Smith, 139–71. Beverly Hills, Calif.: Sage, 1984.

———. "New York City's Informal Economy." In *The Informal Economy: Studies in Advanced and Less Developed Countries*, ed. A. Portes, M. Castells, and L. Benton, 60–77. Baltimore, Md.: Johns Hopkins University Press, 1989.

Sassen, Saskia, and Robert C. Smith. "Post-industrial Growth and Economic Reorganization: Their Impact on Immigrant Employment." In *U.S.-Mexico Relations: Labor Market Interdependence*, ed. J. Bustamante, C. W. Reynolds, and R. A. Hinojosa, 372–93. Stanford, Calif.: Stanford University Press, 1992.

Schlossman, Steven L. "Is There an American Tradition of Bilingual Education? German in the Public Elementary Schools, 1840–1919." *American Journal of Education* 91 (February 1983): 139–86.

Schmalz, Jeffrey. "Hispanic Influx Spurs Step to Bolster English." *New York Times*, October 26, 1988, I1.

Schmidt, Philip. "Ignored Majority: The Moderate Cuban-American Community." Washington, D.C.: Latin America Working Group Education Fund, 2004.

Schneiderman, Howard G. "The Protestant Establishment: Its History, Its Legacy—Its Future?" In *Origins and Destinies: Immigration, Race, and Ethnicity in America*, ed. S. Pedraza and Rubén G. Rumbaut, 141–51. Belmont, Calif.: Wadsworth, 1996.

Schuck, Peter. "The Message of 187." *American Prospect* 21 (Spring 1995): 85–92.

Schwab, John J., and Mary E. Schwab. *Sociocultural Roots of Mental Illness: An Epidemiologic Survey*. New York: Plenum, 1978.

Seeman, Melvin. "On the Meaning of Alienation." *American Sociological Review* 24 (December 1959): 783–91.

Select Commission on Immigration and Refugee Policy. *U.S. Immigration Policy and the National Interest.* Washington, D.C.: U.S. Department of Justice, 1984.

Sellers, Jeff M. "Despite Protestant Growth, Hispanic Catholicism Holds Steady in U.S." *Christianity Today,* February 7, 2003.

Sengupta, Somini. "On One Queens Block, Many Prayers Are Spoken." *New York Times,* November 7, 1999, A1.

Shannon, David A. *The Socialist Party in America.* Chicago: Quadrangle Books, 1967.

Sharma, Miriam. "The Philippines: A Case of Migration to Hawaii, 1906–1946." In *Labor Immigration under Capitalism,* ed. Lucie Cheng and Edna Bonacich, 337–58. Berkeley: University of California Press, 1984.

Shutz, Alfred. "The Stranger: An Essay in Social Psychology." *American Journal of Sociology* 49 (May 1944): 499–507.

Silva-Corvalán, Carmen. *Language Contact and Change: Spanish in Los Angeles.* New York: Oxford University Press, 1994.

Simon, Julian. *The Economic Consequences of Immigration.* Cambridge, Mass.: Blackwell, 1989.

Simon, Rita J. "Refugee Families' Adjustment and Aspirations: A Comparison of Soviet Jewish and Vietnamese Immigrants." *Ethnic and Racial Studies* 6 (October 1983): 492–504.

Smith, James D., and Barry Edmonston. *The Immigration Debate, Studies on the Economic, Demographic, and Fiscal Impacts of Immigration.* Washington, D.C.: National Academy Press, 1998.

Smith, Madorah E. "Some Light on the Problem of Bilingualism as Found from a Study of the Progress in Mastery of English among Preschool Children of Non-American Ancestry in Hawaii." *Genetic Psychology Monographs* 21 (May 1939): 119–284.

Smith, Michael P., and Luis E. Guarnizo. *Transnationalism from Below.* New Brunswick, N.J.: Transaction Publishers, 1998.

Smith, Robert C. "Diasporic Memberships in Historical Perspective: Comparative Insights from the Mexican, Italian, and Polish Cases." *International Migration Review* 37 (Fall 2003): 724–59.

———. "*Los Ausentes Siempre Presentes*: The Imagining, Making, and Politics of a Transnational Community between New York City and Ticuaní, Puebla." Ph.D. diss., Columbia University, 1995.

———. "Mexican Immigrants, the Mexican State, and the Transnational Practice of Mexican Politics and Membership." *LASA Forum* 24 (1998): 19–24.

———. "New York in Mixteca: Mixteca in New York." *NACLA Report on the Americas* 26, no. 1 (1992).

Smith, Timothy L. "Religion and Ethnicity in America." *American Historical Review* 83 (1978): 1155–85.

Smith, Tom W. *Estimating the Muslim Population of the United States.* New York: American Jewish Committee, 2002.

————. "Religious Diversity in America: The Emergence of Muslims, Buddhists, Hindus, and Others." *Journal for the Scientific Study of Religion* 41, no. 3 (2002): 577–85.

Smith, Tom W., and Seokho Kim. "The Vanishing Protestant Majority." *Journal for the Scientific Study of Religion* 44, no. 2 (2005): 211–23.

Smith-Hefner, Nancy. *Khmer-Americans: Identity and Moral Education in a Diasporic Community.* Berkeley: University of California Press, 1999.

Sowell, Thomas. *Ethnic America: A History.* New York: Basic Books, 1981.

Sridhar, Kamal K. "Language Maintenance and Language Shift among Asian-Indians: Kannadigas in the New York Area." *International Journal of the Sociology of Language* 69 (1988): 73–87.

Srole, Leo, Thomas S. Langner, and Stanley Mitchell. *Mental Health in the Metropolis: The Midtown Manhattan Study,* vol. 1. Rev. ed. New York: New York University Press, 1962.

Stark, Oded. "Migration Decision Making." *Journal of Development Economics* 14 (1984): 251–59.

————. *The Migration of Labour.* Cambridge: Blackwell, 1991.

Starr, Paul D., and Alden E. Roberts. "Attitudes toward New Americans: Perceptions of Indo-Chinese in Nine Cities." *Research in Race and Ethnic Relations* 3 (1982): 165–86.

Stein, Barry N. "The Experience of Being a Refugee: Insights from the Research Literature." In *Refugee Mental Health in Resettlement Countries,* ed. Carolyn L. Williams and Joseph Westermeyer, 523. New York: Hemisphere, 1986.

Steinberg, Stephen. *The Ethnic Myth.* New York: Atheneum, 1981.

Stephens, Bret, and Joseph Rago. "Stars, Stripes, Crescent: A Reassuring Portrait of America's Muslims." *Wall Street Journal,* August 24, 2005, editorial page. http://www.opinionjournal.com/editorial/feature.html?id=110007151.

Stepick, Alex. "Haitian Refugees in the U.S." Minority Rights Group Report no. 52. London: MRG, 1982.

————. *Pride against Prejudice: Haitians in the United States.* Boston: Allyn and Bacon,1998.

Stepick, Alex, and Carol Dutton Stepick. "Power and Identity: Miami Cubans." In *Latinos, Remaking America,* ed. M. M. Suárez-Orozco and M. M. Paez, 75–92. Berkeley: University of California Press, 2002.

Stepick, Alex, Guillermo Grenier, Max Castro, and Marvin Dunn. *This Land Is Our Land: Immigrants and Power in Miami.* Berkeley: University of California Press, 2003.

Stepick, Alex, and Alejandro Portes. "Flight into Despair: A Profile of Recent Haitian Refugees in South Florida." *International Migration Review* 20 (Summer 1986): 329–50.

Stevens, Rosemary, Louis W. Goodman, and Stephen Mick. *The Alien Doctors: Foreign Medical Graduates in American Hospitals.* New York: Wiley, 1978.

Stonequist, Everett V. *The Marginal Man: A Study in Personality and Culture Conflict.* 1937. Reprint, New York: Russell & Russell, 1961.

Strand, Paul J., and Woodrow Jones Jr. *Indochinese Refugees in America: Problems of Adaptation and Assimilation*. Durham, N.C.: Duke University Press, 1985.

Suárez-Orozco, Marcelo M. *Central American Refugees and U.S. High Schools: A Psychosocial Study of Motivation and Achievement*. Stanford, Calif.: Stanford University Press, 1989.

———. *Crossings: Mexican Immigration in Interdisciplinary Perspectives*. Cambridge, Mass.: David Rockefeller Center for Latin American Studies, Harvard University, 1998.

———. "Towards a Psychosocial Understanding of Hispanic Adaptation to American Schooling." In *Success or Failure? Learning and the Languages of Minority Students*, ed. H. T. Trueba, 156–68. New York: Newbury House Publishers, 1987.

Suárez-Orozco, Marcelo M., and Carola Suárez-Orozco. *Children of Immigration*. Cambridge, Mass.: Harvard University Press, 2001.

———. "The Cultural Patterning of Achievement Motivation: A Comparative Study of Mexican, Mexican Immigrant, and Non-Latino White American Youths in Schools." In *California's Immigrant Children: Theory, Research, and Implications for Educational Policy*, ed. Rubén G. Rumbaut and Wayne A. Cornelius, 161–90. La Jolla: Center for U.S.-Mexican Studies, University of California, San Diego, 1995.

Sullivan, Mercer L. *Getting Paid: Youth Crime and Work in the Inner City*. Ithaca, N.Y.: Cornell University Press, 1989.

Swarns, Rachel S. "Capitol's Pariah on Immigration Is Now a Power." *New York Times*, December 24, 2005, 1.

Szapocznik, José, Raquel Cohen, and Roberto E. Hernández, eds. *Coping with Adolescent Refugees: The Mariel Boatlift*. New York: Praeger, 1985.

Tabori, Paul. *The Anatomy of Exile: A Semantic and Historical Study*. London: Harrap, 1972.

Tan, Amy. 1989. *The Joy Luck Club*. New York: Putnam.

Taylor, Donald M. "Ethnicity and Language: A Social Psychological Perspective." In *Language: Social Psychological Perspectives*, ed. Howard Giles, W. Peter Robinson, and Philip M. Smith, 133–39. New York: Pergamon Press, 1980.

Taylor, Lowell J., Frank D. Bean, James B. Rebitzer, Susan González Baker, and B. Lindsay Lowell. "Mexican Immigrants and the Wages and Unemployment Experience of Native Workers." Discussion paper PRIP-UI-1. Washington, D.C.: Urban Institute, 1988.

Teitelbaum, Michael S. "Right versus Right: Immigration and Refugee Policy in the United States." *Foreign Affairs* 59 (1980): 21–59.

Thernstrom, Abigail M. "Language: Issues and Legislation." In *Harvard Encyclopedia of American Ethnic Groups*, ed. Stephan Thernstrom, 619–29. Cambridge, Mass.: Harvard University Press, 1981.

Thoits, P. A. "Conceptual, Methodological, and Theoretical Problems in Studying Social Support as a Buffer against Life Stress." *Journal of Health and Social Behavior* 23 (June 1982):145–59.

————. "Undesirable Life Events and Psychological Distress: A Problem of Operational Confounding." *American Sociological Review* 46 (February 1981): 97–109.

Thomas, Brinley. *Migration and Economic Growth: A Study of Great Britain and the Atlantic Economy*. Cambridge: Cambridge University Press, 1973.

Thomas, Hugh. *Cuba: The Pursuit of Freedom*. New York: Harper and Row, 1971.

Thomas, William I., and Florian Znaniecki. *The Polish Peasant in Europe and America: Monograph of an Immigrant Group*. Chicago: University of Chicago Press, [1918–1920]. Reprint, ed. and abridged by Eli Zaretsky: Chicago: University of Illinois Press, 1984.

"Threat to Security Cited in Rise of Foreign Engineers." *Los Angeles Times*, January 20, 1988, I1.

Tienda, Marta. "Hispanic Origin Workers in the U.S. Labor Market: Comparative Analyses of Employment and Earnings." Mimeograph, final report to the U.S. Department of Labor. Madison: University of Wisconsin Department of Rural Sociology, 1981.

Tienda, Marta, and Haya Stier. "The Wages of Race: Color and Employment Opportunity in Chicago's Inner City." In *Origins and Destinies: Immigration, Race, and Ethnicity in America*, ed. S. Pedraza and Rubén G. Rumbaut. Belmont, Calif.: Wadsworth, 1996.

Tilly, Charles. "Migration in Modern European History." In *Human Migration, Patterns and Policies*, ed. William S. McNeill and Ruth Adams, 48–72. Bloomington: Indiana University Press, 1978.

————. "Transplanted Networks." In *Immigration Reconsidered: History, Sociology, and Politics*, ed. V. Yans-McLaughlin, 7995. New York: Oxford University Press, 1990.

Tobar, Héctor. "Salvadoran Loyalties Clash in L.A." *Los Angeles Times*, February 12, 1989, A1.

Tumulty, Karen. "When Irish Eyes Are Hiding." *Los Angeles Times*, January 29, 1989, A1.

"2 in New York Are Top Science Winners." *New York Times*, March 1, 1988, I1.

Tyhurst, Libuse. "Displacement and Migration: A Study in Social Psychiatry." *American Journal of Psychiatry* 101 (February 1951): 561–68.

————. "Psychosocial First Aid for Refugees: An Essay in Social Psychiatry." *Mental Health and Society* 4 (1977): 319–43.

Ugalde, Antonio, Frank D. Bean, and Gilbert Cárdenas. "International Migration from the Dominican Republic: Findings from a National Survey." *International Migration Review* 13 (Summer 1979): 235–54.

United Nations, Population Division. *International Migration Report 2002*. New York: United Nations Publications, 2002.

Unz, Ron. "California and the End of White America." *Commentary* 18 (November 1999):17–28.

Urrea Giraldo, Fernando. "Life Strategies and the Labor Market: Colombians in New York in the 1970s." New York: New York Research Program in Inter-American Affairs, 1982.

U.S. Bureau of the Census. *Ancestry: 2000*. Census 2000 Brief. Release C2KBR-35. Washington, D.C.: U.S. Government Printing Office, June 2004. http://www.census.gov/prod/2004pubs/c2kbr-35.pdf.

———. *The Foreign-Born Population in the United States*. 1990 Census of Population, CP-3-1. Washington, D.C.: U.S. Government Printing Office, 1993a.

———. *The Hispanic Population 2000*. Census Brief C2KBR/01-3. Washington, D.C.: U.S. Government Printing Office, 2001a.

———. *Language Use and English-Speaking Ability: 2000*. Census 2000 Brief. Release C2KBR-29. Washington, D.C.: U.S. Government Printing Office, October 2003. http://www.census.gov/prod/2003pubs/c2kbr-29.pdf.

———. *1980 Census: Detailed Population Characteristics*. Release PC80-1-D1-A. Washington, D.C.: U.S. Government Printing Office, 1984a.

———. *1990 Ethnic Profiles for States*. Release CPH-L-136. Washington, D.C.: U.S. Government Printing Office, 1993b.

———. *1997 Survey of Minority-Owned Business Enterprises*. Washington, D.C.: U.S. Government Printing Office, 1997.

———. *Socioeconomic Characteristics of the U.S. Foreign-Born Population Detailed in Census Bureau Tabulations*. Washington, D.C.: U.S. Government Printing Office, 1984b.

———. *Survey of Minority-Owned Business Enterprises: Blacks, Hispanics, and Asian Americans*. Washington D.C.: U.S. Government Printing Office, 2001b.

———. *U.S. Employment Data: 1950–1997*. Washington, D.C.: U.S. Government Printing Office, 1998.

———. "Voting and Registration in the Election of November 2000." Current Population Reports, Series P-20. No. 542. Washington, D.C.: U.S. Government Printing Office, February 2002.

U.S. Department of Justice. *Immigration Reform and Control Act: Report on the Legalized Alien Population*. Washington, D.C.: U.S. Government Printing Office, 1992.

U.S. Department of Justice, Bureau of Justice Statistics. "Adult Correctional Populations in the United States, 1980–2002." Washington, D.C.: U.S. Government Printing Office, 2004. http://www.ojp.usdoj.gov/bjs/glance/tables/corr2tab.htm.

U.S. Department of Labor. *Report of the Department of Labor Legal Immigration Task Force*. Washington, D.C.: U.S. Government Printing Office, 1988.

U.S. Immigration and Naturalization Service (INS). *1987 Statistical Yearbook*. Washington, D.C.: U.S. Government Printing Office, 1988.

———. *1990 Statistical Yearbook*. Washington, D.C.: U.S. Government Printing Office, 1991.

———. *1993 Statistical Yearbook*. Washington, D.C.: U.S. Government Printing Office, 1994.

———. *1998 Statistical Yearbook*. Washington, D.C.: U.S. Government Printing Office, 1999.

———. *2001 Statistical Yearbook*. Washington, D.C.: U.S. Government Printing Office, 2002.

U.S. Immigration [Dillingham] Commission. *Reports of the Immigration Commission*. Vol. 29, *The Children of Immigrants in Schools*. Washington, D.C.: U.S. Government Printing Office, 1911.

"U.S. Muslim Scholars to Forbid Terrorism." *New York Times*, July 28, 2005. www.nytimes.com/2005/07/28/national/28fatwa.html.

Vargas, Gloria E. "Recently Arrived Central American Immigration: Mental Health Needs." *Research Bulletin*, UCLA Spanish Speaking Mental Health Research Center (Autumn 1984): 13.

Vecoli, Rudolph. "The Italian Americans." In *Uncertain Americans: Readings in Ethnic History*, ed. Leonard Dinnerstein and Frederic C. Jaher, 201–15. New York: Oxford University Press, 1977.

Veenman, Justus. "Ethnic Minorities in the Netherlands." In *Poverty, Inequality, and the Future of Social Policy*, ed. K. McFate, B. Lawson, and W. J. Wilson, 607–28. New York: Russell Sage Foundation, 1995.

Vega, William A., and Hortensia Amaro. "Latino Outlook: Good Health, Uncertain Prognosis." *Annual Review of Public Health* 15 (1994): 39–67.

Vega, William A., Bohdan Kolody, and Juan Ramón Valle. "Migration and Mental Health: An Empirical Test of Depression Risk Factors among Immigrant Mexican Women." *International Migration Review* 21 (Fall 1987): 512–30.

Vega, William A., Bohdan Kolody, Juan Ramón Valle, and Richard Hough. "Depressive Symptoms and Their Correlates among Immigrant Mexican Women in the United States." *Social Science and Medicine* 22 (1986): 645–52.

Vega, William A., and Rubén G. Rumbaut. "Ethnic Minorities and Mental Health." *Annual Review of Sociology* 17 (1991): 351–83.

Vega, William A., W. Sribney, and I. Achara-Abrahams. "Co-occurring Alcohol, Drug, and Other Psychiatric Disorders among Mexican-Origin People in the United States." *American Journal of Public Health* 93, no. 7 (2003): 1057–64.

Vega, William A., George J. Warheit, Joanne Buhl-Auth, and Kenneth Meinhardt. "Mental Health Issues in the Hispanic Community: The Prevalence of Psychological Distress." In *Stress and Hispanic Mental Health*, ed. William A. Vega and Manuel R. Miranda, 30–47. Rockville, Md.: National Institute of Mental Health, 1985.

———. "The Prevalence of Depressive Symptoms among Mexican Americans and Anglos." *American Journal of Epidemiology* 120 (October 1984): 592–607.

Vega, William A., George J. Warheit, and Robert Palacio. "Psychiatric Symptomatology among Mexican American Farmworkers." *Social Science and Medicine* 20 (1985): 39–45.

Veltman, Calvin. *Language Shift in the United States*. Berlin: Mouton, 1983.

———. "Modeling the Language Shift Process of Hispanic Immigrants." *International Migration Review* 22 (Winter 1988): 545–62.

Vigil, James Diego. *Barrio Gangs: Street Life and Identity in Southern California*. Austin: University of Texas Press, 1988.

Wacquant, Loïc J., and William J. Wilson. "The Cost of Racial and Class Exclusion in the Inner City." *Annals of the American Academy of Political and Social Science* 501 (1989): 826.

Wadestrandt, Jacques-Christian. "Lt. General Ricardo Sánchez Named 'Hispanic of the Year.'" *Hispanic Magazine,* December 2003.

Waldinger, Roger. "Ethnic Business in the United States." Mimeograph, Department of Sociology, City University of New York, 1988.

———. "Immigrant Enterprise: A New Test of Competing Theories." Paper presented at the Symposium on Hispanic Enterprise, Arizona State University, April 1987.

———. "Immigration and Industrial Change in the New York City Apparel Industry." In *Hispanics in the U.S. Economy,* ed. George J. Borjas and Marta Tienda, 323–49. New York: Academic Press, 1985.

———. "The Making of an Immigrant Niche." Unpublished manuscript, Department of Sociology, University of California, Los Angeles, 1992.

———. *Still the Promised City? African-Americans and New Immigrants in Postindustrial New York.* Cambridge, Mass.: Harvard University Press, 1996.

Waldinger, Roger, and Michael I. Lichter. *How the Other Half Works: Immigration and the Social Organization of Labor.* Berkeley: University of California Press, 2003.

Waldman, Amy. "Seething Unease Shaped British Bombers' Newfound Zeal." *New York Times,* July 31, 2005, A1.

Walker, S. Lynne. "The Invisible Work Force: San Diego's Migrant Farm Laborers from Oaxaca." *San Diego Union,* December 1822, 1988, A1.

"Wanted: Fresh, Homegrown Talent." *Time,* January 11, 1988, 65.

Wardhaugh, Ronald. *Languages in Competition: Dominance, Diversity, and Decline.* New York: Blackwell, 1987.

Warheit, George J., William A. Vega, Joanne Auth, and Kenneth Meinhardt. "Mexican-American Immigration and Mental Health: A Comparative Analysis of Psychosocial Distress and Dysfunction." In *Stress and Hispanic Mental Health,* ed. William A. Vega and Manuel R. Miranda, 76–109. Rockville, Md.: National Institute of Mental Health, 1985.

Warner, R. Stephen. "Approaching Religious Diversity: Barriers, Byways, and Beginnings." *Sociology of Religion* 59 (1998): 193–215.

Warner, W. Lloyd, and Leo Srole. *The Social Systems of American Ethnic Groups.* New Haven, Conn.: Yale University Press, 1945.

Warren, R. "Status Report on Naturalization Rates." Working Paper #CO 1326, 6/C. Washington, D.C.: U.S. Bureau of the Census, 1979.

Warner, R. Stephen, and Judith G. Wittner, eds. *Gatherings in Diaspora: Religious Communities and the New Immigration.* Philadelphia: Temple University Press, 1998.

Watanabe, Teresa, and Nicole Gaouette. 2006. "Next: Converting the Energy of Protest to Political Clout." *Los Angeles Times,* May 2, A1.

Waters, Mary C. *Black Identities: West Indian Immigrant Dreams and American Realities.* Cambridge, Mass., and New York: Harvard University Press and the Russell Sage Foundation, 1999.

———. "Ethnic and Racial Identities of Second Generation Black Immigrants in New York City." *International Migration Review* 28 (Winter 1994): 795–820.

———. "West Indian Immigrants, African Americans, and Whites in the Workplace: Different Perspectives on American Race Relations." Paper presented at the meetings of the American Sociological Association, Los Angeles, August 1994.

Weber, Max. *The Protestant Ethic and the Spirit of Capitalism*. London: Unwin, [1904] 1984.

———. *The Sociology of Religion*. Trans. E. Fischoff. Boston: Beacon Press, [1922] 1963.

Weeks, John R., and Rubén G. Rumbaut. "Infant Mortality among Ethnic Immigrant Groups." *Social Science and Medicine* 33, no. 3 (1991): 327–34.

Weissman, Myrna M., Jerome K. Myers, and Catherine E. Ross, eds. *Community Surveys of Psychiatric Disorders*. New Brunswick, N.J.: Rutgers University Press, 1986.

Western, Bruce. "The Impact of Incarceration on Wage Mobility and Inequality." *American Sociological Review* 67 (2002): 1–21.

Western, Bruce, Jeffrey R. Kling, and David F. Weiman. 2001. "The Labor Market Consequences of Incarceration." *Crime and Delinquency* 47: 410–27.

Williams, Carolyn L., and Joseph Westermeyer, eds. *Refugee Mental Health in Resettlement Countries*. New York: Hemisphere, 1986.

Wilson, Kenneth, and W. Allen Martin. "Ethnic Enclaves: A Comparison of the Cuban and Black Economies in Miami." *American Journal of Sociology* 88 (1982): 135–60.

Wilson, William J. *The Truly Disadvantaged: The Inner City, the Underclass, and Public Policy*. Chicago: University of Chicago Press, 1987.

Wittke, Carl. *Refugees of Revolution: The German Forty-Eighters in America*. Philadelphia: University of Pennsylvania Press, 1952.

———. *We Who Built America*. Englewood Cliffs, N.J.: Prentice Hall, 1939.

Womack, John. *Zapata and the Mexican Revolution*. New York: Vintage Books, 1968.

Wong, Morrison G., and Charles Hirschman. "The New Asian Immigrants." In *Culture, Ethnicity, and Identity*, ed. William C. McReady, 381–403. New York: Academic Press, 1983.

Woo, Elaine. "Immigrants: A Rush to the Classroom." *Los Angeles Times*, September 24, 1986, I1.

Wood, Charles H. "Caribbean Cane Cutters in Florida: A Study of the Relative Cost of Domestic and Foreign Labor." Mimeograph, paper presented at the meetings of the American Sociological Association, San Antonio, Texas, August 1984.

Wuthnow, Robert. *America and the Challenges of Religious Diversity*. Princeton, N.J.: Princeton University Press, 2005.

Yoon, In-Jin. *On My Own: Korean Business and Race Relations in America*. Chicago: University of Chicago Press, 1997.

Zabin, Carol, and Sallie Hughes. "Economic Integration and Labor Flows: Stage Migration in Farm Labor Markets in Mexico and the United States." *International Migration Review* 29 (Summer 1995): 395–422.

Zamichow, Nora. "No Way to Escape the Fear: Stress Disorder Grips Women Immigrants." *Los Angeles Times*, February 10, 1992, B14.

Zhou, Min. *New York's Chinatown: The Socioeconomic Potential of an Urban Enclave*. Philadelphia: Temple University Press, 1992.

———. "Revisiting Ethnic Entrepreneurship: Convergencies, Controversies, and Conceptual Advancements." *International Migration Review* 38 (Fall 2004): 1040–74.

———. "Straddling Different Worlds: The Acculturation of Vietnamese Refugee Children." In *Ethnicities: Children of Immigrants in America*, ed. Rubén G. Rumbaut and Alejandro Portes, 187–227. Berkeley University of California Press and Russell Sage Foundation, 2001.

Zhou, Min, and Carl L. Bankston. "Entrepreneurship." In *Asian American Almanac*, ed. I. Natividad, 511–28. Columbus, Ohio: Gale Research, 1995.

———. *Growing Up American: How Vietnamese Children Adapt to Life in the United States*. New York: Russell Sage Foundation, 1998.

———. "Social Capital and the Adaptation of the Second Generation: The Case of Vietnamese Youth in New Orleans." *International Migration Review* 28 (Winter 1994): 821–45.

Zhou, Min, Carl L. Bankston, and Rebecca Y. Kim. "Rebuilding Spiritual Lives in the New Land: Religious Practices among Southeast Asian Refugees in the United States." In *Religion in Asian America*, ed. P. G. Min and J. H. Kim, 37–70. New York: AltaMira Press, 2002.

Zolberg, Aristide R. "From Invitation to Interdiction: U.S. Foreign Policy and Immigration since 1945." In *Threatened Peoples, Threatened Borders: World Migration and U.S. Policy*, ed. M. S. Teitelbaum and M. Weiner, 117–59. New York: Norton, 1995.

———. *A Nation by Design: Immigration Policy in the Fashioning of America*. Cambridge, Mass.: Harvard University Press, 2006.

———. "The Next Waves: Migration Theory for a Changing World." *International Migration Review* 23 (Fall 1989): 403–30.

Zolberg, Aristide R., Astri Suhrke, and Sergio Aguayo. *Escape from Violence: Conflict and the Refugee Crisis in the Developing World*. New York: Oxford University Press, 1989.

———. "International Factors in the Formation of Refugee Movements." *International Migration Review* 20 (Summer 1986): 151–69.

Zolberg, Aristide, and Long Witt Woon. "Why Islam Is Like Spanish: Cultural Incorporation in Europe and the United States." *Politics and Society* 27 (March 1999): 5–38.

Zwingmann, C. A., and Maria Pfister-Ammende, eds. *Uprooting and After*. New York: Springer-Verlag, 1973.

Index

Text:	10/13 Sabon
Display:	Akzidenz Grotesk
Compositor:	Michael Bass Associates
Illustrator	Corinne Ovadia, Asterisk*
Indexer:	Herr's Indexing Service
Printer and binder:	Sheridan Books, Inc.